THE LAITY AND THE CHURCH OF IRELAND, 1000–2000

The Laity and the
Church of Ireland, 1000–2000

All Sorts and Conditions

Raymond Gillespie and W.G. Neely

EDITORS

FOUR COURTS PRESS

This book was typeset in 10.5 on 12.5pt Ehrhardt
by Carrigboy Typesetting Services, County Cork for
FOUR COURTS PRESS LTD
Fumbally Lane, Dublin 8, Ireland
e-mail: info@four-courts-press.ie
and in the United States for
FOUR COURTS PRESS
c/o International Specialized Book Services,
5824 N.E. Hassalo Street, Portland, OR 97213

A catalogue record for this title is available from the British Library.

ISBN 1–85182–716–1

Printed in Great Britain
by MPG Books, Bodmin, Cornwall.

Contents

Illustrations

PLATES (BETWEEN PAGE 144 AND PAGE 145)

1   Middle Church, Ballinderry, Co. Antrim, 1668.
2   Waterford cathedral, 1774–92, by John Roberts.
3   Chapel, Dublin Castle, 1807–14 by Francis Johnston
4   St James's church, Ramoan, Co. Antrim, 1848.
5   Interior of St Mark's church, Belfast by William Butterfield, 1876–8.
6   Stained glass, St John's church, Whitehouse, Co. Antrim.
7   Font, St Anne's church, Dungannon, Co. Tyrone, 1875.
8   Windows by Beatrice Elvery, 1908–9, St Magheralin church,
    Co. Down.
9   Stained glass by Harry Clarke, 1919, Holy Trinity church,
    Killiney, Co. Dublin.
10 Stained glass by Evie Hone, 1935, St Beaidh's church,
    Co. Roscommon.
11 St Molua's church, Stormont, Belfast, 1961–2.
12 St Ignatius's church, Carryduff, Co. Down, 1964–6.

CREDITS FOR ILLUSTRATIONS

Dúchas: The Heritage Service (1, 2); Paul Larmour (10–14, 16–22, 24–43, 47,
49–52, plates 1–12); Stephen McBride (23, 24, 48); Professor Adrian Phillips
(9); R.C.B (3, 4, 8).

Abbreviations

B.L.	British Library, London
Cal. S.P. Ire., 1509–73 etc	*Calendar of state papers relating to Ireland, 1509–73* etc. (24 vols, London, 1860–1911)
I.H.S.	*Irish Historical Studies*
Ir. Econ. Soc. Hist	*Irish Economic and Social History*
L. &. P. Hen VIII	*Letters and papers, foreign and domestic, Henry VIII* (21 vols, London, 1862–1932)
N.A.	National Archives, Dublin
N.L.I.	National Library of Ireland, Dublin
P.R.O.N.I.	Public Record Office of Northern Ireland, Belfast
R.C.B.	Representative Church Body Library, Dublin
R.I.A. Procs.	*Proceedings of the Royal Irish Academy*
R.S.A.I. Jn.	*Journal of the Royal Society of Antiquaries of Ireland*
S.P.C.K.	Society for the Promotion of Christian Knowledge, London
S.P. Henry VIII	*State papers, Henry VIII* (11 vols, London, 1830–52)
T.C.D.	Trinity College, Dublin

Contributors

T.C. BARNARD is Armstrong-Macintyre-Markham fellow and keeper of the archives at Hertford College, Oxford. During 1997 to 1999 he was a British Academy Research Reader and in 2001 Tercentary Visiting Fellow at Marsh's Library, Dublin. He has written extensively on Ireland in the seventeenth and eighteenth centuries.

PATRICK COMERFORD is a Church of Ireland priest, Regional Officer of the Church Mission Society, Ireland and a former *Irish Times* journalist. He has written on church history in a number of journals and books. His 'Brief history of Christianity' was published both in the *Irish Times* and in Patsy McGarry (ed.), *Christianity* (Dublin, 2001)

ADRIAN EMPEY is principal of the Church of Ireland Theological College in Dublin and precentor of Christ Church cathedral. He is a distinguished medieval historian who has written widely on the history of settlement in medieval Ireland.

RAYMOND GILLESPIE teaches local history and early modern history at NUI Maynooth. He has written widely on early modern Irish society including *Colonial Ulster* (1985) and *Devoted people: belief and religion in early modern Ireland* (1997).

DAVID HAYTON is Reader in Modern History at the Queen's University, Belfast. He was previously on the staff of the History of Parliament Trust and is the general editor for the volumes on *The House of Commons, 1690–1715*. He has published widely on the political and religious history of Britain and Ireland in the late seventeenth and early eighteenth centuries. He has also edited several collections of essays including *Penal era and golden age: essays on Irish history 1690–1800* (1979).

PAUL LARMOUR is Reader in architecture at the Queen's University, Belfast. His books include *Celtic ornament* (1981), *Belfast: an illustrated architectural guide* (1987) and *The arts and crafts movement in Ireland* (1991)

COLM LENNON, a senior lecturer in the Department of Modern History, NUI Maynooth, specializes in the study of religion and society in reformation and

Counter-Reformation Ireland. He is the author of a number of books including *The lords of Dublin in the age of Reformation* (1989) and *Sixteenth-century Ireland: the incomplete conquest* (1994) as well as several articles. He is a Government of Ireland Senior Research Fellow in 2002–3.

JACQUELINE HILL is a senior lecturer in history, NUI Maynooth, and on the editorial board of *A New History of Ireland*. Her research interests are in eighteenth and nineteenth-century Irish history.

STEPHEN MC BRIDE, vicar of Antrim parish, archdeacon of Connor and precentor of St Anne's cathedral, Belfast, studied architecture at the Queen's University, Belfast and theology at Trinity College, Dublin. His doctoral thesis was an examination of nineteenth-century architecture.

KENNETH MILNE, historiographer for the Church of Ireland, was formerly principal of the Church of Ireland College of Education. He has written widely on both education and the history of the Church of Ireland. He was one of the editors of *As by law established: the Church of Ireland since the Reformation*. His *Irish charter schools* was published in 1997 and *Christ Church Cathedral, Dublin: a history*, which he edited, was published in 2000.

MARTIN MAGUIRE teaches history in Dundalk Institute of Technology and has published articles on the interaction of the identities of class and religion as well as a history of the Local Government and Public Services Union.

W.G. NEELY is rector of the parish of Keady, County Armagh, and prebendary of Swords in St Patrick's cathedral, Dublin. His books include *Kilcooley: land and people in Tipperary* (1983) and *Kilkenny: an urban history* (1989). He is also secretary of the Church of Ireland Historical Society.

JOHN PATERSON was ordained deacon (1963) and priest (1964) for the parish of Drumglass (Dungannon) in Armagh diocese. Since then he has served in Dublin and Kildare and is currently dean of Christ Church cathedral in Dublin. From 1985 until 1991 he was clerical honorary secretary for the province of Dublin in the General Synod of the Church of Ireland.

Preface

From the middle of the 1990s historical interest in the Church of Ireland has perceptibly quickened. Three works in particular have demonstrated this renewed interest in the institution. The first, the proceedings of a 1993 conference, brought together a number of scholars to attack particular aspects of the history of that church from improving bishops to imprudent laity. The result was *As by law established: the Church of Ireland since the Reformation* edited by Alan Ford, James McGuire and Kenneth Milne (Dublin, 1995). The second, rather different, work was Alan Acheson's overview, *A history of the Church of Ireland, 1691–1996* (Dublin, 1997). For those daunted by the 300 pages of this work a more concise statement, dealing with the same broad range of issues, was available in Robert MacCarthy's *Ancient and modern – a short history of the Church of Ireland* (Dublin, 1995). A further approach to the history of the Church of Ireland was provided by another multi-authored work focusing on one institution within the Church of Ireland, *Christ Church cathedral, Dublin: a history* (Dublin, 2000). Yet another manifestation of the growing interest in the past of the Church of Ireland was the establishment of the Church of Ireland Historical Society in the mid-1990s. This present volume, sponsored by the Church of Ireland Historical Society, is intended as a contribution to the growing body of historical writing concerning that church. However it approaches the history of the Church of Ireland from a rather different perspective to earlier histories. It is not focused on an institution. Neither is it an attempt to provide a comprehensive narrative history of the Church of Ireland nor does it deal with the doings of bishops or clergy. Rather it describes aspects of what it meant to be a lay person in the Church of Ireland at different points in its history.

This is a challenging subject which has a complex history. For that reason it is appropriate that any attempt to tackle it should be a collective undertaking which brings diverse skills to bear on a difficult subject. Such collective undertakings are not always as fruitful as they might be and the success of this one has lain in the enthusiasm and commitment of those who have been part of it. Most obviously the contributors have borne graciously editorial demands, unreasonable or otherwise. Similarly the publishers have, with their customary style and efficiency, been responsible for the production of the final handsome product. However, there are others whose part is less visible. Libraries and archives have generously allowed their collections to be used and cited. In particular those who crew the Representative Church Body Library, under the captainship of Dr Raymond Refaussé, have uncomplainingly borne the brunt of the demands of many of the contributors. Others, including the British Library, the National Library of Ireland, the Public Record Office of Northern Ireland, Marsh's Library, the Grand Lodge of Free and Accepted Masons in Ireland and the National Archives of Ireland, have facilitated many of the contributors. We are grateful to the earl of Middleton and the Governing Body of Christ Church, Oxford for permission to cite material and to Dúchas: The Heritage Service for Illustrations 1 and 2. We are also grateful to the General Synod Royalties Fund for a grant towards the costs of publication and to all those at Four Courts Press for their usual efficiency and good humour. Without them this volume would not exist. The book is, we hope, rather more than the sum of its parts. If it conveys something of the problems, possibilities and indeed excitement associated with reconstructing how men and women found their own salvation in the often dangerous worlds of the past then it will have done its work well.

RAYMOND GILLESPIE
W.G. NEELY

Introduction

Raymond Gillespie

> O God, the Creator and Preserver of all mankind, we humbly
> beseech thee for all sorts and conditions of men; that thou wouldest
> be pleased to make thy ways known unto them, thy saving health
> unto all nations.
>
> *Book of Common Prayer*, Morning prayer.

It is one of the enigmas of life in Ireland at the beginning of the twenty-first
century that as support for institutional Christian churches declines interest
in the history of those institutions is expanding rapidly. At local level there is a
profusion of published parish histories and at the diocesan level both the history
of the Catholic diocese of Dublin and the Church of Ireland diocesan cathedral
of Christ Church have recently received scholarly treatment.[1] Methodists,
Presbyterians and the Church of Ireland have also received their share of
attention with general histories being produced in recent years.[2] At the level of
Church of Ireland parishes, lecture series have been hosted to explain the
evolution of the church to the laity and some of these have been published.[3] It
might be tempting to see at least some of this interest as being generated by a
muted milleniarism but if so that has left little trace in the existing writing.

In the case of the Church of Ireland interest in the history of the institution
is not a new development, either within or outside the church.[4] That church's
understanding of itself and its theology has always been intimately bound up
with its understanding of its history. The efforts of the seventeenth-century

---

1 James Kelly and Dáire Keogh (eds), *History of the Catholic diocese of Dublin* (Dublin, 2000);
Kenneth Milne (ed.), *Christ Church cathedral: a history* (Dublin 2000). 2 Alan Acheson, *A
history of the Church of Ireland, 1691–1996* (Dublin, 1997), D.A.L. Cooney, *The Methodists in
Ireland: a short history* (Dublin, 2001); Finlay Holmes, *The Presbyterian church in Ireland: a
popular history* (Dublin, 2000). 3 R.B. MacCarthy, *Ancient and modern: a short history of the
Church of Ireland* (Dublin, 1995) began life as such a series of lectures. The Christ Church
cathedral lunchtime lectures have served a similar role. 4 For a bibliographical survey of

polymath and archbishop of Armagh, James Ussher, in constructing a coherent historical account of how the Church of Ireland in his day related to the early Irish church has shaped the Church of Ireland's view of the Reformation and its role in church and state ever since.[5] Throughout the eighteenth century, for instance, Church of Ireland authors remade the Irish past to accord with their perceptions of it. St Patrick, for example, was carefully remodelled into what the eighteenth-century clergy regarded as proper for the founder of the Church of Ireland.[6] Into the nineteenth century confessional warfare over the issues of episcopal succession and the nature of the early church led Church of Ireland apologists to reach for historical texts to justify their own position.[7]

If ideology and justification of present positions were factors which induced members of the Church of Ireland to take an interest in the evolution of the institution then another was the fact that the church had acquired a tangible reminder of its inheritance as a result of the events of the 1530s. The creation of the administrative structure of the Church of Ireland arising from the Henrician reforms meant that the church inherited a structure of parishes and churches of considerable antiquity. As the established church it became responsible for an administrative structure which continually looked to the past for precedents for present action. Unlike the voluntary religion which characterized the dissenting churches, and emphasized the history of congregations as sometimes temporary gatherings of the godly, the Church of Ireland looked to its administrative structure as a validation of its established position within Irish society. To some extent this has been the origin of some of the harsher verdicts passed on the Church of Ireland by historians, especially those of the eighteenth century. Judged as a national church it clearly failed to fulfil its mission but viewed as a body responsible for the spiritual welfare of a minority within Ireland it can be seen in a more positive light.[8]

The position of the Church of Ireland before 1870 as the established church has ensured that those interested in its history would not be confined to members of that church. The institutional church touched the workings of government at almost every point. Most of the officials in the Dublin administration were members of the Church of Ireland and their actions were, presumably, affected in some way by its teachings. Moreover prelates and clergy took an active part in government as members of the Irish House of Lords before

---

writing on the history of the Church of Ireland, 'The Church of Ireland: a critical bibliography' in *I.H.S.* xxviii (1992–3), pp 345–84. **5** John McCafferty, 'St Patrick for the Church of Ireland: James Ussher's *Discourse*' in *Bullán* iii no. 2 (1997–8), pp 87–101. **6** Bridget McCormack, *Perceptions of St Patrick in eighteenth-century Ireland* (Dublin, 2000). **7** Alan Ford, '"Standing ones ground": religion, polemic and Irish history since the Reformation' in Alan Ford, J.I. McGuire and K. Milne (eds), *As by law established: the Church of Ireland since the Reformation* (Dublin, 1995), pp 5–10. **8** S.J. Connolly, *Religion,*

1800 or as members of the privy council or as lords justice before 1800. The history of the Church of Ireland and the history of Ireland as a whole were inextricably interwoven.

The salient characteristics of this sort of historical approach to the Church of Ireland's past are relatively easily discerned. The targets of historical analysis were senior clergy, the operation of the institution as a whole or the history of theological ideas. From the middle of the twentieth century shifts in both theological thought and the practice of history have served to modify our understanding of how churches worked in past. Ecclesiastical history has increasingly given way to the history of religion. The renewed emphasis on the church as the corporate people of God has served to bring the laity to the fore.[9] Historical practice has move along similar lines, replacing the study of institutions with attempts to reconstruct belief systems and to understand what it meant for the laity to be part of an institutional church. Eamon Duffy's *The stripping of the altars*, for example, vividly recreated what it meant to be part of the pre-Reformation church in England.[10] More recently there have been a number of incisive studies in an English context which have persuaded us to recognize just how seriously many those who lived in the past took their religion and how this was articulated through the frameworks offered by main-line churches. Thus many of those who lived in, for example, early modern England were neither part of a separatist puritan movement nor were they part of some exotic world of folk beliefs which barely touched on orthodox christianity. Many of these people worshipped in an undramatic way according to the Prayer Book and took that tradition within the Church of England seriously.[11]

In Ireland this approach has found fewer advocates. This is not because either historians or churchmen were not persuaded of its value but rather because of the difficulty of reconstructing what in an earlier incarnation was termed 'popular religion'. Indeed such forays into this world as there have been suggested that such an approach could change the way we regard the history of the Church of Ireland. The case of disestablishment in 1870 is an instructive one. While institutionally the removal of the established church status from the Church of Ireland could be seen as a disaster a shift of perspective tells another story. In Dublin some parishes flourished with a new sense of lay empowerment and in other dioceses, such as Kildare, church building activity surged as a result

law and power: the making of Protestant Ireland, 1660–1760 (Oxford, 1992), pp 171–90. 9 For a discussion of the theological trends Fredrica Harris Thompsett, 'The laity' in Stephen Sykes and John Booty (eds), *The study of Anglicanism* (London, 1988), pp 245–60. 10 Eamon Duffy, *The stripping of the altars: traditional religion in England, 1400–1580* (London, 1992). The second part of this work uses rather more traditional approaches to the understanding of the process of the Reformation. 11 Most importantly Judith Maltby, *Prayer Book and people in Elizabethan and early Stuart England* (Cambridge, 1998) and Donald Spaeth, *The church in an age of danger: parsons and parishioners, 1660–1740*

of renewed lay support.[12] Despite the attraction of this sort of approach evidence, particularly for periods before the nineteenth century, is sparse and difficult to handle. Moreover the Church of Ireland contained a remarkably diverse range of voices within a relatively restricted geographical area making it difficult to generalize from sometimes limited ranges of evidence. The point is clearest from the evidence of twentieth-century memoirs. Homan Potterton writing of his Church of Ireland father in the prosperous agricultural county of Meath in the 1950s recorded that he was 'a great man for the church'. This however

> had nothing whatever to do with theology or even doctrine in which he, like everyone else in the Church of Ireland, had absolutely no interest at all. Instead, his practice of religion focused on the Scriptures, prayer, hymn-singing and regular attendance at church: in other words he was 'a devout churchman'.

To this might be added the political life of the Select Vestry and the General Synod. Moreover he did not spare his criticism of the bishop of Meath where he disagreed with him.[13] His picture finds some support in the world of Wicklow where school scripture lessons were banal and theologically suspect but the style of churchmanship encouraged social propriety.[14] In the industrial Belfast of the 1930s Robert Harbison recorded a rather different experience of Church of Ireland life. Here members of the Church of Ireland also attended children's meetings organized by the Plymouth Brethren and services in the local mission hall. As entertainment these vied with the Church Lads' Brigade. Even those homes that were not overtly evangelical were decorated with Protestant godly pictures and the Bible was an object of veneration.[15] A church more different to that of rural Meath both in its churchmanship and outlook would be hard to imagine. The bond that held these very varied Protestant communities together was a fear and a distrust of Catholicism.

Despite the problems associated with lack of sources and diversity of understandings of what constituted the church this volume is an attempt to reconstruct what the religious life of the laity in the Church of Ireland may have been like in the past. The central point of this reconstruction is the characteristic Church of Ireland institution of the parish which provided not only a context for worship but also a framework for lay activity at a local level.

(Cambridge, 2000). 12 John Crawford, *St Catherine's parish, Dublin, 1840–1900: portrait of a Church of Ireland community* (Dublin, 1996); Adrian Wilkinson, 'St Brigid's cathedral, Kildare, and the challenge of disestablishment' in *Journal of the County Kildare Archaeological Society* xix no. 1 (2000–1), pp 96–115. 13 Homan Potterton, *Rathcormick: a childhood recalled* (Dublin, 2001), pp 49–57. 14 Hugh Maxton, *Waking: an Irish Protestant upbringing* (Belfast, 1997), p. 89. 15 Robert Harbison, *No surrender: an Ulster childhood* (Belfast, 1987), pp 52–68.

Moreover the increasing realization that much of the life of the Church of Ireland was found not in spectacular events but in the minutiae of parochial life and Prayer Book worship serves to place the parish at the centre of the religious life of the laity. From a practical point of view the survival of parochial records makes such a local reconstruction possible. While the minutae of vestry minutes, churchwarden's accounts and preacher's books do not make for exciting reading they nevertheless contain the raw material for the recreation of the ordinary world of parochial life which was an integral part of the laity's religiosity in the past. Many of the Irish parochial structures, together with the tradition of lay action, were the inheritance of the medieval period, as Adrian Enpey's essay demonstrates. The succeeding essays by Colm Lennon, T.C. Barnard, Patrick Comerford, W.G. Neely, Kenneth Milne and Martin Maguire all trace the continuing importance of parochial life in shaping Church of Ireland identity from the sixteenth to the twentieth century as it was reshaped to meet the changing priorities of the wider world. It was on the basis of the parochial structures that other frameworks, such as the General Synod, were built and the scale of lay involvement in the government of the church after disestablishment presupposed an active parish life. From this understanding of the parish as the central and distinctive unit of the Church of Ireland this volume moves in two directions. The activities of the parish affected people in a number of ways but their experience of parish life influenced both their public lives and, in the private sphere, their own personal spiritualities, shaped by many factors including corporate parish worship. While many of the essays in this volume touch on the influence of members of the Church of Ireland in the wider world those by David Hayton and J.R. Hill focus particularly on this aspect of the laity's world. They do this by examining the distinctive position of the laity of the established church in secular government while Kenneth Milne discusses the wider impact of Church of Ireland members on Irish society after 1870. If one exploration of the volume is into the secular world the second is into the private sphere of belief and spirituality. The essays by Raymond Gillespie and John Paterson attempt the difficult task of reconstructing the influences which acted on the Church of Ireland laity as they tried to shape their own salvation within the context of corporate worship and private devotion. One specific aspect of this is dealt with by Paul Larmour and Stephen McBride in their reconstruction of the physical fabric of the parish church and how that was deployed in the parish liturgy.

The essays in this volume are in many ways exploratory. Unlike the older tradition of denominational historiography there is neither a reservoir of case studies to draw on for generalization nor the fruit of systematic combing of sources stretching over decades. Although this volume adopts a chronological division which owes much to that older tradition it has tried to move away from a framework of structures to that of belief. Instead of asking the question 'how did the church work?' it poses the problem 'what did it mean to be a member of that church in the complex worlds of the past?'. Until it is possible to understand at least some of the many answers to that historical question our response to that same question in a contemporary context will be much impoverished. While these essays may have a denominational focus the volume has a wider significance. The structure may be that of the Church of Ireland but the issues which the authors address here are applicable to almost every formal religious group in Ireland. If we have helped to move the agenda towards the study of the history of religion rather than the study of church structures then this book will have achieved at least some of its objectives.

The layperson in the parish: the medieval inheritance, 1169–1536

Adrian Empey[1]

'The lawdable costome off this chyrche is to chose the chyrche war-
denys opon the ffyrste Sonday of Maii'. (Account of Thomas Ashe
and James Clynton, proctors of St Werburgh's Church, 1495.)[2]

The 'lawdable costome' of choosing churchwardens on the first Sunday
of May in St Werburgh's parish church, Dublin, bespeaks of a well-
established lay institution, with unmistakable undertones of pride in the office
bestowed upon them. The task of this essay is to examine the evolution of the
medieval parish and to evaluate the significance of lay participation in the life of
the church at its parochial base. In order to place these developments in their
context, it will be necessary to discuss the sources, the origins of parochial
organization, lay piety, lay participation, and lay attitudes to the clergy.

I

Assessing the sources of lay history in the medieval church presents formidable
difficulties for the simple reason that the overwhelming volumes of ecclesiastical records were written by clergy. Although the church rested on a lay
base, the laity were, to all intents and purposes, an invisible people. From the
perspective of the clergy the role of the layman was to service the institution by
dutifully paying his tithes and other dues, and by fulfilling his sacramental
obligations.[3] Beyond that he could play a more positive role by acts of charity,

---

1 I wish to thank Dr Colmán Etchingham for furnishing me with his translation of the
twelfth-century Irish poem dealing with the churches of Dublin, *c.*1121; Dr Raymond
Gillespie for drawing my attention to a number of bibliographical items and Mr Con
Manning of Dúchas for his help with St Mary's Church, Callan. 2 R.C.B., P326/27/1/4,
f.5. 3 See Emma Mason, 'The role of the English parishioner, 1100-1500' in *Journal of*

including the maintenance of the fabric of the parish church and the provision of lights for the interior of the church.

The superiority of the ordained found expression both in liturgical and in architectural developments in the twelfth and thirteenth centuries. Chief among these changes was development of Eucharistic doctrine, culminating in the doctrine of transubstantiation and the feast of Corpus Christi. While such doctrines were not, one presumes, the subject of heated debate in the village tavern, their import was effectively communicated to the laity by ritual means. Durandus, the great Dominican theologian (*c.*1275–1334), known to his contemporaries as the *doctor modernus*, explained that due to sinfulness the laity communicated only once a year at Easter – as provided by the Lateran Council of 1215 – because the priest communicated daily for them. It was enough just to see the host. These changes were communicated to the laity by the growth of the practice of the Elevation of the Host, signalled by ringing a sacring-bell, and the withdrawal of the chalice. The circulation and kissing of the Pax – an object shaped like the Host and inscribed with a crucifix – substituted the reception of communion in parish churches in the fifteenth century, if not considerably earlier. Such was the awe in which the host was regarded that diocesan synods laid down careful rules as to how the *viaticum* – the communion of the sick – was to be transported. A decree of the synod of Paris (1204–5) permitted only priests to carry communion to the sick, not even a deacon save in dire necessity, and never in any circumstance a layman. Other synodal decrees provided that it should be placed in a pyx, accompanied by lighted candles and the ringing of bells.[4] When, in 1324, Bishop Ledrede of Ossory, confronted the seneschal of Kilkenny in the court of the liberty in pursuit of his case against Alice Kyteler, he came armed with the most potent weapon in his ecclesiastical armory:

> Donning his vestments, [the bishop] picked up the host [*corpus Christi*] in its decorated gilt vessel, and went with candles lit in procession to the tribunal of the said seneschal, accompanied by the said prior [of the Dominican convent] and five Dominicans, the warden and five Franciscans, and his own chapter and clerics. As he entered the court, several nobles blocked his way ... he kept on towards the tribunal, and, reverently lifting up the host [*corpus Christi*], he requested from the seneschal, the justiciar, the sheriff and the bailiffs, that in respect and love for Christ, *whom he was holding in his hands* [my italics], he should be granted a hearing in the cause of faith.[5]

Ecclesiastical History, xxvii (1976), pp 17–29.   **4** For a full discussion of eucharistic doctrine in this period see Miri Rubin, *Corpus Christi: the Eucharist in late medieval culture* (Cambridge, 1991).   **5** T. Wright (ed.), *A contemporary narrative of he proceedings against Dame Alice Kyteler, prosecuted for sorcery in 1324, by Richard de Ledrede, bishop of Ossory* (London, 1843), pp 13–14; also L.S. Davidson and J.O. Ward, *The sorcery trial of Alice Kyteler*

Clearly the bishop calculated that no layman would dare oppose him while he bore the greatest and most potent of all relics – the body of Christ himself. His elaborate procession may well have been a conscious imitation of the Corpus Christi rite, which had been introduced into England only six years previously. It is notable that in the account of the incident – almost certainly penned by Ledrede himself – he uses the term *corpus Christi* and not the more usual Latin term, *hostia*. Significantly, he was accompanied by the Dominicans, who were particularly associated with both cultivation and the dissemination of the cult since the Beguine community, which had close ties with the order, in Liège, instigated it.

The gulf between lay and ordained found its expression in architecture with the elongation of the chancel and the insertion of rood screens, but given the limitations of research into the layout of parish churches in Ireland no satisfactory conclusion can be drawn.[6]

There is one exception to this virtual black hole that exists in ecclesiastical sources. As parish churches became increasingly the focus of lay piety and bequests, so too the need to appoint wardens to oversee their investments became necessary. Significantly, the office of warden would seem to have been borrowed from the guild system rather than from clerical models. The fortunate survival of a series of late-fifteenth – and early-sixteenth-century churchwardens' accounts for St Werburgh's parish in Dublin throws considerable light on the place of the laity in the parochial system. Sometimes the verdicts of juries allow us to catch a fleeting glimpse of lay life, while episcopal registers can yield some valuable information, particularly in the later middle ages. The survival of a significant number of wills certainly provides a good index of lay piety. Other potential sources of information could include a systematic study of sepulchral iconography, to say nothing of the large numbers of ruined churches that await detailed examination and excavation. It is surely significant that a report published in 1996 by the Council for British Archaeology on church archaeology ranging across England, Scotland and Wales, contained no contribution on Ireland.[7] Realistically, however, it must be acknowledged that while much remains to be done even within the scope of the evidence that remains, it will almost certainly not be possible to conduct the kind of ground-breaking study on lay religion that has been recently undertaken for the early modern period by Raymond Gillespie.[8] Much of the lay religious experience before the reformation is likely to remain permanently veiled from our sight.

(Binghampton N.Y., 1993), p. 45. **6** See Sinead Ní Ghabhlain, 'Church and community in medieval Ireland: the diocese of Kilfenora' in *R.S.A.I. Jn.*, cxxv (1995), pp 61–84, and particularly her comments on pp 74-5. Unfortunately, the lack of manuscript sources in the Gaelic dioceses renders it extremely difficult to make essential correlations. **7** John Blair and Carol Pyrah, *Church archaeology: research directions for the future* (Council for British Archaeology Research Report 104, 1996). **8** See his *Devoted people: belief and religion in*

II

As the focus of pastoral care, the parish was the basic ecclesiastical unit. It was the base that supported not only the spiritual needs of the laity, but also the administrative structure of the diocese, and even the monastic church which drew much of its wealth from rectorial tithes. Yet the parochial system has been almost completely ignored by ecclesiastical historians, who are for the most part preoccupied with the higher clergy and the monastic church. It is almost as if the parochial system is 'given'. John Watt in his two standard works on the Irish medieval church, while acknowledging the fundamental importance of the parish, devoted only two pages to the subject.[9] Significantly, the groundbreaking research on the formation of the parish, such as it is, has been largely the work of secular historians.[10] This conspiracy of silence among church historians and historians of art is difficult to explain. It may be that the destruction or abandonment so many medieval parish churches outside our towns accounts for their low visibility. On the other hand, the fact that so many churches – unlike England or continental Europe – are ruinous ought to render them all the more accessible to archaeological investigation.[11]

There are, however, encouraging signs that a new debate about the origin of the parish in Ireland is at last under way, most notably among historians of the pre-Norman period, who are asking themselves hard questions about the pastoral care of the laity. The answers, one must add, are proving to be even harder than the questions, but at least some scholars are trying to peer through the monastic mist to discern the shape of things beyond the enclosure. Why such questions have not been posed before may have to do with the nature of the sources, in particular collections of canon and secular law, where it is difficult to distinguish between what is prescriptive and what is actual. It is impossible to do justice to the sophistication of the current debate initiated by Thomas Charles-Edwards and Richard Sharpe in 1992, whose conclusions have

early modern Ireland (Manchester, 1997).   **9** See J. Watt, The church in medieval Ireland (Dublin, 1972), pp 208–9. I can find no reference to parishes in The church and the two nations in Ireland (Cambridge, 1970).   **10** See A.J. Otway-Ruthven, 'Parochial development in the rural deanery of Screen' in R.S.A.I. Jn., xciv (1965), pp 111–22; K.W. Nicholls, 'Rectory, vicarage and parish in the western Irish dioceses' in R.S.A.I. Jn., ci (1971), pp 53–84; Paul Brand, 'The formation of a parish: the case of Beaulieu, County Louth' in J. Bradley (ed.), Settlement and society: studies presented to F.X. Martin, OSA (Kilkenny, 1988), pp 261–75; Mark Hennessey, 'Parochial organisation in medieval Tipperary' in W. Nolan and T.G. McGrath (eds), Tipperary: history and society: interdisciplinary essays on the history of an Irish county (Dublin, 1985), pp 60–70.   **11** Some notable work on the design of such churches has been undertaken by Ana Dolan, 'The large medieval churches of the dioceses of Leighlin, Ferns and Ossory: a study of adaption and change' in Irish Architectural and Decorative Studies, ii (1999), pp 26–65. See also Ní Gabhlainn, 'Church and community in medieval

been subjected to an exacting analysis by Colman Etchingham.[12] All are agreed
that the question of the pastoral care of the laity is central to the debate. All are
agreed that the traditional model of an all-embracing Celtic monastic church is
fundamentally flawed, and that in certain respects the pastoral structures of the
Celtic church may have been much closer to contemporary English and
continental models – for instance the 'minster' system – than has been hitherto
acknowledged. For Charles-Edwards this model took the form of a church with
pastoral responsibilities and duties organized on the basis of the *tuath*, while
Sharpe discerns the outlines of a fundamentally secular church, obscured from
view by monastic terminology, organized in communal groups with a collegiate
pastoral ministry. Indeed, he would 'go so far as to question any genuine
continuance of monastic life in Ireland at this date [ninth and tenth centuries]'.[13]

Whatever systems of pastoral care may have emerged in the ninth and tenth
centuries, it is extremely difficult to find evidence of their existence in the
second half of the twelfth century. Only in Dublin, and perhaps in the other
Norse cities, are there positive indications of pre-conquest non-monastic
churches. In a polemical poem designed to underline the claims of Armagh over
Dublin, which fits the circumstances of a disputed episcopal election in 1121,
there are references to a number of churches, including St Patrick's, St Mary's
and St Brigid's, which surface as parochial churches in early Anglo-Norman
documents.[14] Given the long-established association with Canterbury, to say
nothing of the city's trading links, it is not surprising that the diocese of Dublin
should have fashioned itself on the English, rather than on the Irish, model.
The fact that the first archdeacon to appear in the records bears the Norse name
of Torkill, presumably a member of the Mac Torcaill clan that dominated
Dublin between 1133 and 1170, strongly suggests that the office was pre-
conquest in its origins.[15] The appointment of an Anglo-Norman subprior of

Ireland', pp 61–84.   12 See T. Charles-Edwards, 'The pastoral role of the church in the early
Irish laws' and R. Sharpe, 'Churches and communities in early medieval Ireland: towards a
pastoral model' in J. Blair and R. Sharpe (eds), *Pastoral care before the parish* (Leicester, 1992),
pp 63–80, 81–109; Colmán Etchingham, *Church organisation in Ireland AD 650–1000*
(Maynooth, 1999).   13 Sharpe, 'Churches and communities in early medieval Ireland',
p. 102.   14 See Howard Clarke, 'Conversion, church and cathedral: the diocese of Dublin to
1152' in James Kelly and Dáire Keogh (eds), *History of the Catholic diocese of Dublin* (Dublin,
2000), pp 44–50. I am indebted to Dr Colman Etchingham for drawing my attention to the
poem preserved in the Book of Ui Maine, and for supplying me with his text.   15 A certain
Torquellus, archdeacon, is a witness to a charter granted by Laurence O'Toole to the canons
of Holy Trinity *c.*1178; see M.J. McEnery & R. Refaussé (eds), *Christ Church deeds* (Dublin,
2001), no. 364. For the Mac Torcaill family, see Stuart Kinsella, 'From Hiberno-Norse to
Anglo-Norman, *c.*1030–1300' in K. Milne (ed.), *Christ Church cathedral, Dublin: a history*
(Dublin, 2000), pp 42–6. Margaret Murphy, 'Archbishops and anglicisation: Dublin,
1181–1271' in Kelly and Keogh (eds), *History of the Catholic diocese of Dublin*, p. 87, seems to

Holy Trinity while Archbishop O'Toole was still prior illustrates just how impatient the new ecclesiastical regime was to 'Normanize' the church. The Dublin Norse were certainly not 'the flavor of the month' in the 1170s, so we have good reason to suspect that Archdeacon Torkill was a survivor of the *ancien regime*. 'Parity of esteem' is, after all, a comparatively late arrival on the Irish historical scene.

But if a parochial system, policed by an archdeacon, was already visible in Dublin before 1170, there are several compelling reasons for believing that the same was not true of the rest of the country. There are certain inescapable realities that must inevitably attach themselves to the existence of a parochial or proto-parochial system. Pastoral care of its nature is rooted in the organization of lay society – it cannot be discussed solely as an aspect of ecclesiastical polity. Without going into the remote origins of parochial organization in western Europe,[16] the overarching reality is that it evolved over a period of centuries in a confused process of cellular multiplication inextricably bound up with patterns of lordship. By the mid-twelfth century the great majority of such churches were sponsored and sustained by lords, whether for reasons of piety or profit, for the convenience of themselves and their tenants. In this complex process they acquired various proprietorial rights over the lands and income of *their* churches. Thus the parish church did not exist simply as a subdivision of the diocese: it was bound to the lay world by custom and right, while being simultaneously subject to an episcopal authority. The point at which lay and spiritual lordship intersected was the subject of an intense struggle for supremacy between church and 'state', laity and clergy, which occupied the legal energies of the eleventh and twelfth centuries. Put in this context, we have to ask how any pre-conquest system of pastoral care was related to lay authority on the one hand, and the spiritual authority on the other. To ask the question – what church? – we must be able to answer the prior questions: what lord and what bishop?

Translated into practical terms, this raises the question of who claimed the ownership of tithes, church lands, baptismal and burial rights, not to speak of lesser dues such as 'surplice fees' (dues for baptism, last unction, and burial). As Addleshaw so rightly observed in connection with the Carolingian church:

have missed this reference. I would certainly agree with her that the office of archdeacon was in general introduced into Ireland by the Anglo-Normans, but Dublin is a probable exception to this pattern.   **16** See G.W.O. Addleshaw, *The beginnings of the parochial system* (London, 1953); *The development of the parochial system from Charlemagne (778–814) to Urban II* (London, 1954); and *Rectors, vicars and patrons in twelfth and early thirteenth-century canon law* (London and York, 1956). For a briefer synopsis see Gerd Tellenbach, *The church in western Europe from the tenth to the early twelfth century* (Cambridge, 1993), pp 26–37, 75–90.

Every person had to pay a tenth of the produce of his land or of the profits in trade of commerce, at first it would seem to the bishop of the diocese. *But very soon* [italics mine] *the payment was transferred to the church where the person heard mass and his children were baptized. Along with the glebe it formed the endowment of the church ... Tithe helped too in the formation of parochial boundaries. A church's boundaries came to consist of the sum total of the lands from which it received tithe.*[17]

If such rights and customs belonged to non-monastic churches with some measure of pastoral oversight of the general population, then we should be able to find definite traces of them in the post-conquest sources. A church that had no right to baptism could not have a proper Easter liturgy, since the baptismal liturgy was an integral element in it. Along with the Easter liturgy came Easter communicants, confession, the Maundy Thursday chrism and the anointing of the sick. From the eleventh century onwards the possession of a font was the measure of parochial status.[18] The key question therefore is to whom did such rights belong? Moreover, once they had been established, whether by charter or by prescriptive right, they are not easily alienated from the church to which they are attached. We should therefore expect that disputes over the original ownership of tithes and dues would surface in legal disputes after the conquest, as in fact regularly occurred in England following the disintegration of the old minsters.[19] Given the sweeping changes that occurred in the Irish church after 1170, it is astonishing not to encounter such disputes in Ireland. We certainly hear of numerous disputes over the ownership of church land in the early years of the Anglo-Norman regime, but not a single word about tithes or dues. Similarly, we hear nothing about squabbles over the propriety of burial claims, even though they were recognized – in theory if not in practice – by both Irish law and the Irish canonists as far back as the eighth century.[20] Instead of the sound of constant background radiation, we encounter total radio silence. Something just does not add up.

---

17 Addleshaw *The development of the parochial system from Charlemagne (768–814) to Urban II (1088–1099)*, p. 4.   **18** See Colin Morris, *The papal monarchy: the western church from 1050 to 1250* (Oxford, 1989), pp 296–7.   **19** See, for example, Colin Platt, *The parish churches of medieval England* (London, 1981), pp 9–11.   **20** See Susan Leigh Fry, *Burial in medieval Ireland, 900–1500: a review of the written sources* (Dublin, 1999), pp 108–11. While Leigh is quite explicit about the legal claim, she is correspondingly vague about the precise identity of the 'territorial' church to which such claims theoretically belonged. Curiously, while Sinead Ní Ghabhlain recognizes that baptism and burial in the later middle ages were the prerogative of the parish church ('Church and community in medieval Ireland', p. 66), she does not discuss the question of burial propriety before the advent of the parish in Gaelic

At this point it is appropriate to introduce Gerald of Wales as our star witness. Writing in 1185, his view of the natives was nothing if not forthright:

> This is a filthy people, wallowing in vice. Of all people it is the least instructed in the rudiments of the faith. They do not yet pay tithes or first fruits or contract marriages.[21]

What is at issue is rather more than the moral hygiene of the Irish laity. It poses acute questions about how the laity interfaced with a supposedly non-monastic pre-conquest system of pastoral care, which elsewhere in Europe was inextricably bound up with the payment of tithes. It is not enough to dismiss his observation as sheer bias. The fact that Anglo-Norman lords were able to dispose of tithes to endow their monastic foundations – not merely from their own demesnes but from all the tenements that composed their lordships – can only mean that such tithes had no prior claimants. If they belonged either to churches, whether monastic or secular, or to the bishop, we should certainly have heard about it.[22] Since Gerald was not mistaken about the failure of the Irish to pay tithes, we should be better disposed to his comments about the disinclination of the Irish clergy and their prelates to stray beyond the enclosures of their monasteries to take responsibility for the pastoral care of the people.[23] His comments are doubly curious because it was not the business of monastic clergy to engage in the pastoral care of the laity. They only make sense if they were directed at the monks *in the absence of any alternative system of pastoral care.*

Thus in spite of scholarly efforts of historians of the Celtic period to reconstruct the outlines of non-monastic pastoral ministry, it seems clear that outside the Norse city states there is no evidence of its survival in 1170. Either it had not endured – if it ever existed outside the imagination of the canonists – or it was so defective by the time the Anglo-Normans appeared on the scene that there was nothing for it but to reconstruct it afresh on the tithing base of the manor. What is so striking about the post-conquest parochial system is its remarkable consistency. It lacks the untidiness of the parish system imposed in England and continental Europe by the long-established complications of custom and lordship. It is interesting to note that while the new parish churches, sustained by the tithes of manor, existed cheek-by-jowl with the castle, the

---

Ireland in the thirteenth century.   **21** Gerald of Wales, *The history and topography of Ireland,* translated by J.J. O'Meara (Mountrath, 1982), p. 106.   **22** So great was the control exercised by these new lords that it is possible to reconstruct the geographical extent of their lands by tracing their tithe endowments. I have discussed this question at some length in my article, 'The sacred and the secular: the Augustinian priory of Kells in Ossory 1193–1541' in *I.H.S.* xxiv (1984), pp 132–6.   **23** See my article, 'Gerald of Wales: a case of myopia?' in J.R. Guy and W.G. Neely (eds), *Contrast and comparisons: studies in Irish and Welsh church history*

lord's private chapel never became the parish church. The new parochial structures with their rectories and vicarages exhibit all the order and design of twelfth-century canon law. The timing of the conquest, which coincided with the emergence of a coherent system of canon law governing the pastoral oversight of parishes, was fortuitous.[24] Perhaps the principal defect of the new system lay not so much with the parochial as with the diocesan structures. Since the dioceses were designed on the basis of small Irish kingdoms apparently devoid of a parochial system, they were small by English and continental standards, with the inevitable result that most dioceses were poor and starved of material resources.

III

The primary problem with many questions about the parish church in medieval Ireland is that they have never been asked. We are gazing into a black hole of astronomic proportions. In his three-volume *Irish churches and monastic buildings* Harold Leask devoted a seven-page chapter to parochial churches, entitled 'some parish churches'.[25] The title says it all. Observing *en passant* that most of the larger churches are situated in the towns, 'few of them date in their entirety from the years subsequent to 1400',[26] he gave no explanation as to why it should be so. Similarly we are told that many rural parish churches were rebuilt in the fifteenth century. But given the fact that by the early thirteenth century Anglo-Norman Ireland had established a comprehensive parochial network, why are there no examples – for we are offered none – of earlier structures? Who built them or rebuilt them? Why were they built where they were built? It is as if two centuries of parochial history can be dismissed as of no consequence.[27]

While we know that the Anglo-Norman parish was coextensive with the manor, the tithes of which had initially been granted by the lord to the parish priest or, more usually, to a monastic foundation of his choice, we do not know who endowed the building. The fact that the parish church was invariably located within a couple of hundred metres of the castle, and often much closer, suggests the lord had more than a little to do with it. It can hardly be coincidental that

(Llandysul, 1999), pp 46–9. **24** These changes occurred principally between the council of Nimes (1096) and the fourth Lateran council (1215). **25** H.G. Leask, *Irish churches and monastic buildings* (3 vols, Dundalk, 1955–60), iii, pp 81–8. **26** Ibid., p. 81. **27** Ní Ghabhlain, in her article 'The origin of medieval parishes in Gaelic Ireland: the evidence from Kilfenora' in *R.S.A.I. Jn.*, cxxvi (1996), pp 37–61, has indeed tried to deal with some of these issues, but in the nature of things she is hampered by the limitations of the documentary evidence. Ana Dolan's study of 'The large medieval churches of the dioceses of Leighlin, Ferns and Ossory', pp 26–65, while providing a useful examination of the towns with notable parochial buildings were under the lordship of powerful magnates: Callan, St Mary's, Kilkenny, and New Ross (Marshall); Gowran (Butler); Galway (de Burgh); and Youghal (Fitzgerald), to name a few. The same was probably true of the small rural churches, even though they were usually in the gift of monasteries.

The fact that virtually all parish churches were rebuilt in the fourteenth and fifteenth centuries plainly suggests that the original buildings came to be regarded as inadequate, even though this development occurred mainly in the post-plague period when the population had diminished by a third or more. It is probably true that the buildings that were replaced were extremely modest. Until further research is carried out, along the lines of the archaeological survey of Louth and other counties,[28] we will not know how to define 'modest'. None of the Louth rural parish churches was positively identified as being earlier than the fifteenth of sixteenth centuries, though clearly they would have occupied the site of the thirteenth-century building. Indeed, it may be the case that few thirteenth-century parish churches will ever be successfully identified.[29] If that is true, then it seems likely that the churches of the period were built in wood, as were the great majority of castles and manorial residences in this period. In 1303 the motte castle at Inch in Tipperary included a new hall *cum veteri capella lignea*.[30] There is no reason to presume that the parish church, which stood a few metres away on the site occupied by the present late medieval ruin, would have been built in a grander style than this 'old wooden chapel'. The fact that the rectorial tithes of most parish churches were held by monastic communities meant that much of the income of the parish went to support them, leaving the

buildings themselves, scarcely touches on the wider issues.   **28** Victor M. Buckley and P. David Sweetman, *Archaeological survey of County Louth* (Dublin, 1991), pp 218–66. Much useful data on parish churches, among others, can be found in the series *Archaeological inventories* for the counties of Louth, Meath, Wicklow, Wexford, Waterford, Carlow, Laois, Offaly, Cavan, Monaghan, Galway (2 vols), and Cork (3 vols), published by the Stationery Office, Dublin.   **29** The parish church of Tullaherin, Co. Kilkenny, seems to have thirteenth-century traces. See Conleth Manning, 'Some notes on the early history and archaeology of Tullaherin' in *In the Shadow of the Steeple*, no. 6 (1998), pp 19–39, especially pp 27–8. If this is the case, I would point out that Tullaherin is different from most rural parish churches in that it occupies a pre-Norman monastic site, and that the lord of the manor of Tullaherin was the bishop of Ossory, who had greater resources at his disposal than an ordinary knight. Another example of a village church is Newcastle Lyons, which has been the subject of study by Tadhg O'Keeffe. He concluded that the western tower may be as early as the late fourteenth century, but he assigns most of the windows to the fifteenth century, while not excluding 'the possibility of a date immediately pre-1400 for some of the work'. See Tadhg O'Keeffe, 'Medieval architecture and the village of Newcastle Lyons' in Peter O'Sullivan (ed.), *Newcastle Lyons: a parish of the pale* (Dublin, 1986), pp 45–61.   **30** Extent of the manor of Nyncheaunlef in Newport B. White (ed.), *The Red Book of*

parishes in the charge of an impoverished vicar. Only in the larger towns were there sufficient resources to build significant parish churches.

Two factors in the fourteenth century help to account for the dramatic change in the profile of the parish church. First, reference has already been made to heightened emphasis on the Mass, culminating in the phenomenal development of the Corpus Christi festival and its attendant festivities, to which we shall return. While it would be difficult to pinpoint its knock-on impact on church architecture, no one can seriously doubt that something that had such a powerful hold on the medieval imagination could fail to find expression in bricks and mortar. Second, the horror of the Black Death (1348–50), in which an estimated one third of the population perished, left a profoundly pessimistic mark on the European psyche. The psychological shock waves – something conceivable only on the scale of the impact of a major nuclear holocaust – were registered in the iconography of the period: the grim portrayals of judgement and the horrors of hell were frequently displayed in the portrayals of 'the doom' over the chancel arch, to say nothing of the ghastly cadaver effigial monuments in the side aisles. The shortness and uncertainty of life was deeply impressed on the popular imagination. Getting to heaven, if not for the love of God at least for the fear of hell, was an absolute priority. The legions of the demonic hosts lay in wait to snatch the souls of unsuspecting faithful even at the moment of death. It is against this background that we can understand the extraordinary upsurge of lay interest in, and generosity towards, the parish church.

What is less explicable is why parish churches, as opposed to the monastic church, with the notable exception of the friaries, became the object of lay giving. In the late twelfth- and early thirteenth-century, it was the monasteries that were the focus of lay support to the extent of fleecing the parishioners of their tithes. It is significant that the main beneficiaries of lay piety in the late twelfth- and early thirteenth-century were the Cistercians and the Augustinian canons, yet no new foundations were created after this comparatively short period of hectic activity. Only the friaries maintained their popularity till the end of the medieval period. One notable exception is Christ Church Cathedral, Dublin, which had an Augustinian chapter.[31] Whatever the reasons for the decline of these orders, it would appear that the vacuum was filled to a large extent by the increasing profile of the parish church. It may be that the enormous inflation of memorial masses simply could not be accommodated within the tight schedule of the monastic *cursus*. The secular churches, with their lighter load, were better placed to accommodate the increase in liturgical traffic.

Ormond (Dublin, 1932), no. 17, p. 52.   **31** Raymond Refaussé with Colm Lennon (eds), *The registers of Christ Church cathedral*, Dublin (Dublin, 1998). The cathedral was naturally the focus of much of the civic and religious life of the city.

To attribute the increased profile of the laity exclusively to the impact of the plague would be too simple. The wealth and position of the church was the direct consequence of lay generosity since the reign of Constantine. According to the Kilkenny annalist John Clyn, there was a significant level of church building activity in the city in the first half of the fourteenth century.[32] The new chancel in St Canice's Cathedral was commenced in 1321. Three years later William Outlaw was commanded to cover the cathedral roof and the roof of the lady chapel with lead as a penance for his role in the Kyteler affair. In 1343 a new bell tower was erected at St Mary's parish church, presumably by the parishioners.[33] Four years later, on the eve of the Black Death, he tells us that Lady Isabella Palmer, who had financed part of the chancel in the Franciscan friary,[34] died in the same year that the friars themselves began work on a new campanile. In Dublin, just on the eve of the Black Death, Robert North bequeathed an unspecified sum of money 'for the building of St Warburg's [sic] church and the new chapel of the B.V.M'.[35] The wording of the bequest suggests that building was already in progress. Such signs of activity ought to guard us against oversimplification.[36]

Nevertheless, there can be little doubt that the shock of the plague concentrated lay minds as never before. Instead of belfries and choirs, chapels and chantries became the focus of benefaction. As early as 1350 a royal licence was issued to Richard Wright, chaplain

> To assign to the parson and parishioners of the church of St John the Evangelist of 'Bothestrete', Dublin, for the enlargement of the said church and for a certain chapel to be newly made in honor of the Blessed Virgin Mary, a messuage in St John's parish, bounded in the east by 'Fishamelstrete' ... [37]

Thanks to the preservation of a number of the deeds of the parish, we are able to trace in outline the way in which the chapel attracted lay investment. In 1434

---

32 Richard Butler (ed.), *The annals of Ireland by Friar John Clyn and Thady Dowling, together with the annals of New Ross* (Dublin, 1849).   **33** Clyn was apt to commend pious works. Since he mentioned no benefactor in this context, it is likely that the initiative lay with the parishioners themselves.   **34** Ibid. sub anno 1347 '*que frontem chori fratrum erigi fecit*'. The friars in question must be the Fransiscans, to which Clyn belonged.   **35** In 1346. See *Christ Church deeds*, no. 633.   **36** In Dublin, for example, John de Grauntsete received a licence from the prior of Holy Trinity in 1347 to build a chapel in honor of the Holy Trinity in St Michan's churchyard on the north side of the church (*Christ Church deeds*, no. 236), and in the following year he built the chapel del Marie du Grace on the bridge of Dublin (Mary Clark and Raymond Refaussé (eds), *Directory of historic guilds of Dublin* (Dublin, 1993), p. 32).   **37** J.L. Robinson, 'On the ancient deeds of the parish of St John, Dublin, preserved in the library of Trinity College' in *RIA Procs.*, xxxiii Section C (1916–17), p. 188.

John Lytill bequeathed his body to be buried in the chapel of the Blessed Virgin Mary in the church of St John near the body of his former wife, Eleanor Comyn. To the chaplain, Sir William Fitzwilliam, he left a gown, the bed on which he lay, and his records (*cartae*) 'to remain and be preserved among the deeds of the said chapel'.[38] Moreover, he made provision from his properties to provide an annual income of 40s. per annum

> to provide a perpetual chantry of one priest in the said chapel and choir of St John's Church for the souls of John Lytill and Eleanora, their parents and benefactors; the said Sir William to be the first holder of the chantry, and to appoint his successor.[39]

It may be noted that while the chapel was not up to this point a perpetual chantry, it does seem to have had a corporate existence of some kind since it possessed its own collection of deeds. By a curious coincidence, the only annual account to survive for an Irish chantry in this period belongs almost certainly to St Mary's chapel. Sometime in the 1470s we have a rental of the receipts from the land of the Blessed Mary, amounting to £5 6s. 4d. Expenditure amounted to £1 3s. 3 ½ d., consisting of payments to carpenters, daubers (plasterers), heliers (slaters), masons and other workmen. Other items included new locks and keys, and 16d. for wine for Mass.[40] We are not told who compiled the account. It was usual for religious guilds to appoint wardens to look after the property and finances of the guild chapel, so it is likely that these accounts were rendered by laymen who had to have them audited by the membership of the guild or their representatives, in the same manner as the churchwardens' accounts.

Thus the story of this parochial lady chapel casts a brief ray of light on the process by which the laity evolved from a passive role in the thirteenth century to a highly participative and corporate role by the second half of the fifteenth century, if not somewhat earlier. Beginning with the extension of the church in 1350 as a result of a private bequest, the chapel in time acquired the services of a permanently endowed chaplain, who was paid by what amounts to a guild of lay devotees that administered the finances and saw that everything was kept in due repair. All of this activity was distinct from the duties of the church-wardens, who surfaced regularly in the parochial deeds. It is a paradigm of the development of the lay role. Such activities were replicated in many parish churches *inter Anglicos*.

The degree, if not the measure, of lay investment in the parish church may be gauged from the surviving wills of the late medieval period. Legacies for particular or general work on the fabric of the church, chapels, parochial guilds, vestments, chalices, and liturgical books were a regular feature of wills: indeed,

38 Ibid., p. 198. 39 Ibid., p. 198. 40 Ibid., pp 201–2.

one could almost say they were part of the fixed format. Naturally, the church that the legator designated for burial was usually the primary subject of benefaction, but it was also common to provide additional legacies to several parish churches, the four mendicant orders, and monasteries.[41] The wills of Hugh Galyane (c.1474) and Jonet Cristor (1473) are typical, if more detailed. Hugh's exclusive concern was his parish church:

> I bequeath ... my body to be buried in the church of St Mary of the Dam in the said city [of Dublin]. Item, I leave for the repair of the belfry of the said church 6s. 8d. Item, I leave for the maintenance of the north wall of the said church 6s. 8d. Item, I leave to William Bluet, my parish chaplain 6s. 8d. ... Item, I leave to the works of the church of St Mary of the Dam 6s. 8d.[42]

Jonet, on the other hand, included a wider spectrum of churches in her will:

> I, Jonet Cristor ... do make my testament in this manner: to be buried in the nave of the parish church of Glasnevin before the image of St Mary. Item, I leave 12s. to the said church to buy a cope. Item, I leave to the church of the Holy Trinity, Dublin 3s. Item, to the monastery of St Thomas the Martyr 3s. Item, to the monastery of St Mary the Virgin, near Dublin, 2s. Item, I leave to the parish church of Clondalkin 2s. Item, I leave to the 4 orders of mendicant friars 6s. 8d.[43]

Quite incidentally, wills sometimes yield information about the internal disposition of small village churches. In 1475 Richard Goldynge left various sums to the parish church of Balscadden, including 5s. 6d. to the proctors of the lights of St Mary.[44] References to such confraternities are common, and seem to have been a regular feature of village as well as city churches. It is equally clear that many of these modest churches supported several altars or chapels. In 1471 William Nele bequeathed various sums in his will to the parish church of Clondalkin, including 20d. to the chaplain of St Mary's [altar], a chalice weighing 16 ounces to the altar of St Mary, 6s. 8d. to the altar of St Brigid, and 6s. 8d. 'to the altar of St Thomas ... towards the maintenance of the lights of the said altars'.[45] William seems to have been a tanner by trade, for he bequeathed his tanhouse to his son, Sir John Nele, who was one of the chaplains

41 See H.F. Berry (ed.), *Register of the wills and inventories of the diocese of Dublin in the time of archbishops Tregury and Walton, 1457–1483* (Dublin, 1898), *passim*. For a more detailed analysis of lay bequests see Margaret Murphy, 'The high cost of dying: an analysis of *pro anima* bequests in medieval Dublin' in W.G. Shiels and D. Wood (eds), *The church and wealth: Studies in Church History*, xxiv (Oxford, 1987), pp 111–22. **42** Berry (ed.), *Register of the wills and inventories of the diocese of Dublin*, pp 86–7. **43** *Ibid.*, p. 56. **44** *Ibid.*, p. 121. **45** *Ibid.*, p. 98.

attached to the church. Besides the gift of an expensive chalice to the chapel of St Mary,[46] he also left a bequest for the purchase of an antiphonary.[47] Three years later John Whytoyn, John Eliot, and William Broghe, chaplains, are named as beneficiaries of the will of Nicholas Ketyng:[48] they were, presumably, the chaplains attached to the altars dedicated to the saints in the previous will. Thus we must envisage a village church served by a vicar – the rectory belonged to St Mary's Abbey – and three chaplains, who were probably maintained by lay confraternities attached to each chapel. The perpetual vicar would, of course, have been maintained by the lesser tithes and the parish glebeland.

Two conclusions may be drawn from these developments. First, that much of the late medieval parochial building or rebuilding fever was driven by the inflationary demand for private masses, particularly in the post-plague period. In order to accommodate more chapels staffed by chaplains, each with their attendant lay organizations, it was necessary to extend the modest confines of the thirteenth-century nave. Second, the responsibility of parishioners for the upkeep of the nave in England, and by extension in Ireland, seems to have been firmly established by the thirteenth century.[49] This division of responsibility must have had organizational and architectural consequences. As the pressures on building space became more acute, so too the need for the laity to raise money and administer it grew proportionately. It can be no coincidence that the office of churchwarden emerges into the clear light of day around 1350 in England. Another consequence may have been architectural. In the English context Andrew Brown has underlined the divergent histories of chancel and nave building, drawing attention to the fact that chancels tended to be the least rebuilt part of the parish church after 1350, perhaps because of a decline in the value of rectorial income.[50] Once again, we come up against the problem of insufficient research on Irish parish churches to draw any conclusion.

Since the jury will remain out for the foreseeable future, the only option is to make some general remarks about a particular building. The manor, town and parish of Callan were founded by William Marshall, probably in the last decade

---

46 Valued at 5½ marks (ibid. p. 97). **47** Ibid., p. 98. **48** Ibid., p.113. **49** See Charles Drew, *Early parochial organisation in England: the origins of the office of churchwarden* (London, 1976), p. 8. Also Mason, 'The role of the English parishioner, 1100–1500', p. 23 ff. One curious aspect of this custom is that it is based on English synodal legislation rather than the strict requirements of canon law, whereby the maintenance of both nave and chancel is a rectorial responsibility. For examples of its application in Ireland see Newport White (ed.), *Irish monastic deeds, 1200–1600* (Dublin, 1936), pp 242, 266, 272. **50** See Andrew Brown, 'The late medieval English church: parish and devotion in buildings and landscape' in Blair and Pyrah (eds), *Church archaeology*, pp 65–6. Complaints about the fall-off of tithing income were an unfailing source of clerical lament in Ireland from the mid-fourteenth century onwards. In Ireland, given the prevalence of war and the shrinkage of the land of peace, the decline was certainly more catastrophic.

1   Western tower of St Mary's church, Callan, Co. Kilkenny,
fourteenth century.

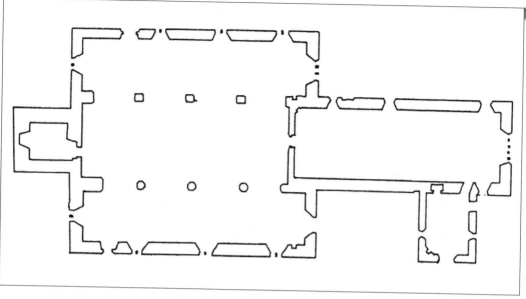

2 Interior of St Mary's church, Callan, Co. Kilkenny.

of the twelfth century. Due to its wealth, Callan was retained in demesne by his successors, lords of Leinster and, subsequently, the liberty of Kilkenny. Even after the tripartite division of the liberty in 1317 between the heirs of Gilbert de Clare, Callan was retained in demesne by the coparceners and their successors, which makes its later history very complex. It is usual to find wealthy parishes associated with the great seignorial manors, and Callan is no exception. With a tithe income valued 50 marks (£33 6s. 8d.) in the taxation of the diocese of Ossory by Bishop Ledrede c.1324, excluding vicarial tithes amounting to a further £8, the parish of Callan was by far the richest benefice in the diocese.[51] The rectorial tithes of the next wealthiest parishes did not equal the value of the vicarial tithes of Callan. It is therefore not surprising that Callan possesses one of the finest fifteenth-century parish churches in Ireland. Except for the tower at the western end of the building, which belongs to a previous phase of the building, the nave, side aisles and chancel belong to the mid-fifteenth century. The nave measures 68 feet in length, flanked by two aisles, each 73 feet. The chancel is no less than 71 feet in length, longer by a slight margin than the nave.

While this is not the place to discuss the architectural merits of the church, two points deserve notice. First, the existence of an imposing tower from an

---

51 'Red Book of the diocese of Ossory', in *10th Report Historical Manuscripts Commission* (London, 1885), appendix 5, pp 234–41.

earlier period, clearly suggests that the rest of the building was razed to the ground in order to accommodate a greatly expanded fifteenth-century nave and chancel. Unfortunately, we have no information about the source of the funds required to build the nave and the aisles. There is, however, a curious mid-sixteenth century list of lands and rents belonging to the church, which are not glebeland. The most likely explanation is that this long list was a checklist for the use of the churchwardens when they were composing their annual account.[52] The number of erasures suggests that it was revised for use in later years. At the very least it is a record of numerous legacies bequeathed by the faithful members of the parish. Considering the twenty-two finely executed memorials of wealthy members of the parish (largely sixteenth century),[53] we cannot seriously doubt that the parishioners themselves were responsible for the construction of the nave and side aisles. Second, the addition of such a long chancel must be related to the wealth of the rector and vicar. Granted that they enjoyed considerably greater incomes than their clerical colleagues in the diocese, they certainly had the means to augment the nave in style. In making the chancel slightly longer than the nave the rector was perhaps making a statement about his status.

Callan is notable for another reason: the apparent absence of any dominant family, which is surprising in view of the remarkable fact that for a town of its size there were no friaries located there before c.1468, when the Augustinian friary was built by James FitzEdmund MacRichard Butler, father of Piers, ninth earl of Ormond.[54] In Gowran, by contrast, Edmund Butler, earl of Carrick (d.1321), his son James, first earl of Ormond (d.1337), and James, third earl of Ormond (d.1405) were buried in the parish church.[55] As lords of the manor and town of Gowran, they clearly had some part in the building and the affairs of the church that was the family mausoleum. In the fifteenth and early sixteenth centuries there are many examples of endowments made by the great in the parish church, especially in the form of collegial chantries: the earl of Kildare (Maynooth, 1518), St Lawrence (Howth, ante 1500), Fleming (Slane, 1512), and Verdon (Ardee, ante 1487), to name a few.[56] Apart from occasional visits to Ireland, on the other hand, the lords of Callan from the beginning were almost

52 White (ed.), *Irish monastic deeds, 1200–1600*, pp 186–90.   **53** W. Carrigan, *The history and antiquities of the diocese of Ossory*, (4 vols, Dublin, 1905), iii. pp 298–308.   **54** Carrigan, *Ossory*, iii, pp 310–14; A. Gwynn and R.N. Hadcock, *Medieval religious houses, Ireland* (London, 1970), p. 297.   **55** Carrigan, *Ossory*, iii, p. 400.   **56** See Mary Ann Lyons, 'Sidelights on the Kildare ascendancy: a survey of Geraldine involvement in the church, c.1470–1520' in *Archivium Hibernicum* xlviii (1994), pp 73–87; Mary Ann Lyons, *Church and society in Co. Kildare, c.1470–1547* (Dublin, 2000), p. 87 ff.; Mary Ann Lyons, 'The foundation of the Geraldine college of the Blessed Virgin Mary, Maynooth, 1518' in *Journal of the Kildare Archaeological Society*, xviii (1994–95), pp 134–50; L.P. Murray, 'The ancient chantries of Co. Louth', in *Journal of the County Louth Archaeological Society* ix (1939), pp 181–208; John Bradley, 'The chantry college, Ardee' in *Journal of the County Louth*

always absentee. It was not until the earl of Ormond purchased the Despenser purparty, which included only a one-third interest in Callan, that the Butlers became directly involved in Callan.[57] It was, in fact, James FitzEdmund MacRichard Butler, deputy of the earl of Ormond, who was in possession of the Ormond interest in Callan, but instead of establishing a college in the parish church he founded the friary, where he was later buried. The absence, no less than the presence, of a powerful lay patron is a factor that deserves close consideration in any full discussion of the development of the parish church. Too often the church building is treated simply as an architectural phenomenon existing somewhere in historical cyber space. Monastic patrons are constantly invoked in monastic studies: the identity of the piper is no less important in the case of parish history.

IV

The origin of the office of churchwarden is inextricably bound up with the development of a participant lay parochial community, since they were elected annually by the parishioners. The remote origins of the office in England need not detain us here, beyond observing that we begin to encounter *procutores* [proctors] or *custodes* [wardens] in the second half of the thirteenth century.[58] The earliest reference that I have found in Irish sources to churchwardens – or proctors as they are usually called – is in connection with St Werburgh's church in 1454:

> Indenture 10 Aug. 32 Henry VI, between John Vale, barber, and William [Cornell], proctors of St Werburgh's church; William Sutton, John Burnell, Thomas Rocheford and Walter Molghane, parishioners, first part; Geoffrey Calfe and William Broun, chaplains, on the other part: witnesses that the said proctors, &c., to farm, let to said chaplains a waste place of said church, on the south, and the house of St Mary del Dam, in which John Andron now dwells, on the north, to hold for 40 years: rent six pence silver to the proctors and their successors at Easter, during the lifetime of said William Cornell and Elena his wife, and the heirs of their bodies. Said Geoffrey and William to build a chamber of oak covered with oak boards, and keep in repair. If William and Elena die without heirs, they to pay 12d. silver at Easter and Michaelmas to the proctors; the latter to pay chief rent, if any.[59]

Archaeological Society, xxii (1989), pp 16–19.   **57** I have examined in detail the division of the de Clare lordship of Kilkenny in my doctoral thesis, 'The Butler lordship in Ireland, 1185–1515' (Trinity College, Dublin, 1970), p. 74 ff.   **58** Drew, *Early parochial organisation in England*, pp 6–7; J.C. Cox traces it to the first canon of the council of London, 1127 (*Churchwardens' accounts* (London, 1913), p. 1).   **59** H.F. Twiss, 'Some ancient deeds of the

This otherwise uninspiring deed is significant for several reasons. First, it is clear that the institution of churchwarden was already a long-established feature of parochial life in St Werburgh's. The wardens plainly acted as the representatives of the parishioners with authority to enter into legal agreements on their behalf. We have therefore no reason to believe that the office was new to Ireland either in the fifteenth or, for that matter, the fourteenth, century. Second, the churchwardens are associated with four named parishioners in the indenture, who were doubtless prominent members of the parochial community, similar to the *laici fidedigni* ['worthy laymen'] commanded by the archbishop of Armagh in 1366 to appear before him or his deputies from every parish in the deanery of Trim, along with abbots, priors, rectors, vicars and parochial chaplains.[60] While no specific office is assigned to the four men, they were probably sidesmen (i.e. synodsmen) who, like the *fidedigni* in the deanery of Trim, attended synods or visitation courts, to support the wardens' presentments.[61] Third, the property leased to the chaplains was owned by the parishioners corporately. Since it was in lay ownership, the acquisition of property on behalf of the parish was possible without infringing the statute of Mortmain (1279), prohibiting land from being alienated to the church without royal licence. Without legal status it is difficult to see how the laity could have received the properties bequeathed to the parish church.[62] In effect, the community of the parish was a guild with the power to appoint officers, to hold property, and to regulate their members.

The liability of the laity to maintain the fabric of the nave and to provide liturgical books, vestments and sacred vessels as laid down by thirteenth-century synodical decrees, together with the financial and liturgical pressures, particularly after the plague, forms the immediate background to the emergence of the churchwardens. The business of levying parish rates, the management of numerous bequests, the collection of rents, ensuring that money was accounted for, books and parish plate were not lost, stolen or alienated, the payment of chaplains and clerks, called for systematization. It should be remembered that these new duties and revenues were not concerned with traditional clerical revenues such as tithes, glebelands and surplice fees that belonged to an earlier phase of parochial evolution. The earliest surviving churchwardens' accounts, which belong to the parish of St Michael without the North Gate, Bath, date from 1349. They reveal that the wardens were charged with duties over and above the care and supervision of the church fabric. They administered rents, managed bequests for memorial masses and obits (anniversary masses on the

parish of St Werburgh, Dublin, 1243–1676' in *R.I.A. Procs.*, xxxv, Section C (1919), pp 288–9.   **60** Brendan Smith (ed.), *The register of Milo Sweetman, archbishop of Armagh 1361–1380* (Dublin, 1996), no. 240.   **61** Cox, *Churchwardens' accounts*, p. 3.   **62** See Drew, *Early parochial organization in England*, pp 22–3.

mind-day of the legator), bought candles, paid wages, maintained liturgical books, and sold church furnishings.[63]

Although England possesses a rich collection of medieval parish archives, almost nothing has survived the ravages of time, mindlessness and destruction in Ireland. The sum of pre-reformation documents is easily reckoned: parish of St John, Dublin (150); parish of St Werburgh, Dublin (40); and the parishes of St Catherine and St James, Dublin (21).[64] Our knowledge of the internal arrangements of Irish parishes would be virtually blank were it not for the fortuitous survival of a series of twelve churchwarden's accounts for St Werburgh's, ranging from 1484 to 1597, eight of which belong to the pre-reformation period.[65] Until a critical edition of these accounts is published, our knowledge will not be as complete as the circumstances permit. It may be said, however, that these quite detailed records are in no way inferior to English records of the same type. They reveal a remarkably well-ordered parochial community in which the laity played an essential role.

A random sample of items that appear on the account of Richard Dowgyne and Patricke Kerde for 1510–11 provides a fairly comprehensive list of the responsibilities of the wardens:[66] quarterly payments of 5s. for the Mary priest (i.e. chaplain to the lady chapel), 'roschis' (rushes) for St Martin's chapel on St Martin's Day (10 November) 2s. 4d.[67]; the quarterly dirge 4d. (for the souls of parish benefactors);[68] bread and wine (for mass) 9d.; the wax maker for the Paschal candle 10d.; to the priests and clerks for Margaret Downis 'mynde' (memorial mass) for dirge and mass 16d. (in fulfilment of a legacy); charges for graves; payments to heliers, carpenters, plumbers, and for poles, lime, laths, pitch, spikes, slates. Receipts included rents for houses, chambers and gardens, grave money at a rate of 3s. 4d. per grave, and 4d. from Thomas Fleming for the loan of a 'ball' (i.e. pall covering the 'hearse').[69] The same account includes an

---

63 Platt, *The parish churches of medieval England*, p. 89.   64 J.L. Robinson, 'Ancient deeds of the parish of St John, Dublin', pp 175–224; J. Lydon, 'A fifteenth-century building account from Dublin' [a short account for repairs on St John's, 1477] in *Ir. Econ. Soc. Hist.*, ix (1982), pp 73–5; H.F. Berry, 'Some ancient deeds of the parish of St Werburgh, Dublin, 1243–1676', in *R.S.A.I. Jn.*, xlv (1915), pp 32–44; H.F. Twiss, 'Some ancient deeds of the parish of St Werburgh, Dublin, 1243–1676', pp 282–315.   65 R.C.B., P326/ 27/1, 1 ff. See also J.L. Robinson, 'Churchwardens' accounts, 1484–1600, St Werburgh's Church, Dublin', in *R.S.A.I. Jn.*, xliv (1914), pp 132–42.   66 R.C.B., P326/27/1/ 8.   67 The provision of rushes 'to strow the church' at festivals is a recurrent item throughout the series of accounts. No mention of seats or pews is made, but pews certainly existed in English parish churches at this period, though often reserved for use by women.   68 Dirge or *Dirige*, the opening word of Psalm 5.8 in the office of the dead. The payment was probably made to the parish clerk or one of the chaplains.   69 Palls, and even coffins of appropriate sizes, were often hired out by the parish as a source of revenue, and, no doubt, convenience to parishioners. The hearse was not a vehicle, but a framework over the coffin, on which candles were place.

interesting inventory of church plate, for which the wardens were responsible, presumably because they were bequeathed:

> Item a cros of sylver gylt with a stone weyng lx uns [ounces]
> Item a senser of sylver gylt weyng xxx uns
> Item a pax bord of sylver gylt weyng v uns iii qtr
> Item a buste of sylver gylt weyng iiii uns di [4 ½]
> Item a chalyse of sylver gylt weyng xv uns
> Item a chalyse of sylver gylt weyng xvi uns qtr
> Item a chalyse of sylver gylt weyng xiii uns
> Item a chalyse of sylver gylt weyng xii uns di
> Item a chalyse of sylver gylt weyng xii uns
>   Summa vii^{xx} xviiii uns. Quit' sunt inde [They are discharged]

The total weight of the collection, amounting to almost 10 pounds of silver, gives a fair measure of the level of lay bequests. That the church had no fewer than five chalices is because the chalice, as the receptacle of the blood of Christ, was a popular focus of lay piety. It was therefore deemed to be a singularly meritorious – in the theological sense of the word – gift. Another curious inclusion were valuable items held in pledge by the wardens:

> Item a mas[er] of sylver gylte with a rose in the mydys and vii spons of sylver wich bethe Phelip Whit in pleg for iii Li iiis [£3 3s.]
> Item a payr of bedys of corall gandeyt with sylver weyng ii unces di et qtr [3/4] wich bethe Alyson Selymanys in pleg for vi s viii d
> Item a crose of sylver gylt wich ys James Westons yn pleg for vi s viii d

It seems that Philip, Alison and James had surrendered their personal valuables to the parish as security for debts due. Equally notable is the fact that two of the pledges were items for private devotional use.

While we have no way of knowing what the medieval church of St Werburgh looked like, we can glean a significant amount of information about its staffing and interior disposition. The parish priest was the perpetual vicar, since the rector was chancellor of St Patrick's cathedral. The vicar lived in a chamber attached to the church, rendering an annual rent in 1496 of ten shillings to the wardens. Unlike the Mary priest, he was not paid by the parishioners since he received the lesser tithes. Strangely, there seems to have been no manse for him to live in, so perhaps there was no glebe. The chaplain of St Mary's chapel, on the north side of the chancel, received a mere forty shillings annually. Like the vicar, he lived in a chamber attached to the church. It is likely that another chaplain served St Martin's chapel on the south side of the chancel. Although he is not mentioned in the accounts, it may be that he was paid by a guild or by private patrons. Since the guild of millers maintained the light in the chapel of their patron saint, it is likely that they maintained their own chaplain there. In 1520 the parish clerk received three shillings per quarter.

Regarding the furnishing of the church, we read about images of St Mary and St Martin, a rood beam supporting the great crucifix, with figures of St Mary and St John on either side. There was also a rood loft. The 'hye quer' (chancel) is mentioned, where the [Easter] sepulchre light was maintained, no doubt in the sepulchre niche on the north side of the high altar. Apart from the saints already mentioned, we hear, not surprisingly, of a 'saynt warbrow ys lyght', but where her image was located is not stated. It is strange that St Werburgh does not seem to have a chapel in the church dedicated in her honor. It may be that her altar stood north or south of the rood screen. The accounts refer to the bells of the church: the sacring-bell (probably over the rood), and the sanctus bell, which announced the progress of the service to those outside the church. No reference is made to 'the doom', the judgement scene often painted above the chancel arch, but silence may only mean that no money was expended on it in the period of the account. Numerous references to wax and candles remind us of the dark interiors of many parish churches, and the fact that some services – for example the early mass (the morrow mass) said at 5 a.m. or 6 a.m. depending on the season – would have been said in the hours of darkness. In sum, it is clear that the interior disposition of the building reflected the normal layout of contemporary English churches.[70]

It is not easy to see the shape of the parochial community that is subsumed in the sources. In 1471 Richard Herford, chaplain, and the two churchwardens of St John's church, William Yong and Thomas Prikker, 'with the consent of the parishioners' leased to John Dromyn a certain property for a term of twenty-one years.[71] Nowhere does it appear how or by whom such consent was given. In a series of ordinances governing procedures in the parish of All Saints, Bristol, we learn that

> It is agreed and assented that from henceforth no proctor set [lease] out of any house for years, nor abate any rent of any house, without the advice and consent of the substance of the parishioners, under the pain of £20.[72]

In an age when elections to parliament were conducted by juries empanelled by the sheriff, and not by anything resembling universal suffrage, we should not

---

70 For this see Platt, and the essential Eamon Duffy, *The stripping of the altars: traditional religion in England c.1400– c.1580* (New Haven and London, 1992). **71** J.L. Robinson, 'Ancient deeds of the parish of St John, Dublin', no. 131 (p. 201). Cf. no. 126 (p.200), no. 139 (p.203). **72** Clive Burgess (ed.), *The pre-reformation records of All Saints', Bristol* [Part I]

expect to find formal bodies such as select or general vestries. The range of trades represented by the churchwardens themselves are probably representative of the classes of people who constituted 'the substance of the parishioners'. Among the deeds of St John's parish a random sample of trades included John Bennet (merchant), William Yong (butcher), Richard White (pewterer); in St Werburgh's, John Vale (barber), William Cornell (armourer), Walter Baldewyn (gentleman), Nicholas Laweles (merchant), Thomas Ashe (baker), Richard Dugyn (glover), and John Elys (goldsmith). It is likely that these men were also senior figures within their respective guilds. While the numbers of people constituting this 'substance of the parishioners' was probably quite small, it seems from the range of professions found among the wardens that there was no marked reluctance to serve in the office, which must have required a heavy commitment. Certainly a warden was responsible personally for any shortfall in his annual account, for his debts were repeated in future accounts. The reference to the annual election on the first Sunday of May (1495) as a 'lawdable costome of this chyrche'[73] suggests that the office was held in some esteem. A further powerful motive to serve the church was the warden's desire to be included among the lists of benefactors whose souls were prayed for at the annual general mind on the Thursday and Friday after Ash Wednesday.[74] An entry in the 1503–4 account touches the heart of late medieval anxiety in the face of the pains of purgatory and the necessity of alleviating them:

> Item, R^d of master felenys [Mr Felenys] to the reparasyon of the cherch & to the entent that he schold be set in the bede Roll xs.[75]

By paying ten shillings towards the fabric fund, Master Felenys earned the right to be remembered at the mind by virtue of being entered on the bead roll [prayer list].

Whether representatives of the 'substance of parishioners' attended the auditing of the accountants is not apparent. Certainly the accounting period, which varied from year to year, was not associated with the date for the annual election of wardens. In their annual account for the period 1 June 1505 to 10 June 1507, the wardens, Thomas Ashe and John Armeror, made reference to a more detailed set of accounts recorded in 'there boke of acquont', which suggests that great care was taken with book keeping.[76] In 1495 Christopher Armorer and Thomas Ashe presented their accounts for audit before the rector

---

(Bristol, 1995), p. 3. **73** R.C.B., P326/27/1/4, f.5. **74** See Burgess, *The pre-reformation records of All Saints', Bristol*, pp xx–xxvii. Burgess lays great stress on the desire to alleviate the pains of purgatory by being included in the list of benefactors. Remembrance was a primary motive in keeping such records. **75** Robinson, 'Churchwardens' accounts, 1484–1600, St Werburgh's church, Dublin', p. 139. **76** R.C.B., P326/27/1/6 (on a loose folio).

and Thomas ffylbert, and were discharged owing arrears amounting to 35*s*. 3 ½ *d*.[77] Two years previously the accounts were presented to the rector, Master ffylbert and Elizabeth Talbote, auditors.[78] The inclusion of a female auditor with two men in clerical orders is unique. One can only speculate that she may have been a significant benefactor of the parish.

What the churchwardens' accounts reveal is the very marked growth of the power and participation of the laity in the life of the parish church over the period extending from the second half of the thirteenth century down to the eve of the reformation. In his ground-breaking article, 'The role of the laity in the parishes of Armagh *inter Anglicos*, 1518–1553',[79] Henry Jefferies has indicated similar developments in County Louth, using the evidence of the diocesan registers and courts. He has drawn attention not only to the role of the churchwardens, but also to the part played by lay parochial representatives in the consultations that took place prior to the appointment of a rector or vicar, to say nothing of their occasional resort to the diocesan courts to seek redress of grievances against the incumbent. Thus it seems that these developments extended generally to the church *inter Anglicos*. What happened in the church *inter Hibernicos*, in the absence of comparable records, is a mystery and may ever remain a mystery. Perhaps a skilful use of more oblique Gaelic sources may yet provide some indications of the nature of lay involvement in these areas.

V

The rapidly growing influence of the laity in the parish was, in the nature of things, more visible than religious formation. In an age when sheela-na-gigs – nude female figurines built into the south walls of parish churches with genitalia exposed – 'flashed' the intending worshipper, one hesitates to be overconfident in assessing the spiritual temperature of 'the man in the pew', to borrow an anachronism.[80] In the world of the late medieval imagination religious orthodoxy, magic, thinly disguised pagan custom, and demonology did not just coexist: rather, they formed an integrated world-view. Caught up in a Darwinian struggle of cosmic proportions, the faithful could trust only in the power of sacraments to defeat the awesome powers ranged against them.

77 R.C.B., P326/ 27/1/4 *coram rectore et Thoma ffylbert auditoribus eiusdem compoti finiti et probati crastino nativitatis sancti Johannis baptiste anno domini m cccc nonagesimo v.* 78 Robinson, 'Churchwardens' accounts, 1484–1600, St Werburgh's church, Dublin', p. 133. 79 H.C. Jefferies, 'The role of the laity in the parishes of Armagh Inter Anglicos, 1518–1553' in *Archivium Hibernicum*, lii (1998), pp 73–84. 80 The purpose of these mysterious figurines was probably an apotropaic or evil-averting function. See Conleth Manning, 'A sheela-na-gig at Ballinaclogh, Co. Tipperary' in G. Mac Niocaill and P. Wallace (eds), *Keimelia: studies in*

The nature of this struggle was grimly proclaimed in the graphic depictions of 'the doom', or Day of Judgement, in many parish churches of the period. None has survived the near total destruction of Irish parish churches, but it would be surprising if they were not common.[81] What we do have is a number of surviving cadaver effigies, designed to evoke terror in the eye of the beholder, moving them to pray for the repose of the soul of the deceased, and serving as a forceful reminder of the need to amend one's life. The most gruesome examples of tomb effigies belong to the late fifteenth and early sixteenth centuries: putrefaction, post-mortem infestation by worms, toads, and serpents, and worse, are portrayed unsparingly. The best examples of this art are to found at Bewley – probably a Plunket tomb – and at Stamullen in the chantry chapel of St Christopher, which belonged to the Preston family. Both effigies were probably executed by the same sculptor. They are best described by Helen Roe:

> Both cadavers pullulate with vermin, extraordinarily various and all presented with great skill and a degree of morbid, even gleeful imitation that is quite astounding. Great serpents bore into the ears; at Bewley small horned 'worms', perhaps the *seps* of the *Bestiary*, fabled to destroy bone and flesh, slide along the lower jaw … On both bodies swollen speckled toads lie upon the breasts; the wasted arms and legs are encrusted with newts, spotted and scaly worms, maggots, small lizards and toads with needle-like noses and beady eyes. Out of the folds of the shroud creep and slither so many and strange sorts of worms, snakes and beetle-like creatures that it would seem the sculptor had supplemented the all too comprehensive catalogue of *vermes* listed in the *Bestiary* with those life-consuming vermin, the palmerworm, the cankerworm, and (at Bewley) the locust as given by the prophet Joel 1:4. Also at Bewley … is a scorpion and tiny dragonlike creature, which I take to be the *draco* of the *Bestiary*, a symbol of evil and death. Still more uncertain is the identification of a small legless creature with a slug-like, speckled body and animal head from whose jaws flames shoot out.[82]

---

medieval archaeology and history in memory of Tom Delaney (Galway, 1988), pp 71–3. **81** The provision of liturgical objects, crucifixes and statues of the saints in parish churches was certainly a concern of Irish church councils in the fifteenth century. It was provided by the council of Cashel in 1453 that the laity were obliged to provide a missal, a silver chalice, an alb, a stole, a chasuble, a surplice, and a font, among other things. Each parish church was to have a statue of St Mary and the patron saint of the church in addition to a crucifix. See Michael A.J. Burrows, 'Fifteenth-century Irish provincial legislation and pastoral care' in W.J. Shiels and D. Wood (eds), *The churches, Ireland and the Irish: studies in church history xxv* (Oxford, 1989), p. 65. **82** Helen Roe, 'Cadaver effigial monuments in Ireland', in *R.S.A.I. Jn.*, xcix (1969), pp 8–9.

If global warming is an obsession of the twenty-first century, it is safe to say that warming of a non-terrestrial variety preoccupied the thoughts of medieval parishioners. It was not death itself, but the horror of what lay beyond. Purgatory and hell did not exist in interstellar space: the hot breath of hell and the ubiquitous demons that inflicted eternal torment on the damned were realities as substantial as the earth itself. But if one could not cheat death, it was still possible to rob the devil of the soul he sought for his infernal pleasure. A ready means to this end was the provision made in one's last will and testament, which we have already touched upon in connection with parochial bequests.

Significantly, the first items in a will concerned the disposal of one's soul and one's body. The soul was bequeathed to God, St Mary and all the saints, for the good reason that the intercession of St Mary and the saints was the prime object of the will. Not enough attention, however, has been paid to the disposal of the mortal remains. Since only the very wealthy could afford the erection of a monumental tomb – the purpose of which was to inspire prayer for repose of the soul – the next best thing was to be buried in the church itself, preferably in one of the chapels. Proximity to an altar was especially desirable. In 1476 Thomas Harrold, prior of Holy Trinity, Dublin, gave leave to Brother John Higley, a canon of the cathedral, to act as executor of his father's will *utilitate ecclesie nostre in ea parte suadente* (bearing in mind the advantage of our church in that respect). What the prior intended by this comment is not clear, but material advantage, perhaps in the form of gifts to the cathedral over many years, seems likely. Whether it was for reasons of compassion, advantage, or both, John's father bequeathed his body to be buried in the chapel of St Mary the Virgin, leaving a rent of twenty shillings to the cathedral, together with an annual pension of 13s. 4d. to his son, the canon, no doubt by way of recognition for his prayers.[83] John's death was recorded among the obits of the cathedral.[84] In the same year Richard Goldynge bequeathed his body to be buried in the chancel – a very rare privilege – of the parish church of Balscaddan. Richard combined this wish with bequests for repairs both to the chancel and the nave, in addition to bequests to three other parish churches, and the four mendicant orders in Drogheda. He did not omit to include the vicar of Balscaddan, and Sir

---

83 Berry (ed.) *Register of the wills and inventories of the diocese of Dublin*, pp 130–4. He charged John and the other executor 'to perform and dispose for the health of my soul, as to them may seem most expedient' (p. 132). For burial and other *pro anima* aspects of medieval wills, see Margaret Murphy, 'The high cost of dying: an analysis of *pro anima* bequests in medieval Dublin', pp 111–22. For a general discussion of medieval burial see Fry, *Burial in medieval Ireland, 900–1500: a review of the written sources*, especially p. 89.   84 Refaussé with Lennon, *The registers of Christ Church cathedral*, p. 55.

Nicholas, the chaplain, in his list of benefactions. He also acknowledged a debt of 5s. 4d. to the proctors of the lights of St Mary, which suggests that the lady chapel was maintained by a guild of which he was member.[85] Richard was not notably wealthy; his burial in the chancel may owe more to a lifetime of devotion to the church than to the value of his bequests. Some measure of the importance attached to burial within the church may be gained from an analysis of the register of wills for the diocese of Dublin between 1457 and 1483, which reveals that whereas fifty specified the church as the place of burial, only sixteen related to the churchyard.[86] The great majority of poor parishioners, not having sufficient means to justify the making of a will, were almost certainly buried in the churchyard. However, such was the pressure to be buried in church where the means were available, and such was the desire of the churchwardens to augment church funds with 'pit money', that the danger of disease must have been ever-present.[87]

Next in order of importance were the provisions for the funeral, both on the day and by way of providing for continuing intercession for the repose of souls. Typically these measures included payment for priests and chaplains, wax for candles, and food and ale for those who attended. In 1471 Alice Bennet made provision for eight priests at her funeral in St Pappan's, Glasnevin, 4s. for wax [candles], 30d. for thirty masses, 5s. for bread and 6s. 8d. for ale.[88] The purpose of providing food and ale was to attract the prayers of those who attended, especially the poor, whose prayers were deemed to be especially potent. Around the same period John Kempe made provision for the attendance of six priests and two clerks. He seems to have made even greater efforts to attract prayers by providing 9s. for bread and ale, in addition to a cow, a hog, five sheep, besides geese and capons:[89] a feast the good people of St Canice's, Hollywood, were unlikely to forget for some time.

Provision for longer-term intercession in the form of memorial Masses varied considerably according to the means of the legator. Only the very wealthy could provide for perpetual intercession by endowment of a chapel or chantry. Others provided for one or more trentals, a 'package' of thirty Masses, or paid a chaplain for a fixed term. In 1471 John Whylde left 30s. for three trentals, and made provision for one chaplain to 'be employed to celebrate in Dublin for one year for the health of my soul and the souls of all the faithful departed'.[90] None,

85 Berry (ed.), *Register of the wills and inventories of the diocese of Dublin*, pp 120–2.   86 Ibid., *passim*.   87 Churches were deemed to be a primary cause of plague in England in the sixteenth and seventeenth centuries. In the case of St Neots, Cornwall, no fewer than 548 corpses were buried in an area 85 ft by 52 ft, not discounting the area occupied by six pillars, over a period of 102 years. See Cox, *Churchwardens' accounts*, pp 168–70.   88 Berry (ed.), *Register of the wills and inventories of the diocese of Dublin*, p. 12.   89 Ibid., pp 14–15.   90 Ibid., pp 16–17.

however, could compare with John Chever, who bequeathed in 1474 the enormous sum of £16 13s. 4d. 'for a thousand Masses to be celebrated for my soul'.[91] In the absence of adequate testamentary material, it is impossible to say whether such provisions were exceptional in Ireland. Certainly it was not so in England. Scanning a random selection of Oxfordshire wills, two examples serve to put the Irish material in the context of the age. In 1395 Sir Robert Bardolf provided funds for 100 'poor innocent boys on the day of my burial to pray for the aforesaid souls'. The will further provided for

> the repair of the said aisle where I shall be buried and to make a tomb above my body there, and for devout prayers to be said £60. To honest priests, secular and religious ... to say 5000 masses for my soul and the aforesaid souls immediately after my decease as soon as they can be celebrated £20 16s. 8d.[92]

Towards the end of the fifteenth century, Sir Edmund Rede, authorized his executors

> to distribute with all speed after my death 1000 groats [i.e. 4000 pence] to 1000 priests, each to celebrate *Dirige* with a mass of requiem for my soul. To each priest present on the day of my burial 12d.; at my soul's mind 12d.; to each clerk singing at my funeral 4d; to every poor person at my funeral praying for my soul 1d. with food and drink in abundance. Two tapers to burn by day and night from the day of my burial until my month's mind, one at the head, the other at the foot of my tomb; the priest in the chapel at the time to pray daily for my soul from the day of my burial for thirty days, saying in the chapel one *Dirige* with a Mass or memorial of requiem; the parish clerk of the said church and two others shall daily at the above times ring the bells and have for their labours 3d. daily.[93]

It is difficult to see how any phrase other than 'terror of death' can adequately explain the motive behind such testaments.

There was, however, a positive side to gloom and doom, which found expression in practical works of charity. In 1471, for example, Richard Boys bequeathed 10 marks [£6 6s. 8d.] 'to buy woollen and linen cloth for clothing poor people in gowns and shirts.'[94] About a year later William Neill, chaplain,

91 Ibid., pp 146–8; see also Murphy, 'The high cost of dying: an analysis of *pro anima* bequests in medieval Dublin', pp 119–20. 92 J.R.H. Weaver, 'Some Oxfordshire wills proved in the prerogative court of Canterbury, 1393–1510' in *Oxfordshire Record Society*, xl (1958), p. 8. 93 Ibid., p. 42. 94 Berry (ed.), *Register of the wills and inventories of the diocese*

Clondalkin, bequeathed 'that the house of the poor of St John without the New Gate, Dublin, have a threefold repast, according to the praiseworthy custom of entertainment which was wont to be given there by others'.[95] In 1476 Joan Steven of Crumlin 'in the course of nature greatly broken by old age, apprehending the destiny of the whole human race, and that the hour of death, uncertain as it is, is threatening me', left her estate, including all outstanding actions for debts due, to her son John Mastoke, provided that he remitted debts 'due by the poor and by people unable to pay, as I, for the health of my soul and that of the said John my late husband, forgive and remit them'.[96] Mature reflection on the parable of the sheep and the goats – the seven corporal works of mercy (feeding the hungry, giving drink to the thirsty, clothing the naked, visiting the sick, relieving the prisoner, housing the stranger and burying the dead) seems to underlie the terms of the will of Nicholas Suttowne, a clerk, who left

> his body to St Warburge's church to be buried, and a crucifix … legacies to the monastery of the monks of the B.V.M., the four orders of friars, his five boys, *the prison at the castle and the lepers, for victuals, the poor of St John without the walls, Dublin, Anne White, Walter Holme, John Waltir, the poor of Rechell Street* [italics mine].[97]

While the teaching of the parables, not least of Dives and Lazarus, with its all-too explicit reference to the discomforts that awaited those who ignored plight of the beggar, inspired such works of mercy, the solid achievement in terms of charitable foundations so characteristic of the period is a deserving tribute to the piety of the age.

VII

If the *communitas parochianorum* – the general vestry in modern parlance – remains a tantalizingly obscure body in late medieval sources, the same cannot be said of the religious guild or confraternity. Their lay provenance is instantly recognizable in their structure, which plainly derives from the craft guild. Headed by a master and two wardens elected annually at the patronal festival, these guilds maintained their own chapel and chaplain in the parish church. Their enormous popularity in western Europe in the late medieval period is the measure of lay spirituality. It cannot be overstated that their formation was rooted in the deeply felt spiritual needs of the laity, for reasons that we have

of Dublin, p. 9.   **95** Ibid., p. 98.   **96** Ibid., pp 160–2.   **97** *Christ Church deeds*, no. 327. For the corporal acts of mercy, see Duffy, *The stripping of the altars*, pp 357–62.

already discussed. Neither the inspiration nor the initiative was clerical. Given that religious movements in earlier centuries were largely inspired by monastic initiatives, the significance of this development has to be seen against that background. Such was their popularity, that many towns could boast of dozens of fraternities: London (about 150); King's Lynn (over 70), Bodmin (over 40); and Great Yarmouth (19).[98]

By comparison the eleven known guilds in the diocese of Dublin – seven in the city and four in manorial villages[99] – seems a modest achievement. This may be a considerable underestimate. The existence of the guild of St Canice, Hollywood, for example, is known only casually in the context of a will in 1471. Besides, lay devotion could take various forms. As we have already noted, even village churches without guilds, for example Clondalkin, supported several altars dedicated to saints and served by a number of chaplains. Devotion to the saints is evident in wills. In 1473 Robert Walshe bequeathed 7d. to the light of St Katherine of Swords. In the following year Dame Margaret Nugent left her body to be buried in the chapel of St Mary the Virgin (St Michan's parish church, Dublin), and the balance of the articles listed in the inventory after her debts were discharged 'to the aforesaid chapel of the glorious Virgin'.[100] Among the items bequeathed were a small brass pot for holy water, and two pairs of coral beads worth 40d. and 5s. respectively, which strongly suggests a life of marked private devotion. Her case is all the more curious because her parish church hosted the guild of St Sythe, to which she bequeathed nothing, and of which, in spite of her evident piety, she does not appear to have been a member. Yet others may have found sufficient outlet for their devotions as members of the craft guilds with their manifold religious affiliations.

Since the organizing principle of the religious guild was to promote the cult of a saint, its primary function was to maintain the guild light in the appropriate chapel. We have already noted that around 1476 Richard Goldynge made provision in his will for the payment of a debt to the proctors of the lights of St Mary in Balscadden church.[101] These proctors – not to be confused with the parish proctors – were elected annually to maintain the guild light and to supervise the income and expenditure of the guild in maintaining and staffing the chapel. So characteristic was this function that in northern France such associations were called *chandelles* or *candailles*.[102] A second function was the procurement of prayers and alms from all members for the repose of the souls of deceased members. For those who could not afford to pay a chaplain or arrange lavish funerals, membership of the guild fulfilled in a public way the

---

98 Duffy, *The stripping of the altars*, p. 142. 99 Clark and Refaussé (eds), *Directory of the historic Dublin guilds*, pp 32–40. 100 Berry (ed.), *Register of the wills and inventories of the diocese of Dublin*, pp 67, 79 –81. 101 Ibid., p. 121. 102 Jacques Heers, *L'Occident aux xive et xve siecles* (Paris, 1963).

function of the private chantry. Members were expected to attend the funerals of fellow members, and make provision from the alms fund for their families in times of hardship. Members were also expected to meet together on the patronal festival for a Mass, the annual guild dinner, and the election of officials. The task of saying numerous Masses for the dead – usually a trental – naturally made the appointment of a chaplain essential. Their maintenance was, of course, a charge on the guild and not on the parish. Thus membership conferred a system of mutual support, particularly for the poor, a resource for intercession for the departed, and a religious discipline. Their importance in the religious formation of the laity is incalculable.

Since religious confraternities were the focus of lay spirituality, it was natural that they should have been beneficiaries of lay endowments in the form of rents and properties. Whether due to legal concerns arising out of the application of the statute of Mortmain, or the potential loss of taxable properties, the mayor and bailiffs of Dublin decreed in 1483 that

> Every citizen may devise lands and rent within the bounds of the city, except to houses of religion, and such as cannot aid the city in time of need; that every such testament should be certified under the seal of the spiritual court to the mayor and bailiffs within the day and year of the testator's death; proclamation thereof should be made on three market days within that period at the high cross of Dublin; twelve citizens before the mayor and bailiffs should find that the testator had good title, such finding to be enrolled in the records of the city; every testament not complying with these conditions to be deemed void.[103]

Concern over the legal status of guild property may explain why some of the more prominent religious guilds sought and obtained incorporation by royal or parliamentary licence. Such licences were certainly extended to a number of prominent guilds, including Corpus Christi (1444), St Anne (1430), St George Martyr (1426), St John the Baptist (1418), St Mary in the parish of St Nicholas Within, Dublin (1470), and St Sythe (1476). That similar charters continued to be issued, as in the case of the guild of the Holy Cross, St George the Martyr, and St Katherine the Virgin in the parish church of Ardee, licensed on 15 March 1534,[104] testifies to the enduring popularity of the guilds.

The internal evidence of the charters has remarkably little to say about the religious objectives of the guild and rather more about the rules governing their corporation and its legal competence. The Ardee charter provided

---

103 *Christ Church deeds*, no. 336.   104 Murray, 'The ancient chantries of Co. Louth', pp 206–7.

that two masters shall govern the guild and protect whatever lands and possessions may be granted to them. They shall have power to nominate other masters and remove them when occasion require, have a common seal to serve for the affairs of the fraternity that shall remain in the custody of the masters. The masters may plead and be impleaded, answer and be answered in all courts secular and ecclesiastical and they may establish a chantry consisting of one or more chaplains to celebrate the divine service in the church of Atherdee forever ... They may acquire lands, tenements, rents and advowsons of churches to the value of £40 a year to be held of the chief lord of the fee thereof by the service thereof due and of right accustomed: they may assemble themselves as often as occasion may require to consult concerning the affairs of the guild, and make rules and ordinances for their better rule and government.[105]

The charter of the guild of St Sythe (parish of St Michan, Dublin) in 1476 contains similar terms, emphasizing more than once the capacity of the guild to hold property, nothwithstanding the statute of Mortmain.[106] The curious thing about St Sythe is that a chantry chapel was established in her honor since 1424,[107] if not earlier. Why wait for another half century to seek incorporation? Besides, we know of royal approval in only six out of a total of eleven identifiable guilds. While it may be that such licences have been lost, a more probable explanation is that the expense of obtaining them discouraged small fraternities from following suit. After all, churchwardens were able to lease or acquire property belonging to the parish without any letters patent or formal act of incorporation, so why should the wardens of small fraternities do otherwise? The explanation is probably contained in the clause of the Ardee charter, which provided that the guild might acquire rents and tenements provided that they were 'held of the chief lord of the fee thereof by the service thereof due and of right accustomed'. By so doing, they were not infringing the provisions of the statute of Mortmain, for the simple reason that the secular charges attached to such properties were not alienated in the first instance. The annual account of the chantry of St Mary (parish of St John, Dublin) c.1477 amounted to only £5 6s. 4d., of which a mere £1 3s. 3½d. was actually expended.[108] In such modest circumstances, it is likely that only the richest guilds found it necessary to seek incorporation to protect assets sufficiently large to attract troublesome litigation. Just as we have no documentary proof that churchwardens existed in most parishes *inter Anglicos* – which they almost certainly did – so too we should

---

105 Ibid., pp 206–7. 106 The text of the charter is printed in Colm Lennon, 'The foundation charter of St Sythe's guild, Dublin, 1476' in *Archivium Hibernicum* xlviii (1994), pp 6–12. 107 Colm Lennon, 'The foundation charter of St Sythe's guild', p. 3. 108 Robinson, 'On the ancient deeds of the parish of St John, Dublin', no. 133, pp 201–2.

not expect to find more than a proportionate ratio of references to religious guilds.

To draw a sharp distinction between religious and craft guilds – as if one was 'secular' and the other 'spiritual' – would be not merely anachronistic but profoundly misleading. All guilds had a patron saint and maintained a chapel. One has only to glance through the accounts of the Dublin guild of carpenters, millers, masons and heliers, which was incorporated by royal charter in 1508 and licensed to call themselves 'the fraternity of the Blessed Virgin Mary of the house of St Thomas the Martyr',[109] to see the degree to which it was integrated into the religious life of the city. Between 1531 and 1536 the following items appear in the guildwardens' accounts:

> xxiii lbs wax @ 2 ½d, 4s 9 ½d [almost certainly wax for the guild chapel]
> wax maker for his labours, 20d
> Spent in wax of our Lady's beam [i.e. candle before the image of St Mary]
> Received at Our Lady time in offering at St Thomas' Court, iiii d ob.
> Costs for gemmeise [hinge or hook] and nails to mend our Lady's coffer 5d
> Making prickets to our Lady altar, 2d
> Bread and ale to the convent of St Thomas Court at our Lady time, 6d
> Bread, ale, and wine to the abbot and convent at our Lady time xvi d
> For paper to our Lady book, 2d [? Missal]
> A pottle of claret and a pottell of romne [a Spanish wine] 12d, spent upon the parson of St Katherine's and upon our brethren at St Thomas' Court in bread, ale, and wine 4s
> Croks and a wire to our Lady tabernacle 3d
> The choir the Assumption day of our Lady, 3d[110]

To all intents and purposes such accounts are indistinguishable from the accounts of 'religious' guilds. The patterns are exactly the same: the maintenance of a chapel light before the image of the patron saint, the costs associated with the furnishings of the chapel (such as the coffer to hold sacred vessels), the altar, the liturgical books, and the tabernacle. Much of the expenditure was on the annual dinner held on the patronal festival – the feast of the Assumption – when elections took place. The abbot and monks of St Thomas's Abbey (who provided the lady chapel) and the parish priest were not overlooked in the general festivity of the occasion. We hear subsequently of a bead roll, recalling, no doubt, the deceased members of the guild, and a payment of 10d for five tapers at the burial of Patrick Tawner.[111] Thus membership of a craft guild

109 H.F. Berry, 'The Dublin gild of carpenters, millers, masons, and heliers, in the sixteenth century' in *R.S.A.I. Jn.*, xxxv (1905), pp 323–4.   110 Ibid., p. 332.   111 Ibid., p. 333.

secured the same spiritual benefits and system of mutual support as a religious guild. Indeed, it may be that members of the latter were composed almost entirely from among those who were excluded from craft associations.

Nothing better illustrates the close ties between the craft guilds and the church than their participation in the annual Corpus Christi pageant. The Chain Book of Dublin contains a set of regulations governing the pageant drawn up in 1496. Where appropriate, the members of the respective crafts played or mimed a variety of biblical or legendary scenes. Thus, for example, the apostles were represented by the fishermen; the mariners, vintners, ship-carpenters and salmon-takers represented Noah and the ark; the goldsmiths represented the Three Kings of Cologne; the skinners, house-carpenters, tanners and browders represented Joseph, Mary and Child; the Corpus Christi guild naturally was designated to portray the Passion of Christ.[112] The guilds might also perform plays of a secular or religious nature on appropriate occasions, such as at a public performance before the lord deputy on Hoggen Green in 1528.[113]

VIII

That lay religious activity enveloped parochial organizations, craft guilds and even civic government is not so remarkable as to evoke astonishment. The parish was, after all, designed to satisfy the demands of the pastoral care of the laity. The liturgy was, by contrast, a strictly clerical sphere of activity. Yet even here the evidence of the *Visitatio Sepulchri* Easter play indicates that lay influence penetrated to the sanctuary itself.

A Latin drama dating from around 1400, the *Visitatio* was not a drama that could be performed independently of its liturgical context.[114] The drama of the three Marys' discovery of the empty sepulchre on Easter morning was specific to the Easter liturgy. It is clear from the detailed directions that the action was designed to take place in the context of the office of matins and before the commencement of the Mass. One by one the three Marys approached the entrance to the chancel, clothed in surplices and silk copes, each bearing a pyx containing spices, each singing a lament. They proceeded slowly towards the altar, eventually finding themselves beside the Easter Sepulchre, normally located on the north side of the sanctuary. There they declared their intention of anointing Jesus with spices, but who will roll back the stone? The angel appears, announcing that Christ is risen. Having 'entered' the sepulchre, the Marys proclaim in a loud voice

112 Clark and Refausse (eds), *Directory of historic Dublin guilds*, pp 44–5.   113 Ibid., p. 12.
114 See Maire Egan-Buffet and Alan J. Fletcher, 'The Dublin *Visitatio Sepulchri* play' in *R.I.A Procs*, xc, Section C (1990), pp 159–241.

Alleluya, resurexit Dominus
Alleluya, resurexit Dominus hodie
Resurexit potens, fortis Cristus [*sic*], filius Dei.[115]

On their return through the chancel they encounter the barefooted Peter, carrying his keys, and John, with a palm in his hand, vested in albs and tunicles, on their way to the sepulchre. A dialogue ensues between the Marys and the apostles, after which the apostles run to the tomb, John entering first, followed by Peter. As the cast of six retires through the chancel, the office is resumed with the singing of *Te Deum*.

It is not without significance that the only two extant manuscripts of Ireland's earliest play belonged to the parish church of St John the Evangelist, Dublin. True, there is no conclusive evidence to prove that it was performed in a parochial setting, but given that it was designed to dramatize the Easter liturgy in a church setting, focusing on the Easter sepulchre, the focal point of Passiontide devotions, it is difficult to imagine a more appropriate setting.

The *Visitatio* raises a number of issues, which need to be asked even if they cannot be answered. Why stage a play in Latin in a parish church on Easter Day before an illiterate congregation?[116] Who were the players? Were they clerical or lay professionals? Was the dramatic inspiration purely liturgical in origin? Or was it derived ultimately from lay performances, and hijacked by the clergy who saw in it a powerful instrument of pastoral instruction? In short, was the church mimicking lay forms of entertainment for didactic purposes? While the text is in Latin, is there any compelling reason to believe that at least the narrative sections could not have been rendered in the vernacular? Or were the actions of the players sufficiently explicit to render the words almost superfluous to the narrative? However one answers such questions, it is difficult to avoid the impression that the lay presence was being acknowledged.

IX

Any attempt to measure lay attitudes to the clergy will inevitably founder on the ambiguous nature of the sources. Much of the surviving evidence – and it is not much – takes the form of verdicts in response to questions that had little or nothing to do with attitudes to the clergy. Given the poverty of most parochial clergy, which was considerably below English and Welsh levels even in the church *inter Anglicos*,[117] it is hardly surprising that their educational and

115 Ibid. p. 214. 116 See Alan J. Fletcher, *Drama, performance, and polity in pre-Cromwellian Ireland* (Cork, 2000), p.77. Fletcher suggests that the canons of Christ Church, who served St John's, are the most likely candidates for the acting roles. 117 See Steven Ellis,

pastoral abilities were almost certainly minimal. The semi-literate status of many diocesan clergy was a source of continual lament by post-reformation bishops, who could not attract educated clergy to impoverished parishes. Even before the reformation, one rarely encounters sons of the gentry in parochial positions, although a small but significant number of parishes were in the gift of such families, as Henry Jefferies has rightly observed.[118]

Just how inadequate some parochial clergy could be may be gleaned from the case of Sir William Magenich, 'chaplain' of the parish of Greenoge, diocese of Meath, who features in the record of the metropolitan visitation of the diocese in 1355.[119] He could not read, sing or even conduct any office properly [*nec aliquid officium congrue facere*], whether by way of baptizing or instructing parishioners. He was a drunkard. Indeed, you name the vice, he had it [*et quicquid est vitium in eo regnat*]. He was always angry with his flock, threatening many of the them with blows. Not surprisingly, he provoked them to anger [*sic provocat suos parachianos continuo ad iram*]. He sold the altar candles and even the consecrated bread to numerous women. When he was finally dismissed by the rector, the abbot of St Thomas', he forced his way into the church by persuading a small boy to get through the chancel window to open the doors, which had been fortified by the new chaplain to exclude him on the instruction of the abbot [*qui firmavit ostia ecclesiam juxta mandatum rectoris*]. He allowed mice and rats to eat the consecrated host. Naturally, the fabric of the church had not benefited from his neglect, as we are informed that it was in a state of poor repair. However bad things were in Greenoge, it is perhaps more significant that although queries about the conduct of the curate were clearly included among the articles of the visitation, no other complaints were made about the clergy in the remaining five parishes recorded in the visitation. Only the abbot of St Thomas' was reprimanded in his capacity as rector of Donaghmore for allowing animals to pasture in the churchyard, resulting in the disinterring of the body of a woman by pigs. Of the ten verdicts of fornication or adultery, no reference was made to members of the clergy. In fact, in three instances the jurors returned a positive verdict: they knew of nothing that was not good [*nichil sciunt nisi bonum*].

Although cases involving clergy occur in the justiciary rolls, it is impossible to say if they were inspired by anti-clerical sentiment. In 1307, for instance, the

'Economic problems of the church: why the Reformation failed in Ireland' in *Journal of Ecclesiastical History*, xli (1990), pp 259–69; James Murray, 'The sources of clerical income in the Tudor diocese of Dublin, *c*.1530–1600' in *Archivium Hibernicum*, xlvi (1991–2), pp 139–60; Lyons, *Church and society in County Kildare, c.1470–1547*, pp 53–108.   118 Jefferies, 'The role of the laity in the parishes of Armagh *Inter Anglicos*', p. 75.   119 Smith (ed.), *The register of Milo Sweetman*, no. 158, p.158. In the province of Armagh, the term 'chaplain' seems to mean an unbeneficed curate, especially where a monastery held the rectory, as was indeed the situation in Greenoge. See Jefferies, 'The role of the laity', pp 73–4.

archdeacon of Limerick was acquitted when charged by Ralph the clerk and Agnes his wife that he took from the wife of Geoffrey Serle twelve gallons of wine in order to certify the bishop that Agnes was an adulteress. Agnes, duly excommunicated, was committed to the king's prison in Limerick, as a result of which she delivered a premature child. The archdeacon admitted that she had been charged before him in his court and convicted of adultery, but that she had been committed to prison by the bishop for failing to perform the prescribed penance for perjury, which did not lie in the competence of the archdeacon's court.[120] It may be that the prying eye of the ecclesiastical courts was deeply resented by the laity, and that Agnes may have hoped to capitalize on this resentment before a jury of laymen. There are sufficient references to the operations of church courts in the justiciary rolls to show that they were often effective, especially with the support of royal officials, in enforcing matrimonial law, but we can only speculate about how they were received by the laity.

Equally difficult to interpret is a pitched battle that occurred in the town of New Leighlin [now Old Leighlin] in 1305 between the inhabitants of the town and the retinue of William, bishop of Ossory. The bishop charged the provost and the commons of the town, as well men as women, with causing the affray, which began over a dog that attacked one of the bishop's valets as they passed through the town. One thing led to another, and before long the bishop's retainers and the people of New Leighlin were involved in a pitched battle, involving weapons as well as stones:

> The bishop being in the outlet of the town perceiving this, peacefully returned, and gave as is customary the benediction, asking those assembled to cease from doing evil to his men, and pledging himself to make satisfaction immediately for any trespasses done by his men to each person of the town. But they, not accepting his request, although often made, surrounding the bishop – and his other valets, attacked them on every side; so that in the conflict a stone was thrown at the bishop, and one of his valets – was struck almost to death, so that his life is despaired of, and it is believed that he will die within three days. And Robert de Racheford was badly wounded with an arrow.[121]

Affrays by their nature have a tendency to get out of hand, which may well be the case in the normally quiet and peaceful environs of New Leighlin. It may be that the bishop was incidentally involved. Equally, it may be that the imperious attitude of his retainers touched some latent anti-clerical resentments lurking under the emotional surface of those who had to bear in silence the arrogance

---

120 *Calendar of justiciary rolls Ireland, 1304–1307*, pp 450–1.   121 Ibid. pp 42–3.

of the higher clergy. Either way, the provost and commons of the town were fined the enormous sum of 100 marks for their presumption.

The verdicts of the grand juries in south-eastern Ireland in 1537 certainly reflect overt resentment, mainly arising from the charges for surplice fees or oblations, but it is far from clear as to whether the resentment was directed at the clergy or the charges. The same presentments produced complaints against the impositions of both the gentry and the great lords, *including* the higher clergy, in the form of coign and livery, but one cannot conclude from the existence of such complaints that the commons were either anti-gentry or anti-noble as a social class. While undoubtedly they would have wished to see the abolition of the charges that inflicted such misery on them, it does not follow that they were longing for social revolution of the kind provoked by millenarium or anabaptist explosions in contemporary continental Europe. Much the same was probably true of their attitude to clergy of every degree.

Oblations in the form of baptismal, marriage and burial fees, which were never regulated by canon law and varied considerably according to local custom,[122] naturally affected most members of the laity. The jurors of County Kilkenny complained in 1537

> that the curates for the moste of every paryshe churche with the countye aforesaide, do take for his crysteynynges of every chylde 12*d*., and for puryficacion 12*d*. or 16*d*., and other exaccions for the admynistacions of sacramentes, ayenst the lawe of Godde, and the mere duetye of every suche curate.[123]

The means used by clerics to secure payment were sometimes less than subtle:

> the said jurye present that the vycar of the towne of Garon [Gowran] wyll not crysten ne baptyse a childe, oneles the frindes [godparents?] of the same childe gyve him his dynnar or money.[124]

While an episcopal visitation might afford a welcome opportunity to complain about the conduct of the clergy, as in the case of Greenoge, it also meant that the bishop and his retinue had to be housed and fed. The jurors of the city of Waterford complained bitterly about such practices:

> Item the said archbishop [of Cashel] useth extorcyon in his visitacyon sometyme cessyng his charges with great somes of money, and suche as

---

122 See James Murray, 'The sources of clerical income in the Tudor diocese of Dublin, *c.*1530–1600', pp 153–5.   123 H.F. Hore and J. Graves (eds), *The social state of the southern and eastern counties of Ireland in the sixteenth century* (Annuary of the Royal Historical and Archaeological Association for 1868–9), p. 93; cf. p. 114.   124 Ibid., p. 133.

refuse to compounde with hym for a certeyn unreasonable some must fynde mete and drinke and lodging for as many as he list to bringe with hyme, and hath retayned one called Dyrmond Doff for his officiall and counsaillor or comissary which entertayneth the kyngs people by color of canon lawe that there can be no more extorcyon comitted by any Irishe brehowne, and polleth the kings subjects as he list, and taketh for fee of sentence of a devorce £10 or more.[125]

Such instances of lay resentments are by no means exhaustive. It is likely that in view of the low income of parochial clergy they inevitably sought to exact what they could in the form of oblations, which would have made them appear rapacious in the eyes of parishioners. Remarkably, in view of the tithe wars of a later age, tithes are never the subject of lay complaint. In fact, the desire to set aside a sum of money in wills to make provision for forgotten tithes is a regular feature of fifteenth-century wills. Failure to pay tithes was an excommunicable offence under canon law, which may be the reason why one should not wish to be interviewed by St Peter on the issue.

Thus while complaints about the clergy are by no means infrequent, one cannot say that resentment against charges that verged on extortion amounted to hatred of the clergy as a social class. Besides, bequests to clergy as individuals are a regular feature of the wills of the period. No doubt the testator desired their prayers, but given the strong sense of corporate belonging engendered by guild and parochial communities it is unreasonable to suppose that clergy were seen as outsiders. It is in the context of these closely-bonded communities that we should interpret the large number of legacies bequeathed to clergy. Besides, these poor, semi-literate clerics were drawn from the same social milieu as most of the laity, particularly the parish clergy, as already noted. Indeed, the sheer familiarity of the parochial clergy may partially explain why they were not singled out by the jurors in 1537 for moral laxity in the same way as the monastic communities. It is hard to credit that parish clergy were more attached to celibacy than the wayward monks. The jurors, however, would seemingly have us believe that fornication was a specifically monastic vice. It was, after all, this semi-literate class of secular clergy that retained the allegiance of the great mass of the Irish population at the end of the sixteenth century, precisely because they were *of* the people.

X

If, in some respects, the spiritual identity of the medieval layman remains elusive due to the nature and ambiguity of the sources, the steady growth of lay

---

125 Ibid., p. 203.

influence from the late thirteenth century onwards is perhaps the most significant development in the history of the church in the late medieval period. The declining influence of the papacy and the monasteries was compensated in a large measure by the rising influence of the laity, characterised by a revitalised programme of building and flourishing parochial organizations. What we are witnessing is a fundamental shift in the church's centre of gravity.

How do we measure the significance of that shift? Perhaps because of the proximity of the Reformation there is a temptation to measure it mainly by reference to subsequent developments. In the eyes of the puritan or the Protestant iconoclast the religion of the late medieval layman was simply a form of idolatry. But neither was it quite the same as Tridentine Catholicism: the forms remained, but the spirit of the Catholic Reformation seems remote from the world of the fifteenth-century layman. Much has been done to re-instate the spirituality of this period, most obviously by Eamon Duffy in his brilliant evocation of late medieval Christianity in *The stripping of the altars*, published in 1992. However, his perspective remains one whereby the achievement of late medieval religion is measured against the loss and destruction wrought by the Henrician and Elizabethan reformations.

There is, I suggest, another perspective from which we can measure the role of the laity in the pre-Reformation period, and that is to measure it against what occurred, or did not occur, *before* such developments took place. I propose as the *terminus a quo* the advent of the Anglo-Normans in the late twelfth century. Only by measuring the multifarious activity of the fifteenth-century parochial laity against the pre-parochial pastorless situation described by Gerald of Wales can we adequately comprehend the scale of the revolution that occurred in the intervening period. It may not be an exaggeration to say that more was achieved *pastorally* in those three centuries than had ever been attempted in the preceding six. The laity had come of age.

Two developments in particular mark the progress of the laity. First, the extraordinary degree to which lay religion and spirituality was integrated into the fabric of society, to the extent that it is difficult to say whether the lay world – supremely in the form of the guild, the model of parochial organization – invaded the sanctuary, or whether the sanctuary colonized the lay world. The Corpus Christi pageant, incorporating the church, civic authority, craft and religious guilds, was a concrete expression of this symbiotic relationship.

Second, the manner in which the imaginative world of Christian story, parable, teaching and sacrament was communicated to a largely illiterate laity was astonishingly effective. In the parish church the central truths of the Easter faith were spelt out in ceremony, symbol and mime, beginning with the 'palm' ceremony on Palm Sunday, through the vigil at the sepulchre to the Easter Day ceremonies. The iconography of the building with its crucifix, images, and presentations of the Doom, the chantries and guilds, all contributed to a three-dimensional representation of Christian teaching. Those who witnessed the *Visitatio Sepulchri* may not have understood the gospel, but the event was vividly portrayed before their eyes. If clerical education left much to be desired, the fact remains that teaching was communicated to the laity less via the pulpit than by ritual, sign and symbol, play and pageant.

The reasons for the abandonment and consequent ruin of so many late medieval parish churches lies beyond the scope to this study. The impact of the suppression of the monasteries has deservedly attracted scholarly debate in recent years, thanks to outstanding contribution of Brendan Bradshaw.[126] Yet the fate of many hundreds of parish churches, impacting on the mass of the population, has raised no dust at all. The time for such a discussion is overdue.

126 Brendan Bradshaw, *The dissolution of the religious orders in Ireland under Henry VIII* (Cambridge, 1974); Brendan Bradshaw, 'Sword, word and strategy in the reformation in Ireland' in *Historical Journal*, xxi (1978); Brendan Bradshaw, 'The Edwardian Reformation in Ireland, 1547–53' in *Archivium Hibernicum*, xxxiv (1976–7).

2

The shaping of a lay community in the Church of Ireland, 1558–1640

Colm Lennon

There were few signs of a cohesive community of the laity in the Church of Ireland by 1558. An extrinsic factor was the smallness of the number of committed lay people, at least until the opening decades of the seventeenth century. The early Reformation under Henry VIII from 1536 to 1547 had been largely devoted to administrative change, affecting the clergy pre-eminently, while ecclesiastical reforms during the reign of his son, Edward VI (1547–53), were implemented extremely patchily. After the reversion to Roman Catholicism in the time of Queen Mary (1553–8), the reign of Elizabeth I represented the first real opportunity for continuous and concerted evangelism of lay people once the Protestantised state church had been established by parliament in 1560.

Moreover, apart from a clustering at Dublin and perhaps in the newly-planted areas of the southern and northern provinces, there was a very thin dispersal of members of the church throughout the country. The number of worshippers in the Anglican rite was swollen periodically in certain places by the enforcement of the Reformation statute of uniformity but the vast majority of these coerced attenders lapsed in their conformity once the legal strictures were removed. A more deep-seated reason for a lack of social cohesion among those who identified with the Anglican church was the division between native converts to Protestantism and the newly-arrived adherents of the state church as established by law. Leaving aside theological dissensions that were, in any case, considered to be essentially a matter for clerical resolution, a range of separate priorities and aspirations fostered scission between Protestants from longer established Irish families and those who had arrived more recently. Differences over municipal, guild and economic privileges, for example, over-shadowed convergent tendencies arising from membership of the same church, to the detriment of a united front in face of a Catholic majority in Ireland. Underpinning these divergences was the factor of national origin, the Irish-born Protestants tending to draw upon their native heritage to identify themselves apart from New English Anglicans as well as from Old English

Catholics. By confounding these sensibilities, the welter of Irish politics in the 1640s and 1650s helped eventually to promote a fusion of the separate elements within the Church of Ireland lay community. By 1660 there was a comparatively large, self-identifying and unified group of Anglican laypeople in Ireland.

By balancing the centripetal and centrifugal forces at work among the Church of Ireland laity, it may be possible to show how a communal ethos was forged, with difficulty, by the mid-seventeenth century. In the process an opportunity may be afforded us to scrutinise something of the tenor of the lives of Anglican laymen and women. Hesitancy on the part of the older Protestants about separating themselves out from their Catholic neighbours may best be understood by advertence to their spatial disposition, and to their immersion in the campaigns of their recusant fellow-citizens to preserve cherished civic and commercial immunities. The process of integration of the older Church of Ireland families with their new co-religionists may have received a fillip from the contracting of strategic marital alliances, sometimes over longer distances, but it was mainly within the existing parochial system that vital social and cultural ties were forged. Increasingly in the early seventeenth century, the parishes with their newly-evolving welfare institutions were the foci of lay commitment, and new and traditional forms of piety were deployed therein to body forth Anglican religiosity. In particular, innovative charitable projects inured the older and more recently-settled Protestant laypeople to working together creatively. Indubitably educational reforms at secondary and university level helped to foster a unified sense of purpose, though attachment to the Irish language as an instrument of evangelisation on the part of some native Protestants rested uneasily alongside the anglicising programme of most English reformers. By way of illustration of the conflicting trends, a case study drawn from the minute lay world of the Church of Ireland in Limerick in the opening decades of the seventeenth century may help to crystallise the main themes of this study.

That there was no critical mass of Church of Ireland laypeople in key locations much before the 1600s militated against the early coalescence of a community of Protestant believers. The expected nodal points for the burgeoning of church organisation were the major towns, but, Dublin aside, promising signs of growth of congregations in the provincial centres seemed to wither in the later Elizabethan years. Bishop John Bale had built a following for Protestantism among the youth of Kilkenny in the early 1550s, but his abrupt departure and the lack of subsequent evangelisation in the city appear to have stunted the development of a native Church of Ireland laity.[1] In Waterford and

---

1 For Bishop Bale's sojourn in Kilkenny, see S.G. Ellis, 'John Bale, bishop of Ossory, 1552–3' in *Journal of the Butler Society*, ii (1984), pp 283–93; and Alan J. Fletcher, *Drama, performance and polity in pre-Cromwellian Ireland* (Cork, 2000), chapter four; for the aftermath of his reforming efforts, see W.G. Neely, *Kilkenny: an urban history, 1391–1843* (Belfast, 1989),

Cork, whatever progress had been made in enforcing conformity to the state church was dissipated by the general growth of recusancy in the 1580s and 1590s.[2] Limerick, like Kilkenny, had a small coterie of Protestant youths, who were, as the papal emissary, David Wolfe, put it pejoratively, 'infected with the Lutheran leprosy' but their presence was scarcely felt in that city at the turn of the century.[3] There were hopes that Galway would become a missionary centre of Protestantism in the west, but these had faded by the end of the sixteenth century.[4] In the town of Youghal, which by the early Jacobean period had a nucleus of 100 English churchgoers, the attempt to graft on a congregation of several hundred Irish people by the use of 'moderate coercion' failed once the pressure was eased.[5] Yet the presence of a cohort of regular, voluntary worshippers in the Munster port indicates the importance of the plantation settlement in the region in delivering lay membership of the Church of Ireland. In Ulster the plantation also stimulated the establishment of groups of Anglican churchgoers, but, apart from comparatively small numbers of Irish conformists, assimilation of Irish converts to Protestantism within the parishes was comparatively rare.[6]

Dublin had by far the largest number of Church of Ireland laypeople by the early seventeenth century. Headed by a coterie of substantial patrician families, the native urban Protestant population was greatly expanded by the influx of English officials in the late Tudor and early Stuart periods. The pattern of settlement of the newcomers may at first have militated against their integration. Although a couple of the dozen or so metropolitan parishes were predominantly Protestant by 1630, the older Church of Ireland families were widely diffused throughout the city and suburbs. St Werburgh's and St John's parishes had a majority of Protestant residents by the 1630s, the households in the former being 80 per cent churchgoing.[7] These districts were heavily settled by state officials who desired proximity to Dublin castle and the Four Courts at Christ Church. In the other parishes, the number of Protestant families varied. In the most prestigious parish, St Audoen's off High Street, sixteen households, slightly less than a quarter, were Protestant in 1630, while the proportion was probably higher in St Nicholas Within and St Nicholas Without, and lower in St Michan's.[8] St Catherine's was unusual in having the large number of 226 recusants in 1617–18, yet, according to Archbishop Bulkeley in 1630, having

pp 41–9.   2 See Alan Ford, *The Protestant Reformation in Ireland, 1590–1641* (Dublin, 1997), pp 32, 36–40.   3 See Brendan Bradshaw (ed.), 'Father Wolfe's description of Limerick city, 1574' in *North Munster Antiquarian Journal*, xvii (1975), pp 47–53; idem, 'The Reformation in the cities: Cork, Limerick and Galway, 1534–1603' in John Bradley (ed.), *Settlement and society in medieval Ireland: studies presented to F.X. Martin, OSA* (Kilkenny, 1988), pp 445–76; Colm Lennon, *An Irish prisoner of conscience of the Tudor era: Archbishop Richard Creagh of Armagh, 1523–86* (Dublin, 2000), pp 29–31, 41–7.   4 See Ford, *Protestant Reformation*, pp 43–5.   5 Ibid., p. 98.   6 Ibid., pp 127–54.   7 M.V. Ronan (ed.), 'Archbishop Bulkeley's visitation of Dublin, 1630' in *Archivium Hibernicum*, viii (1941), p. 60.   8 Ibid., p. 58.

600 Anglican communicants.[9] It may have been that the former liberty of St Thomas court, now possessed by the Brabazon family, attracted New English settlement outside the corporation's jurisdiction (as indeed did the liberties of St Patrick's, Christ Church and St Sepulchre).[10] There was, however, no isolationism among the older Protestant families, as they continued to live in their houses in traditional neighbourhoods. Members of the Ball family and the Usshers of Bridgefoot Street were among the prominent Protestant worshippers in St Audoen's, the Bishop and Ussher families of St Nicholas Street frequented St Nicholas Within, and the Dermotts were associated with St Werburgh's.[11] While the new arrivals, lacking ties to the old urban core, might have been attracted to developing and settling in green-field sites to the south or to the east of the city after 1600, the long-established families who were Protestant, most of them mercantile, needed to remain embedded within the civic nexus with a view to preserving their social, business and commercial interests.

By remaining in communion with their recusant fellow-citizens through residential and matrimonial connections, the Dublin Protestant families continued to participate fully in corporation politics in the decades down to the 1640s. Indeed, notwithstanding their minority position, they came to play a crucial role in the maintenance of Dublin's municipal autonomy. From the early 1600s the state government made determined if sporadic attempts to ensure religious conformity on the part of the urban magistracies in Ireland.[12] The imposition of the oath of royal supremacy on leading officials, and the use of the prerogative court of Castle Chamber to enforce the statute of uniformity of 1560 threatened to disrupt severely the orderly course of municipal adminis-tration. The debarment from office of many Catholic mayors- and sheriffs-elect in the years after 1604 cut across the intricate system of succession by seniority to posts in the corporation. Gradually a strategy was devised whereby coun-cillors who were acceptable to the government because of their religious conformity were presented for election to senior civic positions at times when a policy of severity loomed. Leading Dublin Protestants were thus thrust forward to head the corporation on many occasions when more senior colleagues declined to hold office. Robert Ball, for example, was mayor of Dublin twice during the turbulent decades of the 1600s, and Alderman Richard Forster was described as having performed 'a salmon leap' over several 'grave and grey-headed'

9 Ibid., p. 59; John Meagher (ed.), 'Presentments of recusants in Dublin, 1617–18' in *Reportorium novum*, ii, no. 2 (1959–60), p. 273.   10 Ronan (ed.), 'Archbishop Bulkeley's visitation of Dublin', pp 61–2; Ciaran Diamond, '"God hath commaunded": the established church and its community in Dublin, 1603–41' (M.A. thesis. N.U.I., Maynooth, 1997), p. 26. 11 For details of the cultural and religious ties of the Dublin families, see the prosopography of the bench of aldermen of Dublin, 1550–1620, in Colm Lennon, *The lords of Dublin in the age of Reformation* (Dublin, 1989), pp 223–76. 12 Ibid., pp 174–205.

aldermen who were reluctant to serve as mayor in 1613.[13] Sir James Carroll and Sir Richard Browne served on four and three occasions respectively between 1612 and 1635.[14] Furthermore, a practice was established whereby one of the two sheriffs elected annually would normally be a Protestant who dutifully accompanied the mayor to church while the other was a Catholic who refrained from attending. In 1607–8, for example, the two serving sheriffs were Nicholas Purcell, a noted recusant, and John Lany, a Protestant.[15]

By acting in unison to manipulate the succession to office in times of difficulty, the patricians of Dublin, both Catholic and Protestant, secured the conservation of the city's cherished chartered liberties. In Limerick, too, the careful maintenance of an orderly succession to the highest corporation offices of mayor and sheriff through strict adherence to seniority had come under severe pressure during the period known as 'the battle of the mayors' from 1605 to 1616.[16] A whole series of debarments from office of elected mayors and sheriffs resulted from the imposition of the oath of supremacy by the Munster president but civic government was held together by the juggling of the principal offices among those eligible. These included the well-connected native Protestant, Edmund Sexton, who was advanced to the mayoralty for an unprecedented four times. He claimed that this was done by the corporation leaders 'to save themselves and to excuse their obstinacy'.[17] But Limerick managed to retain its chartered liberties at a time when, for instance, the city of Waterford lost its charter due to patrician 'obstinacy' in the face of government policies. This was despite the fact that three Protestants were hurriedly elected to the corporation of the southern city to provide subscribers to the oath of supremacy. Kilkenny escaped a similar fate notwithstanding the widespread incidence of recusancy among the leading citizens. Perhaps the unprecedented election of Sir Cyprian Horsfall, son of the Church of Ireland bishop of Ossory, as freeman, common councilman, alderman and mayor, all on the same day, averted the threat to municipal autonomy.[18]

There was also close co-operation between the Protestant and Catholic aldermen in respect of the defence of corporate and individual wealth. As an expanding commercial centre after 1600, Dublin was eyed with great interest by English and continental merchants who hoped to gain a foothold in the city's trade. There was therein a danger to the merchant guild's monopolies over commercial activity within the port. The government too aspired to regulate trade in order to generate more revenue for the state coffers, especially by

---

13 Ibid., pp 177, 183, 252.   14 Ibid., pp 235–7.   15 Ibid., pp 184, 259.   16 See Liam Irwin, 'Seventeenth-century Limerick' in David Lee (ed.), *Remembering Limerick* (Limerick, 1977), pp 114–22.   17 Colm Lennon, *The urban patriciates of early modern Ireland: a case-study of Limerick* (N.U.I., O'Donnell lecture, Dublin 2000), pp 8–9.   18 Neely, *Kilkenny*, p. 49.

resuming control over customs dues which the urban merchant classes had traditionally appropriated. Far from breaking ranks for individual benefit, the Protestant families were supportive of the corporatist principles underpinning the municipalities. That there were individualist tendencies on the part of the more entrepreneurial members of the Protestant community was clear in the Elizabethan period. Alderman John Ussher senior proposed a major overhaul of the leather industry which would cut across the interests of the merchant staplers.[19] Alderman Nicholas Weston applied successfully to the crown for an exclusive export licence for sheepskins, wool and tallow.[20]

Yet, although Ussher and Weston were subjected to angry recriminations on the part of their brother-aldermen for their initiatives, both were employed by the civic corporation on separate occasions. They both travelled as envoys to the English court representing the commercial and financial interests of the city to the monarchy, and both served as customers of the city.[21] When the issue of the city's rights to the retention of customs income arose in 1608, the advocate of the Dubliners' case at the court of King James I was Richard Bolton, an English Protestant, who had become a freeman and alderman before serving as city recorder.[22] The appointment by the aldermen of another Protestant, Alderman Richard Forster, as customer of the city may have been a tactical ploy to prevent the loss of privileges.[23] Throughout the period of challenge to corporate trading monopolies down to 1641, members of the Dublin Protestant families were fully participant in the running of the prestigious merchants guild. It appears that from the early years of the seventeenth century one of the two masters elected annually was a Protestant, Robert Ball serving in this capacity on six occasions, for instance, and John Cusack on four. During the particularly fraught period of the 1620s all of the masters were Protestants, but the pattern of shared mastership was reverted to in 1629–30.[24]

As well as providing outlets for pious expression, the confraternities or religious guilds attached to the parish churches had traditionally helped to forge cultural and social bonds among the civic community. With the abrogation of obitual forms of commemoration in the Reformation, the confraternities may have lost their official *raison d'être* but some of them continued to function throughout the early modern period in the absence of an official decree of abolition. The most notable of the Dublin confraternities was St Anne's which

19 'Ussher's scheme for leather export from Ireland in the reign of Queen Elizabeth', ed. A.F. Alexander in *Analecta Hibernica*, no. 12 (1943), pp 69–78.   20 Lennon, *The lords of Dublin in the age of Reformation*, pp 108–9.   21 Ibid., pp 104, 111, 115, 274.   22 Ibid., p. 194; Victor Treadwell, 'The establishment of the farm of the Irish customs, 1603–13' in *English Historical Review*, xciii (1978), p. 593.   23 Lennon, *The lords of Dublin in the age of Reformation*, p. 193.   24 Henry F. Berrry (ed.), 'The records of the Dublin gild of merchants, known as the gild of Holy Trinity, 1438–1671' in *R.S.A.I. Jn.*, xxx (1900), pp 44–68.

had its purpose-built chapel in St Audoen's off High Street. This had become a wealthy corporation by the sixteenth century, supporting six priests who drew their stipends from the large rental income of the guild's extensive properties within and without the walls of Dublin. Even though the guild provided a facade for recusant activity from the late years of the sixteenth century onwards, Protestant families continued their involvement in its affairs, fraternising with Catholic brothers and sisters at meetings and availing of leases of lands and houses. Alderman Walter Ball was a member of the guild alongside his Catholic brother, Alderman Nicholas. Once again a mediating role was played by Alderman Robert Ball, Walter's son, who during his mayoralty in 1605 became a member of the guild and reconciled its ruling group to the parish of St Audoen by procuring a commitment for guild funds for the incumbent, John Richardson. Through the following years of royal investigation of the guild's warrant, both Aldermen Robert Ball and John Cusack retained their membership and joined in the efforts to protect St Anne's charter. In all likelihood the guild was a vehicle for the patronage of Catholic clergy and their mass-house in the parish. Despite a papal bull of 1569 (a copy of which was in the guild's muniments) enjoining Catholic corporations to rent and lease property only to Catholics, St Anne's had as lessees during the early decades of the century Robert Ball (of a house on Merchant's Quay called the 'White Hart'), Dr Henry Ussher, Thomas Challinor, Robert Forster and John Cusack, all members of the Protestant community of Dublin. Right down to the end of the 1630s, when Lord Deputy Wentworth stepped in to regulate the guild and purge its officer-board, Protestants such as Robert and Edward Ball played a full part in the social and commercial world of the St Anne's. Rather like the Grocers' guild in contemporary London, the membership of St Anne's prioritised civic unity and tradition, skating over confessional differences in the interests of continuity and commonweal.[25]

Matrimonial arrangements between families helped to consolidate these interests, and here geographical proximity was an important factor. For example, marriages contracted between members of the Ussher family and their neighbour-families within St Nicholas's parish, Dublin, such as the Stanihursts and Kennedys, were evidently influenced by propinquity. Yet the Church of Ireland families of Dublin were also concerned to foster their faith by arranging unions for their offspring with children of their co-religionists. In spite of the

---

25 Colm Lennon, 'The survival of the confraternities in post-Reformation Dublin' in *Confraternitas*, vi (1995), pp 5–12; idem, 'The chantries in the Irish Reformation: the case of St Anne's guild, Dublin, 1550–1630' in R.V. Comerford, Mary Cullen, J.R. Hill and Colm Lennon (eds), *Religion, conflict and coexistence: essays presented to Patrick J. Corish* (Dublin, 1991), pp 7–12; Joseph P. Ward, 'Religious diversity and guild unity in early modern London' in Eric J. Carlson, *Religion and the English people, 1500–1640* (Kirksville, Missouri, 1998), pp 77–97.

difficulties posed in respect of the smallness of the pool of potential partners and the danger of isolation from the civic mainstream through unduly endogamous marriages, an intricate web of nuptiality enmeshed the older Protestant civic families. Thus, the children of Alderman Walter Ball married into the families of Archbishop Henry Ussher of St Nicholas parish, and Aldermen Richard Barry and Nicholas Weston. There was another wedding between a Ball daughter, Rose, and Lucas Challinor, the Protestant divine and foundation fellow of Trinity College, and nephew of Alderman John. Their daughter, Phoebe, was married to James Ussher who was a foundation scholar of Trinity. Besides being separately allied to the family of Ball, the Challinors and Usshers were themselves interlinked through the marriage of Thomas Challinor and Rose Ussher. Another foundation fellow of the new university, Launcelot Money, was part of this tightly-knit Dublin Protestant nexus. He was the son of Alderman John Money and Rose Ussher, sister of alderman of Alderman John Ussher the younger of St Nicholas's parish. To this network of active supporters and participants in the new university venture could be added Alderman John Forster, the executor of Walter Ball's will. The Forster family contracted marriages with city Protestant families such as that of Alderman William Gough.[26]

By contrast, some of the more recently-arrived Protestant families of Dublin such as Lany and Wiggett attempted to remain outside the network by confining their choice of partners exclusively to their fellow-New English. The marriages of the ten children of Archbishop Adam Loftus display this tendency very clearly. Most of Loftus's sons and daughters were wedded to members of families of the English servitor and planter class which had consolidated its holding in Ireland in the later Tudor period.[27] Among the archbishop's in-laws were the Bagenals of Newry, the Dukes, Hartpoles, Moores and Colleys of the midland plantation settlement, the Colcloughs of Wexford and the Berkeleys, newly-settled in Askeaton, County Limerick. Isabella was the only offspring of Loftus to marry a Dublin-born Protestant, William, son of Alderman John Ussher the elder. All of the eight children of that couple who married, with one exception, were partnered with members of families of the New English Protestant official and settler coterie, such as Crofton, Molyneux and Newcomen. Among the recently-arrived families in the midlands such as the Cosbys, Moores and Colleys, the preference was, where possible, for marital alliances within the Protestant colonial society either in Leinster or farther afield in the other provinces.

In the southern, western and northern regions in particular it was frequently neither possible nor desirable to maintain an isolationist religious or ethnic

26 See Colm Lennon, ' "The bowels of the city's bounty": the municipality of Dublin and the foundation of Trinity College' in *Long Room*, no. 37 (1992), pp 10–16; idem, *The lords of Dublin in the age of Reformation*, pp 137–8. 27 Donald Jackson, *Intermarriage in Ireland,*

policy in respect of marriage arrangements.[28] Moreover, the preservation of Protestantism may have proved to be less potent an impulse in this enterprise than the preservation of property and the advancement of social ascendancy. It is again in the capital city that the devising of means to conserve purity of religious reform is most evident. A balanced strategy of spousal selection from Protestant civic and New English families eventually ensured both the credal position and the survival within the municipality of the older Church of Ireland laity. The marriage of the daughter of Archbishop Adam Loftus, Isabella, to William Ussher, the son of John the elder who had proposed a university project in 1571 and 1582, points up the admixture of interests. Besides being an advocate of the commercial and social wellbeing of the municipality, Loftus had close ties with the Protestant coterie within its ruling group, holding a lease from the corporation of Donnybrook, one of the county estates of All Hallows. A daughter of this marriage between William Ussher and Isabella Loftus, married Charles Forster, of the long-established Church of Ireland family. Forsters had also contracted marital ties with New English families such as those of Huet, Bysse and Thomas.[29]

The process of communal bonding fostered by ties of consanguinity between older- and newer-established families over two or three generations was undoubtedly facilitated by habitual coexistence within the Church of Ireland parish system. The parish as district continued to be as important as ever for the forging of networks of social, economic and cultural connection, but gradual changes in the concept of parochial organisation and functions under the new Anglican regime had added significance for the Protestant laity. The identification with parish for worshippers down to the Reformation (and indeed beyond in some cases) had traditionally been overlain with membership of religious fraternities and combined with allegiances to local monastic houses and friaries, as Adrian Empey suggests in his essay in this volume.[30] With the slow vitiation of the panoply of medieval religious institutions in later sixteenth-century Ireland, the implications for the provision of welfare and charity for the sick and poor and for the practice of new devotions became apparent in the wake of the removal of the old structure. In the transition to a new system of care for the unprivileged and weak, Protestant laypeople played a full part, and the evolution of parish-based welfare schemes enlisted their energies in a creative manner. The painful sloughing off of former fellow-parishioners as well as the abrogation of traditional rituals, decor and furnishings eventually led

1550–1650 (Montreal, 1970), pp 20–8. **28** Ibid., pp 77–80. **29** Lennon, '"The bowels of the city's bounty"', pp 13–14; Jackson, *Intermarriage in Ireland, 1550–1650*, pp 20–8. **30** See above, pp 25–41; cf. the dispersal of bequests among parish churches, guilds and religious houses on the part of testators whose wills are recorded in Henry F. Berry (ed.), *Register of the wills and inventories of the diocese of Dublin, 1457–83* (Dublin, 1898).

to the formation of a different worshipping milieu, reduced in scale, perhaps, but enriched by the engagement with the new Protestant arrivals.

A disproportionately high number of Protestants in Dublin were very active in the provision of welfare schemes for the unprivileged, the sick and the marginalised. The context was the civic community's shouldering of the burden of charitable provision in the wake of the dissolution of the monasteries.[31] A quasi-monastic institution which survived the closure of the religious houses was St Stephen's lazar-house. In spite of the questioning of its warrant, it continued in operation until about the 1620s. The *custodes* appointed by the corporation to run the institution were young scholar-divines with Protestant leanings: Launcelot Money, for example, and Henry Fitzsimon, the future Jesuit who admitted to being a Protestant in his youth. Fitzsimon's father, Alderman Nicholas, and Alderman Walter Ball were both involved in the properties of St Stephen's in the suburbs of Dublin, and Ball was joined by Alderman Giles Allen in investigating the complaints of the lepers in 1591.[32] Private philanthropic enterprises in the older mode continued to be a feature of relief policy among Protestants, no less than their recusant fellow-citizens. In 1578 Alderman Richard Fyan offered to donate the former church of St Andrew which he then possessed to the city as a poorhouse or schoolhouse, and a later donation, that of Ann St Lawrence of £200 (to be invested at a rate of £18 per annum) for the maintenance of six poor widows 'such as goes to church', is confession-specific.[33]

From the Elizabethan period onwards, Protestant citizens of Dublin associated themselves prominently with poor law initiatives, and specifically the implementation of the act for vagabonds of 1541. This legislation divided the poor into the categories of deserving and undeserving, the former being those who were unable to support themselves through infirmity or old age. The existing institutions for reception of the deserving poor, St John's almshouse and St Stephen's lazar-house, were supplemented by a system of outdoor relief, based on a new poor rate levied on the citizenry. In each of the areas of indoor and outdoor relief, Protestant families were directly involved. Aldermen John Ussher senior and Thomas Fitzsimon were deputed to oversee the deserving poor, and to choose two honest men from each parish to require alms from churchgoers on Sundays and holydays. Later Alderman Richard Rounsell and Alderman Walter Ball were appointed as overseers, and Rounsell was delegated

31 Colm Lennon, 'Dives and Lazarus in sixteenth-century Ireland' in J.R. Hill and Colm Lennon (eds), *Luxury and austerity: Historical studies* XXII (Dublin, 1999), pp 46–65. 32 Myles V. Ronan, 'Lazar houses of St Laurence and St Stephen in medieval Dublin' in John Ryan (ed.), *Essays and studies presented to Professor Eoin MacNeill on the occasion of his seventieth birthday* (Dublin, 1940), pp 480–9. 33 J.T. Gilbert (ed.), *Calendar of the ancient records of Dublin* (19 vols, Dublin, 1889–1944) [hereafter cited as *Anc. rec. Dub.*], i, p. 193; iii, pp 346–7.

to collect the money due from citizens to pay for the upkeep of the civic almshouse. A four-man committee set up in the early seventeenth century to monitor the operation of institutions of indoor relief comprised leading Protestants: Aldermen John Cusack, Thomas Bishop, John Ussher the younger and Robert Ball.[34] Newly-arrived and longer-established Protestants were heavily involved in a series of initiatives designed to tackle vagrancy and disease around the turn of the sixteenth century. Sir George Carey's venture of 1602 was one of a number of proposals to deal with the idle or undeserving poor who were becoming more numerous in turn-of-the-century Dublin. His plan lacked focus, proposing as it did that the building could be a hospital for 'poor, sick and maimed soldiers, or other poor folks or a free school or college or else a place for punishing offenders' like the bridewell in London. Perhaps because of its ill-defined function Carey's hospital failed to fulfil any of those uses.[35] A bridewell was in fact built in close proximity to the hospital in 1604–5. The consortium of proposers included the Protestants, Dr Lucas Challinor, fellow of Trinity College, Mr John King, James Ware and Alderman James Carroll. Modelled on its London counterpart, it was to provide a place of punishment and work for idle persons. The building went ahead on Hoggen Green and stocks of materials for the inmates to work were ordered. The purpose was to reform the able poor by labour, and to provide an economic utility. In 1609, however, the city corporation withdrew its permission to make the building a bridewell and allowed it to be put to other uses.[36]

The decay of the long-established houses for the poor and sick and the failure of the new punitive institutions to prosper prompted a concerted effort to tackle the problem of poverty in circumstances of rising population in the later 1620s and 1630s.[37] A fundamental rift with implications for the provision of charitable services for the unprivileged opened between civic magistracies and state and ecclesiastical authorities over the issues of the unit of organisation and the financing of relief. By the 1620s and 1630s the Anglican parish was emerging as an alternative focus to the city ward for the dispensation of charity but, due to friction between the municipalities and the church, lines of administrative demarcation were not clearly drawn.[38] A linked question was whether alms should be raised through voluntary charity in the wards or parishes, or through a levy imposed by the city or the churchwardens of the

34 *Anc. rec. Dub.*, ii, pp 28–9; ii, 128–9; ii, 188; Lennon, *The lords of Dublin in the age of Reformation*, pp 227, 232, 240, 273–4. **35** *Anc. rec. Dub.*, ii, pp 390–2; iii, pp 62–3. **36** *Anc. rec. Dub.*, ii, pp 420, 498. **37** In some of the towns in Munster and Ulster where the influence of newcomers was significant, indoor and outdoor relief schemes for the deserving poor were pioneered, and houses of correction and bridewells for vagrants were established at a comparatively early date: see Patrick Fitzgerald, 'Poverty and vagrancy in early modern Ireland' (Ph.D. thesis, Queen's University, Belfast, 1994), chapters 1–2. **38** Fitzgerald, 'Poverty and vagrancy in early modern Ireland', p. 61.

parishes in the name of the established church. Also the system of collection and the means whereby money should be raised (by voluntary or compulsory giving) were not clearly agreed. The events surrounding the passage of poor legislation through the Irish parliament in the 1630s and early 1640s attest these tensions which bore especially upon the position of Protestants as citizens and parishioners. A bill presented to parliament in 1635 provided for at least one house of correction in each county to be funded by the proceeds of a county rate. It was passed but the operation of the law was to be delayed for five years, because of reservations of some members over the capacity of counties to pay. In 1640 a bill proposing a parish system of poor relief and enshrining the role of churchwardens passed through parliament but seems never to have been persevered with. It is likely that there was substantial opposition to both bills from borough representatives who resented the overriding of the powers of their magistrates in relation to the raising of local taxation and the organisation of internal schemes outside the competence of the corporations.[39]

The position of members of the Protestant community in the debate over the role of the parish is hard to reconstruct but there is little doubt that the emergence of a stronger parochial administrative system in the later seventeenth century assisted them in participating more fully in the distribution of charity and the regulation of vagrancy. By defining the duties and responsibilities of church-wardens and providing for a cess to be levied on parishioners for poor relief, the St Andrew's Act of 1665 set the tone for Protestant philanthropy and organisation within the parochial structure.[40] The nature of the involvement of the precursors of the later seventeenth-century reformers may perhaps be taken as reflective of the integrative nature of this process. Older and more recently-arrived members of the Dublin Protestant community were well represented on the committee of those elected to survey ground at Oxmantown for a municipal house of correction in the 1620s: the participation of Aldermen Richard Barry, Richard Forster and Thomas Evans balanced that of three Catholic city councillors.[41] Churchwardens were drawn from both longer-established and new Protestant families. In the parish of St Werburgh's, the family names included older-established ones such as Dermott and newer ones such as Philpott, Leventhorpe and Edwards.[42]

St Audoen's, Dublin, as has been seen, was the parish in which the guild of St Anne was located. As the Catholic parishioners separated themselves out into

39 For the text of the proposed bill, see Peter Gale, *An inquiry into the ancient corporate system of Ireland* (London, 1834), pp 185, pp clxxix–cxcv. 40 See Rowena Dudley, 'The Dublin parishes and the poor, 1660–1740' in *Archivium Hibernicum*, lii (1999), pp 80–2, and Katherine Anderson, 'The evolution of the parish of St John the Evangelist, Dublin, 1600–1700' (M.A. thesis, N.U.I., Maynooth, 1997). 41 *Anc. rec. Dub.*, iii, 68–9. 42 Henry F. Berry, 'Some ancient deeds of the parish of St Werburgh, 1243–1676' in *R.S.A.I. Jn.*, xlv

a worshipping community based on Mass-houses in the precincts of the church, the guild provided resources for their priests.[43] While the Protestant parishioners continued to participate in the commercial dealings of St Anne's, their eschewing of its religious practices called into question the subsidising of the parish from the considerable funds of the guild. The relatively sound structure of St Anne's chapel within the poorly repaired St Audoen's, with its unpaved floors and parlous steeple in 1632, pointed up the issue of ownership of the hallowed places.[44] Gradually the response of the Church of Ireland parish community became clear, as the older nave of St Audoen's was consolidated and renovated (partially with guild funds). New plate was donated by Peter Harrison in 1624 and new bells acquired at the behest of the prebend in the 1620s and 1630s.[45] The old rood and organ loft was taken down in the same year because, besides being in a dangerous condition, it deprived the congregation of 'sight of the east window and the holy table'. Instead, a 'comely partition' was erected between the nave and chancel, small enough so as not to 'hinder the congregation beholding the minister'.[46] The older Protestant families such as the Usshers and Tyrells and the newly-resident such as the Parrys and the Molyneuxs came to share this worshipping space. While some of the hallowed grounds within the precincts of the churches such as St Audoen's may have continued as places of entombment for the old Catholic and Protestant families, differing beliefs were reflected in the design and iconography of the tombs and plaques of the leading families. The wall-tombs of Protestant parishioners such as those of the Sparkes and Duffes families bodied forth their family pride in the form of effigies and heraldic devices, while the monument of the Catholic family of Malone in St Anne's guild chapel incorporated the motifs of the instruments of the passion.[47]

Through their campaigning for educational advances in support of the Reformation, Church of Ireland laypeople became habituated to working together and with the clergy. Alderman John Ussher senior of Dublin was one of a small but influential group of Dublin Protestants who were dedicated to educational advances at second- and third-level, building on their close inter-familial relations. Ussher had had philanthropic intentions when proposing the

(1915), p. 44. **43** Nicholas Donnelly, *A short history of Dublin parishes*, part viii (Dublin, 1917), pp 168–81. **44** *Irish Builder*, xxviii (1 Feb. 1886), pp 34–6; see also Lennon, 'The chantries in the Irish Reformation', pp 6–25. **45** John Crawford, *Within the walls; the story of St Audoen's church, Cornmarket, Dublin* (Dublin, 1986), pp 36, 39–40; *Irish Builder*, xxviii (15 July 1886), p. 203. **46** *Irish Builder*, xxviii (15 July 1886), p. 202. **47** For a discussion of the monuments and their historical background, see Amy L. Harris, 'Tombs of the New English in late sixteenth and early seventeenth-century Dublin' in *Journal of the Church Monuments Society*, xi (1996), pp 25–41; see also Rolf Loeber, 'Sculptured memorials to the dead in early seventeenth century Ireland: a survey from "Monumenta Eblanae" and other sources' in *R.I.A. Procs*, lxxxi, Section C (1981), pp 267–95.

reform of the leather industry in 1571. He urged that surplus revenue created should go towards the foundation of a university in Ireland for the education of Irish youth at home and the prevention of their imbibing 'notions' at Louvain and Douai.[48] Driven by credal principles in their zeal for the training of ministers of the gospel, these reformers were content to work within the framework of municipal government. Officially Dublin corporation preserved a position of strict public neutrality in respect of religious debate, but the body was susceptible to the lobbying of powerful and well organised coteries. In the case of the 1591 campaign for the siting of a new university on the city's estate of the dissolved monastery of All Hallows, the main protagonist, Archbishop Adam Loftus, enlisted the support within the executive of the city council of leading Protestant aldermen. Most notable among them was Walter Ball, a senior city politician and member of the commission for ecclesiastical causes. Besides speaking out vociferously in favour of the new academy, he was to provide bequests for the education of four scholars at Trinity College, and sent two of his sons, George and John, there. Through marriage he was connected to two of the foundation fellows of the new college: his son, Robert, married a daughter of Archbishop Henry Ussher, and his daughter married Lucas Challinor. On 18 January 1591 a 'godly and Christian motion' was advanced by 'certain well-disposed persons' before the city council for the granting of the precincts of the former All Hallows as a site for the college of a university. Meeting with the 'good liking' of the assembly, the proposal was conveyed as formal petition to Queen Elizabeth for a new university by Henry Ussher, archdeacon of Dublin. Formal ratification of the scheme came with the charter of incorporation of the university in 1592. Obviously the ground had been very well prepared for this smooth procedure. Archbishop Loftus worked effectively with his 'well-wishers' within the civic community to bring it to fruition. Besides being an advocate of the commercial and social well-being of the municipality, Loftus had close ties with the Protestant coterie within its ruling group.[49]

Pedagogical reform at second level was a *sine qua non* of an integrated educational system, as the newly-founded university needed feeder institutions for its student body. Within the context of the drive to foster grammar-schooling within the country, the Dublin city school emerged as the primary focus for educational endowment within the metropolis. Located at Ram or Schoolhouse Lane, the civic academy was run by the corporation in a systematic way from the early Elizabethan period onwards. The Protestant families played a highly supportive role in assisting the municipality's efforts in this respect. Alderman Walter Ball acted decisively at a time perhaps when the schoolhouse may have been in need of financial aid, patronising the newly-arrived James

---

48 Lennon, *Lords of Dublin*, p. 137.   49 Lennon, '"The bowels of the city's bounty"', pp 10–16.

Fullerton as incoming schoolmaster in 1588. During Walter's son, Robert's mayoralty in 1604–5 an indicator of the ethos within the school was given when it was spelt out by the city assembly that the master appointed should abide by the 'king's instructions or establishment touching matters of religion'. It was unusual if not unprecedented for a civic institution to be so overtly identified with the Reformation, but, at a time of testing of religious conformity, it was important that the municipal school be presented as officially orthodox. The Catholic majority on the corporation was complaisant in the appointing of a series of Protestant schoolmasters after the early 1600s. They were drawn at first from the English universities but later were usually graduates of Trinity College. Thus there was a reciprocal relationship between the new university and the city school, the latter providing scholars from among whom school-teachers emerged.[50] James Ussher was the most famous product of the academy, but it is significant that many Catholic families sent their offspring to be educated there. In 1622, commissioners found that the school had 122 pupils, of whom forty-three did not attend church. In the previous twelve years, the school had sent 100 scholars to Trinity; it had also sent 160 overseas, several of whom subsequently returned as priests.[51] Protestant and Catholic children were being educated together before their academic careers diverged into very different university systems.

A notable contribution to Protestant and Irish cultural history was made by John Ussher the elder. Already mentioned as an enterprising businessman and promoter of university education, Ussher, described by Archbishop Loftus as 'a rare man both for honestie and religion', provided leadership of the Dublin Protestant community during its vital incubation period, and he was midwife to a most significant project in his dedication to the Reformation. The fruits of his farsightedness are to be seen on the title page of the first book ever printed in the Irish language, *Aibidil Gaoidheilge agus Caiticiosma* of 1571. While the intellectual vigour was provided by John Kearney, it was Ussher's premises and financial support which made the publication possible. The printing press, using a font of Irish type subsidised by Queen Elizabeth, was set up at Ussher's residence on the island that came to bear his family's name beside the Liffey bridge. Two hundred copies of the catechism were produced in this domestic workshop. Presumably he would have had a direct role in distributing and selling the work through his own mercantile connection.[52] Family continuity in the printing and propagation of Irish religious texts is evidenced by John's son, William Ussher's part in the production of the Gaelic New Testament in 1602. The translator, Uilliam Ó Domhnaill, refers to the 'fervent zeal and Christian

---

50 Michael Quane, 'City of Dublin free school' in *R.S.A.I. Jn.*, xc (1960), pp 163–90.
51 Ford, *Protestant Reformation*, p. 92. 52 See Risteárd Giltrap, *An Ghaeilge in eaglais na hÉireann* (Dublin, 1990).

affection of Sir William Ussher, who following the steps of his religious faith, willingly undertook the greatest part of the charges of this impression'. The groundbreaking work was also printed in the house at the Bridgefoot.[53]

The career of the Limerick Protestant layman, Edmund Sexton (1569–1639), may be adduced to illustrate many of the facets of the lives of his co-religionists in early seventeenth-century Ireland. Born into the leading family among the small Church of Ireland congregation in the city, Edmund was conscious from an early age of his belonging to a minority and of the necessity to struggle for survival in what he saw as a hostile environment. It is from his own notebook and journals that a picture of his Protestantism may be drawn.[54] In the course of his chronicling of the history of Limerick and of his family's contribution to civic affairs, he inserted a chilling account of the disinterment of his grandfather, also named Edmund, by a group of Catholics during the reign of Queen Mary. The elder Sexton's remains were desecrated, his right arm being cut off at the elbow and the rest of his corpse being hanged by the heels above the roof of the chancel of the cathedral church of St Mary. Only when Sexton's widow was being buried in the family tomb was the absence of her husband's body discovered. A fleeing felon found the remains above the church and a reinterment took place, apparently in secret. According to the grandson, this sacrilegious act was perpetrated 'for his religion' because Edmund Sexton senior had embraced the Reformation.[55] In a letter to the Dublin government the younger Edmund claimed additionally that Sexton's physician had been procured by his enemies to 'bleed him to death' because he 'had received the gospel'.[56] Edmund junior went further in his attribution of persecution to the Limerick recusant community: his father, Stephen Sexton, who died in 1593, had his life ended prematurely because of the grief occasioned him through harassment over his claims to former monastic property in the city.[57]

Because of the smallness of the pool of Protestants within the city and its hinterland, Edmund faced a challenge in consolidating his credal convictions among members of his immediate family. His own marriage to Joan, daughter of Justice Gould, a Church of Ireland member, set the tone for the binding of familial ties within a network of co-religionists.[58] The couple had seventeen children between 1597 and 1620, six boys and eleven girls, of whom six died in infancy or childhood.[59] The baptisms of each are recorded as having been

53 Ibid., pp 68–9; Ford, *Protestant Reformation*, pp 107–8. **54** The principal manuscript sources for a reconstruction of Sexton's career are 'Sexton's notebook', *c.*1635 (N.L.I., MS 16085); Papers relating to the Sexton family (B.L., Add. MS 19865); Limerick MSS (N.L.I., PC, 875–9). **55** 'Sexton's notebook', *c.*1635 (N.L.I., MS 16085), p. 49. **56** Limerick MSS (N.L.I., PC, 875–9, 15/35). **57** Ibid. **58** 'Sexton's notebook', *c.*1635 (N.L.I., MS 16085), p. 53. **59** Ibid., p. 143.

performed either by curates of St Mary's cathedral, Nicholas Amery, Humphrey Rastell or Mr Chaff, or by the curate of St John's parish (Sexton's own appointee), Mr Richard Mannering. Of the total of fifty-one godparents listed, only a few had names of long-established Limerick families, and it is most probable that these Lysaght, Comyn and White members were Protestants.[60] The rest included the category of servitors of the crown in Munster or of the earl of Thomond and his family, leading Protestant ecclesiastics such as the dean of Limerick and other members of the chapter of St Mary's cathedral, Limerick, the wives and other female relatives of senior and junior clerics, the domestic staff of Sexton's own household and a select group of civic officials, including the town-clerk, the clerk of the munition and the impost collector. Prominent sponsors included John FitzAndrew Lysaght who stood for three of the children, his wife, Elinor who stood for two, Elizabeth Silvester, lady to Sir Turlough O'Brien, Deans Campbell and Andrews of Limerick, the latter's wife, Elinor, and Mr Richard Fuller, the cathedral organist and his wife. The only corporation magistrate mentioned, Sheriff Robert Lillis, belonged to a Protestant bookselling family. Enclosed within this small world of north Munster Protestantism, Edmund Sexton attempted to control the destinies of his family, also organising weddings for them where possible within the restricted Church of Ireland community.

In characterising the sentiments of the citizens of Limerick towards him, he referred to Psalm 129:[61]

> Ever since I was young, my enemies have persecuted me cruelly, but they have not overcome me. They have cut deep wounds in my back and made it like a ploughed field. But the Lord, the righteous one, has freed me from slavery.

As well as experiencing their 'general hatred against all possessors of the true religion', Edmund Sexton pointed to the 'malice' of the majority towards himself and his ancestors 'only for ... religion and adhering to the state'.[62] Yet he continued to support the institutions of corporate government, even when he may have perceived them as being used to save the ruling coterie from the consequences of non-conformity. In his journal, Sexton vaunted the municipal achievements of the borough of Limerick which culminated in the charter of incorporation in 1609, and his family's participation in urban life. He noted proudly the date of his own enfranchisement as free citizen and enrolment in the panel of householders in 1595.[63] Even during his periods of service as

60 Cf. the approving words of Sexton about these individuals in 'Chronicle of Limerick' in 'Sexton's notebook', c.1635 (N.L.I., MS 16085), pp 35–94.   61 Limerick MSS (N.L.I., PC, 875–9, 15/35).   62 Ibid.   63 'Sexton's notebook', c.1635 (N.L.I., MS 16085), p. 51.

sheriff of the county of Limerick, Sexton was called upon to serve as mayor of the city, an office he occupied for an unprecedented four times between 1606 and 1623. His loyalty to the corporation in acting as chief magistrate at times when central government was insisting on religious conformity ensured that the city's immunities and privileges were maintained. In addition, he served as mayor of the staple in the city, and in 1608, when the customs rights of the municipality were under threat of abolition, it was Sexton, a trained lawyer, and James Galway who travelled as agents of Limerick to the royal court in London to plead the case for retention of the income.[64] Sexton's lavish hosting of Lord Deputy Falkland at his house at Gurtenfluch in 1624 during the latter's visit to the city was important in presenting the civic community in a favourable light to the chief governor.[65]

Thus, even at the height of his personal quarrel with the corporation in the 1600s and 1610s, Edmund Sexton contributed notably to the survival and well-being of the municipality of Limerick. The root of the long-running litigation between the councillors and the leading Protestant of the city lay in the grants of dissolved religious property which had been made to Sexton's grandfather by King Henry VIII. The elder Edmund Sexton had acquired titles to the former Franciscan friary and also the estate of the priory of St Mary. There had been bitter resentment among the leading councillors of Limerick at the transfer of these prime city lands and houses to an *arriviste* who had been catapulted into the mayoralty on the king's orders in the 1530s. In all likelihood, the resultant dispute had its macabre sequel in the disinterment of Edmund Sexton's body in the 1550s.[66] Feelings were no less intense in the second and third generations of the post-monastic era, and the younger Edmund Sexton was obliged to expend a great deal deal of time and money in defending his rights and privileges in respect of his abbey lands. His access to the friary was obstructed by various barriers, corporation workmen intruded upon the possessions and his privileges as the successor of the priors were denied and called into question. The protracted case generated voluminous documentation in the form of letters, deeds and leases, many of which have been preserved in the archives of Sexton's descendants.[67] He travelled to Dublin frequently and enlisted the support of leading provincial and national politicians, including Lord Deputy Chichester

---

64 For details of his political and legal career, see 'Sexton's notebook', *c.*1635 (N.L.I., MS 16085), pp 57–79. **65** 'Sexton's notebook', *c.*1635 (N.L.I., MS 16085), p. 80. **66** *Cf. L. & P. Hen. VIII*, xiii, pt 2, pp 932, 1032; *State Papers, Henry VIII*, iii, pp 107–8; Brendan Bradshaw, *The dissolution of the religious orders in Ireland under Henry VIII* (Cambridge, 1974), pp 80, 102–3, 148–9. **67** See, for example, Papers relating to the Sexton family (B.L., Add. MS 19865), pp 91, 92–6, 101–2, 105–6, 113–19; Limerick MSS (N.L.I., PC, 875–9), 15/30, 31, 35, 47; 19/ 2f; 21/2; 25/31; for a catalogue of the documents that Edmund considered of vital importance, see 'Papers relating to the Sexton family' (B.L., Add. MS 19865), p. 127.

(whose secretary was Edmund's brother, George), in pursuance of his cause. The outcome was satisfactory as far as the plaintiff was concerned when James I issued a letter patent, confirming him in full possession of all the properties over which there was contention.[68]

While the upholding of his proprietorship was a major consideration throughout the legal proceedings, there is little doubt that Sexton regarded his stance as incorporating a shepherding of Protestant interests in Limerick. At a time of increasingly open Catholic reorganisation in the 1610s and 1620s Edmund was ever-vigilant for the re-entry of friars into their former possessions. Thus he took part in the implementation of the regulations against mass-houses within the city and approved of the president of Munster's campaigns to curtail Catholic worship. He noted with approbation, for example, the search for the newly-appointed Catholic bishop of Limerick, Richard Arthur, and had justifiable fears of a recurrence of the revolt of recusants that had occurred on the accession of King James I in 1603.[69] Then, the insurgents had taken over the churches in the name of the papacy, among the ecclesiastical places threatened being Sexton's own.[70] The family tomb in St Mary's cathedral had to be preserved from the intrusions of the Creagh family, among others, and the security of the church of St John in the suburbs, the rectory of which was in his gift, was a matter of great concern to him. The church had been invaded and taken over by the recusants in 1603. He applied successfully for the right to expend recusancy fines charged for non-attendance at divine service on the repair of St John's.[71] Once the premises were safely in his control, however, Sexton was content to let the local families, Catholics as well as Protestants, have access to their traditional places of burial within the church.[72]

Something of the character of Sexton's Protestantism emerges from evidence of his own religious interests and patronage. Richard Mannering, the curate of St John's who had baptised a number of his children, was Sexton's own appointee, as was Roger Herys, who succeeded Mannering on his death in 1624. Sexton was prepared to override the opposition of the bishop in the case of the latter appointment.[73] Edmund's own education in Ireland, Oxford and London had inculcated a breadth of learning and knowledge which becomes clear from the catalogue of his library.[74] The major part of the collection was of books of divinity, comprising 40 per cent of the total. Among the categories was that of scriptural texts and commentaries, including at least three books of his

---

68 See Limerick MSS (N.L.I., PC 875–9), 28/1.   69 See, for example, 'Sexton's notebook', c.1635 (N.L.I., MS 16085), pp 55, 70, 79, 80, 82, 84, 86.   70 Limerick MSS (N.L.I., PC, 875–9, 15/35).   71 'Sexton's notebook', c.1635 (N.L.I., MS 16085), pp 55, 75.   72 'Sexton's notebook', c.1635 (N.L.I., MS 16085), p. 145; Limerick MSS (N.L.I., PC 875–9), 24/5. 73 'Sexton's notebook', c.1635 (N.L.I., MS 16085), p. 80.   74 Papers relating to the Sexton family (B.L., Add. MS 19865), pp 74–8.

grandfather's. Besides the works of leading Protestant and Catholic theologians, there were texts containing disputations between protagonists of both sides and a number of controversialist books in confutation of the claims of the Roman church and Mass. Sexton also possessed several works of spirituality and practical piety including the *Imitatio Christi*, *The practice of piety*, *The sanctuary of a troubled soul* and *The poor man's garden*. His journals suggest a lively interest in the history of the Reformation, there being inserted in his chronicle of world and local events a long discussion of abuses in the church and of the deliberations of the councils of Ratisbon and Trent in the mid-sixteenth century.[75] His son and heir, Stephen, was sent to the Tuam grammar-school run by Isaac Lally, a graduate of Trinity College, Dublin, before beginning his own studies at the university in Dublin.[76] Although Sexton revealed little connection with his own family's Gaelic past, the inscription in his notebook of a version of the ten commandments in Irish may suggest an interest in the Irish language and perhaps an awareness of its place in catechesis within the Anglican mode.[77]

Edmund Sexton's hopes for the transmission of his beliefs through a consolidated family inheritance in Limerick city and its region were severely dented before his death. It was apparent to him that a Catholic resurgence in the later 1620s was threatening the Protestant holding within the city.[78] Among his own kinsfolk a pattern of deaths and 'marrying out' disrupted his plans.[79] The death of his son, Stephen, in 1628 at the age of thirty-one was a blow from which he may never have recovered. He had devoted much time and energy to the formation and training of the young man.[80] His second son, Christopher, was groomed to carry on the traditions but his position in Limerick political life may have been fairly tenuous. Before his death in March 1639, Edmund Sexton had to endure indignities which were reminiscent of the events surrounding his grandfather's demise. According to evidence in a trial in the court of Castle Chamber later that year, two Protestant clergymen, Fursman and Hayes, were denied admission to the dying Edmund by his relatives who 'attempted' him out of the Protestant religion.[81] Fursman did get into Sexton's house but was interrupted as he tried to pray with Edmund. Arising out of the contretemps, Alderman Edmund junior, the dying man's youngest son, his wife, Joan, and two of his daughters, Mary Sexton and Catherine Lysaght (née) Sexton, were found guilty of 'high impiety and inhumanity'. Edmund junior and Joan were

---

75 'Sexton's notebook', *c.*1635 (N.L.I., MS 16085), pp 44–6.   76 Ibid., pp 60, 63, 68, 69.
77 Ibid., pp 133–4.   78 Ibid., pp 86, 90.   79 See, for example, his frustration at the marriage of Mary Gould, the widow of Dr Field, to George Creagh FitzRichard, 'without the consent of her friends'. Creagh had been servant to Geoffrey Galway, a notable recusant: 'Sexton's notebook', *c.*1635 (N.L.I., MS 16085), p. 81; Limerick MSS (N.L.I., PC, 875–9, 15/35).
80 'Sexton's notebook', *c.*1635 (N.L.I., MS 16085), p. 84.   81 *Cal. S.P. Ire.*, *1633–47*, p. 227: I am grateful to Dr Clodagh Tait for drawing this episode to my attention.

fined £5,000 and the others £1,000, and all were put in the pillory for three days, wearing papers on their heads declaring their offence. At least the deceased was accorded a fitting funeral, with all the solemnities the city and county could afford, and he was interred in the family tomb in St Mary's to rest undisturbed.[82]

The fate of the civic-minded Edmund Sexton in having his beliefs subverted on his deathbed is testimony to the fragility of the Protestant base in Limerick. Despite his elaborate efforts to construct a support system through ties of marriage and gossipred, some of his own offspring were revealed as antagonistic to his religious stance and acted to convert him to Catholicism at the end of his life. Eventually the confessional and material inheritance of Edmund Sexton was to be secured after 1660 through the marriages of family-members to the newly-arrived Pery family and the long-established Stackpoles, but the careful balancing of new and old interests was extremely difficult for Edmund to achieve in the earlier decades of the seventeenth century, given the scarcity of Protestants. It was only in Dublin before 1640 that the numbers were great enough to sustain the growth of an integrated Church of Ireland lay community. The 'older' Protestants, by demonstrating their commitment to the civic commonweal, retained the respect of their Catholic fellow-citizens. Yet they gradually forged social and economic ties with members of the new Protestant settlement who became obligated to them for their induction into the privileged world of the municipality. By degrees, recurrent and familiar contact between Protestants engaged in welfare and educational enterprises augmented their common participation in parochial worship and ritual to shape a body of self-confident lay people, secure in both their religious and civic identities.

---

82 'Papers relating to the Sexton family' (B.L., Add. MS 19865), pp 138–9.

3

Parishes, pews and parsons: lay people and the Church of Ireland, 1647–1780

T.C. Barnard

I

Most estimates suggest that at best 10 per cent of Ireland's population throughout the eighteenth century belonged to the established Protestant church. This membership was never spread evenly across the island. Generally it was densest where most English and Welsh immigrants had settled. Also, numbers tended to be highest in towns. In Dublin, indeed, it is agreed that a majority of its inhabitants were Protestants, at least until the middle of the eighteenth century. With a total population estimated at 124,000 in 1732–3, this meant that perhaps as many as 75,000 lived there. Thereafter, both the absolute number and proportion of Protestants drifted inexorably downwards.[1] In the other substantial towns, the proportion of Protestants varied from something between a third and 40 per cent in Cork, through 29.4 per cent in Limerick, 26.5 per cent in Drogheda, 20.5 per cent in Kilkenny to a mere 12.9 per cent in Galway.[2] These estimates lumped all Protestants together, regardless of whether or not they conformed to the Church of Ireland as established by law. It is likely that in the places just enumerated, the overwhelming majority of the Protestants were conformists. As noteworthy is the likelihood that a much greater proportion of the total number of Protestants (including members of the Church of Ireland) than of Catholics inhabited the larger Irish towns. Perhaps as much as a third of the conformist population was made up of town-dwellers. This manner of life in its turn accentuated an already strong sense of

---

1 D. Dickson, 'The demographic implications of Dublin's growth' in R. Lawton and R. Lee (eds), *Urban population development in western Europe from the late-eighteenth to the early-twentieth century* (Liverpool, 1989), pp178–87; P. Fagan, 'The population of Dublin in the eighteenth century with particular reference to the proportions of Protestants and Catholics' in *Eighteenth-Century Ireland*, vi (1991), pp 121–56, reprinted in Fagan, *Catholics in a Protestant country: the papist constituency in eighteenth-century Dublin* (Dublin, 1998), esp. pp 31–7, 43–5. 2 D. Dickson, '"Centres of motion": Irish cities and popular politics' in L. Bergeron and L.M. Cullen (eds), *Culture et pratiques politiques en France et en Irlande*

cultural difference between Irish Catholics and anglicised Protestants. It also accounted for the important variations in outlook and behaviour between urban and rural parishioners of the established church. In the countryside, outside Ulster, Protestants were much more thinly scattered. Only County Wicklow with 33 per cent of the total population, and County Dublin with 23 per cent, contained reasonable concentrations of Protestants.[3] The unevenness with which Irish Protestants were spread led to startling variegations in religious life, whether in the public or the more domestic aspects. However, before exploring those differences, it is first necessary to ascertain what formally was expected of adherents of the state church.

The Elizabethan statute of 1560 required attendance at prescribed worship each Sunday on pain of fines for defaulters. The penalties, intermittently applied, hurt prominent recusants more than Protestant backsliders. Changes in, and uncertainty about, what the state demanded in the way of religious conformity left all Protestants reasonably free between 1647 and 1660 to go wheresoever their fancies listed on Sundays.[4] Thereafter, efforts to reintroduce the earlier severity, embodied in the Act of Uniformity of 1666, failed to curtail the newly-won freedom among Protestant dissenters. This Act in any case aimed chiefly to bring errant pastors back into line.[5] Instead, an alternative method of coercing the reluctant into outward religious conformity was tried. In 1704 a Test Act was enacted in Ireland. Following the precedent of English statutes of the 1670s, entry to a variety of prestigious posts and full enjoyment of civic rights were confined to communicant members of the Church of Ireland, the implications of which are discussed in David Hayton's essay below. The intention behind this measure may have been more negative than positive: less to herd all into the established church than to share the material benefits of membership among a select company. It is also uncertain how rigorously the test was applied once the initial intolerance which had led to its enactment abated.[6]

XVIe–XVIIIe siècle (Paris, 1991), p. 106. **3** Abstract of the number of Protestant and Popish families in the several counties and provinces of Ireland (Dublin, 1736); S.J. Connolly, Religion, law and power: the making of Protestant Ireland, 1660–1760 (Oxford, 1992), p. 146. Communities more sparsely inhabited by Protestants are studied in B. Gurrin, A century of struggle in Delgany and Kilcoole (Dublin, 2000), and W. Gacquin, Roscommon before the famine: the parishes of Kiltoom and Cam (Dublin, 1996). **4** Guides to the variety of religious options available at the time include: St.J.D. Seymour, The puritans in Ireland, 1647–1661 (Oxford, 1921); T.C. Barnard, Cromwellian Ireland (Oxford, 1975). **5** 17 & 18 Car.II, c.6. For the development of Protestant nonconformity: P. Kilroy, Protestant dissent and controversy in Ireland, 1660–1714 (Cork, 1994); R.L. Greaves, God's other children (Stanford, 1997). **6** Assessments of the impact of the Test include: J.C. Beckett, Protestant dissent in Ireland, 1687–1780 (London, 1948); Connolly, Religion, law and power, pp 160–71; I. McBride, 'Presbyterians in the penal era' in Bullán, i no 2 (1994), pp 2–23; T.C. Barnard, 'The government and Irish dissent, 1704–1780' in K. Herlihy (ed.), The politics of Irish dissent,

However, the significance of the Act was to associate sacramental communion according to the rites of a particular confession with political trustworthiness. This invested an action, regarded by the devout as the essence of their faith, with strong secular connotations. It was characteristic of how the sacred and secular interlocked in Ireland during the heyday of the Protestant Ascendancy. Some would go further, seeing this intertwining as the hallmark of a confessional state, many of which already existed across the water in Europe.

Had the Test Act been strictly enforced, then any layman who aspired to salaried office would need to attend and take holy communion, 'in some parish church upon some Lord's day', in order to equip himself with the necessary certificate of conformity.[7] Occasions are recorded on which those about to be sworn as justices of the peace hastened to the apparently sporadic administrations of the sacrament in their local churches. At Kinsale in 1714, the curate and churchwardens attested that fifteen functionaries in the customs 'did receive the sacrament of the Lord's Supper according to the usage of the Church of Ireland ... immediately after divine service and sermon'.[8] The action had to be performed within three months of being nominated to a patentee post.[9] Others about to make leases or conclude other legal contracts needed similarly to enable themselves.[10] No particular spectacles seem to have gathered around this essentially utilitarian action. In this it differed sharply from the theatre of recantation when adherents of the Church of Rome admitted their error and joined the Church of Ireland. Whereas state servants in qualifying themselves for office simply utilised an existing rite (albeit the most important), the Church had devised a special form for those who recanted. The solemnity of public abjuration, before the whole body of the congregation, cannot be minimised. The impact on the watchers and auditors perhaps never equalled that on the recantor. Nevertheless it was a ceremony which enlivened the otherwise predictable annual cycle of liturgical observances.[11]

The church calendar, in Ireland as in England, mingled religious and civil celebrations. Ireland observed such festal days as the deliverance from the

1650–1800 (Dublin, 1997), pp 9–27; D.W. Hayton, 'Exclusion, conformity and parliamentary representation: the impact of the Sacramental Test on Irish dissenting politics', in Herlihy (ed.), *Politics of Irish dissent*, pp 52–71; J.R. Hill, 'Dublin corporation, Protestant dissent and politics, 1660–1800', in Herlihy (ed.), *Politics of Irish dissent*, pp 28–39.   **7** 2 Anne, c. 6, in *The statutes at large passed in the parliaments held in Ireland* (20 vols, Dublin, 1786–1801), iv, p. 23.   **8** M. Mulcahy (ed.), *Calendar of Kinsale documents*, vii (Kinsale, 1998), pp 42–3.   **9** *Statutes at Large*, iv, p. 24.   **10** To the examples in Barnard, 'Protestantism, ethnicity and Irish identities, 1660–1760', in T. Claydon and I. McBride (eds), *Protestantism and national identity: Britain and Ireland, c.1650–c.1850* (Cambridge, 1998), p. 206, n.2, can be added: N.L.I., MS 14101, 1 March 1740[1].   **11** T.C. Barnard, 'The uses of 23 October 1641 and Irish Protestant celebrations' in *English Historical Review*, cvi (1991), p. 907; Barnard, 'Protestants and the Irish language' in *Journal of Ecclesiastical History*, xliv (1993), pp 243–72.

Popish Plot and the accession and birthdays of the sovereign, together with fasts for topical crises and mercies. The enthusiasm with which these imported holy days were commemorated by laypeople varied, and did not always match that which they generated in Britain. Special to Ireland was the feast on 23 October, inserted into the holy year in 1661. Yet, even this uniquely Irish Protestant solemnity waxed and waned in popularity, depending on the sense of present danger from the Catholics.[12] Bit by bit rituals outside the church precincts attached themselves to the most important of these red-letter days: aldermanic processions; mayoral banquets; drunken revels and sectarian brawls. It could be argued that thereby these originally sacred rites were being laicised.[13] As this secular jollity expanded, so (it seemed) the devotions within the walls of the church contracted. Yet the fun, feasting and frenzy on these occasions could not be separated from the construction of a Church of Ireland activist, particularly a Church of Ireland man. The corporate acts of thanksgiving were copied by smaller groups. Some of them continued or reinvented the festivities connected before the Reformation with crafts and guilds. Annually – usually on the patronal day of the tutelary saint – the members of a guild prayed and dined together. Which they regarded as the more important – the spiritual or bodily sustenance – it would be presumptuous to guess. Even if we compare what the dinner and chaplain's sermon cost we are unlikely to learn the correct answer.[14]

The church hosted a series of special events during the year. These brought within its curtilage some who probably did not attend the regular Sunday services. In addition, as the church grew into a more complicated organization, so its multiplying functions led to innovations. These reflected both a new seriousness in attempting to fulfil traditional duties of philanthropy and education, and an increased supervisory role delegated to the parish by the state. It is true that in Ireland the ecclesiastical parish never acquired the multiplicity of powers which burdened it in England.[15] Nevertheless, the authorities in Ireland found it convenient to load regulatory tasks onto the parish. Because of these added responsibilities, the parish as a unit came to bulk larger in the lives of some of its inhabitants.

12 T.C. Barnard, 'The uses of 23 October', pp 889–920.   13 J. Coughlan to R. Musgrave, 20 Nov. 1712 (N.L.I., MS 13242); D. Clarke to W. Smythe, 16 April 1741, 5 Nov. 1743 (N.L.I., PC 447); R. Caulfield (ed.), *The council book of the corporation of Youghal* (Guildford, 1878), pp 382, 409; Barnard, 'Athlone, 1685; Limerick, 1710: religious riots or charivaris?' in *Studia Hibernica*, no. 27 (1993), pp 61–75.   14 Pearse Street Library, Dublin, Gilbert MS 78, pp 139, 141, 178, 179; MS 80, pp 80, 81; P.R.O.N.I., D. 2707/C1/1, 29 Dec. 1757; R.C.B., C 2/2/1 (1), Proctors' accounts, St Patrick's, 12 April 1720, 12 April 1721; T.C.D., MS 1447/8/1, ff. 38v, 48v, 67v, 113v; C.T. Keatinge, 'The guild of the cutlers, painter-stainers and stationers, better known as the Guild of St Luke the Evangelist, Dublin' in *R.S.A.I. Jn.*, 5th series, x (1900), pp 145–6.   15 For the theory and practice in England, see: P. Slack, *From reformation to improvement: public welfare in early modern England* (Oxford, 1999).

The exact tasks of the parish alongside, for example, the summary jurisdiction of magistrates, the continuing work of courts leet and baron or of the municipal authorities are hard to demarcate. Nevertheless, the records of vestries and churchwardens' spending show how rates were levied, collected and then disbursed, primarily to relieve the deserving poor. The last seem to have been defined much as their counterparts in England: in the cycle of life they had reached a stage – youth, old age, chronic illness or widow(er)hood – at which they could not fend for themselves.[16] What is unclear is the extent to which strict confessional tests were applied to the suppliants, thus excluding all but regular communicants of the parish from its charity.[17] On occasion, as during the severe recession of 1720–1 and again in 1740–1, all denominations were reported to have organised relief.[18] Even in these emergencies, help may still have been directed by each to its own. The usually small number in individual parishes relieved suggested that such selectivity kept the burden manageable. The bulk of the indigent, overwhelmingly Catholic, looked elsewhere for doles. Furthermore, when subsistence crises dramatically increased those needing aid, exceptional – non-parochial – measures were taken.

The example of philanthropy emphasises two important ways in which the institutional church touched lives. Increasingly the needy looked to their churches to improve their material as much as spiritual state. As more practical and monetary support was provided, so more was expected. In consequence, the different denominations competed over the services which they could supply to the faithful.[19] At the same time, the need to oversee these activities gave the

16 N.L.I., MS 764, pp 1, 2 (St Peter's, Cork) and MS 5246 (Vestry book of Agher, Co. Meath); R.C.B., P192/5/1, pp 13, 20, 53, 57, 58, 59 (Vestry book of Kells, Co. Meath); P276/8/1 (poor book, St Michan's, Dublin, 1723–34); P317/5/1, pp 38,128,141,144 (Vestry book of Carlow); P326/27/3/76 & 83 (St Werburgh's Dublin); 'A general state of the poor in the parishes of Coleraine and Killowen', P.R.O.N.I., D 668/E/38; E. Parkinson, 'The vestry books of the parish of Down' in *Ulster Journal of Archaeology*, 2nd ser., xiv (1908), p. 155; xv (1909), p. 80.   17 For a suggestion of just such a restriction: R. Malcolmson, *Carlow vestries in the olden times* (Carlow, 1870), p. 15; at Maryborough, proposal of 18 Dec. 1684, Abbey Leix, de Vesci MSS (now in N.L.I.), H/17; and at Buttevant, D. Muschamp to T. Fitzgerald, 21 Jan. 1692[3], ibid., H/2. Non-denominational relief continued in Dublin parishes: R. Dudley, 'Dublin's parishes, 1660–1729: the Church of Ireland parishes and their role in the civic administration of the city' (Ph.D. thesis, Trinity College Dublin, 2 vols 1995), i, p. 175.   18 Abp W. King, 8 April 1721 (T.C.D., MS 2533, pp 216–18); Abp W. King to Abp W. Wake, 23 March 1720[1] (Christ Church, Oxford, Wake MS 13/240) Bp J. Evans to same, 8 April [1721] (ibid., 13/242); Proctors' accounts, St Patrick's Dublin, 17 March 1720[1], 4 Aug. 1729, 16 Jan. 1740[1], 26 April 1741 (R.C.B., C2/1/10(1 & 2)); E. Synge, *Universal beneficence: a sermon preached in the parish church of St Luke, Dublin on Sunday the nineteenth day of March, 1720/1* (Dublin, 1721); D. Dickson, *Arctic Ireland.*   19 T.C. Barnard, 'Identities, ethnicity and tradition among Irish dissenters, c.1650–1750' in K. Herlihy (ed.), *The Irish dissenting tradition, 1650–1750* (Dublin, 1995), pp 46–8.

parish a function distinct from the simple provision of regular worship. Belief in the requirement of civic activism among people of property fused with Christian teaching on benevolence. A type emerged energetic alike in the affairs of corporation, voluntary associations and in the running of the religious parish. Sometimes, indeed, it might be puzzling where a specific concern fitted. The parish, for example, as in England, had long overseen the repair of local highways, organizing levies and navvies for that purpose.[20] After 1698, it also maintained the registers of newly-planted trees, needed if the planters were to be paid the statutory bounties. Vestries were, moreover, the medium through which quotas of saplings to be planted could be aplotted.[21] Just as the possession of a modicum of wealth was required to spare time for citizenship, so, within the parishes, it was again the modestly prosperous who filled the offices. The givers and takers of doles belonged to the same neighbourhood and sacral community. But the inequalities between donors and recipients of alms reinforced other differences. Those charged with raising cesses interested themselves in the vicious behaviour thought to cause rather than to arise from destitution. From time to time, in consequence, parish functionaries investigated vagrancy, 'ill fame', and even brothels: the Dublin parish of St Michan's was employing the aptly named Thomas Vice to do so in 1733.[22] These bad habits were worrying since they threatened not only the affected individuals but also the larger community. If, on the one hand, the managerial elite which had emerged in urban parishes by the eighteenth century felt that its superiority was at root a spiritual one, it also feared lest, by its own neglect of responsibilities or through the provocative misconduct of the unruly, God would punish the whole congregation. Directly, as well as vicariously, the officers of the parish were involved in the plight of the poor and reprobate. The incentives to restrain and reform were strong.

As extra tasks were assumed by the parish, a bureaucracy developed. Where once the incumbent alone, or in tandem with churchwardens and (maybe) the lay patron, had handled the business, it was delegated to a bigger standing committee or to ad hoc panels. Neither the timing nor the processes behind these developments have been much studied. It seems likely that the most precocious in this regard were the populous urban parishes, particularly in Dublin.[23] There, better record-keeping and the survival of those records may

20 N.L.I., MS 5246, 6 Oct. 1747; J. Clelow to ?M. Ward, 10 Oct. 1741 (P.R.O.N.I., D 2092/1/5); R.C.B., P192/5/1, p. 7; J.J. Marshall (ed.), *Aghadow vestry records of the church of St John Parish of Aghadow [Caledon], Co. Tyrone* (Dungannon, 1935), pp 13, 14, 16, 26, 28.
21 10 William III, c. 12; R.C.B., P317/5/1, p. 80; Marshall, *Aghadow vestry records*, p. 10.
22 N.A., M.2549, p. 171 (W. Handcock to St Michan's Church, 8 May 1697); R.C.B., P192/5/1, pp 37, 79; R.C.B., P276/4/1, pp 117–18; R.C.B., P276/8/2, pp 137, 213.
23 Abp of Dublin to W. King, 31 Dec. 1685 (R.C.B., P326/27/3/75); R.C.B., P277/7/1,

distort the picture. Yet, the multiplicity of problems, the availability of numerous helpers and the sise of annual budgets make it plausible to suppose that inner Dublin pioneered administrative innovation. Just how onerous the parochial chores were is also difficult to assess. Apportioning, collecting and spending rates, and chasing defaulters took time and could cause strife. Important in supervising and recording these activities was the parish clerk. Paid a salary – by the early eighteenth-century, varying from anything between an annual £4 and £15 – he provided continuity from year to year as church-wardens and committee-men changed.[24]

Towns at the end of the seventeenth and early in the eighteenth centuries witnessed a craze for rebuilding or beautifying church fabrics. In part, this vogue reflected similar developments in England. Architecture – especially ecclesiastical architecture – was invested with strong ideological connotations. The appropriate style demonstrated both the antiquity of the Protestant church and its continuing links with primitive christianity. It could also express fundamental differences in doctrine and liturgical practices between the established church and its competitors.[25] The Church of Ireland, entrenched in its uniquely privileged position, sought to give physical form to its dominance. In addition, laypeople, familiar in their homes with higher standards of comfort, hoped to introduce them into the houses of God. Pews of greater elaboration, velvet cushions, even 'houses of office' in the churchyard, catered to these wants.[26] More emphatically, with stone spires and porticoes, and in the classical symmetry of the exteriors, the buildings proclaimed a taste and civility to which the meeting house of the nonconformists and the deliberately insignificant chapels of the papists could not aspire. These architectural endeavours necessarily made more work for the busy. Designs were procured, discussed and accepted. Money had to be raised. In the case of several of the most ambitious projects in Dublin and Cork, the burden was spread more widely.[27] Occasionally the state assisted with subventions. But before that kind of help was received, parish worthies had lobbied frenziedly. This kind of labour on behalf of the parish generally fitted into a pattern of activity in which the interests of the

pp 88,167; St Finbarre's cathedral, Cork, 'Caulfield's annals of St Mary's Shandon', pp 1,3; 'Dr Caulfield's annals of the parish church of St Maria de Shandon, now St Ann's Shandon, Cork' in *Journal of the Cork Historical and Archaeological Society*, 2nd series, x (1904), p. 268; Records of Holy Trinity, Cork (R.C.B., P527/1/2), pp 82–90.   **24** N.L.I., MS 764, p. 4; R.C.B., P192/5/1, pp 89,107,114,115; R.C.B., P 276/4.1, P 117; P 276/8.2, pp 306,409; R.C.B., P 276/12/1, P 61; Marshall, *Aghadow vestry records*, pp 26,28; R. Dudley, 'Dublin's parishes', i, pp 83–90.   **25** H.M. Colvin, 'Introduction' in E.W.G. Bill, *The Queen Anne churches* (London,1979), pp ix–xi; P. Judge, 'The state of architecture in Ireland, 1716' in *Irish Arts Review*, iii no. 4 (1986), pp 62–3.   **26** Cloyne Chapter Acts, 21 May 1719, 17 Sep. 1728 (now in R.C.B., C 12/2/1); R.C.B., P276/8.2, pp 49,91; R.C.B., P317/5/1, p. 68.   **27** 6 Anne, c. 21; 2 Geo.I, c. 24.

powerful were solicited for a range of benefits, only a few of which related to the parish.[28]

Ambitious plans to raise new structures affected, at best, only a minority of parishes, usually in towns. Often the motive was ideological, and the prime movers the clergy, such as Archbishop William King of Dublin or Dean Henry Maule in Cork.[29] When rebuilding occurred in country parishes, it was more likely to be inspired and financed by the local lay patron. The social utility of regular episcopalian worship was appreciated by Thomas Wentworth, absentee owner of estates in south Wicklow and north Wexford. His priorities were apparent when he not only subsidised church-building, but despatched to his Irish agent his own and his wife's portraits, 740 copies of a popular catechism and seeds.[30] More modest structural improvements might be financed by humbler parishioners. Thereby their affection for their place of worship was proclaimed and their identification with it strengthened. Particularly visible were funerary monuments, which trumpeted the virtues of individuals or dynasties to their successors and their neighbours.[31] Such boastfulness was not always to the taste of the church authorities, and so, as we shall see, could become a source of conflict between laypeople and clergy. Less contentious were gifts to the parish. Usually these took one of two forms: either silver, pewter or (exceptionally) gold vessels for the celebration of the sacraments – patens, flagons, alms-dishes, candlesticks – were donated in perpetuity for the use of the parish;[32] or land or money in order to generate a revenue which could then be applied to charity.[33]

---

28 R.C.B., P 277/7/1, p. 88; R.C.B., P 317/5/1, s.d. 18 July 1726; K. Severens, 'A new perspective on Georgian building practice: the building of St Werburgh's church, Dublin (1754–59)' in *Bulletin of the Irish Georgian Society*, xxxv (1992–3), pp 3–11. 29 Abp W. King to Bp H. Compton, 2 Aug. 1704 (T.C.D., MS 750/3/1, pp 4–5); same to ?, 14 May 1715 (ibid., 750/4/2, p. 47); H. Maule to R. Stearne, 24 Sep. 1717, same to Abp W. Wake, 25 Sep. 1723 (Christ Church, Oxford, Wake MS 12/354; 14/92): Bp W. Nicolson to Abp W. Wake, 17 Sep. 1723 (ibid., 14/91); petition from St Mary's, Shandon, *c*.1725 (P.R.O.N.I., DIO/4/5/3/92). 30 W. Perceval, *A sermon preach'd at the consecration of Christ-Church, in the county of West-Meath* (London, 1713); R.C.B., P317/5/1, p. 93; T. Wentworth to A. Nickson, 12 July 1715, 2 Aug. 1715 (Sheffield City Libraries, WWM/M. 14/13 & 14); payment on 5 March 1713[14], account of A. Nickson with T. Wentworth (ibid., WWM/A 759, p. 383). 31 R. Gillespie, 'Funerals and society in early seventeenth-century Ireland' in *R.S.A.I. Jn.* cxv (1985), pp 86–91; R. Gillespie, 'Irish funeral monuments and social change, 1500–1700: perceptions of death' in R. Gillespie and B.P. Kennedy (eds), *Ireland: art into history* (Dublin, 1994); H. Potterton, *Irish church monuments 1570–1880* (n.p., 1975). 32 N.L.I., MS 5246; gifts to St Werburgh's, Dublin, 1662 (R.C.B., P326/27/43); J.L. Darling, *St Multose Church, Kinsale* (Cork, 1895), p. 25; J.J. McKenna and C.V. Moore, *The modest men of Christ Church, Cork* (Naas, 1970), p. 3; St.J.D. Seymour, *Church plate and parish records, diocese of Cashel and Emly* (Clonmel, 1930); C.A. Webster, *The church plate of the diocese of Cork, Cloyne and Ross* (Cork, 1909). 33 C. and M. Jackson, 'The Vaughan

The centrality of the church to the lives of the privileged members was constantly demonstrated by its use for secular purposes. Even before municipal office was monopolised by those of the Church of Ireland, town councils borrowed church buildings. The annual ceremonies of mayor-making inevitably involved a religious component, and so included rituals in the parish church. Many corporations integrated official religion more routinely into their practices. The mayor, sheriffs, aldermen and common councilmen were required to assemble each Sunday in their appropriate robes and then process to parish worship. They walked according to their precedence in the council, and were preceded by civic functionaries bearing the insignia of the town.[34] Once in the parish church, the mayor often sat in a designated pew. This could be differentiated from others by its splendour. Moreover, the civic regalia rested before the chief magistrate during the service, sometimes – as at Youghal – in a specially carpentered sword-rest or – in Hillsborough – on the altar itself.[35] The municipality might regard the church as something more than its host. At Youghal in the reign of Charles II, the corporation authorised the sovereign to take up with the bishop the lack of preaching 'in this great congregation'.[36] At Kilkenny, the municipality was paying £25 annually towards a lecturer in St Mary's church in 1716.[37] The presence of the local leaders and beneficiaries of the Protestant interest at worship reminded that established Church and state were indivisible.

What occurred in the incorporated boroughs across provincial Ireland was intended to be replicated in Dublin. There, at the start of each parliamentary session, members of the two houses went – separately – to their devotions: the Lords at Christ Church cathedral; the Commons to St Andrew's. The stated festivals of the Church, notably those with clear public and political connotations, such as 30 January, 30 May, 23 October and 5 November, also called forth congregations of the important. The attendance of the sovereign's surrogate in Ireland, the lords justice or lord lieutenant, set the seal on this association of a Protestant state with a specific denomination. But, in this, as in many other respects, the viceroy failed to uphold the proper values. There were

Charity, 1763–1934' in *Clogher Record*, xii (1986), pp 171–8; J.C.T. MacDonagh, 'A seventeenth-century Letterkenny manuscript' in *The Donegal Annual*, iii (1956), pp 139–41. **34** Waterford City Archives, Waterford Corporation Book 1700–1727, 17 Sep 1711, 28 Feb. 1714[5]; N.A., M. 2549, pp 124, 126; Caulfield, *Youghal*, p. 394; M. Mulcahy (ed.), *Calendar of Kinsale documents, i* (Kinsale, 1988), p. 45; P.D. Vigors, 'Extracts from the book of the old corporation of Ross' in *R.S.A.I. Jn.*, xxxi (1901), p. 59.   **35** Pearse Street Library, Gilbert MS 78, pp 165–6; Caulfield, *Youghal*, p. 412; R. Caulfield (ed.), *The council book of the corporation of the city of Cork* (Guildford, 1879), p. 218; G. O'Brien, *St Mary's parish, Athlone: a history* (Longford, 1989), pp 92–3; R. Richey, 'Landed society in mid-eighteenth-century County Down' (Ph.D. thesis, Queen's University Belfast, 2000), p. 182. **36** Caulfield, *Youghal*, p. 333.   **37** Kilkenny Corporation, Kilkenny Corporation Book, s.d.

eight red-letter days in the year on which he was expected to preside over the sacred-cum-secular celebrations.[38] Often he and his entourage preferred to worship discreetly in the chapel of Dublin Castle. During the 1690s, the primate, Archbishop Marsh made it his business to prod prominent Protestant peers into publicly performing their religious duties. One of the lords justice, Drogheda, was persuaded to communicate in the chapel of Trinity College rather than covertly in the Castle chapel. But the failure of his partner, Mountrath, to do the same worried Marsh and excited comment. As the archbishop observed, 'the common people judge by outward appearance, and if upon that or any other account they should take a conceit that he is not a friend to our church, it might prove of ill consequence'.[39] The viceregal pew at Christ Church suffered from abuses which may have been linked with the declining reputations of the now invariably English lords lieutenant. On behalf of Rochester, the viceroy at the very beginning of the eighteenth century, pursuivants were to guard the stairs to the gallery and thereby prevent the 'disorders and indecencies [which] happen by persons that belong not to the state'. The fact that the directive had to be repeated in 1711, 1713 and 1715 indicated that it had not deterred the intruders.[40]

Except in the largest towns, church buildings offered one of the few – if not the sole – space where the locals could conveniently assemble. In some boroughs, such as Kilkenny, the churchyard was tidied and beautified. Avenues of trees might be planted so that the greensward was turned into an agreeable resort for the *beau monde*.[41] At Dungarvan in 1703, a ferociously contested election was adjourned to the churchyard. Then, too, the militia and other emergency forces raised at moments of danger could be mustered and drilled in the graveyard. Not only did it, as at Ballyclough in the north of County Cork, offer a suitable space, the hours immediately before or after divine service were likely to produce the maximum attendance.[42] Thus, the Protestant community at prayer transformed itself agilely into a group ready to fight. In other ways, the military and ecclesiastical agencies which defended the Protestant kingdom of Ireland overlapped. The garrison frequently marched to, and then participated in, parish worship.[43] Undoubtedly the soldiery swelled the regular congregations. Incumbents could also supplement their stipends by ministering

23 March 1715[16]. **38** Genealogical Office, Dublin, MS 96, p. 133. **39** Abp N. Marsh to Abp T. Tenison, 10 April 1697 (Lambeth Palace, MS 942/133). **40** B.L., Add. MS 4784, ff 248v, 251v; Genealogical Office, Dublin, MS 96, pp 141–2,161; order of 19 July 1715 (Tickell MSS, iii, p. 39, House of Lords Record Office, London). **41** Autobiography of H. Thompson (Bodleian Library, Oxford, MS Eng. Hist. d. 155, f. 40v). See, too, Cloyne Chapter Book, 1 June 1722 (R.C.B., C12/2/1). **42** R. Purcell to Viscount Perceval, 3 Jan. 1745[6] (B.L., Add. MS 47002A, f. 1). **43** Autobiography of J.A. Oughton (National Army Museum, London, MS 8808.36.1, p. 61).

to the local garrison. Yet these arrangements did not always conduce to harmony between the military and churchmen. At Kinsale, for example, the rector, Tom, was paid ten shillings for his services on Sunday. Tom regarded himself as no better than 'a constant drudge to the army there without thanks'. However, the garrison commander seemingly resented the fact that Tom demanded to be paid on the nail, and vented a not altogether jovial anti-clericalism. 'You know the clergy has no faith so wont preach nor pray on tick'.[44] Such animosities disturbed the amity which ought otherwise to have reigned in cities such as Waterford and Limerick, which housed both cathedrals with lordly bishops and obstreperous garrisons.[45] In stations like Kinsale and Youghal, the troops inflated the number of communicants and the frequency of christenings and weddings, as the parish registers attest. But they also introduced, and often left behind them, less welcome traits. Not only might they abet unruly and anti-social habits, but they littered the parish with bastards and abandoned women and children.[46]

Even without the addition of these relics from the military's occupation, most common throughout Irish Protestant parishes were the obligations to relieve the weak and impoverished. These tasks, especially in combination, stimulated parish meetings and the development as an organization of the vestry. The new importance of the latter by the early eighteenth was shown by the designation and construction of rooms, often in or abutting onto the church, where the group could meet.[47] It was but a short step thereafter for the vestry-room to become the site of conviviality. During the 1720s, when the pushy Dublin curate, Pilkington, sought to impress, he did so by entertaining neighbours to an elegant collation 'of fruit, wine, &c.' in this parochial space.[48] It offered an alternative venue to the coffee-houses and taverns of the town for the increasingly varied entertainments with which the polite and genteel diverted themselves. The Church of Ireland, by welcoming the pleasure-bent onto its premises, may have reclaimed some of the leisure of its nominal adherents, thereby checking the secularizing tendencies in contemporary society. At the same time, as critics warned, the Church, by accommodating these novelties, risked being infected by worldliness.

---

44 J. Tom to E. Southwell, 9 Feb. 1704[5], H. Hawley to same, 1 April 1705 (Kinsale Manorial Papers, 1698–1764, National University of Ireland, Cork, Boole Library, U/20). 45 T.C. Barnard, 'Athlone,1685; Limerick,1710', pp 71–5.   46 Parish Register 'B' (Church of Ireland Rectory, Youghal); St Multose's church, Kinsale, Register, 1683–1820; Darling, St Multose church, Kinsale, p. 42; R.C.B., P317/5/1, pp 4, 101; Parkinson, 'The vestry book of Down', p. 26; T.C.D., MS 5301, p. 46.   47 Precisians contended that the parish room should be separated physically from the church itself: W.M. Jacob, Lay people and religion in the early eighteenth century (Cambridge, 1996), p. 204. Cf. R.C.B., P276/8/2, p. 24.   48 A.C. Elias, Jr (ed.), Memoirs of Laetitia Pilkington (2 vols, Athens, Ga. and London, 1997), i, p. 15.

The appearance of dedicated vestry-rooms testified to the new importance of the organization. Just how onerous or honorific were posts such as church-warden, overseer of the poor or vestry-man is harder to ascertain. Indeed, who was permitted to come to the vestry is unclear. In some parishes all adult (and male?) householders may have appeared. Liable to pay the rates levied by the church, presumably a principle of representation entitled them. However, such promiscuous resort to the assembly risked making it unmanageable. To expedite business, the select vestry evolved. Again this could be seen as part of a trend towards oligarchy through which the worthies of the community dominated, in the parish as in the corporation and guilds.[49] In practice, who was welcomed into the vestry varied greatly. Where conformists were few, as in many rural districts, it may have been impracticable to restrict too narrowly membership of the vestry. But then other problems arose. In 1724, Dean Henry Maule of Cloyne was dismayed to discover that Catholics came *en masse* to the vestry of Mourne Abbey in the north of County Cork. The danger that they might swamp the assembly led the bishop to urge a law specifically to debar Catholics. Soon they were statutorily excluded from meetings at which levies for church building were to be agreed. In the shorter term, Maule had responded by tendering to them the oaths of allegiance and abjuration. 'They soon cried pecavi, paid their fines and left the affairs of my church and parish to go in the proper channels'.[50] Elsewhere, especially in eastern Ulster, the threat came from another quarter: the presbyterians. At Bangor in 1739, James Clelow awaited the vestry meeting, apprehensive lest it strip him of his small dues. Two years later, Clelow reported how the local presbyterian pastor had urged his flock to attend the Church of Ireland vestry in order to press or defeat particular measures. Other optional expenditure which the incumbent wished to lay on his congregation, such as recasting a peal of bells, could be rejected by the niggardly vestry.[51] Until debarred by the creation of smaller, select vestries, those otherwise outside public life, Catholics and dissenters, could join in running local affairs. Another group generally excluded from public life – women – may some-times have been admitted to the meetings. However, in comparison with eighteenth-century England, far fewer women appeared. In 1752, Lady Orrery is to be found at the vestry of Aghadow (or Caledon) in County Tyrone. But she seems to have come very much as the substitute for her husband, away in England. At least in the formal workings of the parish, there were depressingly rare outlets for women, and probably none for those of the humbler sort. Given the

49 R.C.B., P276/4/1; R.C.B., P317/5/1, pp 14,24; St Finbarre's, Cork, 'Caulfield's annals', p. 3. 50 H. Maule to Abp W. Wake, 22 Aug. 1724 (Christ Church, Oxford, Wake MS 14/213); J. Smythe to W. Smythe, 'Easter Day' [1745], N.L.I., PC 449; J. Thompson to same, 8 April 1745, N.L.I., PC 445. 51 J. Clelow to M. Ward, 19 Feb. 1738[9], 20 Nov. 1740, 2 March 1740[1], 10 Oct.1741 (P.R.O.N.I., D 2092/1/5, 33, 72, 88 ,98).

importance of vestries as outlets for civic activism, the limited membership denied many a rudimentary political education. Involvement in the regular work of the vestry for members of the Church of Ireland, no less than adherents of the state church in England or North American colonies, may have differentiated the respectable and substantial from the lowlier orders.[52]

In any parish, the undisputed grandees would be expected to serve as church wardens. By doing so they may have honoured the congregation more than they were honoured by the dignity. Yet few parishes, even the smartest in Dublin, boasted so many gentlemen that the choice of functionaries could be confined to them. Thus, traders and craftsmen alternated with the titled, judges, squires and counsellors.[53] The obligation to take one's turn, together with the fact that the vestry annually selected church wardens from its own number, could open the way to the appointment of some not in communion with the established Church. The regularity with which in Ulster the lot fell on presbyterians led to a recognised right to nominate a substitute. Efforts by some early eighteenth-century bishops to end this substitution raised the unwelcome prospect of dissenters as church wardens having to institute proceedings against their non-conforming brethren or themselves risking prosecution when they failed to take the tendered oaths. These scares served to expose doubts about just what oaths could legally be required of the incoming wardens. Even Archbishop King of Dublin felt it better to run a permissive regime in which the scrupulous dissenter could act by deputy or locum. This permissiveness was confirmed by statute in 1720, with the right of nonconformists to appoint surrogates upheld.[54] Laxity later characterised the parish of St Nicholas in Galway in the 1740s and 1750s. Church wardens there were not obliged to subscribe to the Canons of the Church, but merely swore a vague oath to discharge their duties properly. Judging by the names of those who thus equipped themselves in

52 Marshall, *Aghadow vestry records*, p. 30; McKenna and Moore, *Modest men of Christ Church*, p. 26; Jacob, *Lay people and religion*, p. 10; H.R. French, '"Ingenious and learned gentlemen" – social perceptions and self-fashioning among parish elites in Essex, 1680–1740' in *Social History*, xxv (2000), pp 44–66; J.R. Kent, 'The rural "middling sort" in early modern England, circa 1640–1740: some economic, political and socio-cultural characteristics' in *Rural History*, x (1999), pp 19–54; D.B. & A.H. Rutman, *A place in time: Middlesex, County Virginia, 1650–1750* (New York and London, 1984), pp 143–62; K. Wrightson and D. Levine, *Poverty and piety in an English village: Terling, 1525–1700* (New York and London, 1979), pp 103–9. 53 R.C.B., P276/4/1; John Leslie, *Articles to be inquired of by the churchwardens and questmen of every parish in the next visitation* (Dublin, 1667). By 1736 the duties of the post had become so onerous that, at least in Dublin, 'a society' of churchwardens had been formed to coordinate activities. R.C.B., P276/8/2, p. 157; Dudley, 'Dublin's parishes, 1660–1729', i, p. 154. 54 Petition of J. Bell, 1718 (Marsh's Library, MS Z3/1/1, xxiii); Abp W. King to Bp E. Smythe, 5 July 1718 (T.C.D., MS 2535/199); *Statutes at Large*, iv, p. 511; S. Burdy, *The life of Philip Skelton*, ed. N. Moore (Oxford, 1914), pp 78–9.

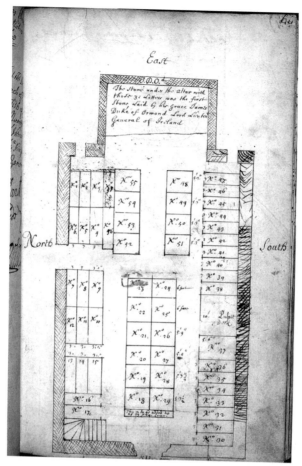

3 Plan of pews in St Peter's church, Dublin, 1693 (R.C.B.).

Galway, this did not lead to Catholics filling the post.[55] In the lowlier jobs, filled by rote from year to year, the respectable among the middling sort were much used. Such dispositions merely recognised the obvious fact that the bulk of Church of Ireland parishioners, particularly in the towns, came from the middling and lower orders.[56]

These basics of social stratification were also displayed, Sunday by Sunday, in the pews. Especially in churches which had recently been rebuilt or re-ordered, pews were sold or leased.[57] In 1709 the incumbent at Wicklow

55 N.A., M. 6947. 56 J. Johnston, 'Clogher parish – some early sidesmen, 1662–1734' in *Clogher Record*, xiv (1991), pp 89–91. 57 R.C.B., P45/6/1, pp 65–73, 84; P276/12/2; P276/4/1, p. 103; P277/7/1, pp 40, 51, 52, 54, 57, 179–82; P317/5/1, p. 86, 18 July 1732;

announced that he was 'settling the parishioners in their respective seats, and fixing the rate of each seat agreeable to the rank and ability of each parishioner' in the new church. Notables availed themselves of the chance to secure, for family and household, permanent seating.[58] This might be differentiated by more ornate joinery or by being situated in the galleries. Nevertheless, the bulk of the reserved pews were possessed by simpler souls, designated as 'gents', tradespeople or widows. The parish of St Werburgh's, close to the castle in Dublin, typified this characteristic. Its pew-holders were, as a parliamentary statute of 1716 alleged, 'mostly shop-keepers and tradesmen'.[59] The willingness of parishes to sell or alienate pews to raise cash stored up trouble for the future. Throughout the eighteenth century, vestries often had to resolve wrangles over the use or sale of particular pews. Frequently a lone parishioner's attachment to property rights warred against the needs of the congregation as a whole. Stubborn owners might refuse to retreat from their pretensions. Thus, unseemly rows could disrupt services, as when claimants continued to sit where they had been banned or forcibly ejected rivals. At Coolkenna in County Wicklow, it was remembered how, in the 1730s, disputes over who should have the right-hand seat in the projected gallery 'put an entire stop' to its being constructed. In 1789, the daughter of Lord Massy, finding another in possession of 'the head pew', demanded it, but in vain. The churchwarden who had denied her what she took to be her proper precedence was threatened first with horse-whipping and then with a duel. In the event, the peer's daughter retreated. Friction over this seemingly trivial matter seldom degenerated to such a low. Against the unedifying fracas can be set the occasions when absent notables happily ceded their pews to underlings on the spot, as with Lord Digby's at Geashill.[60] Yet, these tussles showed how sensitivity over precedence, deference and property were not abandoned when the faithful passed through the door into the church. The most extreme examples of disruption arising from such feelings relate to the few, mainly peers and landlords, and more in the countryside than the principal towns. They had constructed or repaired churches at their own charge. This dependency was frequently repeated in financial arrangements which had alienated impropriations and church property to laypeople and gave to the latter the right of presenting incumbents to livings. It

P527/7/1, pp 81, 84, 85, 86; Parkinson, 'Vestry books of Down', p. 25; Dudley, 'Dublin parishes', i, pp 115–18. **58** C. Whittingham to Abp W. King, 18 March 1708[9] (T.C.D., MSS 1995–2008/1316); N.L.I., MS 764, p. 4; Southampton University Library, MS 64/1/2 (Congleton MSS). **59** R.C.B., P326/13/1; 326/27/2/102; *Statutes at Large*, iv, p. 427. **60** *Retrospections of Dorothea Herbert 1770–1806* (Dublin, 1988), pp 186–8; W. Peard to F. Price, 9 July 1745, 5 Aug. 1748, 24 Feb. 1748[9], National Library of Wales, Aberystwyth, Puleston MS 3579E; N.L.I., MS 6054, p. 8; R. Odlum to Lord Digby, 3 Nov. 1765, Dorset County Record Office, D/SHC, 3C/81.

imbued the Church of Ireland with a markedly seigneurial aspect. An example from County Down illustrates the point.

William Waring had prospered thanks to the opportunities offered by the upheavals of the mid-seventeenth century. They enabled him to transform himself from trader and agent into a landowner on his own account, secure with a rental that steadily rose from £600 a year in the 1690s to £900 by the 1730s. Settling in the countryside, he created the eponymous settlement of Waringstown. There the classic configuration of proprietor's mansion and parish church had appeared by the 1680s. During the Interregnum, Waring had sympathised with the austere religious ethos, and never entirely forsook that austerity, even if, by the 1690s, he conceded that it was old-fashioned. This outlook gave his own life a certain gravity and drabness.[61] It did not, however, prevent him from watching closely over the parish church, visible from the windows of his own residence and very much his personal creation. He expressed his delight at seeing regularly there, 'so full a congregation gathered in a great part by means in a place esteemed once a wilderness'. Having spent heavily, Waring was enraged when the bishop trenched upon his rights. In particular, it seemed, Waring was to be denied the right of sepulture in the building. He raged, 'it will be thought strange to all heaven that a man that hath built a church and reserved it to his family a burying place, shall be disturbed in it'.[62] Others among Waring's landed contemporaries were equally exercised by this question. The learned William Montgomery of Rosemount, also in County Down, surveyed the common-law as well as precedent to determine 'men's rights to dispose of the tombs which they have made and dedicated'. He recorded how many adhered to tradition, and were reluctant to be interred in newly created cemeteries, and himself sympathised with the traditionalists. In cautioning against innovations which might offend, he reminded that 'civil regard is due to dead bodies, especially to those of neighbours, masters, parents, clergymen and honoured persons'.[63] As late as 1739 the issue still concerned the notables of County Down, one of whom was informed confidently, 'whoever has a burying place in the parish church has a right to bury there'.[64] In Ulster, the issue was one which distinguished traditionalist conformists of the Church of Ireland from the zealous who obeyed the ban on intramural burial adopted by the reformed Scottish kirk.

---

61 T.C. Barnard, 'What became of Waring? The making of an Ulster squire' in V. Carey and U. Lotz-Heumann (eds), *Taking Sides?*, (forthcoming). **62** Papers on church at Waringstown (private collection, Co. Down). **63** P.R.O.N.I., D 552/B/4/1/4. p. 9.Cf. petition of John Nettles, St Carthage's cathedral, Lismore, Co. Waterford, Lismore Chapter Book 1663–1829; Sir H. Tuite to Bp H. Maule, 12 April 1745 (N.L.I., PC 449). **64** J. Clelow to M. Ward, 19 Feb.1739[40] (P.R.O.N.I., D 2092/1/5, 33).

The wide spread of this opinion, and also how it could contradict the injunctions of the Church, were most sensationally demonstrated in the first earl of Cork's bid to rear a swaggering monument to himself and his dynasty in St Patrick's cathedral. However, this was but one instance among many of how sharply laity and church authorities might diverge about fitting rites of passage. Intermittent quests to strip away the rituals which had collected around these vital moments in life (and death) intensified as the Reformation and Counter-Reformation reached deeper into Ireland. The revelry and excesses which attended Irish funerals – wakes, keening, extravagant and unseemly feasting – were widely decried.[65] Clergy of all persuasions sought to introduce greater doctrinal correctness into interment. Corpses should no longer be interred within the body of the church.[66] Extra-mural burials, perhaps even in separate graveyards, angered those, such as a Waring or Montgomery, whose own expenditure on the fabric was believed to entitle them to such a privilege. But others than the squirearchy were upset. The clergy, by imposing these prohibitions, might obey the teaching and practices of the primitive Christians. But such doctrinal purity hardly comforted aggrieved parishioners. It was a problem, moreover, which extended beyond the confines of their own denomination. Possessed since the Reformation of most of the earlier buildings, the Church of Ireland thereby acquired custody of numerous sites venerated as the burial-places of locals. In seeking to restrict what were popularly regarded as customary if not legal rights of sepulture, the clergy of the established Church risked unpopularity. Often clerical bans were circumvented, with bodies buried clandestinely at night. But, only gradually did the Church of Ireland relax its claim to a statutory monopoly over the rite of burial: a monopoly from which it aimed to profit handsomely.[67]

Death and burial were only two of the sensitive moments at which laypeople and the church authorities could collide. These wrangles affected many beyond the formal limits of the Church of Ireland, and exposed cultural, economic, ideological and practical differences. Remembering these longer ramifications, nevertheless we need to focus on the impact of practices on the laity of the established Church. They, too, begrudged the fees extorted for occasional but necessary services. The death of one especially rapacious incumbent in Dublin in 1725 provoked a bitter invective. Among the Revd John Clayton's failings, it was recalled,

65 T.C. Barnard, 'Hospitality and display in Protestant Ireland, 1650–1760' in L.W.B. Brockliss and D. Eastwood, (eds), *A union of multiple identities: the British Isles, c.1750–1850* (Manchester, 1997), pp 125–46; Burdy, *Life of Skelton*, pp 121–3; S. Pender (ed.), *Council books of the corporation of Waterford* (Dublin, 1964), p. 42.   66 H.M. Colvin, *Architecture and the after life* (New Haven and London, 1991).   67 Dudley, 'Dublin parishes', i, p. 124; ii, pp 329–31.

His hoarded funds he all by int'rest got
For which poor men in gaol did starve and rot.
When e'er his fees for burials he did want,
Which some perhaps of that was scarce and scant,
Their clothes or treasure they must pledge or pawn
To make him wear fine surplice made of lawn.[68]

For each greedy Clayton, it has to be stressed, there were probably the benevolent, such as Dean Francis or Philip Skelton, who waived what legally was theirs. The underlying point remains that the laity were required to employ the clergy, and to buy their services whether or not they wanted – or approved – them. The charges levied for christenings, marriages and burials, because irregular and unpredictable, never led to the same concerted protests as did tithe-payments. Even so, the effect of these incessant clerical demands could be to alienate even the devout from the formal life of their church. Moreover, it fuelled anticlericalism. The same was true of the church courts which continued to function throughout the century. The contumacious easily enough evaded their jurisdiction. However, the courts' chief sanction – excommunication – was not to be taken lightly, especially by those whose local employment and reputation depended on membership of the established church.[69] The need to secure probate of wills inevitably brought the propertied into contact with the prerogative court. Typical of the labour and expense that could be involved was the complaint of one County Cork gentleman, who, in 1710, grumbled that he had to pay £2 8s. for a *quietus* from the Armagh prerogative court.[70] In any church with a distinct and ordained clergy, the potential for clerical domineering and lay animosity existed. Styles of seventeenth- and early eighteenth-century churchmanship, generally imported into Ireland from England, further stimulated sacerdotalism.[71] High-flying parsons stressed their unique role as intermediaries between God and humankind. They alone could administer the sacraments on which salvation and eternal life depended. A degree of self-interest also obliged incumbents to protect their rights against encroachment and erosion. But, by strictly insisting on being paid their dues, they might

---

68 *An elegy on the Reverend Dean Clayton* ([Dublin, 1725]); dispute of Revd F. Houston and Revd J. Gifford, *c.*1750, P.R.O.N.I., D 668/E/38. **69** Cases before Tuam consistorial court, 1740–2 (N.A., M.6833); Killaloe consistory court papers (B.L., Add MS 31881–2); Chapter book, iii, 1666–1694, p. 201 (St Finbarre's cathedral, Cork); N.A., M.1504, p. 349; *Memoirs of Richard Lovell Edgeworth, esq.* (2 vols, London, 1820), i, pp 70–1; T.C. Barnard, *The abduction of a Limerick heiress: social and political relationships in mid-eighteenth-century Ireland* (Dublin, 1998), pp 26–7. **70** N.L.I., D 13351–D 13422 (6). **71** D.W. Hayton, 'The high church party in the Irish Convocation 1703–1713' in H.J. Real and H. Stover-Leidig (eds), *Reading Swift: papers from the third Münster symposium on Jonathan Swift* (Munich, 1998), pp 117–40.

antagonise parishioners. How this could happen is illustrated again from Waringstown.

In 1712 the incumbent, Henry Jenney, was plagued by complaints which, significantly, were to be adjudicated by the local patron (and magistrate), Samuel Waring (son of William, encountered earlier). The dispute began after a parishioner, Neil, failed to pay tithes for three years. The sum owed totalled 23 shillings. After Neil died, the debt passed to his two sons, and it was they whom Jenney pressed for settlement. One of the boys who had defaulted, Robert Neil, was to be excommunicated by the rector. To avert this threat, Robert Neil's wife, Mary, went to the rector's house and pleaded for leniency. So far from showing it, Jenney promised to procure a writ of excommunication from Dublin and clap young Neil in gaol. At this, Mrs Neil cried, 'if he is put in gaol, she must go begging for money to get him out again, adding that she hoped God Almighty was not so severe and cruel as he was'. Jenney was true to his word, and had sentence of excommunication against the Neil brothers read publicly, presumably in the parish church. Jenney further forbade parishioners to speak with the excommunicates, 'which troubled and terrified them both very much'. These sanctions soon brought the defaulters to heel. The Neils preferred to pay rather 'than to lie under the scandal', or to suffer the boycott 'that no body must speak to him and that he must not buy or sell'. The wife, however, was less submissive. But, before the debt could be fully discharged, Robert Neil fell ill and was unable to ply his craft as a weaver. Now, in a fresh device to extract his money, Jenney secured an order of the civil courts. A sheriff's bailiff was sent to distrain Neil's goods for the outstanding sum. Before this sentence could be executed, the unfortunate Robert Neil expired. He and his wife had refused any ministrations from Jenney. Instead, they had turned in their extremity to the curate. Neil, during the year of his sickness and when facing death, had been denied any consolations from the Church of Ireland. In death, the struggle with the imperious rector continued. Neil's widow and his grieving relations sought to have him interred in Waringstown graveyard alongside his father, grandfather and great-grandfather, and not – as was decreed – in the separate plot for the excommunicated. Once more, the Neils identified Jenney as the villain. It was alleged that he wanted to seal graves such as the Neils' because they obstructed a carriage track which he intended to drive up to the church porch. Neil's widow wept over her husband's grave, only to be removed by the sexton and his daughter, 'who tore some of her clothes and exposed part of her body in view of a great number of inhabitants of the parish who were much offended and moved to pity at so sad a sight'. As a result of this ordeal the Widow Neil seemingly lost her senses, sickened and soon died. From her deathbed, she cursed Parson Jenney, together with his underlings, the sexton and daughter.[72]

72 Papers relating to Jenney and the Neils (Private collection, Co. Down). For other troubles over bringing carriages to the church doors: N.L.I., MS 6054, p. 8.

As told, the unhappy episode imputed personal and petty motives to Jenney in making so public a rupture in his parish. To be sure, it was conceded that he had remitted money owed him for christenings and marriages. Nevertheless, he insisted on the tithes being paid, 'not out of any ill will to them that he prosecuted ... but to deter others'. Whether or not his stand was principled, the antagonisms revealed in Waringstown undid the neighbourliness and harmony which a divine ideally should foster. Furthermore, the power of the incumbent within his locality is conveyed by this account. Jenney thought nothing of appearing in the houses and shops of the village or organizing a boycott of the miscreants. In Waringstown, as elsewhere, the parson knew the circumstances and religious affiliations of the inhabitants. On occasion, this knowledge was channeled into local, diocesan or national enquiries into the confessional composition of Ireland. The clergy of the established church, either on the bishop's or their own initiative, collected the requisite details. As in their other activities they sometimes worked in partnership with the lay officers of the parish; equally, they could tackle the tasks alone. The intimacy of a resident pastor with the peccadilloes of his parishioners could prove claustrophobic or intimidating. A gloss more favourable to Jenney in particular, and the clergy more generally, might be put on the brouhaha at Waringstown. The incumbent could be represented as pressed between the upper millstone of a resident and interfering landlord and the nether stone constituted of unruly parishioners, set on perhaps by the presbyterians to resist legitimate requests. At the same time, unfortunately, the distress caused to the impoverished Neils is inescapable. At points of grief, when they might have looked for solace from the Church, they were harassed.

Clearly to build much on one case, no matter how vividly documented, would be unjustified. As has been suggested already, some incumbents respited what they were owed and succoured their flocks, materially as well as spiritually. Yet, it has also be remembered, that the potential for conflict, such as that which erupted between the Neils and Jenney, was ever present. Indeed, it was endemic in a relationship between clergy and laypeople at root profoundly unequal, but in which (nevertheless) the laity possessed sanctions which could gravely incommode the clerics. Probably the only safe generalization is that relations between lay patron, incumbent and parishioners stretched the full length of a scale between amity and open warfare, and between clerical dictatorship through lordly condescension to self-rule by a parish gerontocracy or plutocracy.

II

In general, what the clergy expected of the laity has left more legible traces than what laypeople wanted of their ministers. In both spheres, the formal requirements were more easily and frequently stated than the informal. Most laypeople still looked first to the church to explain the cosmos, and how they and the visible world fitted into it. They also expected the church to assist and console them in the recurrent crises of individual lives.[73] The established church (and its rivals) had forms for these occasions; they also had tables of fees. It has to be acknowledged that the charges were resented and sometimes evaded. In addition, the churches' expectations of how laypeople should comport themselves diverged markedly from many popular practices. Here the differences between town and countryside, in regard both to precepts and practice, came into play. In the countryside, some fundamentals taken for granted by townspeople might still be wanting. Cures were served intermittently; churches were too ruinous to be used or too remote to be reached by all; sermons could be a rarity. In the absence of a pastor, Protestants might turn to Catholic priests to perform essential functions.[74] What, in these less favourable conditions, the Church of Ireland meant to its country members can be illustrated from two who lived outside Limerick in the 1740s.

For young Lucas, farming in a modest way with his father at Drumcavan in County Clare, the three miles to Church of Ireland worship at Corofin were regularly ridden.[75] Church-going on Sunday was so much a part of his routines that when, on 8 February 1741, he did not go, it was worth mentioning. In addition, when Lucas ambled further afield, on a circuit of kinsfolk and acquaintances, he made a point of hearing divine service at Kilfenora. These sabbath observances were supplemented by attendance at the special services. In the harsh winter of 1741, funerals were frequent. The place of the church in the structure of the Protestant state also impinged on Lucas. On one Sunday, he went to Corofin church to witness a neighbour's receiving the sacrament: an action intended presumably to qualify him for a legal transaction or office. In other ways, the cycles of the church defined the world of the Lucases. Morning service each Sunday was customarily followed by a sociable gathering back at their farmhouse, where others from the small Protestant community were baited. Moreover, in this circle, the children of the local incumbent were valued as friends and visitors. Lucas's telegraphic record of his doings in 1741 reveals a man who certainly went through the motions required by the church. But he drops no clue as to his personal convictions.[76]

The like difficulty of deducing an individual's faith from laconic diary entries and conventionally pious apothegms besets any imaginative use of

---

73 These themes are explored in R. Gillespie, *Devoted people: belief and religion in early modern Ireland* (Manchester, 1997).   74 C. Harrison to Bp W. Smythe, 9 & 25 Dec. 1694 (N.L.I., PC 436); R. Lloyd to F. Herbert, 15 March 1717[18] (National Library of Wales, Powis Castle Correspondence, no. 846).   75 B. Ó Dalaigh, 'Drumcavan, Co. Clare', in P. Connell, D.A. Croinin and B. Ó Dalaigh (eds), *Irish townlands: studies in local history* (Dublin, 1998), pp 99–104; Ó Dalaigh, *Ennis in the eighteenth century* (Dublin, 1995), pp 49–51. 76 N.L.I., MS 14101.

Nicholas Peacock's journal for the 1740s. Throughout the decade, Peacock, living near Adare, a few miles west of Limerick city, described orbits which took him regularly to Church of Ireland devotions, usually at Kildimo, but sometimes at Adare. Peacock seems to have worshipped less often than Lucas, at least if the records of Sunday attendance at church by each man are accurate. Peacock's annual tally of Sunday observances varied from four to eleven. Throughout the winter, at least, it was uncommon for Lucas to miss a Sunday. It could be that Peacock was erratic and inconsistent in noting his church visits. But the patchiness of his record may reflect the uncertain provision of services in his district. On one Sunday, Peacock mentioned how he had arrived at church, but then heard no sermon; on another, he waited but the incumbent never appeared; and on a third, he turned up, but there was no one to unlock the building and admit him.[77] The rising frequency of his recorded visits to church in 1745 and 1746 may owe something to a palpable feeling of international and local danger from Catholicism, which had led to a tougher enforcement of penal measures. Peacock threw himself into the defence of Protestant Ireland and contemplated the possibility of unexpected death. In this mood, his religious affiliation may have bulked larger in Peacock's definition of self. Simultaneously there are signs that he was undergoing a personal crisis, as he tried to amend delinquent behavior and sought a bride.[78] Introspection may have inclined him to attend church more often.

In other of his comments Peacock showed that scriptural language and imagery and Christian categories conveniently expressed his worries, hopes and thanks. Engagingly, although sometimes almost parodying the Calvinist capitalist, he attributed to a generous deity his own good fortune as he listed an enviable stock of linen and livestock.[79] He also entrusted himself to God's care at moments of decision: on making his will; recovery from illness; or marriage.[80] Peacock, by virtue of his main employment as agent to the two local families of Hartstonge and Widenham, often encountered neighbours. Thus, like Lucas, he participated in the numerous dramas of the locale. Christenings and funerals were the chief occasions which brought him – other than on Sundays – into the purview of the church. A meticulous accountant, it is in the nature of the record which Peacock has left that the costs rather than the religious or emotional significance of these events are most strongly conveyed. After he had walked in the cortège of one of his employers, Mrs Widenham, a trace of his regional origins, probably in northern England, not of his faith in the consolations of religion, escapes in his note. 'She was taken out and carried to her long home. I went back to Court [the Widenham's residence] heartily well'.[81]

---

77 N.L.I., MS 16091, 9 Jan. 1742[3], 9 June 1745, 26 March 1749.   78 Ibid., 14 Dec. 1745, 17 Feb. 1745[6].   79 Ibid., 25 Feb. 1742[3], 25 Jan. 1743[4], 3 Aug. 1745, 1 May 1747. 80 Ibid., 18 July 1743, 14 Dec. 1745, 5 May 1747.   81 Ibid., 7 Oct. 1742.

Peacock, enmeshed in a web of business, joined in the government of his church. From time to time he went to vestry meetings, usually when the church rates were to be set or when he was trying to recover debts.[82] In the early 1740s, Peacock was serving as a rate collector for the Kildimo vestry: a task which proved onerous and frustrating. On 19 December 1740, for example, he recorded that he 'walked all day for church rates, but got none'. He was engaged on a similar mission when he visited a fair on 16 March. Then he admitted that he had spent more than he received. However, the following day, St Patrick's, proved more rewarding. He was able to collect six shillings.[83] The church also allowed him modestly to supplement his income. To this end he became a tithe farmer: a function which sat easily enough with his tasks as an agent. From the foregoing it can be seen that the church served a variety of functions in Peacock's already busy life. He was drawn deeper into the business of running the parish via the vestry, partly because it was unavoidable in what could not have been other than a tiny conformist population. Without further clues how to adjudicate between the promptings of civic duty, peer pressure and the lure of profit in explaining Peacock's participation is impossible.

Even in men whose outward circumstances resembled each other's closely, remembering of course the extremely terse nature of the two diurnals, the emphasis given to religion did vary. Perhaps because of the irregularity of services at Kildimo, church-going occupied a less central place in Peacock's week. Nor were there shared meals with other worshippers afterwards. Unlike the Lucases, Peacock did not number the clergy of the established church among his companions. Again this may have reflected the lack of any resident cleric in the parish. More strikingly, the parish priest was twice welcomed at Peacock's home: in 1743, to share Christmas; in the summer of 1751 when he stayed the night.[84] These may have been politic accommodations intended to ease dealings with the locals who were overwhelmingly Catholic. Especially before he married in 1747, something of the isolation of a Protestant in provincial Ireland is evident from Peacock's diary. Sometimes he would sit reading in his small house while his servants went to patterns, fairs and holy wells. He dealt with these differences in a matter-of-fact fashion. Indeed, he often gave the servants money to spend on their jaunts.[85] But, given his tendency to introspection, although language, ethnicity, culture, even the possession of literacy and leisure, all reminded Peacock of how he differed from his modest household or 'family', confession most handily embodied his distinctiveness in a remote environment. On the one hand, he seems to have

---

82 Ibid., 29 March 1741, 26 April 1741, 8 June 1742, 21 May 1744, 3 Sep. 1744, 31 March 1746, 12 May 1746, 17 Feb. 1747[8], 12 March 1749[50], 1 July 1751.   83 Ibid., 16 & 17 March 1740[1].   84 Ibid., 27 Dec. 1743, 8 July 1751.   85 Ibid., 11 July 1741, 15 Aug. 1745, 25 Dec. 1745; Barnard 'Protestantism, ethnicity and Irish identities, 1660–1760', pp 231–4.

exerted himself so that he enjoyed amicable relations throughout the neighbourhood, even to the unusual extent of entertaining the local priest. But Protestant teaching came instinctively to him when he sought to voice gratitude or anxieties. Spasmodic as his devotions seem to have been, even in comparison with the Lucases', Peacock never fell away from them.

The attraction of the rare testimonies such as Lucas's or Peacock's is that they illumine lives below the level of the landed elite. Furthermore, they enable us to reconstruct the part which the church played in the quotidian rounds from their own, and not inquisitive clergymen's, perspectives. But, as has been admitted, they hardly open up the interior spiritual lives of these two men. Even contemporaries acknowledged the difficulty of doing so. Indeed, some warned against trying to. In 1745, a wise bishop contented himself with outward conformity from laypeople. 'Their private thoughts', he added, 'are known only to God'.[86] If the logic of this counsel is followed, then lay attachment to the established church during this period can be measured only by such conventional gauges as tallies of communicants at the principal church festivals. Certainly this is an indicator, but it seldom guides precisely to the proportion of the nominally conformist who actively joined in the central rite of their church. Moreover, it helps hardly at all in establishing how many had been lost to the separatist congregations as a result of the upheavals of the Interregnum or were recovered once the Church of Ireland regained its legal privileges after 1660. An incentive to rebuild or add to urban churches, other than liturgical and architectural fads, was the fear – common to London and other conurbations – that the existing structures could not accommodate all the faithful. Thus, a petition for a new church at Grangegorman outside Dublin mentioned the 300 local families, some of whom, for want of a church, are 'in danger of lapsing into the errors of the Church of Rome or associating with conventicles.' More exhaustive surveys of Dublin parishes in 1718 disclosed that, even after eight new churches had been erected, there was seating for only half the potential worshippers.[87] Similarly, the efforts of bishops throughout this period to ensure that accessible country churches were kept in repair and served regularly spoke of a worry that many in remoter areas were denied essential religious services. Visitations conducted early in the 1730s as far afield as Derry and Ossory revealed large numbers of communicants at Easter. The two churches in the city of Kilkenny, for example, recorded between 270 and 280 who had taken the sacrament. In the nearby borough of Callan, another eighty had done so.[88]

---

86 Bp H. Maule to W. Smythe, 5 April 1745 (N.L.I., PC 449).   87 Petition of the Grand Jury to the Abp of Dublin, c.1715 (N.L.I., PC 449); Monck Mason papers, iii, part i, pp 151–2 (Dublin Public Libraries, Gilbert MS 68); Dudley, 'Dublin parishes', ii, pp 274–80; cf. H.M. Colvin, 'Introduction' in Bill, *Queen Anne churches*, pp ix–xix.   88 N.A., M.2462.

Similarly in Derry, the main urban parish which included the city (Templemore) was believed to contain 500 communicants.[89] This continued to be the pattern. Early in the 1750s, the rector of Kells in Meath was heartened when about 200 took the sacrament at Easter. This occurred at a time when the incumbent was worried about possible losses to the Methodists.[90] Impressive as these totals look, they can be linked only conjecturally with any notional total of Church of Ireland adherents in these places. A guess, not implausible but lacking any solid evidential basis, is that between one-third and one half of potential communicants actually did communicate at Easter.[91]

The traditional festivals retained their appeal, filling pews and bringing suppliants in droves to the communion rail. Efforts to institute extra observations seem to have attracted rather fewer. In 1683 when the elder Edward Synge was ministering at Summerhill in County Meath, he reported how sparsely attended were the afternoon services at which first he catechised and then read Evening Prayer. Attendance improved dramatically once he took to preaching each Sunday afternoon on a section of the church catechism.[92] Sermons, it would seem, were scrutinised critically by later-seventeenth-century congregations. In Derry, for example, the faithful were reported to be hostile to the appointment of 'a sermon-reading bishop', who did no more than read prepared texts, 'for we have too many such already'.[93] During the 1720s articles listed the many shortcomings of the curate of St Michan's, Valentine Needham. Among them was 'going over and over a set of discourses patched up from printed sermons, disguised only by resolving the whole into questions and bringing in scripture by a quaint and free way'.[94] A similar discrimination was said to mark the parishioners at Drummully near Manor Waterhouse in County Fermanagh in the 1740s. The Revd Philip Skelton was forced to preach entirely from the Bible lest he be accused of copying and repeating other men's sermons. The country people in his parish 'would rather hear any nonsense of our own than the best sermons of the most famous writers'.[95] In another of Skelton's cures, the town of Monaghan, he persuaded thirty or forty to pray on weekdays.[96] Less successful were the innovations earlier in the century at Waterford. In 1718 came news that the bishop had started to celebrate holy communion at a new church in the city on each holy day at six in the morning. Other than the bishop's chaplain and the celebrant, the correspondent wrote gleefully, 'about four tradesmen's wives make up the congregation'. Special

89 W. Nicolson to Abp W. Wake, 10 April 1724 (Christ Church, Oxford, Wake MS.14/191); R.C.B., GS 2/7/3/34.   90 Archdeacon J. Smythe to W. Smythe, 'Easter Sunday [c.1750]' (N.L.I., PC 449).   91 Connolly, Religion, law and power, p. 186.   92 Revd E. Synge to Bp A. Dopping, 5 Aug. 1683 (Armagh Public Library, Dopping Correspondence,1/36). 93 C. McNeill (ed.), The Tanner letters (Dublin, 1943), p. 452.   94 R.C.B., P276/12/1, p. 88. 95 Burdy, Life of Skelton, pp 42–3.   96 Ibid, pp 61–2.

factors may have diminished enthusiasm among the laity for this episcopal innovation. The bishop, Thomas Milles, a survivor from the earlier epoch of Tory ascendancy, had long been on bad terms with much of the town and its garrison. Furthermore, the church, St Olave's, where these rites were practised, had been erected by the bishop to free himself from an irksome and disputatious cathedral dean and chapter. It could be that the pious Protestants of Waterford in absenting themselves from early morning communion at St Olave's publicly sided with the dean (a local) against the English-born bishop.[97] The problem was that tussles such as those at Waterford were repeated in many other towns, especially those with cathedrals. Perhaps only in Dublin was it feasible to introduce the crowded regime of public prayers and observances to which Bishop Milles later aspired in Waterford. In 1695 Archbishop Marsh boasted of the intensive religious life in his diocese of Dublin. Almost all the churches had Morning and Evening Prayer every Sunday, save for four of the poorer ones which instead had fortnightly celebrations. In the rural parishes, communion was given four or six times during the year. Marsh intended to increase the frequency to a monthly celebration, 'when the congregation is sufficient'. In the capital itself, the existing monthly communion services were to be changed to weekly ones in the most populous parishes, and every fortnight in the remainder. He also planned to institute a daily reading of prayers in at least one city church. In the countryside, too, he hoped that the practice could be copied: if not on a daily basis, at least on each Wednesday and Friday. The archbishop wished to stimulate a new devotion among the laity. His aspiration smacked of clerical priorities. But it also exploited what Marsh perceived to be a new mood of piety among his people. This he attributed in part to relief and thankfulness for the deliverance from the Catholics' moils under James II. A published list of services in the Dublin churches suggested that the crowded economy noted by Marsh survived at least until 1719.[98] In harnessing the fervour, the clergy did not act alone. A section of the laity was already experimenting with devotional novelties. Unfortunately, as Marsh feared, these sentiments affected only a godly minority and proved depressingly evanescent.

Lay people had always sought to remedy the deficiencies in official religious provision by their own exertions. Again, clerics more often commented on the capacity of their parishioners than vice versa. Sometimes the former were agreeably surprised. At Naas in 1689 the incumbent wrote of a congregation

---

97 H. Alcock to J. Mason, 14 June 1718 (Dromana, Co. Waterford, Villiers–Stuart MSS, T 3131/B/1/9); [W. Dennis], *Address to the bishop of Waterford and Lismore, 21 Jan, 1724/5*; J. Loveday, *Diary of a tour in 1732* (Edinburgh, 1890), p. 34; J.C. Walton, 'The Boltons of County Waterford' in *Irish Genealogist*, vii (1987), pp 186–98.   98 Abp N. Marsh to Bp W. Lloyd, 27 April 1695 (Lambeth Palace, MS 942/96); *An address to absenters from the publick worship of God*, (3rd ed., Dublin, 1719).

assembled in a private house as consisting of '120 understanding parishioners'.[99] The sense of a community under siege may have assisted the rediscovery of a livelier sense of spiritual purpose among these Protestant laypeople. It was monotonously noticed that this awareness all too quickly vanished once the Protestants recovered power in the 1690s. Ignorance also obstructed ministerial efforts at evangelizing. When, in the 1750s, Skelton moved to the Donegal living of Pettigo, its Protestant inhabitants 'scarce knew more of the gospel than the Indians of America'. Equally ignorant, although for different causes, were some of 'the quality' encountered at the local squire's by Skelton. One response of Skelton's was to lock the congregation in the church, catechise them vigorously and then examine them minutely on what they had learnt.

Not all the laity were happy to submit to such clerical high-handedness. They could assert themselves against incumbents whom they regarded as incompetent or negligent. Sometimes it looked as if there was no pleasing exigent laypeople, as in turn they condemned the busy resident and the absentee.[100] For want of the ideal pastor, groups of parishioners might themselves perfect their spiritual awareness. Invariably the church authorities regarded such schemes ambivalently. Much clerical effort had always been devoted to educating parishioners in piety until they were better able to engage privately in their own courses of meditation and prayer. Catechizing was directed in part to this end; so too was the stream of godly tracts which by the 1690s was widening into a torrent. Much of this material, cheap and simple, enabled laypeople to approach the central mystery of communion in a fitting way. Similar efforts had gone into providing versions of the Bible to be read at home. Yet, always there lurked the danger that by putting the weapons into laypeople's hands, they would turn them on the clergy. Moreover, if too great independence was encouraged, then the *raison d'être* of the separate clerical caste might also vanish.[101] These, and other contradictions, were raised by one of the most notable attempts to cater better to the unsatisfied religious yearnings of laypeople. During the 1690s, first Dublin, then a few other Irish towns, saw the establishment of

---

99 Revd J. Brereton to Bp A. Dopping, 13 Dec. 1689 (Armagh Public Library, Dopping Correspondence,1/124).   100 Bp R. Tennison to Bp W. Smythe, 2 & 30 Jan. 1695[6], 7 Feb. 1695[6], 17 July 1696 (N.L.I., PC 436); Burdy, *Life of Skelton*, pp 111–12, 114, 136. 101 T.C. Barnard, 'Learning, the learned and literacy in Ireland, *c.*1660–1760' in T.C. Barnard, D. Ó Croinin and K. Simms (eds), *'A miracle of learning': studies in manuscripts and Irish learning* (Aldershot, 1998), pp 209–35; Barnard, 'Reading in eighteenth-century Ireland: public and private pleasures' in B. Cunningham and M. Kennedy (eds), *The experience of reading: Irish historical perspectives* (Dublin, 1999), pp 60–77; R. Gillespie, 'The circulation of print in seventeenth-century Ireland' in *Studia Hibernica*, no. 29 (1995–7), pp 31–58; Gillespie, *Devoted people*; S. Mandelbrote, 'John Baskett, the Dublin booksellers, and the printing of the Bible, 1710–1724' in A. Hunt, G. Mandelbrote and A. Shell (eds), *The book trade and its customers* (Winchester,1997), pp 115–31.

religious societies. Modelled after English originals, they appealed initially to earnest young men. They tapped fear about both the cosmic and practical consequences of anti-social behaviour, such as drunkenness, swearing or prostitution. They also fostered cooperation between conformists and non-conformists, adjudged appropriate in the light of what all Protestants had lately suffered under James II. Briefly the societies channelled devout aspirations into communal activity. Much of this centred on prayer, singing and discussion. Other objectives included the detection and punishment of sin. Tensions always inherent in the movement, notably between dissenters and conformists and between laity and clergy, soon disturbed the superficial harmony.[102] Lay energies quickly enough were diverted into other institutionalised forms. In particular, the wish to do something to combat ignorance and to tackle the material causes of poverty and crime inspired initiatives. First, parochial schools, then a more systematised network of charity schools; hospitals, especially in Dublin; workhouses; even parochial libraries: all did much to calm lay impatience that the official church was not doing enough.[103] By and large, in these activities, while lay money and time were liberally (even lavishly) expended, the clergy kept a loose rein on what the laity were doing. Certainly these philanthropic efforts broadened the groups among the laity beyond the young men who had been involved in the religious societies The concerned enjoyed better opportunities to mingle civic and Christian impulses. Importantly, much of this was work in which women could join. But, by the same token, it has to be stressed that it was work which could be undertaken only by those with time and money to spare. The management of the charter schools, as of other local charities, tended to be entrusted to those who had subscribed most generously, or their nominees. Much, as a result, devolved on those who already took their turns as churchwardens, sidesmen and select vestry-men.[104]

In the end we are left with the impossibility of seeing the religious lives of the laypeople of the time other than in their multifarious public actions. The Church of Ireland, as should have become clear, encompassed much more than the formal observances on Sunday and other stated festivals. In particular, it was a formidable beam in the elaborate construct of urban society. It also largely controlled the systems through which the knotty questions of life and death were explored and expounded. Alternative explanations gradually started to

102 T.C. Barnard, 'Reforming Irish manners: the Religious Societies in Dublin during the 1690s' in *Historical Journal*, xxxv (1992), pp 805–38.   103 D.W. Hayton, 'Did Protestantism fail in early eighteenth-century Ireland? Charity schools and the enterprise of religious and social reformation, c.1690–1730' in A. Ford, J.I. McGuire and K. Milne (eds), *As by law established: the Church of Ireland since the Reformation* (Dublin, 1995), pp 166–86; Barnard, 'Protestants and the Irish language', pp 263–72.   104 Incorporated Society Records (T.C.D., MSS 5225, 5301, 5597, 5598, 5646); Dudley, 'Dublin's parishes'; K. Milne, *The Irish Charter Schools, 1730–1830* (Dublin, 1997).

permeate the learned worlds; others, ridiculed by the church as superstitious or unscriptural, had never been jettisoned. Ecclesiastical authorities nervous about these challenges, sought to regulate what was imported, published and circulated. At best, they slowed the reception of the ideas of rivals such as the Catholics or presbyterians. On rare occasions, an example could be made of someone who went beyond permissible speculation. Thus, in 1698, John Toland's deist squib, *Christianity not Mysterious*, was condemned and burnt in Dublin.[105] However the acute sensitivity exhibited by clerics about what constituted orthodoxy was seldom shared by the laity, to whom the clear categories beloved of clerical academics meant little. Travellers to Dublin in the 1690s were struck by the lively debates on religious subjects which they heard (and in which they joined). In a city with a rich ethnic and confessional mixture, it was probably inevitable that a variety of religious opinions should be freely expressed, whatever the authorities might wish.[106] For the same reasons, it proved impossible seriously to restrict the import into the island of disparate and sometimes inflammatory publications. Laypeople of the Church of Ireland happily enough connived at this practical liberty. Indeed, they profited from it.

In this matter, lay attitudes ran ahead of those of edgy clerics. The latter constantly watched for new adversaries. In watching they sometimes imagined threats where none existed. Clergymen, told monotonously that they were failing to check the inroads of competitors or to sustain the faith of their own parishioners, blamed much on the wiles of papists, dissenters, deists, libertines and atheists. The offensives mounted by each of these groups against existing members of the Church of Ireland were not designed to convert many; nor did they. Only with the spread of Methodism from the 1740s was the established church seriously endangered by something more tangible than genetic attrition or inertia.[107] Sensational episodes, such as that which demonised Toland, shifted attention away from the structural and cultural shortcomings of the church. As each new generation neared adulthood, greybeards lamented the decay of virtue and piety. English influence and example; foreign travel; imported fashions; affluence; Irish constitutional dependency; the failings of the schools, Dublin university or the clergy: all were blamed. Licence and libertinism undoubtedly had their devotees, especially in smart Dublin society. Church

---

105 For recent reflections on Toland, see: J. Toland, *Christianity not mysterious*, ed. P. McGuinness, A. Harrison and R. Kearney (Dublin, 1997); Toland, *Nazarenus*, ed. J. Champion (Oxford, 1999); also, Barnard, 'Reforming Irish manners', pp 826–34. **106** Verdon's tour (Cardiff Central Library, MS 4,370, p. 36); J. Dunton, *The life and errors* (2 vols, London, 1818), ii, pp 531–8.   **107** For the rise of Methodism in Ireland, see: D. Hempton, 'Methodism in Irish society, 1770–1830' in *Transactions of the Royal Historical Society*, 5th series, xxxvi (1986), pp 117–42; D. Hempton and M. Hill, *Evangelical Protestantism in Ulster society, 1740–1890* (London, 1992).

leaders might reasonably worry how such future leaders of Protestant Ireland would discharge their responsibilities to the state church. Yet, for all the roistering of bucks and the profanities of blasters in the 1730s, these vogues never seriously loosened the grip of the Church of Ireland over its members.[108] More insidious than the misbehaviour of a minority of young bloods was the vogue for intellectual systems which elevated experiment, experience or reason.[109] In practice, in Ireland as in England, the theories of Newton and Locke were deftly annexed to back Christianity, and even to the variety professed by the established churches of the sister kingdoms. Moreover, those who most actively promoted enquiry and experiment in Ireland were drawn disproportionately from the upper ranks of the clergy. Visitors to Hanoverian Ireland remarked on the degree to which learned and polite company was dominated by the clerics.[110]

What laypeople read was suspected of influencing their view of religion. The clergy of the established church, despite their ambitions, never seriously censored the ideas current among the laity. The evidence from surviving lists of books leads uncertainly towards who actually read what, let alone how minds were set. What listings of books owned by lay members of the Church of Ireland do confirm is an attitude at once opportunistic and catholic. Theology, devotion, apologetic and church history certainly formed sizeable sections in laymen's collections. To possess a volume, it hardly needs to be reiterated, did not mean that it had been opened, read or comprehended. If it had, the owner did not necessarily agree with its arguments. In this spirit, room was found on shelves for works from a multiplicity of theological and confessional schools. Often these assorted libraries reflected the accidents which had brought specific, seemingly odd works within grasp. Even among those who benefited from the increasingly good facilities to buy books in Dublin, their wants' lists were rarely dictated by any narrow denominational stance. The sensible precaution of knowing the enemy could justify acquiring standard Catholic, presbyterian and quaker texts. But other classics of theology, homiletic and apologetic, from St Augustine, Aquinas, Calvin to Baxter, Stillingfleet and Tillotson were not felt to be the property of any single denomination.[111] Laypeople may have been

---

108 On unbelief and scepticism: G.E. Aylmer, 'The problem of unbelief' in D.H. Pennington and K.V. Thomas (eds), *Puritans and revolutionaries* (Oxford, 1982); M. Hunter, 'The problem of "atheism" in early modern England' in *Transactions of the Royal Historical Society*, 5th series, xxxv (1985), pp 136–57; M.C.W. Hunter and D. Wootton (eds), *Atheism from the Reformation to the Enlightenment* (Oxford, 1992). 109 Generally: J. Champion, *The pillars of priestcraft shaken: the Church of England and its enemies* (Cambridge,1992); S. Burtt, *Virtue transformed: political argument in England, 1688–1740* (Cambridge,1992). 110 W. Yorke to Lord Hardwicke, 11 Oct. 1743 (B.L., Add. MS 35,587, f. 182) and R. Lowth to M. Lowth, 10 May 1755 (Bodleian, MS Eng. Lett. C.572, f. 26). 111 Barnard, 'Learning, the learned and literacy'; Barnard, 'Reading in eighteenth-century Ireland'; Gillespie, 'Circulation of print'; Gillespie, *Devoted people;* E. Boran, 'Education and dissemination of the word: a

more willing than clerics to ignore the confessional boundaries of the day when reading. (The contents of the book closets of Scottish Presbyterian ministers in Ulster were liable to be inspected by keen-eyed spies from the kirk session in case they harboured the heterodox.[112] This was another aspect of the often uneasy partnership between laypeople and clergy in the affairs of the Church.) Occasionally lay men were scandalised by the musings of the clergy, most notably in the 1750s by Bishop Robert Clayton's questioning in print of the divinity of Christ.[113] The openness to be instructed in piety by any who offered plausible lessons was demonstrated by James Bonnell, probably the most famous lay member of the Church of Ireland at the end of the seventeenth century. Bonnell composed, and eventually published, *Meditations*. These, it was discovered, were closely modelled on Catholic originals: more closely than Bonnell's admirers liked.[114]

James Bonnell brings us to the one Church of Ireland figure of the epoch whose interior life is so richly documented as to raise hopes that we may penetrate the tough carapace of formal doings. Sadly, this belief is a snare, set by those who sought to fashion Bonnell into a Protestant saint. Shortly after he died in 1699, a lengthy biography trumpeted his many qualities.[115] It was as an exemplar that he was intended to stand. He would, it was hoped, continue to inspire the spiritual regeneration and the inter-denominational friendliness which, through his support for the Dublin religious societies, he had done much to promote. But Bonnell belonged to a specific moment, the trauma through which Irish Protestants had lived in the 1680s. The relevance of this to new generations rapidly lessened. Moreover, the irenicism to which he was also committed was not much to the taste of the partisans who dominated ecclesiastical politics and policy in Queen Anne's reign. Thus, much of the public message in the account of Bonnell was ignored as either embarrassing or antiquated. Nevertheless, the minute investigation of this pious paragon continued to be valued as a help in perfecting one's spiritual life, disciplining passions and running a holy household. There were, in addition, less often pondered lessons as how successfully to combine worldly success with estimable conduct. It was a happy partnership which saw the bluff and subtle William Conolly presiding over Protestant Ireland while his brother-in-law and one-time business associate, Bonnell, was being positioned as the tutelary saint for the Protestant worthies of Hanoverian Dublin.

Baptist library in the eighteenth century' in K. Herlihy (ed.), *Propagating the word of Irish dissent, 1650–1800* (Dublin, 1998), pp 114–32.   112 Minutes of the Presbytery of Killyleagh, 1725–32, pp 35, 40, 45, 59, 63, 157 (P.R.O.N.I., D 1759/1D/10).   113 The latest treatment of this affair is C.D.A. Leighton, 'The enlightened religion of Robert Clayton' in *Studia Hibernica*, no. 29 (1995–7), pp 157–84.   114 Barnard, 'Identities, ethnicity and tradition', pp 39–40.   115 W. Hamilton, *The exemplary life and character of James Bonnell, esq.* (Dublin, 1703); Barnard, 'Identities, ethnicity and tradition', pp 38–9.

A clear implication from the efforts which were lavished on keeping Bonnell in the public eye as the pattern of a Church of Ireland layman was that his was an ideal to which few could approach. What sapped lay attachment to the established church was less any intellectual or doctrinal challenge than the insidious spread of a hollow formalism. The minimum which was required of churchgoers was performed. What that minimum consisted of could vary considerably between town and countryside, and then between different districts depending on the strength both of the parson and the church fabric. Since these were visible problems, conscientious prelates (and laypeople) were aware of them. Improvements were certainly accomplished. However, it still remained impossible to coerce the negligent into doing more than the minimum of annual communion to equip themselves for public office. The shrewd were content to have brought those who ruled Ireland into the body of the church. The inner spirit in which they then approached its central mysteries was scarcely to be fathomed. Yet a hope persisted that the lukewarm might suddenly be enthused. Exemplars, such as Bonnell, were intended to aid this regeneration.

New models of piety appeared in the eighteenth century. Perhaps inevitably, they were drawn from the aristocracy or squirearchy. Brockhill Newburgh, squire of Ballyhaise in County Cavan, was promoted in print, and Billy Smythe, inheritor of the Westmeath estate of Barbavilla, revered within his family for unusual devotion. Newburgh, it was noted in 1761, every month treated the poor of the district on 'sacrament Sunday'. Each was given dinner in a purpose-built hall and one shilling. Punctilious over attending worship, he performed domestic devotions with his family or in his closet. He avoided 'cant and sanctified grimace', because 'his piety was too masculine, too much governed by right reason'. Young William Smythe repudiated the habits of his contemporaries at Trinity College during the 1760s, as being 'entirely depraved'. 'They commit all kinds of vice'. To shield himself against these corruptions, he requested from the country his own Bible, *Whole duty of man* and a devotional manual by Thomas Wilson. Lady Arbella Denny, a high-mettled but meddlesome grandee, translated her Christian concerns into philanthropy, notably for penitent prostitutes in Dublin.[116] But such examples throw no light on how the generality regarded their faith. Certainly, at least for men, more opportunities arose to contribute constructively to the life of the Christian community living in the parish. Yet in a more private sphere, the standards outlined in scripture and recommended by the

116 W. Smythe to R. Smythe, 4 & 7 April 1767 (N.L.I., PC 446); *Particulars relating to the life and character of the late Brockhill Newburgh, esq.* (n.p.,1761), pp 16, 28–9; [S.R. Penny], *Smythe of Barbavilla: the history of an Anglo-Irish family* ([Oxford], 1974), pp 67–85; B. Butler, 'Lady Arbella Denny, 1707–1792' in *Dublin Historical Record*, ix (1946–7), pp 1–20; R. Raughter, 'A natural tenderness: the ideal and the reality of eighteenth-century female philanthropy' in M.G. Valiulis and M. O'Dowd (eds), *Women and Irish history: essays in honour of Margaret MacCurtain* (Dublin, 1997), pp 77–9.

4 Lady Arbella Denny (1707–92), Church of Ireland philanthropist
by H.D. Hamilton.

clergy were unattainable. The gulf between what the devout knew they should seek and what was possible for mortal flesh was repeatedly plumbed.

Nothing tested faith more severely and regularly than death. Ever present and unpredictable, the grim reaper cut down children and spouses indiscriminately. Christian resignation to the will of God, as well as the teachings of stoicism in the face of the inevitable, bridled excessive outpourings of grief. However, such composure was difficult to maintain among those denied the vent of hysterical and sometimes stylised grief at 'Irish' funerals. Grandees, from the first duke of Ormond and the first Lord Burlington to the countess of Orrery, struggled to discipline their emotions and so act as their church enjoined.[117] None at this level found it harder to comply with orthodox Church of Ireland teaching than Katherine Conolly, after her husband, the Speaker, died in 1729.[118] She was wealthy enough to be able to divert some of her emotion into an extravagant and

117 T.C. Barnard, 'Land and the limits of loyalty: the second earl of Cork and first earl of Burlington (1612–1698)' in T.C. Barnard and J. Clark (eds), *Lord Burlington: architecture, art and life* (London and Rio Grande, 1995), pp 192–3; Roger Boyle, earl of Orrery, *Poems on most of the festivals of the Church* ([Cork], 1681); R. Gillespie, 'The religion of the first duke of Ormond' in T.C. Barnard and J. Fenlon (eds), *The dukes of Ormonde 1610–1745* (Woodbridge, 2000), pp 101–13.   118 K. Conolly to J. Bonnell, 9 Dec. 1729 (N.L.I., PC 434/5).

much mocked display of mourning. Then she busied herself about ordering from London a suitable effigy of her beloved (and herself). This proved too big to be housed in her parish church and came to rest, incongruously, in a barn. Seekers after church preferment who had clustered around her husband while alive now transferred their hopes of patronage to her. But these distractions, tangentially linked with the church's approved responses to loss, did not assuage her. The submissiveness decreed by the church was not easily achieved. Here, at the heart of human experience, we find how imperfectly the prescripts of an institutionalised church met individual need. Laypeople devised strategies of their own. These, it would seem, were composed of motley. Tatters of biblical and ministerial teaching, approved by the church, were stitched together with more bizarre patches.

4

The development and limitations of Protestant ascendancy: the Church of Ireland laity in public life, *c*.1660–1740

David Hayton

In Irish history the period from the Restoration of King Charles II to the Act of Union is generally defined as the era of 'Protestant ascendancy', marked by the establishment and development of a system of government dominated by Church of Ireland Protestants.[1] A series of penal statutes denied Catholics both the right to hold public office, whether at the centre or in the localities, and the right of representation, in parliament and in municipal corporations. Furthermore, by a clause in one of the most comprehensive of the penal laws, the 'act to prevent the further growth of popery' in 1704, some of these restrictions were extended to Protestant dissenters, by the requirement of a sacramental test (receiving Holy Communion according to the liturgy of the Church of Ireland) for those holding crown or municipal office. The Protestant propertied élite in Ireland had thus created a 'confessional state' *par excellence*; one in which participation in public life depended on a particular religious affiliation, namely membership of the established church. As many historians have observed, this system of government was far from uncommon in *ancien regime* Europe.[2] But there was a distinctiveness about the Irish confessional state, in that political rights and political power were confined to a religious minority; perhaps no more than a tenth of the entire population of the island.

1 I do not propose to enter here into the debate on the origins and use of the term 'Protestant ascendancy', which has arisen from the writings of Professor W.J. McCormack on the political language of late eighteenth-century Ireland. The clearest statement of the positions of the participants is probably the most recent: by James Kelly, in 'Conservative Protestant political thought in late eighteenth-century Ireland' in S.J. Connolly (ed.), *Political ideas in eighteenth-century Ireland* (Dublin, 2000), pp 204–8. Whatever the genesis of the term 'Protestant ascendancy', there can be little doubt that the concept of a confessional qualification for political rights and social privileges was an accepted principle of Irish politics throughout the century. As a historians' construct, rather than a contemporary usage , it does not seem to me to require further justification.   2 See for example S.J. Connolly, *Religion,*

There is a distinct, if seldom appreciated, irony in the fact that these confessional restrictions were being erected and reinforced at the same time as the concept of 'public life' in Ireland was being redefined, and opportunities for participation were changing and expanding. We are confronted here by a process that sociologists, and indeed some historians, would refer to as a general enlargement of the 'public sphere', which encouraged sociability and the exercise of public virtue, and involved an expansion in government bureaucracy, at central and local level; a more active system of political representation, with more frequent parliaments and general elections; and the emergence of new forms of semi-official, even entirely voluntary, organisation, for the administration of public benevolence.

Certain aspects of the development of the Irish 'confessional state' have attracted a good deal of attention from historians. In particular much has been written on the enactment of the penal laws and their supposed objectives and effects, in relation to the Catholic church and community, and the presbyterians of Ulster.[3] Less interest has been shown in measuring the degree to which the regulation of public life established Anglican control over public office and political power; and in examining the ends for which that power was exercised.[4] My hope in this essay is to answer two basic questions about the 'Protestant ascendancy' in the period in which it was becoming established, the late seventeenth and early eighteenth centuries: how exclusive was it, and how far was it distinctively Protestant? We need to know, on the one hand, whether Anglican privilege extended to every corner of Irish 'public life', and whether its benefits were confined only to the propertied classes; and on the other, whether membership of the Church of Ireland meant anything more to the beneficiaries of the penal laws than a ticket of admission to political participation. If indeed, 'all sorts and conditions of men' within the Anglican communion in Ireland enjoyed political rights in this period, did any of them bring to the exercise of those rights a piety and sensibility that was specific to their religious beliefs? In other words, perhaps, the central question should be: what was specifically Protestant about the 'Protestant Ascendancy'?

law and power: the making of Protestant Ireland 1660–1760 (Oxford, 1992), pp 2, 104; C.D.A. Leighton, *Catholicism in a Protestant kingdom: a study of the Irish ancien regime* (Basingstoke, 1994), pp 17–18; I.R. McBride, *Scripture politics: Ulster presbyterians and Irish radicalism in the late eighteenth century* (Oxford, 1998), pp 14–16.   **3** For a sample of this literature, see J.C. Beckett, *Protestant dissent in Ireland 1687–1780* (London, 1948); Gerard O'Brien (ed.), *Catholic Ireland in the eighteenth century: collected essays of Maureen Wall* (Dublin, 1989); Thomas Bartlett, *The fall and rise of the Irish nation: the Catholic question 1690–1830* (Dublin, 1992), chs. 1–2; Connolly, *Religion, law and power*, chs. 5, 7; I.R. McBride, 'Presbyterians in the penal era' in *Bullán*, i no. 2 (1994), pp 2–23.   **4** A significant step is taken in this direction in T.C. Barnard, 'The government and Irish dissent, 1704–1780' in Kevin Herlihy (ed.), *The politics of Irish dissent 1650–1800* (Dublin, 1997), pp 9–27. There is also much useful material

I

The size of the Irish government bureaucracy grew steadily throughout this period, although expansion was not uniform, and was concentrated at two points: the revenue service, and the military. There was little conscious administrative reform; rather a steady accretion of new, active offices alongside traditional sinecures. The patent offices listed in the civil establishment, over 120 in all, maintained their traditional titles, salaries and fees, even though their functions may have disappeared. By the eighteenth century many were being exercised by deputy, and sometimes even the deputyships themselves had become sinecures: the lord treasurership, hereditary in the Boyles, earls of Cork and Burlington, had long since ceased to be an active office, but by 1700 the place of vice-treasurer was also regarded as little more than a lucrative sinecure, with the real work being done by the deputy vice-treasurer. Similarly the post of secretary of state for Ireland was now entirely honorific, while the under-secretary, formerly a glorified clerk, had become the most senior permanent official in the Castle administration.[5] In one important area of civil administration change was more systematic than accidental. The parliamentary grant to Charles II (in perpetuity) in 1662 of the 'new hereditary revenues' necessitated the establishment not only of boards of customs and excise to oversee their collection, but the employment of new customs and excisemen alongside the old patentee customs collectors. Further grants of parliamentary 'additional' revenues after the Glorious Revolution required yet more recruitment. In total the administration of the 'new hereditary' and 'additional' revenues gave employment to thirty-eight collectors, sixty-nine surveyors, twenty-one landwaiters, and a horde of supernumerary local officials, gaugers, tidewaiters, and boatmen.[6] By 1715 it was estimated that as many as a thousand men were employed under the authority of the joint revenue board, with an expenditure on salaries that matched the entire civil establishment.[7] Almost as spectacular was the expansion in the numbers of men on the Irish military establishment: from some 7,000 men in the Restoration period to at least 12,000 in the eighteenth century, following the English parliament's disbandment act of 1699, which obliged King William, if he wished to retain his English standing army,

on the scope of the 'Protestant Ascendancy' in a municipal context in J.R. Hill, *From patriots to unionists : Dublin civic politics and Irish Protestant patriotism, 1660–1840* (Oxford, 1997). **5** T.J. Kiernan, *History of the financial administration of Ireland to 1817* (London, 1930), ch. 10; D.W. Hayton, 'Ireland and the English ministers, 1707–16' (D.Phil. thesis, Oxford, 1975), ch. 2. Patentee offices and office-holders are listed in Rowley Lascelles (ed.), *Liber munerum publicorum Hiberniae* (2 vols, London, 1852). **6** Patrick McNally, 'Patronage and politics in Ireland 1714–1727' (Ph.D. thesis, Queen's University, Belfast, 1993), ch. 3. **7** Archbishop King to Francis Annesley, 24 May 1715 (T.C.D., MS 2536, p. 296); Hayton, 'Ireland and the English ministers', p. 53.

to transfer most of it to Ireland. The bulk of this 'Irish' army was recruited and officered from England, and consisted of English regiments in transit to another posting, but there were a number of specifically Irish regiments, raised by Irish gentlemen, and in addition to the regiments themselves, the increase in the size of the establishment necessitated a larger and more elaborate military administration, the most obvious aspect of which was the network of barracks established across the country in the early eighteenth century, each with its own staff, who were responsible to the barrack master and barrack board in Dublin.[8]

The machinery of local government in Ireland experienced a similar development in this period: a broad but not necessarily uniform increase in the number of officials and in their practical responsibilities. The traditional framework of county government remained intact, with the governor at its apex, the equivalent of the English lord lieutenant, and under him the sheriff and sub-sheriffs, though the governorship was slowly becoming more of a dignity than a duty, and the onerous and unrewarding nature of the shrievalty (except, that is, in general election years, when the sheriff's powers as returning officer gave him considerable political influence) made likely candidates desperate to avoid being pricked (that is, selected by the lord chancellor from a panel of nominees). Justices of the peace were still primarily responsible for public order, appointing parish constables to assist them in their work, but their administrative functions underwent both expansion and erosion through a succession of new statutes after 1691.[9] The number of gentlemen appointed to the commission varied considerably from county to county, over a hundred in County Cork, scarcely more than twenty in County Mayo.[10] The militia, having been reconstituted after the Restoration by Charles II's viceroy, the first duke of Ormond, never really recovered from the trauma of its subsequent disarmament on James II's accession in 1685. In any case, the strengthened military garrison made militiamen less necessary for civil defence. As a result, although commissions continued to be issued after 1691, the militia was only arrayed at times of crisis, in 1708, 1715, 1719, and 1727. Because nothing was done in the intervals the arrays took place amid great disorganisation and even some improvisation, with bodies of 'independent' volunteers intermixed with the legitimate companies.[11] But

---

8 McNally, 'Patronage and politics', ch. 4. See also K.P. Ferguson, 'The army in Ireland from the Restoration to the Act of Union' (unpublished Ph.D. thesis, T.C.D., 1981); A.J. Guy, 'The Irish military establishment, 1660–1776' in Thomas Bartlett and Keith Jeffery (eds), *A military history of Ireland* (Cambridge, 1996), pp 211–30. For the barracks, see also Eustace Budgell to Joseph Addison, 9 Feb. [1715] (B.L., Blenheim papers, Add. MS 61636); Joshua Dawson to Major Francis, 5 Apr. 1712 (Bodleian Library, Oxford, MS Eng. hist. b. 125, f. 29). 9 Edward Bullingbrooke, *The duty and authority of justices of the peace and parish-officers for Ireland* (Dublin, 1766). 10 Commissions of the peace, Cos. Antrim-Dublin, [c.1727] (N.A., M/2537, pp 298–307); commission of the peace, Co. Mayo, 1714 (ibid., M/6236). 11 P.D.H. Smyth, 'The Volunteer movement in Ulster: background and development

elsewhere in local government there was expansion in the eighteenth century: a brief appearance in the 1690s of local commissions to assess the short-lived poll tax and land tax; the rise in importance after 1700 of the county grand jury; and the elaboration of government bureaucracy at the parish level, centred on the vestry and its officers. Most important, perhaps, was the new role enjoyed by the grand juries, which became responsible for public works, in particular the repair and improvement of the roads, for which taxation was supplied locally.[12] Both the collection of the county cess, and its expenditure, required grand juries to develop an administrative apparatus of their own: a county treasurer, clerk of the crown, high constables to collect the cess, measurers to survey and make estimates, and overseers to ensure the work was done. At the lowest level of government there was a similar enlargement in the competence of the parish vestry. As well as levying the parish rates, for the upkeep of the church and its furnishings, and for the maintenance of the poor, it acquired other functions, again through legislation: overseeing the highways, for example, and (under the terms of the timber plantation act of 1698) the power to allocate where saplings would be planted. Consequently, the number of parish officials proliferated: as well as the parish clerk, churchwardens, sidesmen, and parish constables, there were now overseers of the poor, overseers of the highways, even applotters of trees.[13]

Urban growth, though fitful, was none the less a perceptible feature of late seventeenth- and early eighteenth-century Ireland, and with an expansion in the number and size of towns came, naturally enough, an extension in the powers and personnel of urban government. The possibilities for employment in the larger towns were already great; besides the members of the corporation itself, the aldermen, common councilmen and freemen, the borough of Drogheda, for

---

1745–85' (unpublished Ph.D. thesis, Queen's University, Belfast, 1974), ch. 2; Ferguson, 'Army in Ireland', pp 102–6; Jim O'Donovan, 'The militia in Munster, 1715–78' in Gerard O'Brien (ed.), *Parliament, politics and people: essays in eighteenth-century Irish history* (Dublin, 1989), pp 31–47; Connolly, *Religion, law and power*, pp 201–2; Maurice Fitzgerald to David Crosbie, 13 Aug. 1711 (N.L.I., Talbot-Crosbie papers, PC 188); lords justices to lord mayor and commissioners of array of Dublin city, 8 Jan. 1711[/12] (N.A., M/2553, f. 45); Archbishop King to Charles Delafaye, 25 July 1715 (T.C.D., MS 750 (13), pp 58–9). **12** On the grand jury, see Neal Garnham, 'Local elite creation in early Hanoverian Ireland: the case of the county grand jury' in *Historical Journal*, xlii (1999), pp 623–42. **13** The vestry system in the capital has been studied in detail in Rowena V. Dudley, 'Dublin's parishes, 1660–1729: the Church of Ireland parishes and their role in the civic administration of the city' (unpublished Ph.D. thesis, T.C.D., 1995). Extracts from some vestry books have been published: see Robert Malcolmson, *Carlow vestries in olden times* (Carlow, 1870); Charles Scott, 'Vestry book of the united parishes of Ballywalter, Ballyhalbert and Inishargie, in the Ards, Co. Down' in *Ulster Journal of Archaeology*, 2nd ser., v (1898), pp 95–9; Edward Parkinson, 'The vestry books of the parish of Down, 1703–1828' in *Ulster Journal of Archaeology*, 2nd ser., xiv (1908), pp 145–55; xv (1909), pp 20–8, 79–86; J.B. Leslie, *An old Dublin vestry book* (Dublin, 1943); J.J. Marshall (ed.), *Aghadow vestry records ... Co. Tyrone*

example, employed in 1661 a recorder, a treasurer and auditors, two coroners, two sheriffs, constables of the staple, a 'sergeant of the franchises', 'sergeants of the small mace'. 'common appraisers', 'overseers of the crane' , a water bailiff, and proctors of the poor house of St John, a medieval foundation maintained by the corporation. By 1700 there were in addition four overseers of the highways, and in 1727 a keeper for the newly established house of correction, or bridewell.[14] Obviously, the larger the town, the more work there was to be done, and the more people were employed to do it. Dublin was the largest by far, its population of perhaps about 50,000 in the early eighteenth century making it not only elephantine by contemporary Irish standards but the second biggest city of the British empire. Dubliners benefited from a variety of schemes for urban improvement of which urban dwellers elsewhere were deprived, including paving and lighting the streets, bringing in piped water, and the establishment (by a statute of 1704) of a city workhouse for the poor, financed by parish rates but governed by an appointed board of trustees.[15] But even the smaller borough corporations were obliged to take a greater responsibility for the welfare of their citizens and the upkeep of the urban fabric. In Limavady (County Londonderry), for example, the necessity of raising money for various public enterprises, notably road-repairs, required the establishment of new municipal officers, entitled 'assessors', 'appraisers', and 'applotters', to organise the collection.[16] The corporation of Ennis (County Clare), with a majority of non-resident freemen drawn from the surrounding landed proprietors, responded to its proliferating responsibilities by more radical administrative innovation, instituting a 'grand jury' (modelled on the county grand jury) which took charge, *inter alia*, of policing by-laws, appointing minor officials and levying local taxation.[17] And across the kingdom, in boroughs great and small, the maintenance of law and order was assisted by the institution of 'watch and ward', which required the citizenry to do their duty, either in person or by paid substitute, in guarding the peace, not only against insurgency and riot, but increasingly against criminal activity of a non-political nature. So great was the perceived increase in crime in Dublin in the early eighteenth century that, despite the presence of a garrison of regular troops, several anxious city parishes put themselves to the expense of building new watchhouses.[18]

(Dungannon, 1935). **14** Thomas Gogarty (ed.), *Council book of the corporation of Drogheda, vol. 1, from the year 1649 to 1734* (Drogheda, 1915), pp 90, 269–71, 386. **15** David Dickson, 'In search of the old Irish poor law' in Rosalind Mitchison and Peter Roebuck (eds), *Economy and society in Scotland and Ireland 1500–1939* (Edinburgh, 1988), pp 150–1; Maurice Craig, *Dublin 1660–1860* (Dublin, 1980), p. 75. **16** E.M.F-G. Boyle (ed.), *Records of the town of Limavady. 1609 to 1808* (Londonderry, 1912), pp 24, 46, 53, 65. **17** Brian Ó Dálaigh (ed.), *Corporation book of Ennis* (Dublin, 1990), pp 32–3. See also his *Ennis in the eighteenth century* (Dublin, 1995). **18** St Bride's, Dublin, vestry accounts, 19 Mar. 1703, 17 Apr. 1704 (T.C.D., MS 1476); St Catherine's and St James's, Dublin, vestry book, 12 Oct. 1703, 1721 (R.C.B.,

The early eighteenth century also witnessed the emergence of a new form of administrative body, located somewhere between central and local government: the nominated commission, responsible for the disbursement of funds granted under statute for particular local purposes. The first of these was the linen board, established by act of the Irish parliament in 1711, not only to award grants for the encouragement of the linen industry, but to exercise a regulatory authority over manufacture and distribution.[19] Then there were the commissioners appointed under the tillage act of 1729 (3 Geo. II, c. 3), to administer the money collected under the act for the improvement of river navigation; and the various turnpike or highway trusts set up by successive statutes after 1729 (twenty-eight in all, over the next ten years) to oversee specific road improvements.[20] In several respects these innovations were characteristic of the period: the members of the commissions were appointed from the centre, usually by name in the relevant act of parliament, yet their composition recognised and indeed reflected the distribution of power within society at large, since they consisted of leading politicians and landed proprietors, and in the case of the turnpike and highway trusts effectively embodied the local landed elite; the members served for life, with vacancies recruited by co-option; and they were usually unpaid. In other words, this was voluntary public service by the propertied classes: the devolution of power from government to squirearchy, even if it was often power without much profit for those directly involved.

But the sharp increase in opportunities for participation in 'public life' that occurred in Ireland between 1660 and *c.*1740 was more than simply an expansion in government employment, whether central or local, paid or unpaid. In many respects the greatest change that took place in this period was to be found in the health and vigour of representative institutions. The most obvious was the Irish parliament, which prior to the Glorious Revolution had endured an erratic history. Charles II's only parliament had been dissolved in 1666, after granting the king additional customs duties for life, and thus rendering itself financially redundant. James II summoned a parliament in 1689, during his brief rule in Ireland; the so-called 'patriot parliament' of 1689, but it lasted little more than six weeks. Gradually, however, after 1691 parliament became established as an institution. The need for further 'additional' taxation to make

P117/5/2, pp 164, 349); St Paul's, Dublin, vestry book, 7 Sept. 1725 (ibid., P273/6/1, p. 64); St Peter's, Dublin, vestry book, 15 Nov. 1716 (ibid., P45/6/1, p. 176).   **19** List of trustees of linen manufacture, [1711] (N.A., M/2537, pp 272–5); H.D. Gribbon, 'The Irish Linen Board, 1711–1828', in Marilyn Cohen (ed.), *The warp of Ulster's past: interdisciplinary studies on the linen industry* (Basingstoke, 1997), pp 71–91. See also R.B. McDowell, 'Ireland in 1800' in T.W. Moody and W.E. Vaughan (eds), *A new history of Ireland, iv: Eighteenth-century Ireland* (Oxford, 1986), pp 701–2.   **20** See, for example, David Broderick, *An early toll-road: the Dublin-Dunleer turnpike, 1731–1855* (Dublin, 1996); and, more generally, his 'The Irish turnpike road system' (unpublished Ph.D. thesis, T.C.D., 1998).

up the shortfall of government expenditure was met by a succession of short-term subsidies, which guaranteed that MPs would be summoned regularly, and by 1715 a pattern of biennial sessions had evolved. It was now possible to make a political career through a seat in parliament rather than a place at court; indeed, in due course membership of the Irish House of Commons became the recognised avenue for preferment to public office. A new class of 'professional' politicians arose, mostly, though not exclusively, men with a legal training and background, who were the civil servants and administrators of Hanoverian Ireland.

As parliament became more important, so naturally did parliamentary elections. There was not the same frequency of general elections in eighteenth-century Ireland as in England, since, until the passage of the Octennial Act in 1768, the only constitutional limitation on the length of a parliament was the life of the sovereign. Thus the parliament of George I, chosen in 1715, lasted until the king himself died in 1727, and even more remarkably there was no general election between the accession of George II and his death in 1760. But the initial political instability after 1691 meant that there were as many as five elections between 1692 and 1715, and it took some time for Irishmen to get used to the calmer atmosphere under the Hanoverians. The feverish political temperature induced by the violence of 'party politics' under Queen Anne naturally aroused a keen interest in constituency affairs, and in particular in the politics of borough corporations. Many became highly agitated between the 1690s and the mid-1720s. Larger towns, like Dublin, Galway, Kilkenny, and Limerick, were naturally among the most fiercely contested, but many of the smaller corporations were rent by factional strife. Even in the 'rotten boroughs', scarcely if at all inhabited, which enjoyed no meaningful existence as administrative units, the rage of electoral politics sometimes infused corporate institutions with an unexpected vitality.

These constitutional developments were largely political in origin: the result of alterations in the competence and preoccupations of government, and more specifically in the relationship between crown and parliament. At the same time other, equally significant changes were taking place within Irish society which in a rather different way enlarged the scope of public life: the rise in numbers and prosperity of social groups below the level of the great landowners – the lesser gentry in the countryside, professional and commercial men in the towns – and the greater opportunities for economic, cultural and moral improvement opened up by the growth of commerce and education. These changes created the circumstances for an expansion in what might be termed the 'voluntary sector', clubs, societies, even the boards of governors of private philanthropic institutions. There was of course a strong element of conviviality and sociability in such gatherings; but the proliferation of various self-electing boards and fraternities also reflects a greater self-confidence on the part of the educated, landed, commercial and professional, classes, and a determination to become involved in social improvement.

Prior to the Reformation these functions had been served in a different way by the civic guilds of Dublin, Cork, Waterford, and other boroughs. Guilds certainly continued into the eighteenth century, but with one interesting exception they had lost their charitable and pious aspect, and become entirely secular, essentially commercial, institutions.[21] Whereas the medieval guilds had been a setting for the expression of Christian values and communal sentiment, their eighteenth-century counterparts merely regulated admission to trading privileges and undertook some of the more menial duties of municipal administration. The exception was the religious guild of St Anne, based in St Audoen's parish in Dublin. This was predominantly a civic institution, with close links to the city corporation, and even in the middle of the eighteenth century admitted few if any who were not Dubliners. Founded by Henry VI, and open to both men and women (referred to as 'brothers' and 'sisters' respectively), though in practice the membership was dominated by the 'brothers', the guild of St Anne had attracted Catholics as well as Protestants before 1641, and even after the Restoration may have included the occasional Catholic member. By 1700, however, it was entirely Protestant, appointed the vicar of St Audoen's as its *ex officio* chaplain, and among its various philanthropic donations gave a sum to the upkeep of a charity school established in the parish church. From 1694 onwards the guild devoted over half its annual expenditure to the Blue Coat School, itself now a strongly Protestant foundation. The guild of St Anne was unique in early eighteenth-century Dublin in combining piety and philanthropy with sociability: substantial sums were spent on feasts for the brothers and sisters as well as for the relief of distress and the promotion of true religion.[22] Other city clubs and societies – and one would have to include in this generalisation the early masonic lodges, founded in Dublin and elsewhere in Ireland from about 1718 onwards, despite their portentous ritual and pseudo-scientific associations – professed a more obviously and uncomplicatedly convivial purpose.[23]

The guild of St Anne may have been unique in the particular combination of functions it served, but there were other kinds of society which also retained something of the religious and communal spirit of the medieval guilds, albeit with a narrower focus, an altogether more earnest spirit, and a degree of social

---

21 Hill, *From patriots to unionists*, ch. 1, esp. pp 24–32.   22 Accounts of St Anne's guild, 1708–79 (Royal Irish Academy, MS 12/P/1); minutes of St Anne's guild, 1584–1817 (ibid., MS 12/D/1). I am very grateful to Dr Colm Lennon for directing my attention to this important source. On the earlier history of the guild, see Colm Lennon, 'The chantries in the Irish Reformation: the case of St Anne's Guild, Dublin, 1550–1630' in R.V. Comerford, Mary Cullen, Jacqueline Hill and Colm Lennon (eds), *Religion, conflict and coexistence in Ireland: essays presented to Monsignor Patrick J. Corish* (Dublin, 1990), pp 6–25.   23 W.J. Chetwode Crawley, 'Early Irish freemasonry and Dean Swift's connection with the craft' in Henry Sadler, *Masonic reprints and historical revelations ...* (London, 1898).

exclusiveness. Some were explicitly religious groups, with close links to the established church; some were essentially philanthropic, devoting their time to the poor, the sick, and the unfortunate; a few others were coteries of literary, antiquarian or philosophical enthusiasts.

The first religious fraternities to appear were the informal praying and psalm-singing gatherings established in Dublin in the 1680s and 1690s by pious laymen like James Bonnell, on the lines of the so-called 'religious societies' flourishing in England, which in turn drew their inspiration from German pietism.[24] They were followed by the more assertive societies 'for the reformation of manners', another concept introduced from England, which sought to co-ordinate the efforts of vigilant parishioners and sympathetic magistrates in campaigns to stamp out public vices, especially those associated with drunkenness, profane swearing and sexual licence, and to enforce a proper observance of the sabbath. Once again these societies were concentrated in Dublin, though there is evidence of similar activity in other substantial towns within striking distance of the capital, including Drogheda and Kilkenny.[25]

The same concerns which gave rise to the movement for moral reformation through individual prayer or magisterial action were also manifested in the foundation of charity schools, to educate the poor in the rudiments of reading, writing, and religion. At first the charity school foundations were isolated acts of benevolence on the part of private individuals or particular parishes, most notable among them being the 'Blue Coat School' in Dublin and other schools founded by Erasmus Smith in the 1670s.[26] But after 1701 the Society for Promoting Christian Knowledge, newly formed in England, took an interest in developments in Ireland and set up a network of correspondents who eventually coalesced into an Irish society for promoting charity schools.[27] This shadowy organisation, which has left no archive to document its existence, had collapsed by the mid-1720s, but was effectively revived in 1733/4 under a royal charter,

24 Benjamin Scroggs, *A sermon preached before the religious societies in the city of Dublin, on the 29th of Septemb. 1695* (Dublin, 1695); Thomas Emlyn, *A sermon preach'd before the societies for reformation of manners in Dublin, October the 4th, 1698* (Dublin, 1698), p. 20; D.W. Hayton, 'Did Protestantism fail in eighteenth-century Ireland? Charity schools and the enterprise of religious and social reformation, c.1690–1730' in Alan Ford, James McGuire and Kenneth Milne (eds), *As by law established: the Church of Ireland since the Reformation* (Dublin, 1995), p. 173. 25 Bp William King to Bp John Hartstonge, 4 May 1698 (T.C.D., MS 750/1, p. 222); *An account of the societies for reformation of manners, in England and Ireland* ... (3rd ed., London, 1700), p. 12; T.C. Barnard, 'Reforming Irish manners: the religious societies in Dublin during the 1690s' in *Historical Journal*, xxxv (1992), pp 805–38. 26 Sir Frederick R. Falkiner, *The foundation of the hospital and free school of King Charles II, Oxmantown, Dublin, commonly called the Blue Coat School* (Dublin, 1906); Myles V. Ronan, *Erasmus Smith endowment: a romance of Irish confiscation* (Dublin, 1937). 27 Proceedings of the society for promoting charity schools (Marsh's Library, MS Z/1/1/13/97); Hayton, 'Did Protestantism fail?', p. 174.

in the form of the Incorporated Society, responsible for the settlement and encouragement of the so-called 'charter schools', which were such a feature of Irish education for the remainder of the eighteenth and the early nineteenth century.[28]

The first half of the eighteenth century was indeed a great age of philanthropy, much of it inspired by motives of evangelical enthusiasm. Not merely schools but public libraries, like that attached to the Green Coat School in Cork (in imitation of the experiments of the Halle pietists in Germany) or Archbishop Marsh's library in Dublin, workhouses, and hospitals.[29] Between 1700 and 1760 as many as six hospitals were founded in the capital: the Charitable Infirmary (1718), Steevens's (1733), Mercer's (1734), the Lying-in Hospital (the Rotunda) (1745), the Meath (1753) and St Patrick's hospital 'for lunatics and idiots', established by a benefaction in the will of Dean Swift in 1757.[30] All were private foundations, but required trustees to oversee and carry on their work, and thus developed an ethos of communal charitable activity. The governing boards of hospitals like Mercer's provided the opportunity for its members to meet together regularly in a formal setting to practise their public virtue and also, in the organisation of charity concerts and theatrical performances, to raise funds, to enjoy each other's company and to reaffirm their social status.[31]

Finally, there were several antiquarian and scientific societies which flourished in this period, and also combined sociability with a sense of public utility: the Dublin Philosophical Society in the later seventeenth century, the Irish equivalent of the Royal Society in London, which fostered the curiosity of the amateur virtuoso rather than the sophisticated natural philosophy of the professional scientist;[32] the Physico-Historical Society, which emerged in the

---

28 The standard account of the charter schools is Kenneth Milne, *The Irish charter schools 1730–1830* (Dublin, 1997). 29 *Pietas Corcagiensis. Or, A view of the Green-Coat Hospital* (Cork, 1721); Muriel McCarthy, *All graduates and gentlemen: Marsh's Library* (Dublin, 1980); Dickson, 'In search of the old Irish poor law', pp 150–1; St Bride's, Dublin, vestry accounts, 10 Apr. 1683 (T.C.D., MS 1476/28); St Peter's, Dublin, vestry book 1686–1736, pp 104, 106, 110 (R.C.B., P45/6/1); Gogarty (ed.), *Drogheda council book*, p. 270. 30 J.D.H. Widdess, *The Charitable Infirmary, Jervis Street, Dublin, 1718–1968* (Dublin, 1968); T.P.C. Kirkpatrick, *The history of Doctor Steevens' Hospital, 1720–1920* (Dublin, 1924); J.B. Lyons, *The quality of Mercer's: the story of Mercer's Hospital, 1734–1991* (Sandycove, 1991); T.P.C. Kirkpatrick, *The book of the Rotunda Hospital* ... (London, 1913); T.D. O'D. Browne, *The Rotunda Hospital, 1745–1945* (Edinburgh, 1947); Ian Campbell Ross (ed.), *Public virtue, public love: the early years of the Dublin Lying-In Hospital, the Rotunda* (Dublin, 1986); L.H. Ormsby, *Medical history of the Meath Hospital and County Dublin Infirmary, from its foundation in 1753* ... (Dublin, 1888); M.J. Craig (ed.), *The legacy of Swift: a bicentenary record of St Patrick's Hospital, Dublin* (Dublin, 1948); Fred Powell, 'Dean Swift and the Dublin Foundling Hospital' in *Studies*, lxx (1981), pp 162–70. 31 Minute book of the governors of Mercer's Hospital, 1736–72 (Royal College of Surgeons, Dublin, Mercer Library). 32 K.T. Hoppen, *The common scientist in the seventeenth century: a study of the Dublin Philosophical Society*

115

1740s from the circle of antiquarians surrounding the journalist Walter Harris, whose great project was the preparation by its local correspondents of accurate and comprehensive surveys of the history, antiquities and economic potential of the counties of Ireland;[33] and, most important of all, the Dublin Society (later accorded the prefix Royal), established in 1731, which combined an interest in learning and in technology, and was infused with a passion for the 'improvement' of the country through the application of the latest scientific discoveries to Irish agriculture and industry.[34]

II

How much of the expanding 'public sphere' of late seventeenth- and early eighteenth-century Ireland was restricted to members of the established church? Certainly, after the defeat of James II's counter-revolution in 1690/1 there was little chance for Irish Catholics to participate in politics and government. At the Restoration in 1660, a 'Protestant ascendancy' was still far from guaranteed. Catholic landed power had been broken by the Cromwellian confiscations and the ensuing settlement, which had benefited the pre-existing Protestant interests within Ireland, but there was still room for anxiety that the restored monarchy would be able, if it wished, to reverse the process, as indeed happened during the reign of James II, and in particular the lord deputyship of the earl of Tyrconnel, 1687–9. Tyrconnel's remodelling of the Castle administration and the Irish army, and his intrusion of Catholics into local government and in borough corporations, as part of a campaign to 'pack' parliament in the Catholic interest, showed the fragility of Protestant privilege.[35] It was only after the Glorious Revolution and the establishment of a Protestant royal succession that Protestant interests in Ireland could feel secure. However, already in the period 1660–87 a great deal had been done to pave the way for the 'confessional state' which would be completed after 1689. Although there was no Test Act in

---

1683–1708 (London, 1970).   **33** Anne de Valera, 'Antiquarian and historical investigations in Ireland in the eighteenth century' (M.A. thesis, UCD, 1978), ch. 2; G.L.H. Davies, 'The making of Irish geography, part iv: the Physico-Historical Society of Ireland, 1744–52' in *Irish Geography*, xii (1979), pp 92–8; Eoin Magennis, 'A "beleaguered Protestant": Walter Harris and the writing of *Fiction unmasked* in mid-eighteenth-century Ireland' in *Eighteenth-Century Ireland*, xiii (1998), pp 86–111.   **34** H.F. Berry, *A history of the Royal Dublin Society* (London, 1915); Desmond Clarke, *Thomas Prior, 1681–1751: founder of the Royal Dublin Society* (Dublin, 1951); Terence de Vere White, *The story of the Royal Dublin Society* (Tralee, 1955); *The Royal Dublin Society, 1731–1968* (Dublin, 1968).   **35** J.G. Simms, *Jacobite Ireland 1685–91* (London, 1969, repr. Dublin, 2000), pp 32–43; John Miller, *James II: a study in kingship* (2nd ed., London, 1989), pp 216–19; David Dickson, *New foundations: Ireland 1660–1800* (2nd ed., Dublin, 2000), pp 23–9.

Ireland, along English lines, which would have enforced the legal exclusion of Catholics from office, political pressure dictated that few if any Catholics were employed in the service of the crown, other than in a relatively humble capacity, and usually only in the lower reaches of the military. Catholic interests in borough corporations had been directly attacked in the so-called 'new rules' issued by the earl of Essex as lord lieutenant in 1672/3, obliging all municipal office-holders (though not freemen) to take the oaths of allegiance and supremacy, as well as a further oath, denying the right to take up arms against the King, which was designed to apply to covenanting presbyterians.[36]

After 1691, taught by their experience under Tyrconnel, Irish Protestants, in government, in parliament, and in the boroughs, were determined to strengthen their grip on political power. In fact, the first step in the construction of the statutory 'confessional state' was made in England. The oaths act passed at Westminster in 1689, requiring all holders of public office, and members of parliament, to take the oaths of allegiance and supremacy and to make a declaration against transubstantiation, was extended to Ireland; and thus the parliament which met in Dublin in 1692 did not contain a single Catholic. Irish M.P.s followed suit in the poll tax acts of 1695 and 1697, which imposed the oaths and declaration on the local commissioners named in the act. After 1703 another English statute added a further means of discriminating against Catholics in office, in the form of an oath of abjuring the jacobite pretender (and by implication denying the Pope's authority in temporal matters). This too was extended to Ireland, and utilised in the Irish popery act the following year to hinder Catholics from voting in parliamentary elections.[37] In the meantime local, municipal by-laws had stripped voting rights from Catholic freemen across the country, albeit in some cases slowly and 'fitfully', and relegated them to an inferior status.[38] Even where there were no specific requirements for participating in public life, Catholics could be, and were, effectively excluded; that is, the minority of Catholics who had managed to retain their property and social status and thus were not disqualified already on socio-economic grounds. Nominated commissions, of whatever kind, whether it be the land tax commission of 1698, the Linen Board, the various turnpike or highway trusts, the Dublin workhouse trustees, or the governors of Mercer's Hospital, excluded Catholics as a matter of course, and the provisions made for supplying new members to vacancies (co-option or election by the existing commissioners) ensured that Catholics would continue to be kept off.

36 *The statutes at large passed in the parliaments held in Ireland* ... (20 vols, Dublin, 1786–1801), iii, 197–239; Hill, *From patriots to unionists*, pp 52–4. 37 J.G. Simms, 'Irish Catholics and the parliamentary franchise, 1692–1728' in *Irish Historical Studies*, xii (1960–1), pp 28–37. 38 Hill, *From patriots to unionists*, pp 35–9. By 1693 there was only one identifiable Catholic out of 96 freemen in the corporation of Thomastown, Co. Kilkenny: notes on the minute books of Thomastown corporation (N.L.I., Reports on MSS in Private

There can be little doubt that this exclusion of Catholics from public office and political rights after the Revolution was swift and well-nigh complete. It is difficult to find a Catholic in government employ after 1700, not even in the humblest position, except that is for the rank-and-file of the Irish army.[39] Although strictly speaking no Irishmen at all, Protestant or Catholic, should have been recruited, in practice this prohibition proved impossible to maintain. Commanding officers of regiments stationed in Ireland who were desperate to make up numbers before their troops were mustered would naturally take recruits at short notice wherever they could find them. In the civil administration there were occasional accusations that crypto-Catholics had crept into place: opportunists who professed Protestantism and took the requisite oaths while remaining Catholic in their hearts. Anxiety on this score would in due course give rise to further penal laws which imposed restrictions on first-generation converts and in some respects treated them as if they were still Catholics. The evidence of converts' attitudes is difficult to assess, however, largely because it comes from hostile witnesses. During the vicious party conflict in the last years of Queen Anne's reign the Irish Whig opposition accused the Tory ministry of employing recent and dubious converts on a systematic basis, as part of a surreptitious campaign to install Jacobite sympathisers in vital government offices; and it is certainly possible to identify some office-holders and some members of the Irish parliament in 1713 as former Catholics. But without explicit proof we should not be quick to assume that these men had become Protestants simply out of convenience.[40] There were a few 'new converts' – Lords Bellew and Fitzwilliam for instance – who became zealously Whiggish in their politics.[41] Others like Sir Redmond Everard of Fethard, County Tipperary,

Collections, no. 207). The corporation of Clonmel, Co. Tipperary, issued an order in 1713 reaffirming the regulation that no Catholic could be admitted as a freeman (W.P. Burke, *History of Clonmel* (Waterford, 1907), p. 145). **39** For the army, see Guy, 'Irish military establishment, 1660–1776', pp 217–18; Thomas Doyle, 'Jacobitism, Catholicism, and the Irish Protestant elite' in *Eighteenth-Century Ireland*, xii (1997), pp 43–4. For a possible exception in the revenue service, one Denny Connor in Co. Kerry, who was certainly a jacobite if not a Catholic, see James Forth to Paul Whichcote, 25 Sept. 1722 (N.L.I., MS 16007, pp 104–5). Maighréad Ní Mhurchadha, *The customs and excise service in Fingal 1684–1765: sober, active and bred to the sea* (Dublin, 1999), p. 43, notes the dismissal of a Catholic boatman at Malahide in 1741. **40** As did contemporaries: see *The resolutions of the House of Commons in Ireland, relating to the Lord-Chancellor Phips, examined ...* (London, 1714), pp 22–3; Bp Evans of Meath to [Abp Wake of Canterbury] 16 Oct. [1717] (Christ Church, Oxford, Wake MS Arch. W. Epist. 12 (unfoliated)). For calculations of the number of 'new convert' M.P.s in 1713, see J.G. Simms, 'The Irish parliament of 1713' in G.A. Hayes-McCoy (ed.), *Historical Studies iv* (London, 1963), p. 84; D.W. Hayton, 'The crisis in Ireland and the disintegration of Queen Anne's last ministry' in *Irish Historical Studies*, xxii (1980–1), p. 203. **41** Bellew represented the Sussex borough of Steyning in the British Parliament in the Whig interest from February to May 1712. For Fitzwilliam, see 'A list of

and his chief creditor, the attorney Cornelius Callaghan (formerly O'Callaghan), confirmed popular assumptions (about Catholic converts and also about the Tory party) by voicing extreme Tory opinions. However, not even a Tory political allegiance necessarily proves the existence of residual Catholic sympathies, for while the bankrupt Everard fled the country in 1715 and became a jacobite exile, Callaghan remained in Tipperary and fathered a long line of Protestant gentlemen, eventually raised to the Irish peerage as Lords Lismore. Indeed, the surviving list of Callaghan's private library, with its battery of Protestant sermons, histories, and devotional works, and complete absence of Catholic theology, might be taken to indicate that here was a man who had taken his conversion seriously.[42]

Where one can find some evidence of Catholic participation is at the lowest levels of corporate or parish government, and until 1728 in voting in parliamentary elections for county seats. In those boroughs with trade guilds a Catholic might be admitted as a 'quarter-brother' on payment of a fee (known as quarterage), which would entitle him to ply his trade but did not confer any voting rights or make him eligible for guild or civic office. In fact, so petty were the benefits in relation to the quarterly fee demanded that 'quarterage' came to be regarded by Catholic tradesmen as a tax and a grievance rather than a privilege.[43] In towns with few Protestant inhabitants and a strong Catholic commercial interest it was not always possible to exclude Catholics entirely from civic life. In Galway and Kilkenny, for example, in the early eighteenth century, there were allegations of clandestine Catholic influence, through the infiltration of the corporation by 'new converts' or indirectly through the presence of papist or Jacobite sympathisers among the ultra-Tories. Both corporations were remodelled by statute in 1717 to confine power in reliable Whiggish hands.[44] In

---

the peers of Ireland ...' and analysis of the Irish House of Lords, [1715] (B.L., Blenheim papers, Add. MS 61640, ff 27–32).   **42** For Everard, see D.W. Hayton, 'Dependence, clientage and affinity: the political following of the second duke of Ormonde' in T. Barnard and J. Fenlon (eds), *The dukes of Ormonde, 1610–1745* (Woodbridge, 2000), pp 227, 235, 239; for Callaghan, *The conduct of the purse of Ireland: in a letter to a member of the late Oxford convocation ...* (London, 1714), p. 30 ('a new convert lawyer, bred at St Omers'); 'inventory of Con. Callaghan's effects', 1737 (Tipperary S.R. County Museum, Clonmel, Acc. 1985: 65).   **43** Maureen Wall, 'The Catholics of the towns and the quarterage dispute in eighteenth-century Ireland' reprinted in O'Brien (ed.), *Catholic Ireland in the eighteenth century*, pp 61–72; Leighton, *Catholicism in a Protestant kingdom*, ch. 4; Hill, *From patriots to unionists*, pp 31–2, 38, 130–5. In Cork Catholic quarter-brothers were subjected to further restrictions; for example in 1706 their rights to take apprentices were reduced, because of a perceived threat to the Protestant trading interest: see Richard Caulfield (ed.), *The council book of the corporation of the city of Cork ...* (Guildford, 1876), pp 294, 311, 319–20, 328.   **44** James Kelly, 'The politics of the "Protestant ascendancy": County Galway 1650–1832' in Gerard Moran (ed.), *Galway: history and society* (Dublin, 1996), pp 239–43; W.G. Neely,

Ennis Catholic influence was institutionalised and controlled through admission to the grand jury, which undertook the humbler duties of municipal government under the direction of the sovereign (chief magistrate) but had no access to the parliamentary franchise.[45]

Elsewhere in local government, the lowest stratum of administration remained open to Catholics even after the Popery Act of 1704, which specifically exempted from its provisions the offices of high or petty constable, tithing-man, 'head-borough', overseer of the poor, churchwarden, surveyor of the highway, or 'like inferior civil office', though a subsequent act of 1716 did deprive them of the right to serve as constable. In practice, the admission of Catholics to any of these offices would have been at best sporadic, and would have depended on the confessional balance of population, and the willingness of Protestants to serve: in Drogheda, for example, Catholics may well have continued to be appointed as overseers of the highways as late as 1709, though probably not thereafter.[46] Where the hardship of an office outweighed its advantages, as in the case of 'watch and ward', efforts were made to oblige Catholics to the performance of their civic duty, and to prevent them from acting by deputy, as seems to have been the usual practice with many local offices.[47] Of course, in emergencies Catholic hands would not be regarded as safe, and an Irish act of 1716 forbade them from being employed personally on the watch 'in times of tumult and danger', though they were still required to pay for loyal Protestants to do the duty for them.

Finally, there is the question of the parliamentary franchise. Although notionally excluded by the legal imposition of the oaths of allegiance and abjuration, some Catholics do seem to have been polled at elections, especially in county constituencies. The execution of the law depended on the intentions of the returning officer, who could choose to question suspected Catholic voters as to whether they had taken the oaths, or leave the matter to conscience.

Kilkenny: an urban history, 1391–1843 (Belfast, 1989), pp 138–44; T.P. Power, 'Parliamentary representation in County Kilkenny in the eighteenth century' in William Nolan and Kevin Whelan (eds), *Kilkenny: history and society* (Dublin, 1990), pp 312–13. In Limerick and Waterford, too, party-political conflicts gave rise to accusations of collusion with Catholic interests: see Éamon O'Flaherty, 'Urban politics and municipal reform in Limerick, 1723–62' in *Eighteenth-Century Ireland*, vi (1991), pp 108–9; T.P. Power, 'Electoral politics in Waterford city, 1692–1832' in William Nolan and T.P. Power (eds), *Waterford: history and society* (Dublin, 1992), pp 230–1, 233. **45** Ó Dálaigh (ed.), *Corporation book of Ennis*, pp 29–33. **46** Gogarty (ed.), *Drogheda council book*, p. 304. For evidence of the legal prohibition on Catholic constables being honoured in the breach rather than the observance, in this case in the barony of Lecale in County Down, see Robert Ward to Michael Ward, 14 Apr. 1744 (P.R.O.N.I., Castleward MSS, D/2092/1/6/1, p. 121). The fact that an important local landowning family, Savage of Portaferry, had remained Catholic presumably accounts for the presence of 'papist constables' (and, according to Ward, Catholic militiamen too). **47** For example, see Richard Caulfield (ed.), *The council book of the corporation of Kinsale …*

Returning officers were rarely immune from political pressure or partisanship, so whether a Catholic registered a vote depended on the identity of the candidate or candidates for whom he wished to vote. Before 1728, and their final statutory exclusion on the basis of their religion rather than through the application of oaths, there is evidence of Catholic freeholders being canvassed in such counties as Clare, Waterford, or Kerry, and even allegations of Catholics being polled in some of the larger boroughs, for example in Kilkenny city, where the High Tory and 'new convert' interest was strong.[48]

The Protestant 'confessional state' did not just exclude Catholics. The 'new rules' of 1672/3, like Wentworth's 'black oath' before the Civil Wars, had also been aimed at the more extreme and irreconcilable Ulster presbyterians. *Anglican exclusiveness* was extended by means of a clause in the Irish Popery Act of 1704, which imposed a sacramental test on all occupants of crown and municipal office, though again this did not apply to constables and other 'inferior civil offices'. The requirement to receive the sacrament of Holy Communion according to the liturgy of the Church of Ireland, and to obtain a certificate to that effect from a justice of the peace, was aimed principally at Ulster presbyterians, perceived by High Churchmen in the early 1700s as constituting a serious threat to the establishment in church and state, because of their rapidly expanding numbers, their cohesive ecclesiastical and social organisation, and their powerful sense of separate identity, part ethnic or national, and part religious. The main area of Anglican concern was local government: in the counties, where presbyterian justices of the peace protected their co-religionists, and presbyterian militia officers presided over armed troops of their own choosing; and in those borough corporations where there was a very real possibility of presbyterian economic muscle being translated into political power. There was a comparatively large dissenting population in Dublin, presbyterians and Independents for the most part, though constituting no more than substantial minority among the Protestant freemen. Several northern constituencies also boasted a strong presbyterian electoral interest, and in a handful of Ulster corporations (Belfast, Carrickfergus and Derry) Presbyterians were dominant by 1704.[49]

This was where the test was intended to bite; and bite it most certainly did. The presbyterians in the north, unlike their fellow Protestant dissenters in the south, eschewed as a profanation the practice of 'occasional conformity'

(Guildford, 1879), p. lxxxi.   **48** Sir John Ainsworth (ed.), *The Inchiquin manuscripts* (Dublin, 1961), p. 114; John Hore to Roger Power, 29 Aug. 1703 (N.L.I., Lismore papers, MS 13243); David Barry to David Crosbie, 5 Dec. 1710 (T.C.D., Crosbie papers, MS 3821/124); *The journals of the House of Commons of the kingdom of Ireland* (3rd ed., 20 vols, Dublin, 1796–1800), ii, 612.   **49** Connolly, *Religion, law and power*, pp 159–71; D.W. Hayton, 'Exclusion, conformity and parliamentary representation: the impact of the sacramental test on Irish dissenting politics' in Herlihy (ed.), *Politics of Protestant dissent*, pp 57–70; Jacqueline R. Hill, 'Dublin corporation, Protestant dissent and politics, 1660–1800' in Herlihy (ed.),

developed by conservative nonconformists in England, to evade the terms of the English test and corporation acts by taking communion in the parish church once a year and then returning to worship at the meeting house.[50] Presbyterian aldermen in Belfast, Derry and other towns, and presbyterian justices of the peace resigned their offices rather than take holy communion from the hands of a Church of Ireland parson.[51] With the loss of J.P.s went the eclipse of dissenting influence on county grand juries. There were even greater dividends for the Church interest in the long term, as presbyterian gentlemen, no doubt persuaded by the political advantages as much as theological arguments, drifted into conformity with the established church.[52]

It would be misleading, however, to over-estimate the extent of Protestant dissenters' exclusion from public life. To begin with, the effects of the sacramental test were limited. The law exempted the place of constable and the various parish offices,[53] and although presbyterians in Ulster seem to have preferred on the whole to execute such offices as churchwarden and sidesman by deputy, an option given statutory force in the toleration act of 1715 (and indeed to have protested if they were obliged to attend in person),[54] they made their presence felt on vestry boards, which levied and spent the church and poor rate, dominating many northern parishes by the 1770s, when parliament passed the notorious vestry act to prevent them from serving. Nor is it easy to gauge the impact of the test in the areas of the administration to which it did apply. There is at least one attested example of a dissenter holding a lowly administrative place without having taken the sacrament.[55] More generally, despite the technical prohibition on any but communicating Anglicans holding militia commissions, the Ulster presbyterian community responded with enthusiasm and promptness at times of perceived national crisis: during the Jacobite invasion scares of 1715/16 and 1719, some presbyterians risked prosecution by taking their places at the array, while others organised

Politics of Protestant dissent, pp 28–37.   **50** John Flaningam, 'The occasional conformity controversy: ideology and party politics 1697–1711' in *Journal of British Studies*, xvii (1977), pp 38–62; Barnard, 'Government and Irish dissent', pp 24–5. For a single example from Dublin, Alderman Thomas Bell, see Dublin corporation Monday book (1658–1712), p. 130A (Dublin City Archives, MR/18).   **51** Hayton, 'Exclusion, conformity and parliamentary representation', pp 59–69. There were also occasional resignations in a few other boroughs: for an example, see the minute book of the corporation of Belturbet, Co. Cavan, 24 June 1708 (N.A., M/3572, unfoliated).   **52** Alexander McCracken to Robert Wodrow, 11 Nov. 1710 (National Library of Scotland, Wodrow MSS, Letters Quarto II, f. 154). See also T.C. Barnard, 'Identities, ethnicity and tradition among Irish dissenters, *c.*1650–1750' in Kevin Herlihy (ed.), *The Irish dissenting tradition 1650–1750* (Dublin, 1995), pp 34–5; Hayton, 'Exclusion, conformity and parliamentary representation', pp 69–73.   **53** And also, evidently, the sheriff's deputy or 'sub-sheriff': see deposition of James Smyth of Ballintoy, Co. Antrim, 28 Feb. 1715/16 (Marsh's Lib., MS Z3/1/1/12).   **54** Representation of James Bell, [?1717] (Marsh's Lib., MS Z3/1/1/23).   **55** A gunner's place in Derry: Barnard, 'Government and

independent companies of volunteers.[56] The Irish parliament offered a retrospective indemnity to these militiamen after 1715 and further indemnity acts were passed after 1719 (though dissenters wishing to benefit were still obliged to take the test).[57] But the area in which presbyterian disabilities have been most frequently and seriously exaggerated by historians has been the parliamentary franchise. The effects of the test were certainly devastating to presbyterian political interests in two or three northern boroughs, but presbyterians were not deprived of the vote, as has sometimes been alleged. They could and did poll in county elections, and were a force to be reckoned with in counties like Antrim, Armagh, Donegal, Fermanagh, Monaghan and Tyrone;[58] and they could still be admitted as borough freemen and vote as such in the larger freeman boroughs like Carrickfergus, Derry, and of course in Dublin.

Overall, the term 'Protestant ascendancy' is a little misleading. In so far as the penal laws excluded Catholics from almost every area of public life in early eighteenth-century Ireland, we should really be talking of a Protestant monopoly rather than an ascendancy. Even in relation to the Protestant dissenting communities, the control exercised by the Church of Ireland laity over public office and political participation, the so-called 'confessional state', if less than complete, was still remarkably extensive. Nor, if we look closely at the social composition of the Protestant political classes do we find a 'Protestant ascendancy' in the accepted, textbook view, which characterises Irish Protestant society in terms of its elite of larger landed proprietors, the world of the Anglo-Irish nobility and gentry in the 'big house'. Undoubtedly much of Irish public life was indeed the province of the landed elite, which occupied the great offices of state, sat in Parliament, ran county government and controlled many of the smaller borough corporations, and predominated in the more important voluntary societies and charitable trusts. But equally important were the civic elites, in Dublin especially, and other major towns: the greater merchants and financiers,

Irish dissent', p. 9.   **56** Bp John Stearne to Abp William King, 12 Sept. 1715 (T.C.D., MS 1995–2008/1723); *Whalley's News-Letter*, 21–4 Sept. 1715; [Henry Joy,] *Historical collections relative to the town of Belfast* (Belfast, 1817), pp 89–90; Robert McBride, *A sermon preached at the desire of the Belfast independent company of volunteers, May 28, 1716* (Belfast, 1716).
57 Beckett, *Protestant dissent in Ireland*, chs 7–8; Connolly, *Religion, law and power*, pp 166–7.
58 For Antrim, see William Tisdall, *The case of the sacramental test stated and argued* (Dublin, 1715), pp 48–9; for Armagh, Henry Boyle to Sir Archibald [Acheson], 22 Mar. 1753 (P.R.O.N.I., Gosford papers, D/1606/1/1/12); for Donegal and Tyrone, William Stewart to Lord Abercorn, 25 Feb. 1768 (ibid., Abercorn papers, T/2541/IA1/8/27) and James Hamilton to same, 16 July, 5 Aug., 11 Sept. 1768 (ibid., T/2541/IA1/8/75, 80, 86); for Fermanagh, 'Falkland' [J. Scott], *Parliamentary representation: being a critical review of all the counties, cities and boroughs of the kingdom of Ireland, with regard to the state of their representation* (Dublin, 1790), p. 36; and for Monaghan, Bodleian Lib., MS Eng. hist. d. 155, pp 22–3 (I owe this reference to Dr Raymond Gillespie).

who enjoyed the status and influence associated with important municipal dignitaries, and, in the case of the Dublin aldermen in particular, were able to enhance their reputation by participating in major charitable enterprises. (Though whether a clear distinction should be made between landed magnates and merchant princes in this period is a difficult question to answer, given the speed with which commercial wealth was invested in land.) Still more important is the way in which Protestant privilege percolated down the social order. Artisans as well as aristocrats partook of Protestant ascendancy: an army of minor officials, clerks, barrackmasters and revenuemen; the parliamentary electorate, freeholders in the counties and freemen in the boroughs; and at parish level the petty constables, churchwardens and vestrymen. In the more fashionable Dublin parishes the vestry might be composed of the social elite – peers, baronets, members of parliament – but this was certainly not the case in the countryside, especially in parishes in the north, where vestrymen can be found (some, perhaps, presbyterians) who were unable to sign their names to the minutes.[59]

III

It would be unreasonable to assume that the Church of Ireland laymen who benefited from the establishment of an essentially Anglican 'confessional state' in the decades after the Glorious Revolution were unanimously and invariably devout. Undoubtedly, for some, and not just the hastily converting Catholic or the wearily conforming dissenter, adherence to the established church was not much more than a ticket of entry into public life; a badge of privilege which enabled him to hold public office, or to vote. At the same time we should not be too cynical, or generalise too freely. The Church of Ireland laity, at all levels, included many men and women who took their religion very seriously and strove to live according to its precepts; men and women who would have echoed the heartfelt prayer of James Bonnell, that God would 'enable me to reform myself, and then vouchsafe to make use of me for Thy glory, in the way Thy wisdom has ordained for me.'[60] The question must be, whether such aspirations were satisfied by attendance at church and private prayer, or whether they infused conduct in politics and government. To quote Bonnell again, 'where do we see piety practised in all its parts, private, domestic and public?'[61] Among the propertied classes, even those lacking in spiritual fervour could appreciate

---

59 For contrasting examples, see St Bride's, Dublin, vestry accounts (T.C.D., MS 1476); parish of Culdaff, Co. Donegal, vestry minutes (P.R.O.N.I., D/803/1). 60 William Hamilton, *The life and character of James Bonnell esq, ...* (Dublin, 1801), p. 61. See also Mrs Jane Bonnell to John Strype, 13 June 1699 (Cambridge University Library, Add. MS 2, ff 344–5). 61 Hamilton, *Life and character of James Bonnell*, p. 58.

the social importance of religion in reaffirming common values and discouraging criminal and subversive behaviour. Many country gentlemen cherished the ideal of a peaceful Anglican polity, with harmony between squire and parson and a unanimous acceptance of the general order of men and things.

Both before and after the Glorious Revolution there were Irishmen who defined their political principles in terms of their own adherence to the established church, and their opposition both to Catholicism and to Protestant dissent. During the early 1680s, in the aftermath of the Exclusion Crisis and of the covenanting uprising in Scotland, the first duke of Ormond, as lord lieutenant, undertook a policy of repression directed at presbyterian interests in the north of Ireland, which attracted significant support from Anglican gentlemen. But it was during King William's reign, when for many Church of Ireland laymen fear of popery was replaced by a new anxiety at what appeared to be the inexorable rise of presbyterianism, that popular concern for the main-tenance of the church establishment was translated into the appearance of an Irish parliamentary faction distinguishing itself as 'the Church party', or Tories, with the accompanying development, in parliamentary debates and in the press, of a political rhetoric based on sectarian animosities. In the Irish parliamentary sessions of 1703–13 the conflict between the Tories and their Whig opponents rose to such a pitch as to dominate business, and it became impossible for members to escape the acquisition of a party label. Outside parliament, the virus of party spread into the constituencies and into society at large. Coffee-houses and taverns acquired a Tory or Whig complexion; theatrical perfor-mances might be ruined by political demonstrations. And of course the clergy were drawn into the struggle, almost always on the Tory side, preaching in favour of Tory politicians and Tory measures, appearing at elections to support Tory candidates, and contributing to the vituperative polemical literature spawned by the conflict between Tory and Whig, church and dissent.[62]

Despite the close involvement of the clergy as political auxiliaries of the Tory party, the ecclesiastical dimension to the Tory campaign in parliament and in the constituencies was surprisingly limited. The principal issue at stake between the parties in the House of Commons was the exclusion of Protestant dissenters from political rights: the imposition of the test in 1704, and abortive attempts to repeal it in 1707 and 1709. Constructive reform of church organisation or finances was largely ignored: left to the clergy themselves in convocation. In Anne's reign parliament passed only four public acts to benefit the church, three of them in the session of 1703/4, when Tory enthusiasm was at a high point: 'to quiet ecclesiastical persons in their possessions' (1704), to facilitate the exchange of glebe land (1704), and for building parish churches in

62 Connolly, *Religion, law and power*, ch. 3.

more convenient places (1704, 1710), as well as several private acts for the division or uniting of particular parishes. None of these measures, however, had taken its rise in the House of Commons, beginning instead in either the Irish Privy Council, or in the Lords, where one must presume that episcopal influence was decisive. Outside parliament Tories were most publicly involved in campaigns for the repression of dissent by judicial means, as magistrates pursued presbyterian ministers and members of their congregations for various offences arising from the practice of their religion. What most distinguished a fervent Tory was the depth of his enmity towards dissenters in general and Ulster presbyterians in particular, and an emotional recklessness of language: in a Dublin coffee-house in 1714, for example, the leading Tory Lord Anglesey declared that 'there was no difference between papists and presbyterians, and that jumbled together they would make an excellent salad for the devil'.[63] This was a colourful but by no means an isolated example. The motto of the parliamentary party was less likely to be 'may the church flourish' so much as 'may dissenters perish'.

It would be wrong, however, to cast too many aspersions on the churchmanship of Irish Tories, for a number were also demonstrably devout Anglicans. They included a few with strong clerical associations: Samuel Dopping, Henry Maxwell and Henry Tennison, three of the most strenuous defenders of the sacramental test in the House of Commons, were all sons of bishops; Marmaduke Coghill, another resolute Tory, and a member who worked in the House for ecclesiastical interests, was a civilian who held the place of registrar of the consistory court of the archbishop of Armagh and was returned for Armagh borough on the episcopal interest.[64] Others had no such familial or vested interest yet still demonstrated a personal piety or genuine concern for the church's welfare. Anglesey, for example, the scourge of presbyterians in and out of parliament, was a generous benefactor of his parish church and a keen supporter of the establishment of charity schools.[65] His cousin Francis Annesley, a barrister and a member

---

63 [Alan Brodrick] to [Thomas Brodrick], 14 June 1714 (Surrey History Centre, Woking, Midleton papers, 1248/3, f. 187).   64 Anderson Saunders to Edward Southwell, 10 July 1707 (Leicestershire R.O., Finch papers, box 4950, bundle 22); same to same, 17 July 1707 (B.L., Southwell papers, Add. MS 9715, f. 176); D.W. Hayton, 'A debate in the Irish House of Commons in 1703: a whiff of Tory grapeshot' in *Parliamentary History*, x (1991), p. 161. For Maxwell's devotion to the church, see also Archbishop King to Edward Southwell, 15 Oct. 1715 (T.C.D., MS 2533, p. 106). On the other hand, Archbishop King observed in 1715, 'I do not remember any High Churchman that contributed much to any of my churches except Sir William Founds [Fownes], who effectually forwarded Wicklow'; King to Bp Stearne, 9 Sept. 1715 (T.C.D., MS 2533, p. 82).   65 Arthur Annesley (later Lord Anglesey) to Arthur Charlett, 12 Apr. 1705 (Bodleian Library, Oxford, MS Ballard 10, ff 167–8); J.B. Leslie, *Ferns clergy and parishes* ... (Dublin, 1936), pp 263–4; Sir Charles S. King (ed.), *A great archbishop of Dublin William King D.D. 1650–1729* ... (London, 1906), pp 296–8;

of both the Irish and English parliaments, acted as an adviser to the Irish bishops in their attempts to secure enabling legislation.[66] Other Tory gentlemen became actively involved in charitable foundations of a strongly Anglican character, such as Edward Southwell and Michael Ward in County Down, Sir John Perceval in County Cork, and the absentee peers Lord Digby in King's County and Lord Weymouth in County Monaghan.[67] And at a parochial level, there are numerous attested examples of Tory squires donating plate and paying for adornments to their parish churches,[68] providing glebe land for the incumbents, and in some cases even rebuilding churches at their own expense, as Lord Massereene did in County Monaghan, and the O'Haras in County Sligo.[69] Despite the caricature of the Anglo-Irish landed elite as roaring 'squireens', wasting their lives in hunting, drinking, swearing and duelling, eighteenth-century Ireland could boast its quota of God-fearing country gentlemen, like the Veseys at Lucan in County Dublin (themselves the descendants of an archbishop), genuinely devoted to the maintenance of the parish church and the moral welfare of its congregation.[70]

Hayton, 'Did Protestantism fail?', p. 186. For Anglesey's willingness to assist the established church through his parliamentary influence, see Francis Annesley to Archbishop King, 2 Sept. 1710 (T.C.D., MSS 1995–2008/1382).   66 See Annesley's letters to Abp King in T.C.D. MSS 1995–2008, and especially Annesley to King, 21 June 1704 (MS 1995–2008/1091); also Richard Mant, *History of the Church of Ireland from the Revolution to the union of the Churches of England and Ireland, January 1 1801* ... (London, 1840), p. 220.   67 For Southwell, see certificate for building charity school at Downpatrick, Nov. 1724 (B.L., Southwell papers, Add. MS 2113, f. 80); John Trotter to Edward Southwell, 30 Sept. 1728 (ibid., f. 110); Southwell to Dean Daniel, 15 Oct. 1738 (ibid., f. 122). For Ward, see *Methods of erecting, supporting and governing charity-schools: with an account of the charity-schools in Ireland* ... (2nd ed., Dublin, 1719), pp 21–2; Robert Ward to Michael Ward, 9 Apr. 1733 (P.R.O.N.I., Castleward papers, D/2092/1/4/1, p. 94); Richard Daniel to same, 3 Feb. 1736/7 (ibid., D/2092/1/5/1, p. 20) For Perceval, see Sir John Perceval to Berkeley Taylor, 25 June 1720 (B.L., Egmont papers, Add. MS 46971, f. 62); R.G. Macpherson (ed.), *The journal of the earl of Egmont; abstract of the trustees' proceedings for establishing the colony of Georgia 1732–1738* (Wormsloe Foundation publications, no. 5, Athens, Georgia, 1962). For Digby, see Howard Erskine-Hill, *The social milieu of Alexander Pope: lives, example and the poetic response* (New Haven, Conn., 1975), ch. 5; For Weymouth, trust act, Carrickmacross school (P.R.O.N.I., Armagh diocesan registry papers, DIO/4/8/11/1); Weymouth to Robert Nelson, 6 July 1700 (S.P.C.K. archives, London, Wanley papers, CS3/1, entry book, p. 52); same to Mr Fitch, 8 Mar. 1705/6 (Longleat House, Bath papers, 179, f. 127).   68 Leslie, *Ferns clergy and parishes*, pp 258–64; idem, *Derry clergy and parishes* ... (Enniskillen, 1937), pp 311–19.   69 Letters of Lord Massereene to Abp King, Bp Pooley of Raphoe and 'Jack' Smith, 2 Nov. 1713, and to Bp Crowe of Cloyne, 4 Nov. 1713 (P.R.O.N.I., Massereene/Foster papers, D/562/195); Bp Downes of Elphin to Kean O'Hara, 16 June [?1718] (ibid., O'Hara papers, T/2812/8/45).   70 T. Hawley to Agmondesham Vesey, 16 June 1708 (N.A., Sarsfield-Vesey Correspondence, 100); Charles Otway, *A tour in Connaught* (Dublin, 1839), p. 7.

There was thus some justification for the Tories to entitle themselves 'the Church party', and to call on the support of the clergy at elections, even if the mainspring of Toryism was a fear of dissenters that was as much political as religious in origin. It may also be argued that making the conflict of church and dissent the centre of political argument, whatever the underlying motive, served to focus enthusiasm for the established church on the part of those who identified themselves as Tories. Of course, the emergence later in the eighteenth century of an evangelical element among the Church of Ireland laity, whose religious commitment was manifested in ostentatious piety and charitable works, would be independent of 'party' politics. It was also largely coincidental that in our period some of the most active patrons of charity schools and other philanthropic enterprises should also have been Tories in their politics. Others, such as Lord Kildare, Lord and Lady Lanesborough, or the Rawdons of Moira (County Down) were either mildly apolitical in this period or even Whiggish in their partisan inclinations.[71] If piety and Toryism did coincide, the interests of the church could only benefit. It was presumably just this kind of nexus which helped to promote the acts against the profanation of the sabbath (1695), profane swearing (1695) gaming (1698, 1711) and lotteries (1707, 1711), and other, unsuccessful, bills of a similar nature. When such moralistic (and overtly Christian) measures were successful in parliament part of the reason may well have lain in the pricking consciences of those Tory M.P.s who had identified themselves publicly as defenders of the church.

Once the Tory party began to decline as a force in Irish politics, the effects were strongly felt by the church. This decline was rapid after 1714. The greater importance of the succession issue in Irish politics made it difficult, indeed almost impossible, for Irish Tories to be jacobites, and the invasion of 1715 and subsequent evidence of Tory conspiracy in England tarred the party as a whole with the suspicion of treason. Tories lost heavily at the Irish general election of 1715, and when it became obvious that the party could no longer compete for power, many of its more moderate (or opportunist) members deserted to the Whigs. For some time, and possibly as late as 1727, there remained a rump of

---

71 For Kildare see Henry Maule to Mrs Jane Bonnell, 31 Dec. 1722 (N.L.I., Smythe of Barbavilla papers (P.C. 435)). For the Lanesboroughs, see Abp King to Alderman Francis Stoyte, 20 Feb. 1704/5 (T.C.D., MS 750/3/1/8); Alderman John Page to Lord Lanesborough, 26 Jan. 1705[/6] (Marsh's Lib., MS Z/2/3/1/1/147); 'Abstract of the account from the corporation of the poor at Bristol for the use of the Irish corporation for the poor ...' (N.L.I., Lane papers, MS 8645/1); religious notebook (ibid.). For the Rawdons, see Thomas Prior to Sir John Rawdon, 20 Jan. 1718[/19], 20, 27 June 1719 (Huntington Library, San Marino, California, Hastings papers, MSS HA 15566, 15579, 15581); S.P.C.K. minute book, 3 Nov. 1720 (S.P.C.K. archives, min. bk 9, p. 121); Sir John Rawdon to Prior, 20 Mar. [?1738] (P.R.O.N.I., Johnston papers, T/1839, pp 41–3); *Methods of erecting, supporting and governing charity-schools ...*, p. 22.

Tories in the Irish parliament, but their numbers were steadily diminishing and indeed their sense of group identity, based on loyalty to the established church and hatred of dissenters, was also fading as the Ulster presbyterians in particular no longer seemed so menacing (following the subscription controversy of 1721–5 and the beginnings of presbyterian emigration out of Ireland to colonial America).[72]

With the decline of Toryism in parliament, and more generally in the country, the Church of Ireland could not speak so loudly in secular politics. Convocation, whose continued existence under Queen Anne had been sustained by the mutual support its high church party and the Tories in parliament gave each other, paid the price of over-politicisation and was not called again after the accession of George I. The ecclesiastical hierarchy, which soon became predominantly Whiggish or low church in complexion as the old high church bishops died off and were replaced by more politically accommodating appointees, came to terms with the Hanoverian regime, and, in the person of Archbishop Boulter of Armagh (1725–42) enjoyed a significant influence in both government and parliament. Indeed, there were on average far more statutes passed in favour of the church after 1715 than in the parliaments of 1692–1713, including public acts facilitating the union and division of parishes (1715, 1723, 1735), confirming royal grants from the first fruits (1715), securing advowsons (1719), enabling the better maintenance of curates (1719, 1728, 1729), facilitating the restitution of impropriations (1719), assisting clergy to reside (1721), repairing churches (1725, 1729), improving church lands (1725, 1735), encouraging the recovery of tithes (1728), and improving livings (1728); and a battery or private measures, among them acts to enable the erection of the Green Coat School and workhouse in Cork. But overwhelmingly this was a legislative programme devised by the government and the House of Lords rather than the Commons, and much of its success must be attributed to the commitment and energy of Boulter and his colleagues on the episcopal bench. Moreover, the House of Commons did not always nod through bills of this nature: in 1732, for example one bill from the Lords to improve clerical residence was allowed to drop in the Commons, while another, to continue the act for the division of parishes, was thrown out on a division. From time to time there were even outbreaks of open hostility between clergy and laity, usually on issues with financial implications. In 1720 a bill to provide more glebe land for parish incumbents was rejected in the Commons on the rather Whiggish grounds that it would make more clerical freeholders to vote in parliamentary

72 D.W. Hayton, 'The beginnings of the "undertaker system" ' in Thomas Bartlett and D.W. Hayton (eds), *Penal era and golden age: essays in Irish history 1690–1800* (Belfast, 1979), pp 45–6; Patrick McNally, 'The Hanoverian accession and the Tory party in Ireland' in *Parliamentary History*, xiv (1995), pp 263–83.

elections, but the low church Archbishop Synge of Tuam reported that the real reason was 'because many, even Churchmen, are of the opinion that the clergy have too much already'.[73] A year later another Whig bishop wrote that the Commons 'will not suffer any church bill to pass that may do us good'.[74] Not surprisingly, tithes were a particular source of friction, and the condemnation by the House of Commons in 1736 of the hotly disputed 'tithe of agistment' (levied on pasture, and only recognised in 1722 by a decision in the Exchequer) was enough to provoke Swift to one of his bitterest political satires, in which the leading M.P.s opposed to the tithe were ridiculed as members of the 'Legion Club'.[75] Thus although both houses of parliament continued to resist attempts to repeal the test, in 1719, 1731 and 1733, the interests of the church were only patchily maintained under the Hanoverians; indeed, the hotter Tories of Anne's reign would have regarded the toleration act of 1719, the various indemnity acts to cover infringements of the sacramental test, and the statutory indulgence afforded to Quakers to 'affirm' solemnly instead of having to take oaths, as undermining the integrity of the confessional state they had helped to construct.

But while a self-consciously 'church party' declined after 1714 and eventually disappeared in the 1730s, a distinctively Anglican political interest did survive into the middle of the eighteenth century. We can trace its presence in the activities of particular individuals, who continued to promote bills in the Irish House of Commons which would advance the interests of the church, or the moral reformation of the kingdom: Henry Maxwell, for example, who in 1725 successfully piloted through the Commons an act for the regulation of free schools, and Serjeant Richard Bettesworth, who in the same session was unsuccessful in his attempt to introduce a measure for the better maintenance of curates (though he later fell out with Swift on the issue of tithe).[76] Men like these were also interested, more broadly, in the 'improvement' of Ireland, through fostering trade and manufactures, building roads and canals, and developing agriculture, as well as educating the people in literacy, numeracy, and the habits of industry. Their enthusiasm for economic development sometimes brought them up against the vested interests of the clergy (as in the

---

73 Abp Synge of Tuam to Abp Wake (Christ Church, Wake papers, Arch. W. Epist. 13, quoted in L.A. Landa, *Swift and the Church of Ireland* (Oxford, 1954), p. 98).   74 Bp Godwin of Kilmore to Abp Wake, 23 Dec. 1721 (Christ Church, Wake papers Arch. W. Epist. 13, quoted in Landa, *Swift and the Church of Ireland*, p. 98).   75 Mant, *History of the Church of Ireland*, pp 554–5; Landa, *Swift and the Church of Ireland*, pp 135–50; Irvin Ehrenpreis, *Swift: the man, his works, and the age* (3 vols, London, 1962–83), iii, pp 828–31. One of Mrs Bonnell's many pious female correspondents wrote to her from County Armagh in October 1736, 'We have nothing among us now but bitter railing at all clergy and religion' (Mrs Jane Hamilton to Mrs Bonnell, 11 Oct. 1736 (N.L.I., Smythe of Barbavilla papers (P.C. 435)).   76 Ehrenpreis, *Swift*, iii, 768–71; Andrew Carpenter (ed.), *Verse in English from eighteenth-century Ireland* (Cork, 1998), p. 227.

various bills brought into parliament to exempt flax growers from tithe), but the general drive for improvement had a strong moral and religious basis. The charity and charter schools which were to bring up a generation of industrious boys and girls, taught their charges not merely reading, writing, and weaving, but the catechism of the established church. Protestantism was an essential concomitant of 'improvement'. The connexion is plainly visible in the careers of some of the most notable 'improvers' of the 1720s and 30s: the pamphleteers Arthur Dobbs, David Bindon and Henry Maxwell, all three of whom were active both in the press and in the Irish House of Commons;[77] and their fellow parliamentarians Richard Bettesworth, David Chaigneau, Sir Richard Cox, Thomas Lehunte, Sir John Rawdon, Thomas Trotter and Michael Ward, whose names can be found on drafting committees, or presenting bills to parliament for the encouragement of trade, the relief of the poor, or the regulation of abuses in the activities of government or the market.

The constructive 'patriotism' of these economic improvers, concerned above all for the betterment of Ireland, could sometimes lurch over into the more traditional, Anglophobic kind of political 'patriotism' associated with parliamentary oppositionists, with which it undoubtedly shared some common features: a concern for the preservation of *Irish* interests against economic oppression from Westminster, actual or potential, and a distaste for political corruption, which would undermine the public virtue necessary for the full and proper development of the kingdom. In this respect the 'patriot' interest formed a natural destination for those M.P.s whose families had once been Tories, and who since 1715 had been in permanent opposition. But there was more to this kind of 'patriotism' than simply hatred of administration, and indeed it drew in several establishment figures: Maxwell and Trotter, henchmen of Speaker Conolly (1715–29); Bettesworth and Lehunte, both stalwarts of the Court party in the 1730s, Ward, a justice of King's Bench. A strong common feature was personal religiosity and commitment to the established church: Trotter, a civilian and vicar-general of Dublin diocese; Maxwell, the bishop's son; Rawdon and Ward, the pious, paternalistic landlords who sought to encourage not only the economic advancement but the moral health of their tenants; and Ward's cousin Arthur Dobbs, the future governor of North Carolina, who combined a militant Protestantism with a remarkably enlightened view of the value of religious toleration to social progress. The distinctively Anglican tinge to their

---

77 For these writers in general, see Caroline Robbins, *The eighteenth-century common-wealthman* (Cambridge, Mass., 1959), pp 149–52, 157–9; Patrick Kelly, 'The politics of political economy in mid-eighteenth-century Ireland' in S.J. Connolly (ed.), *Political ideas in eighteenth-century Ireland* (Dublin, 2000), pp 105–29; and Gerard McCoy, 'Local political culture in the Hanoverian empire: the case of Ireland, 1714–60' (D.Phil. thesis, Oxford, 1994). For Dobbs in particular, Desmond Clarke, *Arthur Dobbs esquire 1689–1765* ... (Chapel

economic views is further highlighted if we consider the company they kept: the clergyman pamphleteer Samuel Madden, whose writings on improvement were every bit as prolific as those of Bindon or Dobbs; Bishop Henry Maule, the charity-school enthusiast; Walter Harris and his friends in the Physico-Historical Society, whose writings identified Protestantism with improvement; and Thomas Prior, formerly an agent for the Rawdons and active in promoting educational initiatives before publishing his famous attacks on absenteeism and helping to set up what became the Royal Dublin Society.[78]

There was in fact considerable overlap between these various circles of social 'improvers': the 'patriots' in parliament bringing forward legislative measures to promote prosperity and eradicate corruption; the pamphleteers and amateur scientists and agronomists who through the press and through their learned societies were arguing for change and seeking to popularise the latest technical discoveries; and the philanthropic and inveterately public-spirited individuals who involved themselves in voluntary enterprises of social reform, founding schools, almshouses, workhouses and hospitals. What united them was the religious framework in which they operated. In all these enterprises we may find clergymen active alongside the laity; and all were animated by a spirit of 'improvement' which combined material gain with moral edification.

IV

The Anglican 'confessional state' as it had emerged in the early eighteenth century was more extensive than an 'ascendancy', even if it fell a little short of a complete monopoly at borough and parish level. One interpretation would see it as in essence a political system, designed for political ends. But the religious element of the 'confessional state' was more than surface colouring. Admittedly the Church of Ireland laity as a body were not anxious to use their privileges to assist the church itself or to forward its ideals; for many, if not most, of those who benefited, their Anglicanism was in this context little more than a necessary qualification for political rights. The short-lived Tory party in the Irish parliament, the most obvious example of a political movement embodying religious, or at least sectarian loyalties, was concerned to defend the church as a bastion of political power rather than advance its material interests or proselytise its beliefs. Those who took a more constructive approach to the church's problems were very much a minority, but paradoxically they seem to

Hill, N. Carolina, 1957).   78 Robbins, *Eighteenth-century commonwealthman*, p. 157; T.C. Barnard, 'Protestants and the Irish language, c.1675–1725' in *Journal of Ecclesiastical History*, xlv (1993), pp 263–5; Thomas Prior to Sir John Rawdon, 20 June 1719 (Huntington Lib., Hastings papers, HA15579); Clarke, *Thomas Prior*.

have become a more influential minority as time went by and the divisions within Irish Protestant politics became less obviously based on religious allegiances. An essentially Anglican pietism became a significant element in general calls for the 'improvement' of Ireland which attracted social theorists, philanthropists, and a new generation of parliamentary 'patriots'.

Perhaps it was in the 'voluntary sector' of private benevolence that the expanding 'public sphere' in the first half of the eighteenth century gave the greatest opportunity to concerned and pious Anglican laymen to play a useful part in public life. Organised, institutionalised, and communal, the charitable societies, boards and trusts, and the scientific and antiquarian fraternities provided a range of activities and gratifications to those participating in them: the performance of their Christian duty (or perhaps only the salving of conscience), the exercise of public virtue, the assertion of power, the opportunity to establish and cultivate social status, even the simple pleasures of polite social intercourse. On the other hand, these various bodies were essentially sectarian rather than communal, and they were also socially exclusive, attracting the eighteenth-century equivalent of 'the great and the good', peers, baronets, members of parliament, privy councillors, gentlemen and ladies, aldermen, and of course bishops, deans, and archdeacons. The less well-to-do might participate, but only through subscriptions and donations. In this respect, at least, Protestant domination of the expanding 'public sphere' in Ireland may properly be regarded as an 'ascendancy'; snobbish, no doubt, and smugly self-referential, but perhaps a rather more attractive and certainly a more obviously *Anglican* phenomenon than the reactionary 'ascendancy' that the political changes of the late eighteenth century were to redefine and ultimately to demolish.

5

Lay spirituality and worship, 1558–1750: holy books and godly readers

Raymond Gillespie

In 1683 Bishop Edward Wetenhall of Cork took up his pen to describe the spiritual condition of his age. He portrayed a laity not so much hostile to the Church of Ireland as apathetic. He complained of those who 'too often heedlessly mutter over' prayers read by the minister 'with what understanding appears (commonly) by their repeating what they should not (the ministers part, absolutions etc), as well as what they should'. During lessons they whispered and observed strangers or their neighbours and the sermon had barely begun before 'some have plainly and designedly composed themselves for sleep' while others censured the preacher or were engaged in 'mutual caresses'.[1] Others concurred. The archbishop of Dublin, Narcissus Marsh, complained in the 1690s that there was 'whispering, sleeping or gazing about on everyone that comes in' during worship and according to the London bookseller, John Dunton, people in the Dublin churches happily wandered about the church during the service.[2] However not all failed the clerical test of their spiritual state. A few years after Wetenhall's comments the archdeacon of Armagh, William Hamilton, prepared one of the earliest pieces of Protestant hagiography extant in Ireland. The subject was the late comptroller general, James Bonnell. Bonnell was the sort of layman of whom clergy approved. He attended his parish church on Sunday and received the sacrament after careful preparation throughout the week. On weekdays he also attended worship, read the Bible and had an active prayer life. Bonnell's surviving prayers printed by Hamilton indicate a man who took the practice of his religion seriously with much of his devotion concentrated on confession and preparation for the Sunday Eucharist.[3]

---

1 Edward Wetenhall, *A practical and plain discourse of the form of godliness visible in the present age* (Dublin, 1683), pp 111–12. 2 *A charge given by Narcissus Marsh, lord archbishop of Dublin, to the clergy of the province of Leinster* (Dublin, 1694), p. 25; Edward Mac Lysaght, *Irish life in the seventeenth century* (3rd edn, Shannon, 1969), p. 381. 3 William Hamilton, *The life of James Bonnell, late accomptant general of Ireland* (3rd edn, London, 1703). For other

There is little doubt which of these two forms of religious practice the professional representatives of the institutional church approved of. In the late seventeenth century the influence of the Caroline divines was growing in Ireland, first in Dublin and later in the provinces, with a consequent emphasis on the Eucharist and the orderly conduct of public worship. Manuals, such as that of Wetenhall, instructing the laity on how to behave in the formal setting of worship became more common and clerical toleration of aberrant behaviour declined. However, that should not blind us to the fact that the clerical construction of religiosity was only one possibility among many articulations of spirituality. Many who sat in the pew devised a set of ideas about God and their relationship to Him which made sense in the world which they inhabited but these were informed by the teachings of the church to which they belonged. Such conceptions were often based on the same assumptions as those of the formally educated clergy but were articulated in a rather different way. They were informed by their reading, especially of the Bible, and their experience of worship but those ideas were rarely formally systematised in a formal philosophical system as clerical thought often was.[4]

Such differences often turned on the divergence between experience and the theoretical construction of theological systems. A case in point is the understanding of how God worked in the world. The early seventeenth-century Church of Ireland, heavily influenced by the ideas of Calvinism, saw God working directly in the world through special providences which could be interpreted by individuals. In the later part of that century theologians drew back from that understanding, afraid of the highly individualistic form of sectarian religion which the 1640s and 1650s had produced. Instead they preferred to emphasise the importance of general providence which God used to govern the world. The result was a reduced emphasis on the importance of the miraculous. The age of miracles had passed with the early church 'and no longer occurred, their being not the like use or occasion for them'. What was now required was sound doctrine and edification.[5] However in 1665 and 1666 a minor Wexford landowner and member of the Church of Ireland, Valentine Greatrix, began effecting a series of miraculous cures. He preached no new doctrine but claimed his powers came from God through 'an impulse or strange persuasion in my own mind ... which did very frequently suggest to me that

positive comments about behaviour at worship, F.R. Bolton, *The Caroline tradition of the Church of Ireland* (London, 1958), pp 144–5, 148. 4 Raymond Gillespie, 'The religion of Irish Protestants: a view from the laity' in Alan Ford, James McGuire and Kenneth Milne (eds), *As by law established: the Church of Ireland since the Reformation* (Dublin, 1995), pp 89–99 and more generally, Raymond Gillespie, *Devoted people: belief and religion in early modern Ireland* (Manchester, 1997). 5 Henry Leslie, *A discourse of praying with the spirit* (London, 1660), pp 7–8; Edward Nicholson, *An answer to Mr Asgill's book* (Dublin, 1702), pp 16–17.

there was bestowed on me the gift of curing the king's evil'. His method of healing emphasised its divine origin for he used spittle as in Matthew 7:33 or Mark 8:23 and used the words 'God almighty heal thee for His mercy's sake' in the curing ritual. Despite his profession of orthodoxy he was ordered by Michael Boyle, archbishop of Dublin, to stop his activities but he continued with a large measure of popular support. In Cork Lord Broghill, for instance, declared after witnessing Greatrix's activities 'I do now believe he can do miracles'. The result was, as Greatrix recorded, 'I have made the greatest faction and distraction between clergy and laymen than anyone these 1,000 years'.[6] The experience of the power of God manifested through Greatrix's activities was valued by many laity above the abstractions of theology. However at no time did Greatrix renounce his membership of the Church of Ireland. He claimed his activities were not contrary to its teachings and that he had absorbed his ideas from the clergy. His was a lay spirituality constructed from ideas acquired from clerical sources.

Such a focus on the experience of the laity in their construction of a spirituality presents considerable analytical problems for the historian. Such a spirituality was rarely articulated into a formal theological system. It was intended not to be neat but to be workable and as such could have many loose ends. Moreover there could be as many spiritualities as there were individuals which means their common experience is not easily reconstructed. There were obvious divergences between women and men and the educated and the illiterate. From the surviving evidence four individuals who have left some personal record of their religious belief can be selected to stand for many others. The first is Eleanor Stringer, the wife of a carpenter from Cork. In 1642 when asked by a Catholic priest what religion she was she replied, 'she was of that religion wherein she had been bred and would live and die'.[7] The second individual, a Mr Dean, was also from Cork. In 1645 when he asked some of the Catholic Irish rebels why he was being persecuted

> they answered ... he was a Protestant and a Roundhead. He replied I take it upon my death I know not what those words mean but I am of the religion that both the king and the lord lieutenant general of Ireland profess which is the true Protestant religion and if I suffer I know not what I die for ...[8]

The third person is Henry Blaney, a Monaghan landlord, who told rebels in 1641 'I am of the true church and so assured of my salvation. That though you would spare my life yet I will not alter my faith'.[9] The final example of religious

6 For the episode, Gillespie, *Devoted people*, pp 120–1.   7 T.C.D., MS 826, f. 244.   8 T.C.D., MS 826, f. 299.   9 T.C.D., MS 834, f. 143.

discussion comes some years later in 1686 when two Church of Ireland members of the Irish gentry, Henry Piers, a Westmeath landowner, and Sir James Leigh, talked about religion. Leigh suggested that saints and angels could intercede with God and could be prayed to. Piers told him that this was a ridiculous idea. He said saints and angels could not hear our prayers. Leigh retorted that 'in this I was contrary to our own divinity. I told him that I had never met with anything in any of our divines that would favour the doctrine'. He advanced the proposition based on Matthew 11.28 that Christ invited those who were burdened to come to Him for rest, 'but find not that he invites any to address in this case to His mother or any other saint'. He quoted Augustine to support the case. Leigh countered by dismissing Augustine as a Catholic and replied to the text from Matthew with one from Paul. The discussion became confused and ended when the men agreed to consult a bishop when next they were in Dublin.[10] For some religion was a matter of custom, for others loyalty and for yet others a matter of conviction. For some it was a clearly defined set of doctrines and for others a matter of debate and doctrinal uncertainty.

However, devotion was not entirely shaped in an individualistic way. It was expressed in common forms such as worship. One such common form can be found in the tacit agreements which people brought to the interpretation of key texts such as the Prayer Book or the Bible and how they shaped their lives around those interpretations. Indeed for many of those who belonged to the Church of Ireland in the seventeenth and eighteenth centuries, books lay at the core of their devotional life. The reform movements of the sixteenth century had collapsed a wide range of sacramental and devotional practices, many sanctioned only by custom, into two sacraments, a range of devotional activities set out in the Book of Common Prayer and the reading of the Bible to understand Divine will. This emphasis on books took hold only slowly and was limited by problems of low literacy levels and difficulties in the distribution of printed works. It did not entirely displace older means of encouraging devotion and setting an orthodox framework of interpretation within which the devout could understand what they had read. Books and reading, however, did become a central part of shaping devotional lives of members of the early modern Church of Ireland. Indeed much of the educational work of the late seventeenth and early eighteenth centuries by the Church of Ireland clergy was focused on establishing functional literacy among the members of the church. In the 1660s the young James Barry of Dublin, awakened to a sense of religion, described his experience as 'I became very bookish, looking into almost every book wherever I came to try whither I could meet with any help which might forward me in my new trade of religion'. He retired to his room to read and pray, his prayers being shaped by his reading since 'to my course of reading and

10 Armagh Public Library, Dopping MSS, no. 50.

praying by those forms of prayer in the Common Prayer Book and the *Practice of piety* I joined very strict and severe fasting'. When doubts assailed him both the parish clergy and the bishop recommended further books for reading.[11]

Bishops and other clergy distributed cheap pious books to their flock and pious laymen followed their example. James Bonnell, for example, according to his contemporary biographer 'was continually dispersing good books among young people, his clerks and poor families'.[12] However not all might come into contact with print in this direct way. The contents of books might be encountered orally. For those who attended church the reading of the Bible was an important part of the liturgy. The godly were also expected to share what they read. The rules laid down for the Societies for the Reformation of Manners established in Dublin in the 1690s provided that while they waited for the meeting to begin the godly were to 'discourse of what sermons they have heard, what good books they have seen and read or upon any other pious subject'.[13] Others would see books in another form as they watched or took part in the liturgies set out in the Book of Common Prayer either on a weekly basis or more occasionally in baptisms, marriages or burials.

Thus we might understand the spiritual lives of the Church of Ireland laity in seventeenth- and eighteenth- century Ireland as the result of the reading of key texts agreeing on their meaning through a series on micro-societies. Two of the most important texts were the Prayer Book and the Bible. Reading in these texts does not imply literacy, although an increasing number of people could decode the symbols which reading involved, since both texts appeared in many forms. In many ways these two key texts diffused themselves into a wide range of human experience and their meaning for everyday life was decoded.

I

Perhaps the text which most influenced the lives of members of the Church of Ireland in the early modern period was the Bible. The Bible was a text which was not confined to the closet or study for it clearly had a public function when read in church or in family worship and hence would be encountered by those who were both literate and illiterate or who could not read for some other reason.[14] The blind aunts of James Ussher, the future archbishop of Armagh,

---

11 James Barry, *A reviving cordial for a sin-sick despairing soul in the time of temptation* (2nd ed? Edinburgh, 1722), pp 22–4, 31, 36.   12 Raymond Gillespie, 'Circulation of print' in *Studia Hibernica* no. 29 (1995–7), pp 51–2; Hamilton, *Life of James Bonnell*, p. 213.   13 B. Scroggs, *A sermon preached before the religious societies in the city of Dublin on the 29th of September 1695* (Dublin, 1695), p. 39.   14 For a much fuller discussion of the role of the Bible, Raymond Gillespie, 'Reading the Bible in seventeenth-century Ireland' in Bernadette Cunningham and

were said to have 'such tenacious memories' that whatever they heard of scripture 'they always retained and became such proficients that they were able to repeat much of the Bible by heart'.[15] Moreover it also served as a symbol of the importance of the individual reading and judgement within the belief system of Church of Ireland laity. It was displayed in churches and at least some of laity carried their Bibles with them to church.[16] Most importantly the Bible was intended as a text which would be read by an individual as a standard of belief and a way of increasing religious understanding of the world. As the early seventeenth-century polemicist Barnaby Rich put it 'if thou hearest tell of a vision or miracles ... bring them to the touchstone and compare them with the word of God'.[17]

For some the Bible was the only book which they owned while others owned several copies as part of a larger library.[18] Since the printing of Bibles was restricted most of the Bibles owned by the members of the Church of Ireland were imported from England although a few may have been illegal imports from Holland. In 1698 one Dublin merchant, sensing a profitable line, tried to break the London monopoly by printing a New Testament in Dublin but the enterprise was stopped.[19] It was 1714 before a Dublin edition of the Bible appeared but after that ten Dublin printings of the complete Bible had appeared by 1750 and eight editions of the New Testament appeared over the same period. There were certainly complaints about the problems of obtaining cheap Bibles in eighteenth century Ireland but this does not seem to have hindered its circulation greatly.[20] In the 1620s a full Bible could be had for 8s. in Dublin and a New Testament for 3s. although cheaper editions were also available.[21] Over time prices seem not to have risen. A second hand market may also have existed since even lower prices are recorded. Giving Bibles as presents and as legacies in wills was also common, further increasing the circulation of the text.[22] Such widespread distribution of the text meant it was encountered in many ways. It was, for example, widely used to teach children to read and seventeenth-century autobiographies do record that of those who learnt to read many used the Bible.[23] Even basic readers, such as hornbooks or primers, used Biblical short texts to teach reading.

Máire Kennedy (eds), *The experience of reading: Irish historical perspectives* (Dublin, 1999), pp 10–38.   **15** Richard Parr, *The life of the most reverend father in God James Usher* (London, 1686), p. 2.   **16** [Robert Ware], *The second part of foxes and firebrands* (Dublin, 1683), p. 112. **17** Barnaby Rich, *A short survey of Ireland* (London, 1609), p. 55.   **18** Gillespie, 'Reading the Bible', p. 14.   **19** Mary Pollard, *Dublin's trade in books* (Oxford, 1989), pp 9–10.   **20** Henry Maule, *Pietas Corcagiensis* (Dublin, 1721), p. 8; William King, *A discourse on the inventions of men in the worship of God* (Dublin, 1694), pp 89–90; Scott Mandlebrote, 'John Baskett, the Dublin booksellers and the printing of the Bible' in A. Hunt, G. Mandelbrote and A. Shell (eds), *The book trade and its customers* (Winchester, 1997), p. 117.   **21** Raymond Gillespie, 'Irish printing in the seventeenth century' in *Ir. Econ. Soc. Hist.* xv (1988), p. 88.   **22** Gillespie, 'Reading the Bible', p. 14.   **23** C.S. King (ed.), *A great archbishop of Dublin* (London, 1908), p. 3; Parr *Life*

Reactions by members of the Church of Ireland to reading the Bible varied dramatically. At one level Ezekiel Hopkins, the late-seventeenth-century bishop of Derry, commented that some of his congregation had stopped reading the Bible since it 'posseseth them with strange fears and fills them with incredible terrors. It raiseth up the dreadful apparition of hell and the wrath of God makes then a terror to themselves'.[24] Another bishop noted that children in his diocese read the Bible for stories of wars or fabulous occurrences such as 'the strength of Sampson, the bigness of Goliath and the age of Methuselah' rather than for moral stories.[25] Such examples illustrate the diverse ways in which the Bible could be read among members of the Church of Ireland. Some read it simply for the story. In the early seventeenth century Sir Charles Calthorpe, an Irish judge, filled his commonplace book with genealogies constructed from the Old Testament on the basis of his Bible reading and the pious James Bonnell attempted to conflate the gospels into a narrative life of Christ.[26] Other members of the Church of Ireland adopted a more atomistic reading of the Bible, reading not for the plot but analysing individual verses for their meaning.[27] Yet others might read the Bible more meditatively. Alice Wandesford, the daughter of the Irish lord deputy in the 1630s, recorded that on reading Luke 2:49 she fell into a deep meditation on her ignorance and her desire for salvation.[28] Others might well read the Biblical text not for history or spiritual enlightenment but for moral guidance. What is important about these different styles of reading was that they were not mutually exclusive. An attentive reader might well deploy all these strategies for reading the Bible.

The balance between the different strategies clearly depended on theological and cultural background. A person who only heard the Bible read would have understood it in a different way to one who examined the printed text minutely. Moreover the balance between reading strategies was also influenced by political concerns. While the more godly laity of the early seventeenth century might read verse by verse this was discouraged by the late seventeenth century since it could produce the sort of heterodox ideas which had flourished in England in the 1650s. An understanding of text which derived moral meanings was encouraged. The Bible and the way in which it was read was not left to chance. Sermons and other godly books, such as the catechism, tried to inculcate into the laity a correct way of reading to prevent the over exercise of enthusiasm and as a result being carried away by the language of scripture without appreciating its meaning, as Henry Dodwell warned in the 1670s. The Church of Ireland way

of Ussher, p. 3; T.C.D., MS 1050, p. 14. **24** *The works of the rev. and learned Ezekiel Hopkins, lord bishop of Londonderry* (London, 1710), p. 710. **25** Samuel Foley, *An exhortation to the inhabitants of Down and Connor concerning the education of their children* (Dublin, 1695), pp 19–20. **26** T.C.D., MS 676, pp 323–9; Hamilton, *Life of Bonnell*, p. xiii. **27** Gillespie, 'Reading the Bible', p. 23–4. **28** Charles Jackson (ed.), *The autobiography of Mrs Alice*

was that Bible reading 'should be performed with gravity and a principal attention to the coherence of things and the junctures of the discourse which is of special use in discovering the true sense of the Scriptures'.[29] The success of these activities is difficult to measure but for many they probably proved a useful guide for what one author called 'the hard places' of scripture.[30]

II

Reading and hearing the Bible certainly acted as a devotional aid to many members of the Church of Ireland in the early modern period but it also served to place the church within a wider Protestant tradition in which the supremacy of the Bible was opposed to the corporate tradition of the Catholic church. However the experience that convinced most that they were not simply Protestants but members of the Church of Ireland, with links to the Church of England, was their encounter with the Book of Common Prayer. The reading and use of this text served to shape a specifically Church of Ireland identity. The occasional services such as those for baptism, marriage and burial were not only familiar to members of the church but encompassed powerful rituals. For many of the laity the failure of the clergy to use those rituals was a source of concern. In 1634, for instance, it was objected that one minister in Wicklow refused to bury his parishioners with the appropriate ritual arguing that 'they [the dead] need not any such ceremony in their burial, that prayers were for the living and not for the dead'. The consequence of this behaviour was that 'divers English Protestants have forborne their habitations within that parish saying they desire to live where they may be buried like men and not like dogs'.[31] Again in the Dublin parish of St John parishioners in the 1660s complained that their incumbent had failed to baptise children and administer holy communion.[32] The significance of the rituals in the Book of Common Prayer as a mark of Church of Ireland identity made those rituals sensitive areas which were contested between the different denominational groups in Ireland. Catholics objected to their use and at the burial of James Barnewell's mother at Balrothery in 1608, assaulted the minister reading the burial service and 'struck the Book of Common Prayer from his hand and trod it disdainfully under foot'.[33] A similar incident seems to have taken place at Kilmallock in 1685 when the Church of Ireland minister was assaulted by a young Catholic priest while he was reading the burial service.[34] As Protestant dissent grew more confident in

Thornton (Durham, 1875), p. 13.   **29** Francis de Sales, *An introduction to the devout life*, ed. Henry Dodwell (Dublin, 1673), sig. b4.   **30** Gillespie, 'Reading the Bible', pp 26–7. **31** B.L., Harley MS 4297, f. 111v.   **32** R.C.B., C6/1/7/2, ff 161v, 172.   **33** Historical Manuscripts Commission, *Report on the manuscripts of the earl of Egmont* (2 vols, London, 1905–9), i, p. 33.   **34** Historical Manuscripts Commission, *Calendar of the manuscripts of the*

the late seventeenth century and entered into controversy with the Church of Ireland the matters of debate were not those of high theology but rather the rituals associated with the Book of Common Prayer. Thus in the public debate between the presbyterians and Bishop Leslie at Belfast in 1636 the issues for debate included kneeling at Communion and the ritual of the Common Prayer Book.[35] The same issues were to reappear, together with others such as the sign of the cross at baptism, 'body worship' and the legality of singing, in the debate between William King, bishop of Derry and the presbyterians in the 1690s.[36]

The Book of Common Prayer was therefore a central text in shaping not only the worship of the Church of Ireland but also providing a sense of corporate identity. The text itself was identical to that of the Church of England and its history similar.[37] The first Edwardian book was certainly used in Ireland and an edition was printed in Dublin in 1551. The second Edwardian Prayer Book however does not seem to have been in use for long enough to be adopted in Ireland. Certainly in 1553 when John Bale was consecrated bishop of Ossory in Christ Church cathedral, Dublin, the second Edwardian Prayer Book was not used since it had not been authorised for Ireland.[38] Following the reign of Mary the Elizabethan Prayer Book was adopted in Ireland in 1560 and remained the standard of Church of Ireland worship until it was proscribed by the parliamentarian regime in 1647 although it does seem to have been used occasionally throughout the 1650s. In a significant deviation from the English norm the Latin version of the Prayer Book was authorised for use in Irish parish churches where English was not spoken whereas in England the Latin text was confined to non-parochial uses. The English Restoration Book of Common Prayer was again adopted in its entirety by the Irish church and was retained until disestablishment. Additional services were added to meet specifically Irish needs, most importantly the thanksgiving for 23 October and a liturgy for the reconsecration of churches were added, though not always included in the published Book of Common Prayer.[39] Liturgies for specific occasions, such as fasts and thanksgivings, tended to be printed separately and distributed to individual bishops for use in their dioceses.[40]

It seems that the Book of Common Prayer was widely diffused within the Irish church. The visitation returns of the 1630s suggest that most functioning churches had a copy. In the early 1640s reports of its destruction as a mark of

marquess of Ormonde new series (8 vols, 1902–20), vii, pp 346–7, 355, 364.   35 J.S. Reid, History of the Presbyterian church in Ireland (3 vols, Belfast, 1867), i, pp 523–42.   36 Phil Kilroy, Protestant dissent and controversy in Ireland, 1660–1714 (Cork, 1994), pp 175–80. 37 The standard history remains William Reeves, The Book of Common Prayer according to the use of the Church of Ireland: its history and sanction (Dublin, 1871).   38 John Happé and John King (eds), The vocacyon of John Bale (New York, 1990), p. 52.   39 Harry Boone Porter, Jeremy Taylor, liturgist (London, 1979), pp 146–53.   40 T.C.D., MS 1995–2008/147.

Protestantism come from Waterford, Cavan, Kilkenny and Westmeath.[41] Unlike
the Bible the Dublin presses could produce editions of the Book of Common
Prayer. Editions appeared in 1551, 1621, 1637, 1665, 1666, 1668, 1680 and 1700.
Between 1701 and 1750 a further thirty one reprints issued from the Dublin
presses. An Irish translation appeared in 1608 and this was still in use among
Highland Scots in Ulster in the 1690s.[42] Since the text was the same as the
service book for the Church of England imports from England were a strong
possibility. Indeed according to Archbishop King in 1715 'our Prayer Books are
generally printed in England'.[43] The size of Irish editions and the scale of
English imports can only be matters of speculation. However in the 1560s there
are indications that there was a significant trade in Books of Common Prayer
between Ireland and England. In 1560 863 copies were sent to Ireland and by
1566 another 600 copies had been consigned to Humphry Powell, the queen's
printer in Dublin.[44] By the 1580s the Prayer Book in its Latin form seems to
have been fairly widely disseminated but whether or not it was read is a more
complex question. One observer, Anthony Trollop, commented in the 1580s
that many Catholic clergy forced to go to church 'carry with them a book in
Latin of the Common Prayer' which they used a prop from their sermons but
certainly did not use for other rituals.[45]

As distribution mechanisms for print developed in the seventeenth century
so the availability of the text grew. One indication of this is that in the early
seventeenth-century churches, such as St John's in Dublin, repaired their one
copy of the Bible and the Common Prayer on a number of occasions while in
the latter half of the century they simply bought new copies.[46] By the middle of
the eighteenth century a few of the wealthier prostitutes admitted to the
Magdalene Asylum in Dublin carried copies of the Book of Common Prayer
with them but it had not yet become part of the baggage of the poor.[47]

As with the Bible economies of scale ensured that the volume could be made
available relatively cheaply. About 1620 the communion book, probably
containing the weekly services, was available in Dublin in three formats, quarto,
octavo and sextodecimo. Such formats lent themselves to portability and
cheapness, prices ranging from 2s. 4d. to 5s.[48] Larger formats also existed for
churches in a bewildering range of styles and costs. The cathedral church of

---

41 T.C.D., MS 820, f. 211; MS 832, f. 69; MS 812, f. 213v; MS 817, f. 148v.   **42** T.C.D., MS
1995–2008/366, 407.   **43** Richard Mant, *History of the Church of Ireland from the Revolution
to the union of the Churches of England and Ireland* (London, 1840), p. 254.   **44** D.B. Quinn,
'Information about Dublin printers 1556–1573 in English financial records' in *Irish Book
Lover* xxviii (1942), p. 113; Northampton Record Office, Fitzwilliam of Milton MSS, Irish
no. 64, f. 133.   **45** W.M. Brady (ed.), *State papers concerning the Irish church in the time of
Queen Elizabeth* (London, 1868), pp 39, 118.   **46** Gillespie, 'Circulation of print', p. 31.
47 R.C.B., MS 551/1/1, nos. 83, 114, 123, 127.   **48** Gillespie, 'Irish printing', p. 88. The
parish of St Werburgh's paid 3s. 6d. and 5s. in 1585 and 1593 for copies R.C.B.,

Cloyne paid £1. 2s. 0d. for two Common Prayer Books in 1667 but the Dublin parish of St Michael's could get two copies for 4s. 6d. by 1670. The more normal cost for a church copy of the Book of Common Prayer in the late seventeenth century lay between 6s. and 10s. depending on the edition and the quality of the binding.[49] While price trends are difficult to gauge on the basis of a small sample of prices it does seem that, if anything, prices fell over the seventeenth century as Books of Common Prayer became more readily available.

However, price was not the only variable in the circulation of the text. Books of Common Prayer also made fashionable and practical presents. Bishops, such as Dives Downes of Cork, dispensed copies at confirmations and at parochial visits and copies certainly passed through wills.[50] Similarly in the eighteenth century charity schools often gave presents of Prayer Books to those children leaving the school to take up a trade and those leaving the Magdalene Asylum in Dublin in the 1760s and 1770s were all give the Prayer Book as well as other godly works.[51] Certainly by the middle of the eighteenth century the Book of Common Prayer was a commonplace in most houses of the middle and upper reaches of Irish society so that a young county Down girl could comment casually in 1764 of 'my own garments and sundry articles such as Prayer Books, stays, ornaments, comfit boxes, fans [and] purses'.[52]

The distribution of copies of the Book of Common Prayer is a poor measure of its impact. Like the Bible the varied contexts in which it was used meant that it reached an audience much wider than simply the literate who could read the text. Those contexts of reading the text in different types of interpretive communities ranged from liturgical performance, accessible to both literate and illiterate, to personal devotional reading. The widest context was the liturgical use of the Book of Common Prayer both on a Sunday basis but also for baptisms, marriages and burials and most members of the church witnessed all these regularly. Such hearing of the text read was clearly what the Dublin polemicist Barnaby Rich envisaged when he referred to the Irish translation of the Book of Common Prayer as 'that as well the lettered sort that can read their own language as also the unlettered sort that can but understand what they hear others read'.[53] Here oral and textual worlds crossed and the meaning of the text was explained by the clergy in the context of performance which at least some of the laity watched carefully. The Dublin poetess Laetitia Pilkington described the celebration of the Eucharist in St Patrick's by Dean Swift noting

P326/27/1/17, 20.   **49** R.C.B., C12/1/1, account for 1667; P118/5/1, f. 74; P328/5/1 accounts for 1667–8, 1647 and 1678–9; P117/5/1, pp 25, 27; P327/4/1, f. 19v; P351/4/1, f. 60.   **50** T.C.D., MS 562, ff 41, 51v, 52v, 56v, 69.   **51** For example, Maul, *Pietas Corcagiensis*, p. 74; R.C.B., MS 551/1/1.   **52** Cleone Knox, *The diary of a young lady of fashion in the year 1764–5* ed. A.B. Kerr (London, 1927), p. 33.   **53** Barnaby Rich, *A new description of Ireland*

particularly that 'another part of his behaviour on this occasion was censured by some as savouring of popery, which was that he bowed to the Holy Table'.[54] Interpretation of the text could also be provided by the officiating clergyman editing the text in a number of ways. In Dublin Castle at the beginning of the seventeenth century, according to Sir John Harrington in his description of Ireland, interpretation went as far as to remove the entire Book of Common Prayer and for the chaplain to pray extempore.[55] In other cases where words or phrases could cause difficulty new interpretations were offered. In 1638 it was alleged that one native Irish minister in county Cavan, Murtagh King, had used the words in the administration of Holy Communion 'Eat this according to our Saviour's meaning'.[56] A similar problem of belief lay behind the omission of parts of the liturgy by one clergyman in 1709.[57] In another case the text was added to in order to explicate its meaning more clearly. Revd Dr John Yarner, minister of St Bride's, Dublin, in the 1660s included in his notebook a number of supplementary prayers used particularly with the office for the visitation of the sick.[58] In these ways the meaning of the Prayer Book could be negotiated or in some cases subverted. However there were constraints on the clergy's freedom to tamper with the text. Where a congregation did not approve of such deviation of the text, which many clearly knew, complaints could well result as in the Wicklow case cited above. Moreover in the years after 1660 deviation from the accepted text of the Book of Common Prayer by clergy was much less tolerated by the church authorities. The spread of the ideas of the Caroline divines led to a growth in celebrations of the Holy Communion which required the use of the full text of the Prayer Book.[59] Increasingly awareness of the importance of the liturgy and its proper performance was urged on members of the Church of Ireland. William Beveridge's 1681 English sermon *A sermon concerning the excellency and usefulness of the common prayer* was reprinted in Dublin in 1698 and again in 1700, 1719, and 1747. This guide to the Prayer Book which provided a commentary on the services, explained the layout of churches and enjoined devout behaviour in church probably received a wide distribution within Dublin. According to the Dublin printer

> his Grace the archbishop of Dublin, having approved of the design its hoped he will be pleased to recommend to his clergy the buying of some dozens of them to be distributed among their poor parishioners so that

(London, 1610), p. 34.   **54** A.C. Elias (ed.), *Memoirs of Laetitia Pilkington* (2 vols, Athens and London, 1997), i, p. 27.   **55** John Harrington, *Short view of the state of Ireland written in 1605* ed. W.D. Macray (Oxford, 1879), p. 16.   **56** *Cal. S. P. Ire., 1633–47*, p. 206.   **57** Historical Manuscripts Commission, *Egmont MSS*, ii, p. 243.   **58** Raymond Gillespie, 'Rev. Dr John Yarner's notebook: religion in Restoration Dublin' in *Archivium Hibernicum* lii (1998), pp 36–8, 40.   **59** Gillespie, *Devoted people*, pp 97–8.

Plate 1 Middle Church, Ballinderry, Co. Antrim, 1668; restored 1902. The interior contains an original pulpit and high box-pews of Irish oak.

Plate 2 Waterford cathedral, 1774–92, by John Roberts. The classical style, which Wren had pioneered in the Church of England, dominated church architecture in Ireland in the eighteenth century.

Plate 3 Chapel, Dublin Castle, 1807–14, by Francis Johnston. The first neo-Gothic church to be built within Dublin, it displays a very ornate interior.

Plate 4 St James's church, Ramoan, Co. Antrim, 1848 by Joseph Welland. A very typical example of early Victorian Gothic Revivalism, with the different parts of the church given clear expression outside.

Plate 5 St Mark's church, Belfast, 1876–8, by William Butterfield. The colourful treatment of the interior is typical of the High Victorian phase of the Gothic Revival.

Plate 6 Stained glass windows in St John's church, Whitehouse, Co. Antrim. The medieval revivalism of many Victorian churches was reinforced by such memorial windows designed in neo-Gothic style.

Plate 7 The font in St Anne's church, Dungannon, Co. Tyrone, erected to the memory of the earl of Ranfurly in 1875. A memorial font or lectern was often a useful alternative to a stained glass window as a means to commemorating a prominent or wealthy member of the laity.

Plate 8 Windows showing St Columbanus and St Gall, in Magheralin church, Co. Down, by Beatrice Elvery of the Dublin stained glass studio An Túr Gloine (The Tower of Glass), 1908–9. Some of the most attractive stained glass windows in the early twentieth century are those depicting Irish saints.

Plate 9 Stained glass window showing 'The Angel of Hope and Peace', in Holy Trinity church, Killiney, Co. Dublin, by Harry Clarke, 1919. Like many church memorials to the laity, this one commemorates a death in the Great War.

Plate 10 Stained glass window showing St Bridget, St Patrick, and the Eucharist, in St Beaidh's church, Ardcarne, Co. Roscommon by Evie Hone, 1935. Church of Ireland churches contain some of the best examples of modern stained glass art to be found anywhere, such as the work of this internationally renowned Irish artist.

Plate 11 St Molua's church, Stormont, Belfast, 1961–2 by Denis O'D. Hanna.
Tradition and modernity are here combined in an impressive interior
dominated by a mural painted by Desmond Kinney.

Plate 12 St Ignatius's church, Carryduff, Co. Down, 1964–6, by Donald Shanks.
This is a notable example of a modern church in the 'contemporary style' of the time.

they, as well as the rich, may not be without so useful a book in their families.[60]

Whether or not the scheme succeeded is not known but given the subsequent reprints of the work it is likely that it had some measure of success given that the technique of passing out free samples of religious literature was well established in Dublin.[61]

The second context within which the printed text of the Book of Common Prayer could be understood was to hear it being used in the context of family prayers by the head of the household. Family prayers seem to have grown in popularity as the Prayer Book became increasingly widely used in the late seventeenth century. Thomas Pollard's 1696 sermons on family prayers in St Peter's, Dublin gained a wider audience through their publication.[62] By the early eighteenth century many of the landed families seem to have established the custom of family prayers for both servants and immediate family. The duke of Ormond's library list suggests one cluster of Common Prayer books which might represent the site of the domestic chapel. It is difficult to measure the devotional impact of such family prayers, and the catechising which might accompany them. For some they may well have been genuine worship while for others custom and the preservation of social order was the motive behind them.[63]

The third context within which the text of the Book of Common Prayer might be understood was meditative reading by an individual, usually alone. Such introspective reading leaves little trace in the surviving evidence. Only occasionally are direct glimpses of this sort of activity apparent as in 1641 when a number of Galway rebels threatened to kill a Tuam merchant 'because he read a Prayer Book on the Sabbath day'.[64] There is some indirect evidence for this sort of reading. The prayers composed by Jane Bingham, the wife of the landlord of Castlebar, in 1693–4 contain phrases from the Prayer Book as do some of the prayers of the duke of Ormond composed in the late seventeenth century.[65] These might well be remembered from formal liturgical settings or from family prayers but it is also likely that they represent an attempt to individualise a text intended for corporate worship and personalise it. To do this readers constructed their own sets of prayers and meditations for circumstances which affected their own lives using the language and phraseology of the Book of Common Prayer. Others, however, turned to a range of devotional books,

60 William Beveridge, *A sermon concerning the excellency and usefulness of the common prayer* (Dublin, 1698), sig. A2v. **61** Gillespie, 'Circulation of print', p. 51. **62** Thomas Pollard, *The necessity and advantages of family prayer in two sermons preached in St Peter's*, Dublin (Dublin, 1696). **63** Historical Manuscripts Commission, *Ormond MSS* n.s. vii, p. 526. For some eighteenth-century examples Sean Connolly, *Religion, law and power: the making of Protestant Ireland, 1660–1760* (Oxford, 1992), pp 191–2. **64** T.C.D., MS 830, f. 172. **65** T.C.D., MS 4468; N.L.I., MS 19,465.

such as the prayers gathered together by the countess of Morton and widely on sale in Dublin in the late seventeenth century.[66] One other element in the individual devotional use of the Prayer Book may lie in the use of illustrations. The Dublin stationer William Winter advertised in 1685 that he had for sale 'Common prayers of all sorts and sizes, with or without [wood]cutts'.[67] It seems that Prayer Books available in Ireland were increasingly illustrated in the late seventeenth century. Edward Wetenhall complained of the practice asking 'What is the meaning of filling the people's common prayer books with pictures? Our church books have none. How came these into the hands of Protestants at their devotions?'[68] Since texts provided for the communal liturgical round did not have such illustrations these illustrated texts were clearly directed at individuals who used the volume privately. For Wetenhall the practice of using such images in the context of prayer was popish but for at least some of the users of the text the images may have helped them to construct their own understanding of the text.

III

The Bible and the Book of Common Prayer were the mainstays which shaped the spiritual life of the laity in the early modern Church of Ireland but they were not alone. There were also available to those who wanted to read them a range of sermons, catechisms and devotional books, some of which had very long lives indeed. From the 1590s Francis Seager's *School of virtue*, a small didactic work for children dealing with religion, morals and social behaviour was available in the Munster port towns.[69] By the beginning of the seventeenth century some of the lay inhabitants of Dublin could borrow religious works from the library of Christ Church cathedral or from the extensive collection of James Ussher, then a professor in Trinity College, Dublin.[70] Perhaps typical of the sort of collection of books which the more affluent members of the Church of Ireland could assemble is the library of the Limerick lawyer Christopher Sexton, dating to the 1630s. This collection had some 131 titles of which a third

66 Advertised by Robert Thornton in John Sheffield, duke of Buckingham and Normanby, *An essay upon poetry* (Dublin, 1683), p. 15 and by William Norman and Ephial Dobson in Neal Carolan, *Motives of conversion to the catholic faith as it is professed in the reformed Church of England* (Dublin, 1688), p. 68.   **67** Michael [Boyle], *Rules and orders to be used and observed in the high court of chancery in Ireland* (Dublin, 1685), sig A3v.   **68** Wetenhall, *A practical and plain discourse*, p. 178. These would seem to have been imports since none of the surviving copies of the Dublin printings of the text have woodcuts.   **69** Raymond Gillespie, 'The book trade in southern Ireland, 1590–1640' in Gerard Long (ed.), *Books beyond the pale: aspects of the provincial book trade in Ireland before 1850* (Dublin, 1996), pp 5–6.   **70** Raymond Gillespie, 'Borrowing books from Christ Church cathedral, Dublin, 1607' in *Long Room* no.

were religious. Apart from Bibles and sermons, Lewis Bayly's *The practice of piety* and the late medieval work of Thomas à Kempis, the *Imitation of Christ*, are prominent.[71] Both works would continue to be in demand throughout the seventeenth century with Robert Southwell in Cork using a London agent to acquire a copy of the *Imitation of Christ* for him in the 1680s.[72] *The practice of piety* was an equally popular work. Its moralistic tone together with prayers for use on particular occasions ensured its continued popularity and it was a work which the young James Barry 'dearly loved' as he began to discover religion in his teens.[73] By the latter half of the century Bayly's work was being edged out by a more modern text *The whole duty of man* which explained the duty of an individual not only to God but to his neighbours and superiors. When doubts assailed Barry it was to *The whole duty of man* he was referred by his bishop.[74] Again in the 1670s Robert Perceval of Cork was reading the book as a way of amending his life and Samuel Ladyman of Clonmel left his son 20s. in his will to buy not only a copy of Bayly's work but also a copy of *The whole duty of man*.[75] The book clear had considerable popularity in Ireland at the upper social levels but was also aimed at the lower ends of the social order. The first edition of 1700 was attractively priced at 6*d.* bound according to the title page.[76] Pre-1750 Dublin editions followed in 1714, 1717, 1720, 1733 and 1737. *The whole duty of man* was a work more in keeping with the ideas of the Caroline divines which grew in importance in late seventeenth–century Ireland and it deeply influenced significant political figures such as the first duke of Ormond, who drew some of his private prayers from the text.[77]

There can be little doubt that devotional works, such as those described above, were of considerable importance in shaping the outlook of members of the Church of Ireland in the early modern period. The pious James Bonnell, for instance, was deeply affected by Lewis Bayly's work which he read when young.[78] They were not, of course, all that churchgoers read. Some encountered religious works by dissenters and Catholics which they also read. In the 1660s James Barry became enamoured with Richard Baxter's *A call to the unconverted* which he declared 'the more oftener I read it the more I was enamoured with it'.[79] Barry was not alone. Others also read widely.[80] Much of what they read

43 (1998), p. 17; Elizabethanne Boran, 'The libraries of Luke Challoner and James Ussher, 1595–1608' in Helga Robinson-Hammerstein (ed.), *European universities in the age of Reformation and Counter Reformation* (Dublin, 1998), pp 111–14.   71 B.L., Add. MS 19,865, ff 74–8.   72 B.L., Egerton MS 1672, f. 30v.   73 Barry, *A reviving cordial*, p. 23.   74 Ibid., p. 36.   75 Historical Manuscripts Commission, *Egmont MSS*, ii p. 41; W.P. Burke, *History of Clonmel* (Waterford, 1907), p. 333.   76 Edmond Stacey, *The whole duty of man epitomiz'd for the benefit of the poor* (Dublin, 1700).   77 Raymond Gillespie, 'The religion of the first duke of Ormond' in Toby Barnard and Jane Fenlon (eds), *The dukes of Ormond, 1610–1745* (Woodbridge, 2000), pp 108–9; N.L.I., MS 19,465, pp 1–3.   78 Hamilton, *Life of Bonnell*, pp 7–9.   79 Barry, *A reviving cordial*, p. 23.   80 Gillespie, *Devoted people*, pp 9–10.

was of a devotional rather than a confutational nature and was intended to strengthen their faith within a Church of Ireland context rather than to promote conversions. That most of that material before the 1690s was English imports was crucial in ensuring that the Church of England and that of Ireland would move along parallel paths. A significant omission from the canon of devotional works which shaped the Church of England sense of itself was John Foxe's *Acts and monuments* which rarely featured in an Irish context. The only copy which appears in a book collection was in the Dublin parish of St Catherine in 1659.[81] It was the orthodox works of the English church that shaped the devotional life of the Church of Ireland. A case in point here is the use of the catechism. Catechisms were cheap works, often advertised in other popular works such as almanacs suggesting they were aimed at a large market. Moreover catechesis was of considerable importance in shaping identities since it was an oral activity in which the contents of a printed book could be made known to those who could not necessarily read. By such means the young learned standard phrases which created shared bonds of religious identity. Anthony Dopping, in the late 1670s rector of Summerhill in county Meath and later bishop of Meath, fully appreciated the importance of the catechism in shaping confessional identities. As he wrote in 1670 of presbyterian catechisms

> since Christianity hath been broken into parties and divisions the heads of [the] catechism are swollen into too intense a bulk and they do not so much labour to inform their proselytes in the principles of religion as to make them speak the language of their own parties and suck in the principles which are peculiarly adapted to the shibboleth of every communion.[82]

Until 1699 Ireland lacked an English language catechism specifically for the use of the Church of Ireland and hence it was difficult to teach its members the language of that party. In that year one was issued for the diocese of Dublin with the imprimatur of Narcissus Marsh, archbishop of Dublin, and possibly written by him.[83] There had been earlier catechisms, notably that by Edward Wetenhall, bishop of Cork, which had an Irish context but these were directed to the wider English church. In the main the Irish church survived with catechisms intended to inculcate the principles of the Church of England and hence shaped itself in that image.[84]

Important as such pious works seem to have been in promoting devotion and shaping identity it is difficult to be precise about their influence for two reasons.

81 R.C.B., P117/5/1, pp 6, 14, 34.   82 T.C.D., MS 2467, f. 14v.   83 *The Church catechism explain'd and prov'd by apt texts of scripture* (Dublin, 1699).   84 For a list of Irish catechisms Ian Green, "'The necessary knowledge of the principles of religion": catechisms and catechising in Ireland, 1560–1800' in Ford, McGuire and Milne (eds), *As by law established*,

The first is that little is known about their distribution in the years before 1750. In the early part of the seventeenth century libraries with religious books tended to be small. The library of Lettice Digby of Geashill, county Offaly held twelve books of which the only sign of religious reading was the Bible and the Book of Common Prayer.[85] Lady Ann Hamilton in Dublin in 1639 had fourteen books including a Bible and also a number of standard godly works including Lewis Bayly's *The practice of piety*.[86] However such godly works were more likely to be lent and borrowed than the more personal Bibles and Prayer Books. As the volume of print in Ireland grew so godly books could be found in increasing numbers both in booksellers advertisements and library lists. By the 1690s Bishop Foy of Waterford could claim that John Rawlett's *Exhortation to a holy life* had sales of 20,000 copies.[87] The rise of subscription publishing in the early eighteenth century certainly helped target book sales. By the early eighteenth century Dublin merchants were subscribing to godly books published in Wales and the subscription list for Joseph Harrison's *A scriptural exposition* issued in Dublin in 1738 commanded 1,250 subscribers of whom 215 were women.[88] The rise of parochial libraries in the eighteenth century probably helped to make texts more easily available. That at St Mary's in Cork contained a wide range of devotional material, some in multiple copies, which had been donated by prominent lay members of the church and certainly made such texts available locally.[89] If the availability of such godly texts increased over the early modern period access to them by the illiterate was more problematical. Such works did not receive the sort of oral performance which the Bible or the Book of Common Prayer did but one of Bishop Dopping of Meath's resolutions on entering into his first living was to read a chapter of *The whole duty of man* to his congregation and to exhort them to buy the book.[90] At the other end of the social scale domestic chaplains charged with educating children might well have read pious books aloud to them. Steven Jerome, chaplain to the earl of Cork in the 1630s, recorded of the children in the family under his care that 'no day being permitted wherein besides domestic prayer with the family and private in your chambers the scriptures with the best sermons and theological tractates were not read by you or to you'.[91] The result was that the children of the earl of Cork proved singularly pious in later life. Some learning to read in the parochial and Charter schools of the eighteenth century would also come into contact

---

pp 84–5.   85 B.L., Add Charter 13340, m4d.   86 Dublin City Archives, MS C1/J/2/4, p. 228.   87 T.C.D., MS 1995–2008/272.   88 Geraint H. Jenkins, *Literature, religion and society in Wales, 1660–1730* (Cardiff, 1978), p. 292; Máire Kennedy, 'Women and reading in eighteenth-century Ireland' in Cunningham and Kennedy (eds), *Experience of reading*, p. 89. 89 Maule, *Pietas Corcagiensis*, pp 37–47.   90 Cambridge University Library, Add. MS 711, p. 232.   91 S[teven] J[erome], *The soul's centinel ringing an alarm against impiety and impenitencie* (Dublin, 1631) dedication.

with such religious works as *The whole duty of man* and other godly texts were used to teach reading and similar skills.[92]

The second problem in making any detailed assessment of the importance of these devotion works is that little is known about how they were read by contemporaries. As with the Bible there were a variety of reading strategies at play in the reading of devotional works but these are difficult to reconstruct. In one case, however, it is possible to know at least what the author's expectations were of his reader. In 1673 the Church of Ireland layman Henry Dodwell prepared Francis de Sales's *An introduction to the devout life* for the use of an Irish Protestant readership. His preface was intended 'to prepare the reader for the book' and so it is possible to obtain at least a glimpse of what was expected of the reader of such devotional works. The reader of godly books, according to Dodwell, was to approach the task not as he or she would approach other books giving them only a cursory glance. This would be unfruitful and 'endeavours of a practical persuasion and suitable affections were required' since the reader was more concerned with the 'edification of their affections' rather than 'informing their understanding'. Godly books needed to be read slowly and often and the various meanings, moral and metaphysical, of the stories presented in godly books needed to be considered along with the literal meaning. The godly reader was to be an attentive reader rather than a casual one deploying not only the intellect but the emotions also.[93]

IV

It is possible to catch a glimpse of one member of the Church of Ireland reading in the life of Elizabeth Freke, born in London in 1642 and who married Percy Freke in 1672. Percy held Cork property from the Boyle family and Elizabeth spent a number of substantial periods, four and a half years in one case, in Cork. She moved easily between the two worlds of England and Ireland and between the two established churches with their identical liturgies and stock of godly literature. She was clearly a pious woman who recorded in her 'Remembrances' the blessings of God and the trials which she endured looking to the providence of God to sustain herself in these periods of difficulty.[94] When she listed her books in 1711 they contained a substantial number of religious works together with histories, romances, poems and works on gardening, law and medicine. Hardly surprisingly there was a Bible (which had been her mother's), a New Testament and a Psalter 'with [wood]cutts'.[95] She

92 Kenneth Milne, *The Irish charter schools* (Dublin, 1997), pp 123, 126–8.   93 de Sales, *An introduction to the devout life* ed. Dodwell, sig a6v–f4v.   94 Raymond Anselment (ed.), *The remembrances of Elizabeth Freke* (Cambridge, 2001).   95 Ibid., pp 173–6.

was clearly an attentive reader of the Bible since she composed a number of 'emblems' or poems based on biblical texts.[96] In these she selected a text and in some cases developed it by constructing a dialogue around that text in which she teased out the meaning of that text for her and in the process used other verses of Scripture to develop the meaning of the text she meditated on. In the same way she used the language of the Book of Common Prayer to explain her own situation. Thus when her brother died in 1696 she echoed the words of the burial service when she noted 'it pleased God to take to himself my dear brother Austin'. Again in 1709 she echoed the words of the Litany when noting 'from such friends and friendship, good Lord deliver us'.[97] The Bible and Prayer Book were clearly texts with which Elizabeth Freke was very familiar and entered into her daily life as a result of meditative reading. The other godly books in her collection, including *The whole duty of man* and works by Archbishop Ussher have left fewer textual traces in her writings suggesting that they were, perhaps, read less frequently or in a less meditative way than the others.

V

This essay has not attempted a comprehensive overview of the religious lives of the members of the Church of Ireland in early modern Ireland. Such a task would be impossible. There are too many gaps in the evidence as contemporaries failed to commit to paper their assumptions about their spiritual lives. Moreover religious belief varied a great deal from individual to individual and to incorporate all the variants within one essay would be impossible. Rather this essay has concentrated on one of the key elements in shaping the beliefs of those within the Church of Ireland: the medium of print. The Bible and Book of Common Prayer, with their wide circulation both in print and for the illiterate in performance formed the focus of Church of Ireland religiosity. Around this was built a shell concocted from other godly works from both Church of England and other sources. However reading these works was a complex business and individual readers understood the texts before them in slightly different ways. What held them together was the materials which they used to shape their beliefs and the common interpretative framework of a community which held certain books to be important. In that lay the achievement of the Church of Ireland in the early modern period.

---

96 Ibid., pp 133–9. 97 Ibid., pp 66, 260.

6

Protestant ascendancy challenged: the Church of Ireland laity and the public sphere, 1740–1869

Jacqueline Hill

Although the period covered by this essay amounted to little more than a century, it witnessed a complete transformation in the public position of the Church of Ireland. In the 1740s the established church was the very embodiment of the confessional principle that was so ubiquitous in the Europe of the ancien régime.

The idea that religion properly permeated all aspects of life, and that accordingly church and state were intimately linked, was still generally upheld by those in authority in the western world. Of course there were disagreements over such issues as doctrine, the role of the pope, and church government, but ideas associated with the Enlightenment, the new science and the cult of reason, were for the most part themselves permeated with Christian assumptions. In the Hanoverian dominions, although ideas of religious 'toleration' were spreading, even advanced thinkers were apt to make exceptions for those whose religious tenets might represent a danger to the state. For Protestants, Roman Catholicism seemed doubly dangerous, since the Pretender to the throne of Great Britain and Ireland was a Catholic, and it was widely believed that Catholicism was incompatible with both civil and religious liberty.

From this general consensus flowed the multiple privileges of the established church – its near monopoly of public life, both in national and local government, as outlined in David Hayton's essay above; its dominance in the field of education; its ability to exact tithes from those of all denominations – and all this while representing a minority (perhaps around 10 per cent in the 1730s of the people of Ireland).[1] Paradoxically, in certain respects its minority position enhanced the church's status. For instance, compared with Britain, where churchmen ceased to feature as cabinet ministers after the early 1700s, in Ireland churchmen were to be found in the highest executive positions down to the very end of the eighteenth century. No fewer than three archbishops served

---

1 See Alan Acheson, *A history of the Church of Ireland 1691–1996* (Dublin, 1997), p. 19.

as lords justices at some time during the 1740s, and as late as 1795 Archbishop William Newcome of Armagh filled the position. During the 1790s Archbishop Charles Agar of Cashel was one of a handful of key politicians consulted by the viceroy.[2] However, by 1870 the legal foundations of the church's privileges had disappeared, and its members' control of public life had been considerably reduced. Parliamentary representation was no longer a Protestant preserve, and in local government (at least in the towns of the three southern provinces) Catholics had come to predominate. The right to levy tithes had been commuted, and in 1869 the very principle of an established church in Ireland was abandoned by the government of the day. These changes were prompted by various considerations, including military requirements, the rise of liberalism, and a shift on the part of the state towards a more impartial position. Because of the nature and scale of the changes involved, it will be convenient to divide the period into three, and look at each separately, begining with the period 1740–92.

I

It is a commonplace that the Anglican establishment in Ireland represented the dominance of a minority over other sections of the population, notably the Catholics and presbyterians. While this was certainly the case, a number of further considerations (beyond the confessional principle discussed above) should be noted. First, the fact that land was largely in Protestant (especially Anglican) hands lent a certain coherence to the system. Everywhere in Europe land ownership and political power usually went hand in hand. Moreover, the presence of a class of middling Protestant gentry meant that in most parts of the country the numbers (not large, but adequate) existed to supply magistrates, churchwardens, and other middling officials. The same was true of the towns. Although outside Ulster Protestants did not form majorities, they were overrepresented in the towns of the other three provinces, and comprised about one half of the capital city's population.[3] Again, this meant the availability of a class including merchants, shopkeepers, and artisans to supply the 'body corporate' and middle-ranking officials in towns as well as in parish and county government.

It was the very existence of such middle-ranking Protestants that made possible some of the most significant developments in public life in this period. In a hierarchical age, it was the aristocracy and greater gentry – those whose

2 R.B. McDowell, 'Reform and reaction, 1789–94', in T.W. Moody and W.E. Vaughan (eds), *A new history of Ireland: iv. Eighteenth-century Ireland 1691–1800* (Oxford, 1986), p. 309.
3 Patrick Fagan, 'The population of Dublin in the eighteenth century with particular reference to the proportions of Protestants and Catholics' in *Eighteenth-Century Ireland*, vi (1991), pp 121–56.

wealth and status enabled them, if they wished, to spend time in England as well as in Ireland – who took the lead in public life. The gentry dominated representation in the House of Commons, and, at local government level, membership of grand juries. And because most of the towns were governed by 'close' corporations whose members held their positions for life, the gentry were able to exercise influence over town politics. However, from mid-century onwards oligarchy was being challenged, sometimes successfully, both at national and local level.

The challenge was most dramatic in Dublin, one of the few 'open' boroughs in the country. Even as the dynastic threat to the Anglican establishment in church and state was being vividly demonstrated by the Jacobite rising in Scotland (spring 1745), a campaign was under way in Dublin to overturn the oligarchical powers of the aldermanic board. The self-selecting board of twenty-five members dominated the city's corporation, and hence controlled local government in a city whose population over the previous eighty years had trebled to reach 110,000. Led by the apothecary Charles Lucas and the merchant James Digges La Touche, the campaign appealed to 'ancient rights' and used a variety of contemporary 'opposition' languages, notably the civic republican ideal of the virtuous citizen whose exercise of the franchise must be conducted at the highest level of 'independence' and integrity.[4] There was a temporary check when Lucas, standing for parliament in a Dublin by-election, offended the Irish parliament and the lord lieutenant by his trenchant criticisms of parliament's failure to stand up for its rights in dealings with its British counterpart. But the freemen of Dublin (members of the guilds, whose representatives formed the lower house of Dublin corporation) had been aroused, and on Lucas's return to Dublin following the accession of a new king (George III) in 1760, the freemen elected him to represent the city in parliament. At the same time the aldermanic oligarchy was dealt a blow by legislation that enabled the freemen (rather than the aldermen) to choose their own guild representatives on the corporation, and to participate in the election of civic officials, including the lord mayor, sheriffs, and aldermen.[5] Since there were between three and four thousand Dublin freemen, exclusively Protestant, with members of the Church of Ireland constituting about four-fifths, this represented a significant broadening of the civic elite.

Lucas's eirenic attitudes towards presbyterians had been the object of suspicion in some church circles, reinforced by the prominence of certain presbyterians in the campaign for civic reform. However, not all Anglicans were hostile to support from such quarters, and the campaign paved the way for greater dissenting participation in civic life. The sacramental test (1704) for

4 Jacqueline Hill, *From patriots to unionists: Dublin civic politics and Irish Protestant patriotism, 1660–1840* (Oxford, 1997), ch. 3.   5 Dublin city corporation act, 33 Geo. II, *c*.16 (17 May 1760).

officials at local and national level was still in place, but since 1719 a series of indemnity acts had weakened the thrust of the measure, and in 1758 the first presbyterian to breach the Church of Ireland monopoly of Dublin city's representation in parliament, James Dunn, was elected.[6]

These Dublin successes gave heart to those in other towns who had reason to resent the oligarchical nature of town governments. In Limerick, for instance, the dean of St Mary's, Charles Massy, found the corporation to be failing in its obligations to certain educational charities; he joined forces with other critics who complained of excessive muncipal tolls. Some limited success was achieved, although legislation to increase the power of the freemen was halted by the English privy council in 1762.[7] In Waterford an investigation began in the 1750s into the city's ancient charters; and in Cork a 'Friendly Club' was established in the 1760s, with some effect, to counteract the influence of Lord Shannon.[8] These cases indicate that while urban governments, with the possible exception of some of the lowest positions, were exclusively Protestant, there was a vibrant opposition to oligarchy from within the established church itself, sometimes with the support of other denominations.

In the countryside too such trends were reflected in the formation during the 1750s of 'independent clubs'; these marked a new assertiveness on the part of the lesser gentry, including dissenters. By the 1760s electors in many constituencies were displaying an unwonted degree of independence of former patrons,[9] and the octennial act of 1768,[10] which introduced regular general elections, ensured that these developments would be lasting. The Irish parliament itself had gained a higher profile, thanks to constitutional disputes with the crown over treasury surpluses in the 1750s, the outcome of which was to make M.P.s more willing to vote funds for projects likely to promote 'improvement'. All this had the effect of creating a broader 'public opinion', and hence served to dilute the corporatist nature of the state, in which political privileges were confined to members of orders or associations regulated by the crown.[11] There was some overlap between membership of the new political clubs and others formed for practical purposes, such as the farmers' societies (modelled on the Dublin Society) that sprang up around the country in the 1750s and the chambers of commerce formed in some of the larger towns, dating from the 1780s.[12]

6 Jacqueline Hill, 'Dublin corporation, Protestant dissent, and politics, 1660–1800' in Kevin Herlihy (ed.), *The politics of Irish dissent, 1650–1800* (Dublin, 1997), pp 28–39.   7 Éamon O'Flaherty, 'Urban politics and municipal reform in Limerick, 1723–62' in *Eighteenth-Century Ireland*, vi (1991), pp 105–20.   8 T. Cunningham (ed.), *Magna charta libertatum civitatis Waterford* (Dublin, 1752); Ian d'Alton, *Protestant society and politics in Cork 1812–1844* (Cork, 1980), p. 93.   9 W.H. Crawford and B. Trainor (eds), *Aspects of Irish social history 1750–1800* (Belfast, 1969), p. ix.   10 7 Geo. III, *c*.3 (16 February 1768).   11 Jacqueline Hill, 'Corporatist ideology and practice in Ireland, 1660–1800' in S.J. Connolly (ed.), *Political ideas in eighteenth century Ireland* (Dublin, 2000), pp 64–82.   12 Crawford and Trainor,

The aspect of the Church of Ireland's public position that provoked most hostility during this period was tithes. This was not exceptional; all over Europe tithes were a contentious issue, sometimes compounded by confessional conflict. All the main Christian churches upheld the levying of tithes, and there was little outright opposition to the system as such, but from the 1750s onwards, when greater prosperity spurred the clergy to try to exact their share of higher output, there was organised opposition among various agrarian groups. Tithes were one factor in the agitation associated in the 1760s with the Hearts of Oak (drawing support from presbyterians, Anglicans and Catholics) in Ulster, and the Whiteboys (mainly Catholics) in Munster.[13] The violent methods adopted by such groups provided an excuse for the authorities to respond in kind: draconian legislation was introduced in 1776, and that year witnessed the execution of some twenty Whiteboys convicted of capital offences. It has been pointed out that the growth of the Volunteer movement under gentry leadership in the late 1770s was prompted as much by a desire to control the Whiteboys as to provide an alternative to the regular soldiers who had been withdrawn from the country to fight in the American war.[14] The next wave of agrarian unrest, that associated in Munster with the Rightboys in the 1780s, also sought to reduce the level of tithes and church dues; this time the use of violence was generally avoided. Since the Rightboys received some support from the local Protestant gentry, aware that reductions in tithes would make it easier for their tenants to pay rents, this phase was in some respects a more formidable threat to the church, and a reform of the tithe system was attempted in parliament. However, the challenge provoked a successful counter-response, notably from the bishop of Cloyne, Richard Woodward, whose *The present state of the Church of Ireland* (1786) contained a powerful restatement of the grounds for the link between church and state, and warned that if the existing established church were overturned, the state would soon share its fate.[15]

Although there was no legislative reform of tithes in this period, during the 1770s and early 1780s there was a significant relaxation of the penal laws that concerned Catholics in the sphere of freedom of worship, the right to buy and sell land, and conduct schools, while Protestant dissenters had the satisfaction

---

Aspects of Irish social history, p. 8; L.M. Cullen, *Princes & pirates: the Dublin chamber of commerce, 1783–1983* (Dublin, 1983), pp 45, 58. John Patrick, one of the founders of the Dublin chamber of commerce in 1783, was secretary of the Dublin City Constitutional Society in 1785 (*Letters of an Irish helot, signed Orellana* (Dublin, 1785 ed.), p. 6.   **13** See J.S. Donnelly, jr, 'Hearts of Oak, Hearts of Steel' in *Studia Hibernica*, no. 21 (1981), 7–73; id., 'Irish agrarian rebellion: the Whiteboys of 1769–76' in *R.I.A. Procs*, lxxxiii, Section C (1983), pp 293–331.   **14** Donnelly, 'Irish agrarian rebellion: the Whiteboys', p. 329.   **15** Richard [Woodward], *The present state of the Church of Ireland* (Dublin, 1787 edn), p. 7; J.S. Donnelly, jr, 'The Rightboy movement' in *Studia Hibernica*, nos. 17–18 (1977–8), pp 120–202.

of seeing the repeal of the sacramental test.[16] The main impetus for these reforms was not so much the growth of toleration as military considerations: throughout the century the size of armies in Europe had been growing. As noted in the previous chapter, despite the fact that it was illegal for Catholics to bear arms, some limited numbers did enter the army rank-and-file. Although the ban was not formally lifted until 1793, the alleviation of certain penal laws during the American war of independence was expected to improve relations with the Catholic gentry and hence to promote recruitment.[17] At local level, some Volunteer corps were prepared to admit Catholics. However, these moves stopped short of conceding political rights. The issue of the vote for Catholics was raised briefly during the short-lived reform era that followed on the winning of Irish legislative independence in 1782/3, but the matter was so sensitive that it was not pursued.[18]

By 1790, therefore, the elite in Ireland had become less exclusively Anglican, and less corporatist. It was now more broadly Protestant in character, and rested on a wider body of public opinion.

II

The period 1792–1829 was dominated by the revolutionary wars that began in Europe in 1792; in February 1793 France declared war on Great Britain, and British (and Irish) involvement lasted until the final defeat of Napoleon in 1815. Counter-revolutionary and military considerations thus featured among the principal developments affecting Ireland in this period, including the extension of political rights to Catholics and the passing of the act of union, both of which had implications for the established church in the public sphere.

By the beginning of the 1790s the British government's commitment to the principle of an exclusive church establishment in its overseas empire, most recently restated in respect of Quebec following the seven years war (1756–63) had long been compromised. During the 1760s the government had in effect accepted the recommendations of those charged with the government of Quebec that an exclusive establishment was not only inappropriate in local conditions, but counter-productive at a time when the crown's Protestant subjects in the thirteen colonies were becoming restive. Roman Catholics, who formed the great bulk of Quebec's population, were alleged to be potentially

16 Thomas Bartlett, *The fall and rise of the Irish nation: the Catholic question 1690–1830* (Dublin, 1992), chs. 4–5. 17 Robert K. Donovan, 'The military origins of the Catholic relief programme of 1778' in *Historical Journal*, xxviii (1985), pp 79–102. 18 James Kelly, 'The parliamentary reform movement of the 1780s and the Catholic question' in *Archivium Hibernicum*, xliii (1988), pp 95–117.

loyal and peaceable subjects as long as they were not stirred up by the introduction of penal laws and other disabilities.[19] Accordingly, concessions were made to the Quebec Catholics culminating in 1791 in the extension of representative government: Catholics were admitted to the franchise and to office-holding on the same terms as Protestants.[20]

The government's willingness to think flexibly about the principle of church establishments had not hitherto extended to Ireland. But in the aftermath of the apparently successful Canadian precedent, and in view of what seemed increasingly persuasive arguments from the pen of Edmund Burke and others about the counter-revolutionary potential of Irish Catholics (which might be jeopardised unless concessions were made), during the winter of 1791–2 British ministers began to entertain fresh thoughts on the subject. What was more, ministers were prepared to urge their views on the Irish executive.[21] Thanks to resistance in Irish government circles, the first legislative signs of this momentous shift were limited. In 1792 Catholics were admitted to practise at the bar.[22] However, in the following year far more extensive concessions were made. The parliamentary franchise (on the same terms as Protestants), membership of guilds and corporations, the right to take degrees at Trinity College, to bear arms, and to hold most civil and military offices, were all granted.[23] As the wartime climate became increasingly inimical to constitutional innovation, and following the rebellion of 1798, progress towards full civil equality (or 'emancipation' as it came to be called) was halted, but after 1793 there were few remaining Catholic disabilities, the most important being the right to sit in parliament.

The practical results of these changes were mixed. Where landlords were confident that their Catholic tenants would cast their votes in a spirit of deference the necessary freehold tenures were recognised and Catholics gained the right to vote. The way was also cleared for Catholics to enter the army in large numbers (between 1793 and 1815 an estimated 200,000 Irish recruits joined the British army and navy, the bulk of whom were Catholics). Catholics were also permitted to take out commissions in the army (although owing to the absence of a similar reform in England, such commissions were not recognised there).[24] And the 1790s witnessed the first batch of Catholics studying in and obtaining degrees from Trinity College.

However, in other fields the effects of the legislative changes were much more meagre. In towns and cities with fairly large Protestant minorities, the

19 Jacqueline Hill, 'Religious toleration and the relaxation of the penal laws: an imperial perspective, 1763–1780' in *Archivium Hibernicum*, xliv (1989), pp 98–109.   20 J.M. Ward, *Colonial self-government: the British experience 1759–1856* (London, 1976), pp 15–18. 21 Bartlett, *Fall and rise of the Irish nation*, ch. 8.   22 32 Geo. III, *c.*21 (18 April 1792).   23 33 Geo. III, *c.*21 (9 April 1793).   24 Bartlett, *Fall and rise of the Irish nation*, pp 287, 323.

number of Catholics gaining admission to guild and civic freedom were generally limited, leading disappointed aspirants to contemplate legal remedies or a radical reform of the existing political system in order to exercise their rights.[25] In government circles few Catholics were appointed even to lowly positions in the public service, although there were some limited moves in this direction, and other conciliatory gestures, during the tenure of pro-emancipation ministries.[26] In certain parts of the countryside the spectacle of Catholics bearing arms was deeply unsettling to Protestants, and had the effect of heightening sectarian tensions. Also unsettling was the novel phenomenon of Catholic spokesmen, buoyed up by their own counter-revolutionary credentials, being openly dismissive of the established church. One such case involved the Roman Catholic bishop of Waterford, Thomas Hussey, who in a pastoral delivered in the spring of 1797 contrasted his own church ('the *catholic*, or universal religion', destined to extend 'from the rising to the setting sun') with 'a small sect ... [regulating] its creed and form of worship, according to the shape and form of government of the limited boundaries where that sect arose, exists, and dies away'.[27]

The government's conversion to Catholic political rights was bound to be controversial, striking as it did at the very essence of Ireland's system of government since the 1690s. This was not simply because the elite – even in its less oligarchic and more broadly-based form at the end of the century – was still representative only of a minority of the Irish population, though that was part of the problem. There was also the suddenness and extent of the changes, for which the public had been ill-prepared, against a background of international revolutionary upheaval. To the government in London, Irish Catholicism might appear destined to be a counter-revolutionary force; to many in Ireland the reality seemed much more ambiguous, particularly when attention was directed towards the Defenders, a mainly Catholic secret society whose members by the early 1790s were expecting radical change in respect of rents, tithes and other dues. Under the circumstances it was not surprising that debate should centre on the issue of 'Protestant ascendancy'. The term iself was of recent origin (it had first been used extensively by Bishop Woodward of Cloyne in his defence of tithes in the 1780s), and the fact that so many commentators now attempted

25 For Dublin see Jacqueline Hill, 'The politics of privilege: Dublin corporation and the Catholic question, 1792–1823' in *Maynooth Review*, vii (1982), pp 17–36; for Cork see d'Alton, *Protestant society and politics in Cork*, p. 112. See also David Dickson, '"Centres of motion": Irish cities and the origins of popular politics' in *Culture et pratique politiques en France et en Irlande xvie–xviiie siecle* (Paris, 1990), pp 101–22. 26 N.L.I., Richmond papers, MS 60, nos. 258, 264; Bartlett, *Fall and rise of the Irish nation*, pp 285–6; Allan Blackstock, *An ascendancy army: the Irish yeomanry 1796–1834* (Dublin, 1998), pp 281–2. 27 For the pastoral see Richard Musgrave, *Memoirs of the different rebellions in Ireland* (2nd ed. Dublin, 1801), App. xxi, no. 11, pp 170–5, at pp 173–4.

to introduce some specificity into the term testified to the fact that although it was indeed descriptive of the eighteenth-century polity, it was only when that polity came under attack that it became necessary to define it.[28]

The debate marked the fracturing of Protestant opinion in Ireland, hitherto essentially united in support of the Protestant monopoly of public life. Recriminations and counter-recriminations abounded. One politician who backed the new policy, Henry Grattan, claimed that opposition to Catholic political rights had been stirred up by Dublin Castle, through its encouragement of what he called 'the high church party' to assume the name of 'Protestant ascendancy'.[29] In other words, Grattan was implying a degree of continuity between the Tories of the early years of the century and the opponents of Catholic rights in the 1790s. How accurate was such a verdict? There were undoubtedly some parallels. One was the emergence late in the century of a movement for the reformation of manners, similar to those that had flourished in the 1690s and later. The Association for Discountenancing Vice and Promoting the Practice of the Christian Religion was formed in 1792; like its predecessors it was concerned primarily with Protestant renewal rather than the conversion of Catholics. Its early aims were to spread religious knowledge, restore sabbath observance, and to reform the criminal poor. And it certainly embodied the Anglican tradition: its founders were members of the established church, clerical and lay, and they attempted to guard against the introduction of any tenets hostile to the church. It had a membership of over five hundred by 1796, including large numbers of clergy and three-quarters of the fellows of Trinity College, as well as many prominent citizens.[30]

But if the Association for Discountenancing Vice represented a movement for corporate Anglican renewal, the circumstances of the 1790s were far removed from those of the beginning of the century. The sacramental test, for instance, had been repealed in 1780, and there was no likelihood that it would be revived. In any case, other societies were far more important in marking out a determination to defend, as far as possible given the legislative changes, the Protestant nature of the polity. The Orange Order, founded in 1795, was foremost among such societies, and it had no precedent in the earlier era of party politics. Of course the Order had masonic antecedents, and also had forerunners in the shape of the various Boyne and Aughrim societies that had

---

28 Jacqueline Hill, 'The meaning and significance of "Protestant ascendancy", 1787–1840' in *Ireland after the union: proceedings of the second joint meeting of the Royal Irish Academy and the British Academy* (Oxford, 1989), pp 1–22; James Kelly, 'Eighteenth-century ascendancy: a commentary' in *Eighteenth-Century Ireland*, v (1990), pp 173–87. 29 Henry Grattan, *Memoirs of the life and times of the Rt. Hon. Henry Grattan, by his son, Henry Grattan, M.P.*, (5 vols, London, 1839–46), iv, pp 32, 56. 30 Joseph Liechty, 'Irish evangelicalism, Trinity College Dublin, and the mission of the Church of Ireland at the end of the eighteenth century', (Ph.D. thesis, N.U.I.Maynooth, 1987), pp 96–101.

flourished in certain towns since the early part of the century. Nor was its social mix particularly novel. However, what set the Orange Order apart was its combination of the features of a federated secret society and an unyielding political agenda: from the outset membership was confined to Protestants, and the oath of allegiance to the king was originally conditional upon the maintenance of a Protestant constitution.[31] And although its origins lay in the disturbed conditions of County Armagh – against a background of clashes between (mainly Catholic) Defenders attempting to hold armed demonstrations and Protestants determined to prevent them – the Order soon spread to become a national movement, notably after the formation of a gentleman's lodge in Dublin in 1797. Nor were its members confined to Anglicans; some presbyterians were apparently involved in the early years of the Orange Order, although the numbers are still obscure. Following the rebellion of 1798 and Emmet's rising in 1803 more presbyterians were won over. The existence of the evangelical movement helped foster the broad 'Protestant' nature of the membership. By the early years of the nineteenth century the Order was spreading in England and to other parts of the British empire.[32]

The formation of an organised opposition to 'Catholic emancipation' clearly dealt a blow to the hopes of those ministers in London who had come to regard political rights for Irish Catholics as a counter-revolutionary strategy. However, it is difficult to escape the conclusion that one of the contributory factors in the growth and tenacity of such opposition in the nineteenth century was the absence of any clearly defined relationship between the state and the Catholic church. For most of the eighteenth century, during which there had existed no mechanism by which Catholics could testify their loyalty to the Protestant monarchy, and while Catholic bishops (nominated by the Pretender) could be deemed to be passive, if not active, jacobites, their church had been officially proscribed. Following the ending of the Vatican's recognition of the jacobite claim in 1766, and the formulation in 1774 of an oath whereby lay Catholics could attest their loyalty to the crown,[33] proscription was abandoned. But this raised the question of what new relationship should reflect the changed circumstances. In Quebec, for instance, when the British government dropped its original commitment to an exclusive Protestant establishment and consented to recognise the Catholic church (alongside a technical establishment of the Anglican church),[34] the state had entered into a formal relationship with the Catholic church. In an arrangement accepted by Rome, the bishop of Quebec

---

31 See Rules of the Orange Society, 1798, reproduced in Hereward Senior, *Orangeism in Ireland and Britain 1795–1836* (London & Toronto, 1966), App. A, p. 298.   32 Senior, *Orangeism in Ireland and Britain*, pp 75–6, 155–9; Blackstock, *An ascendancy army*, pp 136, 275–6.   33 13 & 14 Geo. III, *c*.35 (2 June 1774).   34 J.H. Stewart Reid, K. McNaught, and H.S. Crowe, *A source book of Canadian history* (Toronto, 1959), p. 62.

(who was officially to be known as 'superintendent' of his diocese) could exercise administrative jurisdiction in his see only with the consent of the governor. Moreover, the bishop received a stipend from the crown (£200 per year in the 1760s, rising to £1,000 after the war of 1812), and the governor exercised some influence (effectively a veto) in the selection of new bishops.[35]

That Rome was prepared to accede to such provisions in the case of the church in Quebec is an indication that church–state relations of this kind were not exceptional, even in cases where the monarchy was Protestant. And the issue naturally arose in Ireland, where Protestants were apt to regard the Catholic clergy as exercising altogether too much influence, of a despotic kind, over their flocks. As early as the 1780s there was discussion of the crown obtaining a role in the choice of Irish bishops, and in 1791 it was further suggested that the government might acquire some influence over the Catholic clergy, in effect to 'bribe them by the prospect of an annual allowance'.[36] Nothing was done, but in 1799 both a state provision for the clergy and a government veto over episcopal appointments were raised with the Catholic hierarchy during negotiations over the act of union; and at that time, with the prospect of complete 'Catholic emancipation' in view, almost all the bishops were prepared to look favourably on such proposals.[37] However, the union passed without bringing emancipation in its wake, and when the issue was raised again in what became known as the 'veto controversy' almost a decade later, the circumstances were very different. In 1808 a 'no popery' ministry was in power in London; there was no prospect of emancipation being granted in the short term; and the publicity that attended the revelation in parliament that ministers had the backing for a veto from English Catholics failed to stem (perhaps even enhanced) the outcry from lay Catholics in Ireland. This response was, undoubtedly, in part a manifestion of Catholic nationalism;[38] but its intensity also reflected an awareness of an aspect of the veto that Edmund Burke had highlighted earlier. If government gained a veto over episcopal appointments, those who would be advising ministers on appointments would, in all likelihood, be Irish Protestants who would be perceived by Catholics as having an animus against their church. Thus Protestants would be gaining new powers of interference in an area where the interests of the Catholic laity, clergy and bishops were delicately balanced.[39]

35 Reid, McNaught, Crowe, *Source book*, pp 65–6; Hugh J. Somers, 'The legal status of the bishop of Quebec' in *Catholic Historical Review*, xix (1933–4), 167–89; Ivanhoe Caron, 'La nomination des eveques catholiques de Quebec sous le régime anglais' in *Memoires de la Société Royale du Canada*, section 1, 3rd ser., xxvi (1932), 1–44.   **36** Bartlett, *Fall and rise of the Irish nation*, p. 189; D.J. McDougall, 'Some problems of church and state in Canada and Ireland, 1790 to 1815' in *Canadian Catholic Historical Association Report* (1940–1), pp 21–33, at p. 33.   **37** Bartlett, *Fall and rise of the Irish nation*, pp 250–1.   **38** Ibid., p. 294.   **39** McDougall, 'Some problems of church and state', p. 23; C.D.A. Leighton, 'Gallicanism and the veto

At all events, in 1810 the bishops reversed their earlier decision and rejected a government veto. The episode had important effects; it heralded the beginning of an estrangement between Irish and English Catholics, and between Irish Catholics and the Whig opposition that had helped keep the issue of emancipation alive in parliament since the 1790s. And the revelation in 1814 that senior cardinals in Rome were prepared to accept a government veto merely intensified the popular reaction in Ireland against it.[40] Because the supporters of emancipation in parliament continued to take it for granted that some sort of government regulation must be agreed in return for the right to sit in parliament, debates over the 'securities', as the veto, state payment of clergy salaries, and other safeguards came to be known, persisted into the 1820s.

The refusal to accept any of the 'securities' played into the hands of those who insisted that Irish Catholics could not be trusted with full participation in a free Protestant constitution, since while they would obtain the right to influence the established church they would concede nothing on their own side.[41] Royal opposition to further concessions also hampered the prospects for emancipation, as did the long duration of the war, which necessitated keeping the largely Protestant yeomanry force in being. Along with the Orange Order, the yeomanry, first set up in 1796, became one of the chief vehicles for the expression of a defensive anti-Catholicism; the legacy of the 1790s had made the corps more rather than less exclusively Protestant in membership and outlook.[42] And the Act of Union of 1800, which might have been expected to draw the sting of sectarian prejudice by reassuring Protestants that they were now secure in a United Kingdom with a huge Protestant majority, failed to have that effect. The fact that parliament was now in remote London, rather than in Dublin; that Catholics had acquired some sort of electoral influence by obtaining the vote in 1793, and were beginning to stress their numbers and abandon the deference of earlier eras; all this contributed to maintaining a sense of distrust and insecurity among Protestants. Aware of their minority status, many Protestants clung to the Orange Order and the yeomanry as vehicles for defending traditional values, and for displaying them in the public sphere. In the post-union period anniversaries, fairs, even funerals became occasions for assertions of an exclusive Protestant loyalty. Anxious not to offend Catholic susceptibilities, some ministries attempted to curb such demonstrations, but with limited success.[43] However, one notable turning point was the 1822 ban on

controversy: church, state and Catholic community in early nineteenth-century Ireland' in R.V. Comerford, M. Cullen, J. Hill and C. Lennon (eds), *Religion, conflict and coexistence in Ireland* (Dublin, 1990), pp 135–58, at p. 150. 40 Leighton, 'Gallicanism and the veto controversy', pp 138, 156; Bartlett, *Fall and rise of the Irish nation*, 291–5, 308. 41 See, e.g., speech of Dr Patrick Duigenan in the House of Commons, 13 May 1805 (*Hansard 1*, iv, 865–917, at 891). 42 Blackstock, *An ascendancy army*, pp 269–78. 43 Ibid., pp 278–85.

the decoration of the statue of King William in College Green for anniversary occasions, which (following a notorious defiance of the lord lieutenant by Orangemen at a Dublin theatre) had the effect of ending the era in which Dublin Protestants of the lower orders could periodically assert their dominance in the streets of the capital.[44]

A climate of caution among Protestants fostered by war and post-rebellion defensiveness meant that Catholics could scarcely maintain the very modest gains they had made in the mid-1790s, let alone build on them. Membership of guilds and corporations, with few exceptions, remained closed to them. And although not all statesmen shared the distrust of Catholics, it was prevalent enough to hamper moves to introduce Catholics into the public service, which remained overwhelmingly Protestant, particularly at the middle and higher levels. It was claimed in parliament in 1825 that in the Irish customs and excise departments there were 591 Protestants and a mere eighteen Catholics.[45] At best the period before 1829 witnessed from time to time some attempt by the authorities to prevent public patronage being engrossed by notoriously hard-line Protestants.[46] If anything, the Act of Union had made the task of reform more difficult. Engagements entered into by government when ministers were trying to win support for the act meant that during the 1810s the Irish pension fund was £80,000, compared with £90,000 for the whole of England, Scotland and Wales. As chief secretary from 1812 to 1818 Robert Peel found that some Irish M.P.s had come to regard local appointments as their exclusive right, and did not even have the grace to lend support to government when key political issues were being debated in parliament.[47]

When Catholic emancipation eventually came in 1829, the contrast with the first granting of Catholic political rights could hardly have been greater. Instead of a few ministers in London taking a decision and pressing it upon a reluctant and sceptical (Irish) parliament, the Catholics themselves deferentially in the background, during the 1820s the Catholics had seized the initiative and demonstrated through disciplined organisation that they could render the electoral system unworkable. Certainly, they had allies among liberal Protestants, who during the 1820s had consistently voted to pass bills for emancipation; it had been the king and the house of lords that had held out against the concession. But such was the Catholic euphoria at the final victory (despite the government's attempts to neutralise the measure by disenfranchising the forty-shilling freeholders) that the old liberal Protestant allies were deemed expendable in the next phase of Catholic political agitation: for repeal of the union.[48]

44 Hill, *From patriots to unionists*, pp 325–9.   45 Senior, *Orangeism in Ireland and Britain*, p. 214.   46 Ibid., p. 178.   47 Robert Shipkey, 'Problems of Irish patronage during the chief secretaryship of Robert Peel, 1812–18' in *Historical Journal*, x (1967), pp 41–56, at pp 43, 47. 48 For liberal Protestant reluctance to join the repeal movement in the early 1830s see Oliver

III

After 1829 Irish Catholics were on a virtually equal footing, in terms of political rights, with members of the established church and other Protestants. Despite the notoriety that was to be gained by the repeal campaign in the early 1830s and 1840s, the main issue on the political agenda in the post-1829 decades was not the repeal of the union but the breaking down of entrenched Protestant privilege. While some liberal Protestants were prepared to work with Catholics towards this goal, most Protestants took a defensive stand. Political parties, which became much more important from the 1830s onwards, tended to reflect these divisions. The Conservative party, dedicated to defending Protestant interests and resisting liberal reforms, succeeded in winning the support of most Protestants. It was helped by an informal alliance with the Orange Order, which had been formally dissolved following the unlawful societies act of 1825.[49] When the grand lodge was reconstituted in 1828 clergymen of the established church filled fifteen of the twenty-five committee positions; they were particularly concerned about the threat emanating from the Whig ministries of the 1830s to the Church of Ireland.[50] And although many reforms were passed, including the Church Temporalities Act of 1833 which abolished ten bishoprics, and a measure of tithe reform in 1838 which converted tithe into a rent charge,[51] the defensive stand of the Conservative party achieved considerable success in the period down to disestablishment.

One of the most important legislative enactments of the first half of the nineteenth century was the reform of the franchise in 1832.[52] By substituting a uniform property franchise for the boroughs, that measure swept away one of the most characteristic features of the old regime in Ireland and Britain, the ramshackle complexity of franchises, often under the control of local patrons, which had grown up since medieval times and had been little modified since the Stuart era. In Ireland the Act of Union had already brought about a modicum of reform in this sphere, by disenfranchising some of the smallest boroughs, but many small boroughs had retained their powers intact.[53] The requirement in the 1832 Act that voters be registered was one factor in the growth of political parties, which could offer services in this field; and the very existence of larger numbers of voters was an inducement to parties to devise political programmes and manifestos. The 1832 Act for Ireland did not restore voter numbers to their pre-1829 levels, but did bring about some increase.[54]

MacDonagh, *O'Connell: the life of Daniel O'Connell 1775–1847* (London, 1991), pp 319–29. **49** 6 Geo. IV, *c*.4 (9 Mar. 1825). **50** Senior, *Orangeism in Ireland and Britain*, p. 237. **51** 3 & 4 Will. IV, *c*.37 (14 Aug. 1833); 1 & 2 Vict., *c*. 109 (15 Aug. 1838). **52** 2 & 3 Will. IV, *c*.88 (7 Aug. 1832). **53** Peter Jupp, 'Urban politics in Ireland 1801–1831' in David Harkness and Mary O'Dowd (eds), *The town in Ireland* (Belfast, 1981), pp 103–23, at pp 103–4. **54** The electorate rose to 92,141.

Daniel O'Connell's announcement in 1830 that he would proceed directly to work for repeal of the Union was not simply the product of post-emancipation euphoria but owed something to the knowledge that the Union was far from popular in certain Protestant circles. This was notably the case in Dublin, which still contained the largest concentration of Protestants in the country (in the 1830s members of the Church of Ireland in Dublin alone outnumbered the entire population of Belfast). However, the Protestant freemen of the guilds, who continued to enjoy the parliamentary franchise after the 1832 reform act, proved reluctant to support a repeal campaign led by O'Connell: following emancipation a restored Irish parliament would in all probability contain a Catholic majority.[55] In any case, O'Connell found it difficult in the 1830s to mobilise Catholics in support of repeal. Consequently the issue arose of cooperation with other parties, and in 1835 O'Connell and his party entered into an arrangement with the Whigs and radicals under the Lichfield House compact. From the O'Connellite point of view the main object was to obtain reforms that would enable Catholics to exercise their political rights.[56]

The later 1830s proved to be highly productive for the O'Connellites. With Whig governments in power from 1835 to 1841, a number of high-profile Catholic appointments were made, and some key reforms obtained. These included, after a protracted struggle, a municipal reform act in 1840 that placed the local government franchise in corporate towns in the hands of the middle classes.[57] The effect, in most of the corporate towns outside Ulster, was to transfer control from Protestants to Catholics; O'Connell's election as lord mayor of Dublin in 1841 was the most striking sign of this. O'Connell was aware of the negative publicity that would attach to the prospect of a Protestant monopoly simply being replaced by a Catholic one; he urged that the Dublin mayoralty should rotate between Catholics and Protestants, and something like this system did operate at least intermittently down to the early 1880s, although it was not apparently replicated in any other town or city.[58] And irritants remained; Catholics were not permitted to attend church services wearing their robes of office – a provision introduced in the emancipation act and not repealed until 1867.[59]

In addition, the new poor law of 1838 afforded opportunities for those outside the established church to aspire to and attain office as poor law guardians, and both Catholics and dissenters were among those appointed to be poor law commissioners. Reform of the constabulary came in 1836, creating a centralised executive under an inspector general, and opening the force to Catholic recruitment. By 1870 Catholics made up 70 per cent of the force. In

55 Hill, *From patriots to unionists*, pp 345–54.   56 MacDonagh, *O'Connell*, ch. 17.   57 3 & 4 Vict., *c.*108 (10 Aug. 1840).   58 Mary E. Daly, *Dublin the deposed capital: a social and economic history 1860–1914* (Cork, 1985), pp 209–11, 214.   59 W.E. Vaughan, 'Ireland *c.*1870' in id. (ed.), *A new history of Ireland: v Ireland under the union, I, 1801–70* (Oxford, 1989), pp 735,

the field of education, by mid-century the non-denominational national school system set up in the 1830s had given way (under pressure from Catholics and presbyterians) to state-funded schools that were effectively under denominational control. Catholics were also represented among the commissioners of national education. The Church of Ireland clergy preferred to maintain their own educational system, the Church Education Society, founded in 1839. It flourished for a decade before running into serious financial difficulties by the early 1860s. Civil service recruitment also came in for reform during this period, with the introduction of competitive examinations, opening up career to talent. By 1870 the Protestant proportion of the civil service had shrunk to about one-half.[60]

In the towns of Leinster, Munster, and Connacht, where liberal reforms typically involved a transfer of power in local government from Catholic to Protestant hands, the speed and scale of change posed difficulties for the poorer classes of Protestants, and those artisans who were losing status as a result of the industrial revolution. Meanwhile in Belfast the rapid growth of the Catholic population (from 6 per cent in the mid-eighteenth century to 31 per cent by 1834 and to 43 per cent by 1848) raised tensions and fostered the territorial rivalry, on sectarian lines, that became so entrenched in the nineteenth-century. In ordinary times such anxieties would have swelled the ranks of the Orange Order, but the Grand Lodge had dissolved itself again following the 1835 report of the select committee on Orangeism: the report had exposed the Order to attacks from radicals by confirming the existence of Orangeism in the army.[61] The Order was not reconstituted until 1846. Accordingly, during the 1830s and early 1840s many lower-class Protestants joined 'Protestant operative societies', which fulfilled some of the same functions as the Orange Order, especially by boosting morale. They also served to put pressure on politicians, and drew the attention of wealthier Protestants to the plight of their poorer brethren. Inevitably, they were drawn into the orbit of the rising Conservative party, but were never to be taken for granted in their support.[62]

In the countryside the changes were less dramatic. In general Protestants retained control of grand juries, the effective vehicles of local government; change was delayed until the coming of elected county and district councils in 1898.

One further feature of political life in this period is worth noting: the breaking down of barriers between different Protestant denominations, under

---

737. 60 Vaughan, 'Ireland c.1870', p. 741; D.H. Akenson, 'Pre-university education, 1782–1870' in *A new history of Ireland: v Ireland under the union, I*, p. 535. 61 Senior, *Orangeism in Ireland and Britain*, p. 268; Sybil Baker, 'Orange and green Belfast, 1832–1912' in H.J. Dyos and Michael Wolff (eds), *The Victorian city: images and realities* (2 vols, London, 1973), ii, pp 789–814, at p. 793. 62 Baker, 'Orange and green Belfast', p. 795; Jacqueline Hill, 'The Protestant response to repeal' in F.S.L. Lyons and R.A.J. Hawkins (eds), *Ireland*

the influence of a widespread antipathy to the O'Connellite repeal movement and the Whig reforms of the 1830s. The emancipation campaign had already witnessed the alienation of many Ulster presbyterians from the liberal and radical camps (if they had not already defected in the rebellion period), and the process of convergence with Anglicans may have been aided by the spreading influence of evangelicalism. The government's plan for non-denominational national schools, for instance, was anathema to many presbyterians as well as Anglicans. In 1834, following a series of large Protestant meetings, members of the Conservative party organised a large gathering at Hillsborough, County Down, at which the high point was an announcement by Dr Henry Cooke, leader of the dominant subscribing wing in the synod of Ulster, of what he called 'the banns of marriage' between presbyterians and Anglicans.[63]

By this time members of the nobility and gentry, many of them former supporters of Catholic emancipation, were coming to support the Conservatives. Throughout the 1830s the party built up its profile at elections, and continued to perform well in the 1840s and 1850s; at the 1859 general election it succeeded in winning a majority of the Irish seats, and during the 1860s it never won fewer than one-third of the seats.[64] Moreover, members of the landed class continued to dominate the Conservative parliamentary representation. Since the electorate was predominantly Catholic, it is apparent that some of the party's support was coming from Catholic voters. If this seems surprising, it has to be remembered that the electorate was still very small and deference had not been entirely eroded; after a further extension of the franchise in 1850 only one in six adult males had the vote,[65] and the secret ballot was not introduced until 1872.

For Church of Ireland women during this period philanthropic activities remained the most common form of participation in public life.[66] During the great famine there was a Church of Ireland input, alongside women from other denominations, into the organisation of famine relief. Philanthropy often provided a route into other social and political causes, and by the 1860s some women had begun to campaign for reforms in the law on married women's property (an essential prerequisite for any significant change in women's role in public life) and for votes for women.[67] During this period women continued to be excluded from the universities, though by the 1860s provision for girls' secondary and technical education was improving; the establishment of Victoria

under the union (Oxford, 1980), pp 35–68.   63 Gilbert A. Cahill, 'Some nineteenth-century roots of the Ulster problem, 1829–48' in Irish University Review, i (1971), pp 215–37; S.J. Connolly, 'Mass politics and sectarian conflict, 1823–30' in A new history of Ireland: v Ireland under the union I, pp 76–7.   64 B.M. Walker (ed.), Parliamentary election results in Ireland, 1801–1922 (Dublin, 1978).   65 K.T. Hoppen, Ireland since 1800: conflict and conformity (London & New York, 1989), p. 114.   66 See Maria Luddy, Women and philanthropy in nineteenth-century Ireland (Cambridge, 1995).   67 Rosemary Cullen Owens, Smashing times: a history of the Irish women's suffrage movement, 1889–1922 (Dublin, 1984).   68 Maria Luddy,

College in Belfast in 1859 and Alexandra College in Dublin in 1866 were important stages in this process.[68]

By the time of disestablishment, therefore, the dominance of the established church in public life had been considerably diminished. The advent of stipendiary magistrates, the wide range of liberal reforms, the extension of the franchise in 1832, 1850, and 1867; all these developments helped to weaken the church's grip on public life. However, because property, and particularly landed property, retained a major place in the political system, members of the Church of Ireland continued to be markedly over-represented in such fields as the civil service, the professions, and local government in the countryside.[69]

'An agenda for women's history, 1800–1900' in *Irish Historical Studies*, xxviii (1992), pp 19–37, at pp 34–5. **69** Vaughan, 'Ireland *c.*1870', p. 741.

7

An innovative people: the Church of Ireland laity, 1780–1830

Patrick Comerford

The period between 1780 and 1830 was one of great transformation, change and turmoil for the Church of Ireland. From being a confident church, assured of its place in the established order, it would see its privilege and position challenged by revolution in the southeast and the northeast of Ireland, followed quickly by the Act of Union and amalgamation with the Church of England. Eventually, the church would face threats financially and politically from, on the one hand, the Tithe Wars of the 1830s, and on the other from both Catholic Emancipation and the legislative moves commencing ecclesiastical reform, reducing the number of diocesan sees and paving the way to disestablishment. The period opened with Henry Grattan and Henry Flood at their most influential phase in the Dublin parliament, and those who advocated toleration and co-operation dominated political life. Those early years saw the organisation and formation of the Volunteers, with the Ulster Volunteer Convention at Dungannon in 1782 representing the zenith of the phase of liberal Protestant activity.[1] However, the outbreak of the Rightboy disturbances in 1784 was perceived by some of the laity as an attack on the Church of Ireland itself. George Ogle from County Wexford interrupted a debate in the House of Commons on 6 February, 1786 to protest that 'the Protestant establishment in church and consequently in state' was being endangered. Ogle, who regarded the preservation of the 'Protestant Ascendancy' as his primary political objective, warned that 'the landed property of the kingdom [and] ... the Protestant ascendancy' were under threat.[2]

In the same decade, the Catholic Church was becoming more confident, a confidence that was illustrated in a new drive in church building. The depth of disquiet among Protestants was revealed in Austin Cooper's reflection, in

1 James Kelly, 'The genesis of "Protestant ascendancy": the Rightboy disturbances of the 1780s and their impact on Protestant opinion' in Gerard O'Brien (ed.), *Parliament, politics and people* (Dublin, 1989), pp 97–8. 2 Ibid, pp 95, 101–2; *Parliamentary Register* (Irl.), vi,

observing the enlargement of St Paul's, Arran Quay, Dublin, that 'Protestants yet unborn' would 'execrate' the new policy of 'inconsiderable toleration'.[3] Indeed, in County Wexford for example, many landlords, in their eagerness to defend the 'Protestant ascendancy' and the interests of 'Protestants yet unborn', took a stand against the building of Catholic churches in places such as Poulfur, Newtownbarry, Crossabeg and Gorey, at a time when new churches were fast replacing the old, thatched mass-houses.[4]

The decades that followed saw the organisation of the United Irishmen and the Orange Order. Soon, the 1798 Rising, with reports, often exaggerated, of sectarian massacres at Scullabogue and Wexford Bridge, would shake the confidence of many Protestants.[5] The Act of Union (1800), Catholic Emancipation (1829), and the first moves towards Disestablishment would see a liberal Protestant church and its laity move into retreat and become decidedly more conservative. It could be said the political and social upheavals reflected the great demographic changes taking place at the time. But, despite the changes in population in those fifty years, the number of dioceses and archbishops and bishops remained unaltered at twenty-two. At the beginning of this period, members of the church, laity and clergy, were unshaken in their assurance of their place and the place of their church in the established order. Despite the population changes in the fifty years that followed, including the rapid growth of the cities of Belfast and Dublin, the church structures had become ossified and proved ill suited to changing circumstances, not to be altered until the Church Temporalities Act of 1833.[6]

For the landed aristocracy and the key political families, church and state were linked intimately, not only in the political order, but in their own family lives too. This was symbolised succinctly in the person of Richard Robinson, who was created Baron Rokeby of Armagh in 1777, and was archbishop of Armagh from 1767 to 1794.[7] For the leading political families, with names such as Beresford, Jocelyn, Knox, Loftus, Maxwell, Ponsonby and Trench, or the emerging banking and mercantile elites among the Guinness, La Touche, Marlay and similar families, there was an inseparable link between prominent lay members of the church and those who exercised ecclesiastical power, a link provided by family members on the bench of bishops or among the senior

85–7. 3 Kelly, 'Genesis of "Protestant ascendancy"', p. 101. 4 Kevin Whelan, 'The Catholic community in eighteenth-century County Wexford' in Walter Forde (ed.), *Memory & mission: Christianity in Wexford 600 to A.D. 2000* (Castlebridge, 1999), p. 38. 5 See Richard Musgrave, *Memoirs of the Irish rebellion of 1798* (eds) Steven W. Myers and Delores E. McKnight (4th ed., Fort Wayne and Enniscorthy, 1995). Fuel was added to W.H. Maxwell's sectarian account of the rising with the illustration of later editions by George Cruickshank's racist cartoons; see W.H. Maxwell, *History of the Irish rebellion in 1798* (6th ed., London, 1864). 6 K. Theodore Hoppen, *Ireland since 1800: conflict & conformity* (London and New York, 1989), p. 71. 7 *Dictionary of National Biography*, xvii, pp 39–40.

clergy. For the other social classes, as James Godkin would observe later, becoming a minister of the established church was a sure way of securing 'the social status of a gentleman'.[8]

The Beresfords illustrate how one leading family in church and politics could yield disproportionate influence in the life of the church, steadily increasing its hold on the highest offices in this period. In 1780, there was one Beresford among the bishops, William de la Poer Beresford, appointed to Dromore that year. William, who later became archbishop of Tuam and became a peer as Baron Decies, was a younger brother of two of the most powerful political figures in the land, John Beresford, who dominated the political clique in Dublin Castle at the end of the eighteenth century, and the first marquess of Waterford; members of the Beresford family alone accounted for almost one tenth of the episcopal appointments made over the next fifty years;[9] those bishops included George Beresford, described by William Stuart, archbishop of Armagh, as 'one of the most profligate men in Europe'. Archbishop Magee, observing the numerous well-placed and well-paid clerical members of the family, commented wryly, 'The production and maintenance of Beresfords is not the final cause of the Irish Church'.[10]

Among the leading political lights of the day, John Foster (1740–1828), the last Speaker of the Irish Commons, was a nephew of Thomas Foster (1709–86), rector of Dunleer, County Louth, brother of William Foster (1744–97), successively bishop of Cork, Kilmore and Clogher, brother-in-law of Henry Maxwell (d. 1798), bishop of Meath, and uncle of William Foster (1796–1826), vicar of Collon, County Louth; and he was related distantly or by marriage to Alexander McClintock (1775–1836), the rector of Newtownbarry, County Wexford, who was at the centre of the tithe battle known as the 'Battle of the Pound', Percy Jocelyn, disgraced bishop of Clogher, and the third earl of Roden and the fifth Lord Farnham, two of the leading evangelicals among the laity at the beginning of the nineteenth century.[11] Similar family connections linked many members of the landed aristocracy and the political elite with the life of the church. And so, just as it was impossible for many to contemplate a separation of church and state, it would have been difficult for many of the most influential laity to think of the clergy as a class apart. Church preferments were often a useful acknowledgement of political service and favour. In the

8 James Godkin, *Ireland and her churches* (London, 1867), p. 217.   9 Ossory 1782, Tuam 1794, Clonfert 1801, Cork 1805, Raphoe 1807, Kilmore 1802, Clogher 1819, Dublin 1820, and Armagh 1822; figures compiled from Henry Cotton, *Fasti Ecclesiae Hibernicae* (5 vols, Dublin, 1847–60) and *Crockford's Clerical directory*, various editions. See also James Godkin, *The religious history of Ireland* (London, 1873), pp 241–2.   10 Quoted in James B. Leslie, *Ossory clergy and parishes* (Enniskillen, 1933), p. 346.   11 A.P.W. Malcomson, *John Foster, the politics of the Anglo-Irish ascendancy* (Oxford, 1978), appendices and tables between pp 450–1.

political debates of the 1780s and 1790s, the term 'Protestant ascendancy', first used hesitantly by Boyle Roche in 1782 in support of Catholic Relief, gained political currency among those clergy and laity who agreed with Richard Woodward, bishop of Cloyne, who in 1787 equated 'Protestant ascendancy' with control of the land and the constitutional link between church and state.[12]

According to a later primate, William Alexander, 'those were the days of a silken prelacy, a slumbering priesthood, a silent laity'.[13] But, although it might be argued that the church had been badly served by a silken prelacy and, to a lesser degree, by a slumbering priesthood, was Alexander less than kind in referring to a silent laity? For the political elite and the landed aristocracy, the church provided an extension of their power throughout all sections of society; but for others among the laity, particularly those among the rising middle classes and the burgeoning business sector, the church inspired and provided an outlet and opportunity for their piety and religion to be expressed in works of charity, in evangelical fervour, and in an enthusiasm for education and mission.

I

At the beginning of the nineteenth century, a Beresford remarked, 'When I was a boy, the Irish people meant the Protestants; now it means the Roman Catholics'.[14] It was never true to say that Protestants formed a majority on the island, but in this fifty-year period there was a perceptible change in the balance in society that saw control of political, economic and social life beginning to slip away from the leading families among the laity of the Church of Ireland. Throughout the eighteenth century, the Church of Ireland never accounted for more than ten or eleven per cent of the population. The changes in population meant the number of people living in Dublin had quadrupled from 51,000 in 1700 to 191,000 in 1800, and while in 1700 an estimated 70 per cent of the city's population was Protestant (mainly members of the Church of Ireland), by 1800 these proportions had been reversed dramatically so that 70 per cent of the city was Catholic and only 30 per cent was Protestant. Shortly after the end of this period the Commissioners for Public Instruction reported the Church of Ireland proportion of the population of the whole island had fallen to less than 11 per cent.[15] These demographic changes alone must have been harbingers of things to come. Nevertheless the diocesan and parochial structures remained unchanged and immune to the changing needs of a shifting population and the urban laity.

12 Kelly, 'The genesis of "Protestant ascendancy"', pp 93 ff, 115, 126–127.   13 Eleanor Alexander (ed.), *Primate Alexander* (London, 1913), pp 108–9.   14 J.C. Beckett, *The Anglo-Irish tradition* (London, 1976), p. 10.   15 Hoppen, *Ireland since 1800*, p. 60.

With the growth of the cities, the neglect of the urban poor by parochial structures became more obvious. In his memoir of the Church of Ireland, R.S. Brooke describes the eight clergy who worked among the poor in the Liberties of Dublin under the leadership of the dean of St Patrick's as a knot of true brethren who kept 'hundreds of poor Protestants from sliding into Romanism, the natural consequence of neglect'.[16] Yet, in Dublin, both cathedrals were falling into decay, and the parochial structures were crumbling: the archdeacon of Dublin held St Peter's and Donnybrook, a parochial union that was, in effect, the largest parish in the diocese, extending from Aungier Street to Donnybrook, Booterstown, Taney (Dundrum) and Rathfarnham. Although served during this period by St Peter's and the ancient but inadequate St Kevin's, it was only in the 1810s and 1820s that a number of chapels of ease were built in outlying reaches of the parish, including Christ Church, Taney, St Stephen's, Mount Street Crescent, St Philip's and St James's, Booterstown, Sandford, Holy Trinity, Rathmines, and St Mary's, Donnybrook.[17] Belfast was served by only one Church of Ireland parish church after the corporation church, the so-called 'English church' was taken down in 1774. In 1776 an order in council changed 'the parish Church of Belfast, which is Shankill, to the town of Belfast' and St Anne's was built in Donegall Street by the lay rector, the earl of Donegall. St Anne's remained the only Church of Ireland church in the city until the early nineteenth century when St George's was built as a chapel of ease on the site of the old corporation church in 1813–16.[18]

The neglect of the urban poor was prevalent in other towns and cities too. Revd Adam Averell observed in 1795 that while population and industry had increased in Galway during the previous twenty years, Protestantism was in retreat due to the zeal of the Catholic clergy and to the 'vile sloth' of the clergy of the Church of Ireland. In Limerick city, there were only three churches in 1830, the parish of St Laurence had no church at all, and the sale of Lord Limerick's private chapel, St Michael's, to the Provincial Bank the following year left a parish of more than 3,000 Protestants without a church. In Wexford town, a complicated amalgam of more than a dozen parishes, there was only one church until St Selskar's was rebuilt in 1818, but the rector was still inducted first in the rural parish of Rathaspeck, and only afterwards in the other churches in the town.[19]

16 Quoted in W.G. Neely, *The shaping of the church: a history of the Church of Ireland* (Dublin, 1994), p. 124.   **17** Peter Costello, *Dublin churches* (Dublin, 1989), *passim*; John Crawford, *Around the churches: the stories of the churches in the St Patrick's cathedral group of parishes* (Dublin, 1988), p. 60; Deirdre Kelly, *Four roads to Dublin: the history of Ranelagh, Rathmines and Leeson Street* (Dublin, 1995), pp 110–12, 230. Taney and Rathfarnham did not receive separate parochial status until 1851, Donnybrook in 1864, and Rathmines as late as 1883. **18** Alan Acheson, *A history of the Church of Ireland, 1691–1996* (Dublin, 1997), p. 93. **19** Ibid., pp 92–4; Elizabeth Browne and Tom Wickham (eds), *Lewis's Wexford* (Enniscorthy,

If the parochial system and non-resident and pluralist clergy had failed the urban poor in many parts of the larger cities, they had failed them in rural Ireland too: in 1799, the new rector of Aughaval (Westport), Thomas Grace, found the 'scanty and 'scattered' Protestants of his County Mayo parish were at risk of being drawn into the Catholic Church,[20] while in neighbouring County Sligo, Albert Best, recalled that many Protestant families in Connacht had been obliged to have recourse to Catholic priests because of the shortage of Church of Ireland clergy.[21] In the mid-eighteenth century, it was estimated that half the population of Connemara belonged to the Church of Ireland, but by the time Revd James Daly of Galway toured Connemara in 1813, he found that the poor had lapsed from the Church of Ireland for want of a minister from their own church to 'baptise their children, to marry their daughters, and to bury their dead'.[22] This poor supply of clergy in the west was in sharp contrast to the over-supply in under-populated rural parishes in the east. In the diocese of Ossory in 1795 Robert Alexander, rector of Kilbride and Kilcoan, described his parish as a 'sinecure', with no church, no glebe house and no resident Protestant family. His neighbour, William Barker of Kilmocar, derived £26 a year from his 'perfect sinecure' with no church, glebe or Protestant parishioners. Similar reports came from the incumbents of Aglishmartin, Dunmore, Listerlin and Rosconnel while Samuel Madden of Kells had no legal vestry for want of parishioners.[23] And yet, even in under-populated parishes, the clergy, including non-resident pluralists, could be conscientious in attending to the needs of the laity. George Stevenson (1744–1825) was both rector of Callan, County Kilkenny, and dean of Kilfenora. Although he was non-resident in his Ossory parishes he kept two resident curates to attend forty-one Protestant families, one at £50 a year and the second, who acted as schoolmaster, at £40 and they reported fifty communicants at Christmas, forty-one at Easter and twenty-six on Whitsunday.[24]

In an effort to meet the needs of an expanding population in Dublin, some of the churches on the fringes of the city were rebuilt. In 1784, Revd Philip Homan of Rathfarnham laid the foundation stone for a new church on the village green to accommodate a growing population. From the 1820s on, older churches were being rebuilt and new ones were being erected in the countryside around Dublin. The old, decaying St Maelruain's in Tallaght, close to the archbishop's palace, was torn down and a new church by John Semple was built

1983), pp 150–1; Norman Ruddock and Naomi Kloss, *Unending worship: a history of St Iberius Church, Wexford* (Wexford, 1997), passim. **20** J. D'A. Sirr, *A memoir of Power Le Poer Trench, last archbishop of Tuam* (Dublin and London, 1845), pp 309–10. **21** M.C. Motherwell, *A memoir of Albert Blest* (Dublin, 1843), pp 9–10. **22** Acheson, *A history of the Church of Ireland*, p. 108. **23** Leslie, *Ossory*, pp 96, 165, 194, 205, 247, 287, 306, 308–9, 317–18, 344; J.B. Leslie, *Ferns clergy and parishes* (Dublin, 1936), p. 126. **24** Leslie, *Ossory*, pp 214–15, 217.

in 1829 with rubble from the old church and funds from the Board of First Fruits.[25] But many of the new churches were provided not at an official level by the church but through the enthusiastic efforts of committed laymen. For evangelical clergy who often found their path to the pulpit blocked by the senior ranks of clerical and lay patrons alike, the new trustee and proprietary chapels provided a welcome opportunity to have their voices heard. The building of the Bethesda Chapel in 1784 in Dorset Street in Dublin's north inner city marked the arrival of the evangelical revival and the early nineteenth century saw committed laymen enthusiastically involved in financing and supporting new chapels such as the episcopal chapel in Baggot Street and the chapel attached to the Molyneux Home. In the suburbs and beyond, Whitechurch was erected for Tallaght parish on land provided by John La Touche of Marlay Park in 1825 and Sandford church was built in Ranelagh in 1826 by Robert Newenham, who secured a site for an evangelical chapel and school from George Sandford, Baron Mountsandford. The same year saw the erection of St Philip's and St James's in Booterstown through the combined efforts of James La Touche and the earl of Pembroke. Later, Trinity church was built in Lower Gardiner Street specially to provide a pulpit for the future bishop of Cork, John Gregg (1798–1878), a popular, forceful and eloquent preacher who also endowed the episcopal chapel at North Strand. Similar lay efforts to supply churches in neglected urban areas could be found in towns and cities around the country, such as Samuel Lane's church at Frankfield in Cork.[26]

Charles Loftus, first marquess of Ely, serves to illustrate the privileged place of influence members of the landed aristocracy held within the church, and the power these privileged members of the laity exercised when it came to appointments in the Church of Ireland. Charles Tottenham, the grandson of Charles Tottenham, the MP for New Ross known as 'Tottenham in his Boots', changed his name to Loftus when he inherited Rathfarnham Castle and extensive estates and property in Dublin, County Wexford, and County Fermanagh following the death of his maternal uncle, Henry Loftus (1709–83), earl of Ely. The Loftus family was descended from Adam Loftus (1533? –1605), archbishop of Armagh and Dublin, lord chancellor of Ireland and first provost of Trinity College Dublin. Through his mother, Loftus was related also to Charles Este, bishop of Ossory (1736–40) and of Waterford and Lismore (1740–45), while the clergy connections on the Tottenham side of the family were numerous too.[27]

---

25 Costello, *Dublin churches*, pp xi, 196; William Domville Handcock, *The history and antiquities of Tallaght* (Dublin, 1991), pp 37–43; Violet Broad et al., *Rathfarnham: gateway to the hills* (Dublin, 1990), pp 12–13; W.R.J. Wallace, *St Maelruain's church, Tallaght, 1829–1979* (Dublin, 1979), pp 7–10.   26 Costello, *Dublin churches*, pp 148, 162, 192, 222; Deirdre Kelly, *Four roads to Dublin*, pp 110–12; Broad et al., *Rathfarnham*, p. 7.   27 *Burke's Peerage*, various eds, s.v. Ely, Hutchinson; Tottenham; Leslie, *Ossory*, pp 26–7, 194, 363.

Following his succession to the Loftus estates and his change of name, Loftus was soon promoted in the ranks of Irish politics and in the peerage, becoming in quick succession Baron Loftus (1785), Postmaster-General and Viscount Loftus (1789), earl of Ely (1794) and, with the passage of the Act of Union, marquess of Ely in the Irish peerage and Baron Loftus in the peerage of the United Kingdom, with a seat in the new House of Lords. Ely also controlled eight seats for six boroughs in the Irish Commons: in County Wexford alone, he was patron of three of the eight boroughs, and shared the patronage of New Ross and Wexford. With a keen eye on church affairs, Ely and his family built a new church in New Ross, held the tithes of a number of parishes in the diocese of Ferns, he was patron of the living at Hook, and he supported public schools at Fethard-on-Sea and New Ross.[28] Ely appears to have been on good terms with the local Catholic parish priest, Canon Thomas Broaders, who, according to local tradition, exorcised the devil at Loftus Hall.[29] However, when the Catholic chapel of Poulfur was being built the Loftus family insisted that it should be located in a hollow and that it should have false chimneys to make it look like a mere dwelling house to the passerby. Similarly, the Lysters of Sion Hill in Kilpatrick parish insisted that the chapel at Crossabeg should be located in a hollow so that the windows would not be visible from the 'big house'.[30]

During the 1798 Rising, Ely was vigorous in his pursuit of the rebels: Austin Ledwitch of Knocklyon, a nephew of the parish priest of Rathfarnham and a member of Ely's constabulary, changed sides and was hanged with other deserters at Queen's Street Bridge, Dublin.[31] At this time, Ely was learning bitter lessons about the difficulties facing those who exercised patronage in the church; in 1797, he presented Revd Thomas Brooke Clarke to Inishmacsaint in Clogher diocese, but within weeks met with refusal when he tried to insist that Clarke should either reside in the parish or raise the salary of his two curates. The bishop of Clogher, John Porter, also failed to move Clarke, and the problem was not solved until Hugh Hamilton was presented in 1824.[32]

Ely used the Act of Union to promote his family's interests on the bench of bishops. Having used the eight votes at his command in the Commons to support the Union, he had been promised a post in the Treasury for his elder son, Lord Loftus, and a bishopric for his younger son, Lord Robert Ponsonby Tottenham (1773–1850). The Tottenham portion of the family estates had devolved on Lord Robert, who retained the Tottenham name; in 1802, his father

28 Browne and Wickham *Lewis's Wexford*, pp 32–3, 40, 72, 75, 101, 124–5, 138, 145. 29 W.H. Grattan Flood, *History of the diocese of Ferns* (Waterford, 1916), pp 112–13, Thomas P. Walsh , 'The history of Loftus Hall', *Journal of the Old Wexford Society*, no. 5 (1974–5), pp 33–7. 30 Kevin Whelan, 'The Catholic community', p. 38; Browne and Wickham, *Lewis's Wexford*, pp 95–6. 31 Musgrave, *Memoirs of the Irish rebellion of 1798*, pp 191, 201, 297; Pat Bradley et al., *Knocklyon – past and present* (Dublin, 1992), p. 25. 32 Acheson, *A history of the Church of Ireland*, p. 112.

sought the vacant see of Clogher for him, but it went instead to the bishop of Ferns, Percy Jocelyn. A year later, Tottenham had reached the age of thirty, the minimum canonical age for episcopal consecration, and soon after Ely unsuccessfully tried to secure for him the vacant see of Clonfert. When Down and Dromore fell vacant in 1804, a stubborn Ely and his elder son, Lord Loftus, now a lord of the Treasury and MP for Wexford, proposed Tottenham, but the archbishop of Armagh, William Stuart, replied that he would prefer anyone else as Tottenham was 'utterly unacquainted with his profession, never having performed any clerical duties'. Stuart suggested a southern diocese instead and so Tottenham was consecrated for Killaloe in 1804. Two years later Ely died on 22 March 1806 with the family titles, estates, church interests and political offices safe in the hands of his eldest son and satisfied that his younger son had been elevated at last to the episcopate.[33]

II

To paraphrase the Canadian church historian Gerald Cragg the Georgian era could be described as the 'golden age of philanthropy'.[34] In the Church of Ireland, this golden age coincided with an evangelical revival that took a firm hold on the laity, encouraged by John Wesley's twenty-one visits to Ireland in the forty-two-year period up to 1789. The evangelical revival saw a parallel growth in charities and causes supported vigorously by the laity, while the growth in charitable foundations and voluntary organisation, and a sharpened interest in education, provided new opportunities for the religious and pious among the laity to give expression to their deepest Christian values.

At the highest institutional levels of education, the church was most closely identified with Trinity College Dublin, and with schools such as the Royal School at Portora, near Enniskillen, or the new Blue Coat School, opened in Dublin in 1783, where the headmasters were, generally speaking, in holy orders. But while the charter schools, Erasmus Smith schools, and private schools were at their height, the church was failing to provide a system of education for the populace at large. With few exceptions, parish and diocesan schools had been of very little use. A survey of the clergy in 1799 and 1800 found less than one-third of children 'fit for school' were receiving any education at all, and those who were largely attended hedge schools. As Kenneth Milne says, the clergy

33 D.N. Akenson, *The Church of Ireland: ecclesiastical reform and revolution, 1800–1885* (New Haven and London, 1991), pp 77–9; Desmond Bowen, *The Protestant crusade in Ireland 1800–70* (Dublin, 1978), pp 40–1, 44–5; Edward Brynn, *The Church of Ireland in the age of Catholic Emancipation* (New York and London, 1982), pp 51–7 ff., 188.   34 Gerald R. Cragg, *The church and the age of reason, 1648–1789* (London, 1983), p. 129.

had palpably failed in their duty to provide a network of schools throughout the land, and the church failed to remedy the situation.[35]

Two societies sought to remedy this situation. The Association for the Promotion of Christian Knowledge (A.P.C.K.) was founded in 1792 as the Association for Discountenancing Vice and Promoting the Knowledge and Practice of the Christian Religion. The A.P.C.K. was incorporated in 1800 and. from 1803 on, began to play a major role in education, paying schoolmasters' salaries and attracting government funding for its projects. The Society for Promoting the Education of the Poor, also known as the Kildare Place Society, was founded in 1811 with the object of furthering Protestant education and the Protestant religion. The first committee of the Kildare Place Society included leading lay luminaries, such as William Lee Guinness and three members of the La Touche family, and attracted Catholic support from the beginning. By 1825, the society was supporting 1,490 schools with 100,000 pupils, was employing Catholic school inspectors, and was receiving government grants.[36]

In addition there were many voluntary schools, such as the inter-denominational school near Castleboro, County Wexford, established by Lady Carew, or the school run by Lady Shaw and James Grattan. Maria Shaw was the wife of Sir Robert Shaw (1774–1849), M.P. for Dublin and one of the leading evangelicals. Her school at Bushy Park in Terenure, Dublin, had 210 children, most of them Catholics. James Grattan of Tinnehinch, M.P. for Wicklow and a reformer who tried to be a 'godly squire', organised non-sectarian schools, and preferred the teachers to 'attend in the first instance' to the children's minds 'rather than to their religious education'.[37] But despite the efforts of a small number of the well-intentioned and pious among the laity, the church was found wanting in the field of education. In 1825, a government report found the A.P.C.K. schools were too few in number and too Protestant in character, and that the church was totally inadequate in the provision of education.[38]

The late eighteenth century also saw the development of charitable institutions with close church links, with new philanthropic endeavours springing up, particularly in Dublin. Earlier decades had seen the foundation and building of hospitals, including Cook Street, Dr Steeven's, Mercer's, Donnybrook, the Meath, Swift's and the Rotunda, and the beginning of charitable ventures such

35 Kenneth Milne, 'Principle or pragmatism: Archbishop Brodrick and church education policy' in A. Ford, J. McGuire, and K. Milne (eds), *As by law established: the Church of Ireland since the Reformation* (Dublin, 1995), pp 188–91.   36 Ibid, pp 193–4; for a detailed study of the Kildare Place Society see Harold Hislop, 'The Kildare Place Society, 1811–31: an Irish experiment in mixed education' (Ph.D. thesis, Trinity College Dublin, 1990). 37 Browne and Wickham, *Lewis's Wexford*, p. 87; R.F. Foster, *Charles Stewart Parnell, the man and his family* (Hassocks, Sussex, 1979), pp xvii, xix.   38 Milne, 'Principle or pragmatism', pp 193–4.

as the Claremont Home for the Deaf in Glasnevin and the Magdalene Asylum in Lower Leeson Street, Dublin. With the inmates screened out of sight, the Magdalene Chapel became one of the most fashionable churches in Dublin. It was a pattern that followed with later foundations: when the episcopal chapel was built in Baggot Street, it was annexed to the Asylum for Penitential Females, while the Molyneux Chapel in Bride Street was attached to an 'asylum for the female blind' from 1815.[39]

One foundation stands out as a symbol of the beginning of the evangelical revival in the Church of Ireland: the Bethesda Chapel, was founded in 1784, the year of Wesley's first ordination, on the corner of Granby Row and Dorset Street, by a wealthy Dublin merchant, William Smyth. Close to fashionable Rutland Square, it came to symbolise in bricks and mortar that the evangelical revival had taken its hold on the fashionable laity of the city. Despite the refusal of successive archbishops to licence the chapel, it attracted the support of prominent members of the commercial, mercantile and land-owning classes, including the conservative Lord Roden and the charitable Arthur Guinness. With Revd Benjamin Mathias exercising a dynamic ministry there from 1805 until 1841, the Bethesda was the centre for evangelical life in Dublin, and it gave tangible expression to the charitable concerns of evangelicals when the Dorset or Lock Penitentiary and an asylum for female orphans was attached, the orphan girls living in a room above the chapel itself and singing at its services.[40]

A leading Dublin businessman of the day, Arthur Guinness (1768–1855), was an example of how many of the leading laity could still devote their time and money to promoting education, supporting charitable foundations, and being attentive to the needs of the poorer sectors of society. Born on 12 March 1768, Guinness was the second son of the founder of the brewery, Arthur Guinness (1725–1803), who benefited from a £100 bequest in the will of Arthur Price, archbishop of Cashel (1678–1752). The immediate heir to the family's business interests, the founder's eldest son, Hosea, decided to seek holy orders and became incumbent of St Werburgh's, Dublin. The younger Arthur Guinness inherited the brewery, and was well connected with leading church families through his mother Olivia Whitmore, a cousin of both Henry Grattan and Revd Edward Smythe of the Bethesda Chapel.[41]

Guinness was prominent in public life for half a century: he was governor of the Bank of Ireland and an alderman and deputy lieutenant for the city of Dublin, served as president of the Dublin Chamber of Commerce, was a member of the Dublin Ballast Board, and a director of the Corn Exchange

39 Costello, *Dublin churches*, p. 222.   40 Acheson, *A history of the Church of Ireland*, pp 98–9, 122, 137, 157.   41 Michelle Guinness, *The Guinness legend* (London, 1990), pp 1–13; Michelle Guinness, *The Guinness spirit: brewers and bankers, ministers and missionaries* (London, 2000), pp 15–34.

Buildings. He gave his energies to a number of civic and charitable causes, including the Farming Society of Ireland, the Dublin Society (later the Royal Dublin Society), the Society for Bettering the Conditions of the Poor of Ireland, the Society for Improving the Conditions of Children Employed as Chimney Sweepers, and the Meath Street Savings' Bank, and was a governor of the Meath Hospital. He was an early and keen supporter of both the Hibernian Bible Society and the Irish branch, or Hibernian district, of the Church Missionary Society (C.M.S.), serving for many years on their committees. He became a 'faithful friend' of Michael Solomon Alexander, first Protestant bishop of Jerusalem (1841–6), who reported to him with some cheer, 'We are daily enjoying your excellent porter, which I think has done much to keep up our strength … I have no doubt that you will be pleased that your excellent beverage has found its way to Jerusalem'.[42]

As Alan Acheson points out, Guinness was a layman who in his piety linked both church and chapel. He was a life-long parishioner of St Catherine's, serving both as churchwarden and treasurer. There in 1786, with the curate, Robert Raikes, he co-founded the parish Sunday School, the second oldest Sunday School Society in Ireland. With Guinness as its first lay superintendent, the school grew to such numbers that it became obvious the area was in urgent need of a day school too. In 1798, the Dublin Free Day School, with accommodation for 1,500 children, was established in a building adjoining Guinness's Brewery.[43] Guinness was also a trustee of the North Strand episcopal chapel, with its Sunday and day schools, and an accustomed worshipper at the Bethesda Chapel. There he was committed to its charities, and was involved in the rescue operation mounted in 1805 when John Walker seceded from the church but tried to remain as chaplain of the penitentiary. Later, with Lord Roden, he was among the trustees of a fund to buy up livings so that evangelical incumbents could be appointed to parishes.[44]

In October 1813, a piece of doggerel in the *Milesian Magazine* described Guinness as 'the heresy beer that was made to poison the Pope', and a certain Dr Brennan claimed that in brewing their porter the Guinnesses had impregnated it with heretical poison by pouring in tons of Bibles and cartloads of Protestant catechisms and Methodist hymnbooks to subvert the Catholic faith and to produce a disposition 'to singing praises of the Lord through the nose' – an implication that evangelicals sang hymns with an English accent.[45]

42 Jack Hodgins, *Sister island: a history of the Church Missionary Society in Ireland, 1814–1994* (Belfast, 1994), p 2; Guinness, *The Guinness legend*, p. 43; Crawford, *Around the churches*, pp 15–7. **43** Acheson, *A history of the Church of Ireland*, p. 99; Crawford, *Around the churches*, pp 15–16. **44** Acheson, *A history of the Church of Ireland*, pp 99–100, 183. **45** Guinness, *The Guinness legend*, pp 36–7; Frederic Mullally, *The silver salver: the story of the Guinness family* (London, 1981), p. 14.

But Guinness was an early supporter of Daniel O'Connell, and organised support in St Catherine's Parish for Catholic Emancipation. With Catholic Emancipation in 1829, Guinness joined the celebrations and told a public meeting, 'I am much joyed ... for hitherto although always a sincere advocate for Catholic freedom, I never could look my Catholic neighbour confidently in the face.'[46] When Guinness died on 9 June 1855, the minister of the Bethesda Chapel, Revd W.H. Krause, delivered a patronising eulogy ascribing his liberal political and social views to 'a judgement not yet fully enlightened in divine truth, and therefore without the perception of their error and evil tendencies'. The evangelical faith of Guinness and his certainty that God had prospered him in his business life was expressed in a letter to his brother Benjamin '... the continued good account of our business calls for much thankfulness to almighty God while we humbly ask for the infinitely higher blessings of His grace in the Lord Jesus Christ'.[47]

III

Coupled with the growth in charitable organisations and voluntary foundations, the evangelical revival brought with it an increased concern among the laity for mission at home and overseas. The earliest Anglican missionary societies were the Society for the Promotion of Christian Knowledge (S.P.C.K.), and the Society for the Propagation of the Gospel (S.P.G.), which received a royal charter in 1701. The S.P.G. came into being in Ireland with an auxiliary society in 1714, and from its earliest days it relied essentially on the high church party for support and its early missionaries.[48] The evangelical revival saw a fresh enthusiasm in Ireland for mission at home and abroad; at home, this came to mean the conversion of Catholics to the established church, but mission overseas, which under the S.P.G. once simply involved providing chaplains for English-speakers in the colonies, took on a new and dynamic meaning with the newly-enthused laity involved in founding new missionary societies.

By the end of this period, five national societies had been established in the Church of Ireland mostly to distribute Bibles and tracts, and one of them to provide literature in the Irish language. These missionary societies to the Catholics were sustained mainly by lay voluntary work and gifts of money, and in general operated outside the parochial structures.[49] Among the new missionary

---

46 Guinness, *The Guinness legend*, p. 38.   47 Mullally, *The silver salver*, p. 14.   48 Harry Vere White, *Children of St Columba: a sketch of the history, at home and abroad, of the Irish Auxiliary of the Society for the Propagation of the Gospel* (Dublin, 1914), p 11; T.E. Yates, 'Anglicans and Mission' in Stephen Sykes and John Booty (eds), *The study of Anglicanism* (London, 1988), pp 429–41.   49 P.M.H. Bell, *Disestablishment in Ireland and Wales* (London, 1969), p. 34.

and evangelistic societies were the Hibernian Bible Society, founded in 1806 'to encourage a wider circulation of the Holy Scriptures, without note or comment, in Ireland'; the Sunday School Society for Ireland, formed in 1809; the Irish auxiliary of the London Society for Promoting Christianity Among the Jews (1810); the Hibernian Church Missionary Society (1814); the Religious Tract and Book Society, formed in 1817; and the Irish Society for Promoting the Scriptural Education and Religious Instruction of Irish Roman Catholics, Chiefly through the Medium of their Own Language (1818). The Irish Society spent £4,000 a year in providing Bibles and teachers. Many of these societies were interdenominational and owed their inspiration, financing and organi-sation to the enthusiasm of the laity of the Church of Ireland. Alone among them the Church Home Missions Society, founded in 1828 to preach the Gospel throughout Ireland, was unique in having clergy only as management and staff, although its mission workers were sustained by voluntary work and donations and their work lay outside the parochial structures. The Hibernian Bible Society had a clergyman, Benjamin Mathias, as its first secretary but the rest of these societies had lay secretaries.[50]

The new evangelical movement brought with it a new enthusiasm for overseas mission. The C.M.S. was founded in London in 1799, and the very first contribution from Ireland to the C.M.S. was made by a layman, William Hall of Dublin, who sent two guineas early in 1802 to London, and Arthur Guinness is noted in the C.M.S. report of 1809–10 as sending £10.[51] Through the efforts of Lady Charlotte O'Brien of Dromoland Castle, County Clare, a Dublin Ladies' Association of C.M.S. was formed on 11 June 1814, eleven days before the men formed an Irish branch or 'auxiliary', later known as the Hibernian Church Missionary Society, at a public meeting in the Rotunda on 22 June. The formation of the new missionary society was mainly an endeavour of the prominent laity of the day: among the twelve speakers at that meeting was Arthur Guinness, but only two senior clergy gave their support, George Maunsell, dean of Leighlin, and Viscount Lifford, dean of Armagh. The first president of the new society was Viscount Lorton, the vice-presidents included the lord mayor of Dublin and two members of the La Touche family, while the vice-patrons included eight peers, of whom only one, Lifford, was a clergyman and the society would remain without episcopal patronage until 1820. By 1823 John Pierce, a teacher from Kilkenny, had become the first lay missionary from the Church of Ireland and the third Irish missionary from the C.M.S. to be sent overseas.[52]

However, not all the home missions were evangelical in their emphasis. In the southwest a new interest in mission was encouraged by John Jebb (1775–1833),

50 Acheson, *A history of the Church of Ireland*, pp 121–2.   51 F.E. Bland, *How the Church Missionary Society came to Ireland* (Dublin, 1935), p. 60; Hodgins, *Sister island*, p. 2.
52 Bland, *How the Church Missionary Society came to Ireland*, p. 158; Hodgins, *Sister island*,

who became bishop of Limerick in 1823. Jebb was one of the pioneers of the Oxford Movement, along with his friend Alexander Knox (1757–1831), a pious high church layman and author of *Use and import of the Eucharistic symbols* (1824). Knox, once an early member of the United Irishmen, has been described as 'a most important precursor of the early Tractarians and therefore of the Oxford Movement', and it was said, 'If Mr Knox be Socrates, Mr Jebb is Plato'.[53] Jebb encouraged a cluster of prominent high church sympathisers in the Limerick area, including the poet Sir Aubrey Hunt, later Sir Aubrey de Vere (1788–1846), William Monsell (1812–94), later Lord Emly, and Monsell's brother-in-law, Edwin Quin, Lord Adare (1812–71), later third earl of Dunraven. Jebb was strongly opposed to Catholic Emancipation, and approved of the great number of conversions that took place in 1827 and later, including the conversion of 410 Catholics at Askeaton, seeing in them a thirst for knowledge unaffected by any scheme for proselytizing. Through the interest in mission of this group of high church Limerick laity St Columba's College was subsequently founded.[54]

IV

The leading evangelicals often were connected by networks of kinship and support and through marriage alliances. A member of a prominent evangelical family, Lord Jocelyn (later the third earl of Roden), illustrates the enthusiasm and passion for mission of many of the leading laity during this period. Robert Jocelyn, who was born on 27 October 1788, came from a strong clerical background: his maternal grandfather, Robert Bligh, was dean of Elphin, and he shared many of the family connections of his kinsman, Speaker Foster.[55] As Lord Jocelyn, he entered public life in 1806, when he was elected for the borough of Dundalk, County Louth, and immediately earned a reputation as an ardent conservative. But he was also active in church life. He was 'converted' at the annual meeting of the Hibernian Bible Society, having followed the crowd into the Pillar Room of the Rotunda in Dublin out of curiosity. From then on, he was an active evangelical, regularly conducting services and delivering addresses in his private chapel at Tullymore Park, near Castlewellan, County Down. The vicar of Dundalk, Elias Thackery, upbraided him for contributing towards an Independent or Congregational chapel in the town on the grounds

pp 14.   **53** Peter Barrett, 'Alexander Knox: lay theologian of the Church of Ireland' in *Search* xxiii no.1 (Spring 2000), pp 40–50; I am grateful to Dean Barrett for a copy of an earlier draft of his paper.   **54** Barrett, *passim*; Neely, *The shaping of the church*, p. 120; R.B. McDowell, *The Church of Ireland, 1869–1969* (London, 1975), p. 23.   **55** *Dictionary of National Biography*, xiii, p 76; *Burke's Peerage*, various editions, s.v. Roden, Darnley;

that he was 'a pillar of the established church' and lay rector and patron of the parish.[56]

Roden's strong family connections with the leading evangelical families – he was the brother in-law and father-in-law of two successive Viscounts Powerscourt – helped reinforce his commitments and made him the most prominent evangelical laymen of his day. A supporter of the Bethesda Chapel and the Adelaide Hospital, and of the Evangelical Society, he was one of a group of eminent laymen who unsuccessfully petitioned Primate Beresford to license the Bethesda – the others included the earl of Wicklow, Judge Daly, Sir Robert Shaw, and Robert La Touche.[57] From 1819, he was involved in the work of the C.M.S., and he cast his net widely when it came to overseas missionary interests, regularly visiting the Waldensian Church in the Piedmontese valley, reporting on the missionary work of Colonel John Beckwith, and leading a European delegation to Italy to secure the release of Rosa and Francesca Madiai, imprisoned in Tuscany for their preaching.[58]

In 1820, he succeeded his father as third earl of Roden, and that year actively helped the promotion of his uncle, Percy Jocelyn (1764-1843), bishop of Ferns, to the see of Clogher. However, the bishop was said to be mentally imbalanced, and it was soon reported that he had sold off the furnishings of his new palace. In 1822, the bishop was caught in intimacy with a 'common sailor' in the White Hart public house, London. The sailor, John Moverley, was committed to prison, but Jocelyn was granted bail, and only after lively correspondence involving the viceroy, the chief secretary, the prime minister and Primate Beresford was he quietly deprived of his office in a return for a commitment from Roden to keep him out of sight. The disgraced bishop ended his days as a layman, working as a butler in his nephew's own household and one of the few examples of a member of the clergy being forced to become one of the laity in the Church of Ireland.[59] The reputation of the Irish clergy suffered as a result: Peel wondered whether it was advisable to appoint any of them to a bishopric but Roden showed no embarrassment at the behaviour of the uncle he protected. While his evangelical influence continued into old age Roden's political reputation was damaged by the consequences of his openly avowed Orange sympathies. An Orange grand master, he was censured by a commission of enquiry for his conduct during the affray at Dolly's Brae on 12 July 1849 and lost his license as a justice of the peace. He died on 20 March 1870.[60]

Malcomson, *John Foster* appendices and tables; Hoppen, *Ireland since 1800*, p. 71. **56** Acheson, *A history of the Church of Ireland*, pp 21, 126. **57** Ibid., p. 137. **58** *Dictionary of National Biography*, x, pp 837–8. **59** Bowen, *The Protestant crusade*, pp 44–5; Brynn, *The Church of Ireland in the age of Catholic Emancipation*, pp 79, 340–1. Brynn incorrectly describes him as Roden's brother. **60** Desmond Bowen, *Souperism: myth or reality?* (Cork, 1970), pp 41, 194.

Peers like Ely and Roden were confident of their role in church and politics alike, and many leading politicians of the day had close church connections. But those outside the political establishment were often equally well connected and pious in their religious life. Despite the popular images of a rising led by presbyterians in the north-east in 1798 and by Catholic priests like John Murphy in the south-east, many of the leading members of the United Irishmen and their sympathisers were prominent members of the Church of Ireland, often finding inspiration for their revolutionary ideals in their religious beliefs and maintaining close links with church life.

Prominent among the United Irishmen was Lord Edward FitzGerald (1763–98), whose uncles and cousins included Dives Downes, bishop of Cork (1699–1710), Revd George Tisdall (1736–72), of Shandon, Cork, and Michael Tisdall, archdeacon of Ross. The brothers Sheares, Henry (1755–98) and John (1766–98), were the most noticeable of United Irishmen who were parishioners of St Michan's, Dublin; both were hanged publicly on 14 July 1798. Other leading United Irishmen had intimate church connections too: Theobald Wolfe Tone's wife Matilda was a clergyman's granddaughter; Beauchamp Bagenal Harvey, commander of the Wexford rebel forces, was the grandson of two clergymen in the diocese of Ferns and the nephew of a third; and Cornelius Grogan of Johnstown Castle was conscientious as patron of Ardamine and churchwarden of Rathaspeck. As Grogan went to his death on Wexford bridge, accompanied by the rector of Wexford, John Elgee, 'the sailors of the Royal Navy who hanged him were amazed when ... they heard him recite Protestant prayers'.[61] In the northeast it is often forgotten that the hero and heroine of the battle of Ballynahinch, Henry Monroe and Betsy Gray, were both members of the Church of Ireland. It is an irony that this memory of the contribution of active members of the laity to the United Irishmen remained largely forgotten in the church. Two figures symbolise this amnesia. John Kelly, celebrated in folklore and ballad as 'Kelly the boy from Killanne', is commemorated with a large Celtic cross in St Anne's churchyard with a Gaelic inscription which might imply that he was a Catholic but for many years in the decades before the rising he was churchwarden of Killanne. The heroine of the ballad 'The boys of Wexford' is an unnamed woman from the Church of Ireland, known only in the opening lines as 'the captain's daughter' – being a woman and a member of the Church of Ireland was a double jeopardy when it came to securing memory for future generations.[62]

61 Ruddock and Kloss, *Unending worship*, p 20; Patrick Comerford, 'Church of Ireland clergy and the 1798 rising' in Liam Swords, (ed.), *Protestant, Catholic and dissenter: the clergy and 1798* (Dublin, 1997), p. 241.   62 See Anna Kinsella, 'Nineteenth century perspectives: the women of 1798 in folk memory and ballads' and John D. Beatty, 'Protestant women of county Wexford and their narratives of the rebellion' in Dáire Keogh and Nicholas Furlong (eds), *The women of 1798* (Dublin, 1998), pp 113–36 and 188.

Many of these laymen and women had been fired in their revolutionary zeal by their religious convictions. Among those religious United Irishmen was the revolutionary millenarian, Thomas Russell (1757–1803). Known in song and folklore as 'The man from God-knows-where', Russell combined his revolutionary politics with a strong visionary brand of millenarianism and pious sacramentalism, and his knowledge of the Bible was so exact that he could argue with professional theologians on interpretations from both Greek and Hebrew. Russell was born near Mallow, County Cork, the son of an army doctor. Both Russell and his father had considered seeking holy orders, and it is said Thomas Russell went to the Isle of Man in the late 1780s, intending to receive ordination at the hands of the bishop of Sodor and Man, Claudius Crigan.[63] Russell grew up with a sympathy for the Irish language and openness to Gaelic culture, and collaborated with Edward Bunting and Whitley Stokes, both members of the Church of Ireland, in collecting Irish music and on a new Gaelic translation of the Bible. By 1791 he had formed his lasting attachment to radical Christianity. Influenced by the recently published works of the Jesuit Pierre Francois Xavier de Charlevoix, Russell considered the comparatively beneficial system of government instituted by the Jesuits in Paraguay as 'beyond compare the best, the happiest, that ever has been instituted'. On the other hand, he contended, tyranny had endeavoured to support itself 'by perverting Christianity from its purposes and debasing its purity'.[64] Russell was a founder member of the Society of United Irishmen in 1791 along with Wolfe Tone and Simon Butler.[65] Among those who were invited to join the Society in its early months were Whitley Stokes and the barristers Thomas Addis Emmet, elder brother of Robert Emmet, and Peter Burrowes, brother of the rector of Kilmuckridge, who was among the first to be killed during the rising in Wexford.[66] After the Society had been proscribed Russell climbed Cave Hill outside Belfast in June 1795 with Tone, Samuel Neilson, Henry Joy McCracken, the Simms brothers and 'one or two others' and there solemnly swore never to desist in their efforts until they had subverted the authority of England over their country and asserted her independence.[67]

Russell was arrested before the 1798 rising began, and his writings in Newgate prison, Dublin, exhibit deep, self-examination coupled with a strong personal faith:

---

63 Denis Carroll, *The man from God knows where, Thomas Russell 1767–1803* (Dublin, 1995), pp 12–19. **64** Ibid., pp 32–3. **65** Ibid., p. 41. For Simon Butler's connections with the Church of Ireland see my 'Simon Butler (1757–1797) and the forgotten role of the Church of Ireland during the 1798 rising' in *Journal of the Butler Society*, iv no. 2 (2000), pp 271–9. **66** Brian Cleary, *The battle of Oulart Hill* (Oulart, 1999), pp 41–50; Patrick Comerford, 'Euseby Cleaver, bishop of Ferns, and the clergy of the Church of Ireland in the 1798 rising in Co. Wexford' in *Journal of the Wexford Historical Society*, no. 16 (1996–7), p. 79. **67** A.T.Q. Stewart, *The summer soldiers, the 1798 rebellion in Antrim and Down* (Belfast, 1991), p. 72.

O Lord God … it is not from thy justice
before which I stand condemned
that I expect salvation,
but from thy mercy that I expect pardon and forgiveness,
my Lord and Saviour Jesus Christ.[68]

The keeper of Newgate was Tresham Gregg, father of the controversial millenarian preacher of the mid-nineteenth century, Tresham James Gregg. In gaol, Russell comforted the condemned leaders of the rising, FitzGerald and the Sheares brothers, and even shared discussions on the apocalyptic prophecies in the Bible with a government negotiator, Francis Dobbs, who would later oppose the Act of Union not on political grounds but because it ran counter to Biblical prophecies.[69] In March 1799, Russell was transported from Belfast Lough to Fort George in Scotland with the other key surviving leaders of the United Irishmen. Of the twenty prisoners on board the *Ashton Smith*, four were Catholics and six were presbyterians; but half of those key rebel leaders were members of the Church of Ireland: Thomas Russell, Thomas Addis Emmet, Matthew Dowling, Arthur O'Connor, Edward Hudson, Roger O'Connor, John Chambers, Hugh Wilson, William Dowdall and Robert Hudson.[70] On his release in 1802, Russell went to Paris, where he attended Mass in the Jansenist church and received Communion at Christmas.[71] There he met Robert Emmet and together they plotted another rebellion in Ireland. Russell was arrested in Dublin in September 1803 and taken to Downpatrick to stand trial. Prior to his execution on 21 October Russell received Holy Communion twice with 'apparently great devotion' according to the prison chaplain, Foster Archer. Archer and Russell had a lengthy discussion of Biblical Greek in regard to the 'end of the age' and Russell remained convinced that the French Revolution and his own political activities were heralding 'the kingdom of Jesus [and] fulfilling the Prophecies'.[72] In his last hours he was translating from his Greek New Testament verses from the Book of Revelation that summarised his politically beatific and visionary millenarianism: 'And I saw a new heaven and a new earth; for the first heaven and the first earth were passed away' (Revelation 21: 1) Russell entrusted his last remaining possession, a Greek New Testament, to his distant cousin, Revd Arthur Forde, who attended him on the scaffold. He was buried in the grounds of Downpatrick Cathedral.[73]

68 Carroll, *The man from God knows where*, pp 131–2.   69 Ibid., pp 141–51.   70 Musgrave, *Memoirs of the Irish rebellion*, pp 590–1.   71 Carroll, *The man from God knows where*, p. 197. 72 Ibid., pp 186–98.   73 Ibid., pp 7, 12–14, 19, 167, 206; *D.N.B.*, xviii, pp 473–5; C. Dickson, *Revolt in the north* (London, 1960), pp 205–8. I am grateful to Revd F. John McDowell of Ballyrashane, County Derry, for additional insights on Russell.

V

J.C. Beckett has described the eighteenth century as the 'century of Swift and Berkeley and Burke, of Goldsmith and Sheridan, of Flood and Grattan; the century of Wolfe Tone and Robert Emmet'.[74] All were born into the Church of Ireland, and throughout the fifty years between 1780 and 1830, lay members of the church contributed liberally to the lasting cultural heritage of the island through literature, music, architecture and the other arts. Henry Loftus (1709–83), earl of Ely, employed the best architects, artists and craftsmen in the building of Ely House, Dublin, and the restoration of Rathfarnham Castle at the end of the eighteenth century. By the time of his death, the townhouse was praised for its stucco interiors by Michael Stapleton, while the castle was famed for its rooms by William Chambers and James 'Athenian' Stuart (1741–88), its furniture, gardens, aviaries and menageries, and its family portraits by the 'Muse of Rome', Angelica Kauffmann (1741–1807). The most famous woman painter of the day, Kauffmann was hailed by poets and philosophers, including Goethe, as the most cultivated woman of all Europe. Ely's neighbour, the banker David La Touche, also decorated his homes with paintings by Kauffmann, travelled through Italy collecting art for his town house and also employed Stapleton to provide stucco interiors for 25 St Stephen's Green, later the offices of the Representative Church Body. The evangelical Wingfields of Powerscourt lived surrounded by Breughels and Tintorettos in the finest town house in Dublin and the most sumptuous country house near Enniskerry, County Wicklow and their travels took then to St Petersburg in Russia, Canada, the United States and Mexico. They and La Touche were clear illustrations that evangelicals of their day were well travelled and did not despise the arts.[75]

Like Oliver Goldsmith before him, the actor and dramatist Richard Brinsley Sheridan (1751–1816) came from a clerical family.[76] Among the writers of the day, Maria Edgeworth's *Castle Rackrent* (1800) and Sydney Lady Morgan's *Wild Irish Girl* might be described as the first Irish novels. Lady Morgan (1783?–1859) personified the renewed interest in Irish music when she erected her monument to Turlough Carolan (1670–1738), the blind harpist, in St Patrick's cathedral, Dublin.[77] Edward Bunting (1773–1843), the Armagh-born pioneer collector of Irish folk music, first studied music under his brother, an organist in Drogheda, and then moved to Belfast, where he was friendly with leading United Irishmen, including the McCrackens and the Joy family, and worked as an assistant to William Wall at St Anne's, before becoming the organist at

74 Beckett, *The Anglo-Irish tradition*, p. 44.   75 Foster, *Charles Stewart Parnell*, p. xviii; Broad et al., *Rathfarnham*, p. 7; *Dictionary of National Biography*, x, pp 1129–32; *Dictionary of National Biography*, xix, pp 6–88.   76 *D.N.B.*, xviii, p. 88.   77 *D.N.B.*, xiii, pp 924–6; xiv, pp 792–4.

Rosemary Street presbyterian church and then at the newly-built St George's in High Street. In 1792, he was moved by the celebrated Belfast Harp Festival to start collecting Irish music that he published in a three-volume collection. Bunting ended his days in Dublin as the organist at St George's, Temple Street, and the newly built St Stephen's in Mount Street.[78]

Two poets at the beginning and the close of this era, from two contrasting backgrounds, Gaelic Irish and Huguenot, illustrate the rich tapestry that was being woven in the cultural life of the laity: Piaras Mac Gearailt and Joseph Sheridan Le Fanu. Mac Gearailt (Piers FitzGerald) (1702–95), was an accomplished poet in Irish and leader or 'high sheriff' of a famed court of poetry near his home in Ballymacoda, now the last remaining Gaeltacht district in east County Cork. When he conformed to the Church of Ireland, he was abused and attacked in verse by Thomas Barry of Clonmel, County Tipperary. But Mac Gearailt's poetic reply in Irish, *An Answer to Thomas Barry*, showed his personal faith and trust in Christ had remained unchanged:

> Do not harbour anger
> in your minds for me,
> Enough that Heaven's wrath
> Is launched, my friends,
> And to guard the soul
> I urge the Son of God;
> Though I am a sinner
> Sunk in the world's mire,
> Fettered in the world's chains,
> Still to the mild nurse
> Of Christ I cry
> 'Dispel my sighs,
> Relieve me of this curse!'[79]

Joseph Sheridan Le Fanu (1814–73), the novelist son of the chaplain to the Royal Hibernian Military School, Thomas Philip Le Fanu, later dean of Emly, and nephew of Richard Brinsley Sheridan, set his novel, *The House by the Churchyard*, in Chapelizod as he had known it in his early childhood in the 1820s. The novel features the churchyard and village on the outskirts of Dublin, replete with rumbustious Catholic priest and sensitive young Anglican clergyman. Le Fanu was proprietor and editor of the *Dublin University Magazine* and of the *Dublin Evening Mail*.[80] His posthumously published poems often exhibit

---

78 *D.N.B.*, iii, p. 273.   79 See Patrick Murray, *The deer's cry* (Dublin, 1986), pp 73–4. 80 J.S. Le Fanu, *The house by the churchyard* (3 vols, London, 1863); W.J. McCormack, *Sheridan Le Fanu and Victorian Ireland* (Oxford, 1980), pp 15, 138–9; *Burke's Irish family*

the piety with which the laity of his generation had been imbued in their childhood. His *Hymn*, from *Beatrice*, combines a surprisingly high piety, with its invocation of the angels, Mary, and (using Italian names) the apostles, with a simple, child-like, personal and evangelical faith in Jesus:

> Hush! oh ye billows,
> Hush! oh thou wind,
> Watch o'er us angels,
> Mary, be kind!
>
> Fishermen followed
> The steps of the Lord;
> Oft in their fishing boats
> Preached He the Word.
>
> Pray for us, Pietro,
> Pray for us John,
> Pray for us, Giacomo,
> Zebedee's son.
>
> If it be stormy,
> Fear not the sea;
> Jesus upon it
> Is walking by thee.
>
> Billows, be gentle,
> Soft blow the wind,
> Watch o'er us angels,
> Mary, be kind!
>
> Soft be the billows,
> Soft blow the wind,
> Watch o'er us angels,
> Mary, be kind![81]

Until the late twentieth century, all women in the Church of Ireland remained members of the laity. But it would be too easy to say that the voices of women were heard in the church only when they sang the canticles and hymns, confided in their clerical husbands, or, like the orphans in the Bethesda who sang for their keep or the women of the Molyneux and Magdalene asylums,

records, s.v. Le Fanu.   81 Murray, *The deer's cry*, p. 112.

who had become the objects of evangelical charity. It must be remembered that the vast majority of laymen were voiceless in the church too: those laymen whose voices were heard in the church were usually those who exercised patronage, who had strong family connections with clerical life, and those whose wealth and privilege ensured their influence in all sectors of life. Nevertheless, a number of women were influential in church life from the mid-eighteenth century on following the foundation of the Molyneux Asylum by Lady Arabella Denny. Through their access to political power, women also influenced the course of church affairs, sometimes even overseas. Lady Frances Cole was the wife of Sir Lowry Cole of Enniskillen, governor of the Cape Colony from 1828 to 1833. Shortly after her arrival at the Cape Lady Cole provided detailed information to Bishop Turner of Calcutta on the nine Anglican missionaries working at the Cape, including two from Ireland, Revd Francis McClelland from Longford at Port Elizabeth and Revd William Wright from County Cork at Bathurst.[82] Wright antagonised the Coles by supporting Black rights and the wrote to the Secretary of State for the Colonies demanding his resignation. In 1829 the S.P.G., acting perhaps on Lady Cole's report, directed Wright to move to Grahamstown.[83]

At home, the greatest influence women yielded in the church during this era was, undoubtedly, through the prominent roles many played in the evangelical revival. Charlotte O'Brien of Dromoland Castle, was the mother of the M.P. and deported Young Irelander, William Smith O'Brien (1803–64). In 1814, as evangelical men faltered in the face of episcopal disapproval, Lady O'Brien and her friends, the 'great Dublin dames', seized the initiative and formed the first Ladies' Association of the C.M.S.[84] Her friends and collaborators included Lady Lucy Barry, wife of the future Lord Farnham, Lady Margaret Molyneux, and Sir Lowry Cole's sister, Lady Florence Balfour. That year, Lady Lucy enlarged the school house on her husband's estate at Newtownbarry, and presented it with a lending library of 200 volumes.[85] Lady Florence, who became a vice-president of the C.M.S. Ladies' Association, was the grandmother of Francis Townley Balfour (1846–1924), a missionary bishop with the S.P.G. in southern Africa and the first bishop to be consecrated for what is today's Lesotho.

Another network of evangelical women emerged in east County Wicklow. The three Howard sisters of Bushy Park, County Wicklow, Frances, Isabella

---

82 C.F. Pascoe (ed.), *Two hundred years of the S.P.G.: an historical account of the Society for the Propagation of the Gospel in Foreign Parts, 1701–1900 (based on a digest of the Society's records)* (London, 1901), pp 270–1, 1316 n. 9; Cecil Lewis and Gertrude Edwards (eds), *Historical records of the Church of South Africa* (London, 1934), pp 19–20.   83 Pascoe (ed.), *Two hundred years of the S.P.G.*, p. 270; Lewis and Edwards (eds), *Historical records of the Church of South Africa*, pp 15, 19.   84 Acheson, *A history of the Church of Ireland*, p. 126. 85 Browne and Wickham, *Lewis's Wexford*, p. 114.

and Theodosia, were first cousins of Lord Roden. In 1810, the eldest sister, Frances, married William Parnell Hayes (1777–1821) of Avondale, County Wicklow, and was the grandmother of Charles Stewart Parnell. Her husband, usually known as William Parnell, was the author of *An historical apology for the Irish Catholics*, and caused a storm with his anonymous novel *Maurice and Berghetta or the priest of Rahery* (1816). During the famine of 1817, through his influence, meat and soup was provided twice a week for four months at the expense of his parish. Parnell was a brother of Thomas 'Tract' Parnell and uncle of John Parnell, second Lord Congleton, who travelled to Baghdad on an evangelical mission with Francis Newman, brother of Cardinal John Henry Newman. On his return to Europe he became a leading light in the Plymouth Brethren, living out his last days in the Spartan style of a missionary.[86] The second Howard sister, Isabella, married Admiral Greville Leveson Proby, later third earl of Carysfort. After his secession from the Church of Ireland the evangelical hymn writer, Revd Thomas Kelly, whose daughter was related by marriage to the Howard sisters, built one of his four churches on the Proby estate at Carysfort Avenue in Booterstown, County Dublin. Five of Kelly's hymns have survived into the latest edition of the Church of Ireland's *Church hymnal*.[87] The most influential of the Howard sisters was the youngest of the three. In 1822 Theodosia married the widowed Richard Wingfield, fifth Viscount Powerscourt and already one of the leading evangelicals of his day. Lord Powerscourt had strong family connections with the other main Irish evangelicals. And his first wife, Lady Frances Theodosia Jocelyn, was Lord Roden's sister. Both Powerscourt and his younger brother Edward Wingfield, were converted to evangelicalism through the preaching of the rector on their estate, Robert Daly, later bishop of Cashel. Edward subsequently became the first evangelical incumbent of a Dublin parish when he was presented as rector of St James's by his uncle, the earl of Meath. In 1830 his half brother, Revd William Wingfield, married a daughter of the hymn writer, Thomas Kelly.[88]

Perhaps through the influence of her sister's brother-in-law, Thomas 'Tract' Parnell, Lady Powerscourt became interested in the Plymouth Brethren, whose origins can be traced to Dublin in the 1820s. Other early figures in the new movement included John Parnell, Henry Hutchinson, and Nelson's godson, Revd John Nelson Darby (1800–82), who had recently arrived in Ireland. In 1829, Darby resigned as curate of Calary, County Wicklow, and was soon holding millenarian meetings in the drawing room of Powerscourt House.

---

86 Foster, *Charles Stewart Parnell*, pp 16–17, 40, 56; *Burke's peerage*, various eds, s.v. Congleton.   87 Costello, *Dublin churches*, p. 230; *Burke's peerage*, various eds, s.v. Carysfort, Wicklow; *Church hymnal*, (5th edn, Oxford, 2000), nos. 248, 269, 275, 285 and 339. 88 Acheson, *A history of the Church of Ireland*, pp 113–16; Crawford, *Around the churches*, p. 20; *Burke's peerage*, various eds, s.v. Powerscourt.

Despite the best efforts of Daly to keep Lady Powerscourt within the Church of Ireland, Darby and his followers succeeded in persuading their hostess to join the new sect. The dissension that followed put an end to the drawing room meetings, and Darby's quarrels with his followers led to schism and the formation of a new sect in Plymouth in 1835, a year before Lady Powerscourt's death.[89] If there were any lessons for the Church of Ireland to learn from the sad experiences of Theodosia Powerscourt they were lessons that took generations to take hold: women had valid religious experiences of their own, had voices that needed to be heard within the church rather than outside it, and had a ministry that went beyond the pious female members of the laity playing host at evangelical drawing room tea parties and discussions.

A closing pen picture of an unusual layman, the first earl of Kilmorey (1748–1832), serves to illustrate the cumbersome and antiquarian church structures of this period and points to the need for extensive reforms throughout the church at the beginning of the nineteenth century, despite the changes being introduced with the reforms in education, tithes and diocesan structures. Born on 5 April 1748, Francis Jack Needham eventually succeeded his two elder brothers as twelfth viscount Kilmorey. As General Francis Needham, he had carved out a successful career, rising from the rank of cornet to general. He fought in the American War of Independence, but is best known for his role in the 1798 Rising. He defeated Father Michael Murphy at the Battle of Arklow, County Wicklow, on 9 June, and was then sent by General Lake to hem in the rebels on Vinegar Hill, overlooking Enniscorthy. There, Needham arrested the loyalist parish priest of Litter (Kilmuckridge), Michael Lacy, who was at Vinegar Hill to intercede, successfully, on behalf of his Protestant neighbours. On the word of two arrested United Irishmen who turned informer, Needham pursued four other Catholic priests, Francis Kavanagh of Gorey, his curate John Redmond, Philip Roche of Gorey and Nicholas Stafford of Riverchapel (Ballygarret). Both Stafford and Roché were sworn United Irishmen but Redmond was known for his loyalty and Needham's pursuit of Kavanagh and Redmond and his insistence on hanging them can only be ascribed to his sectarian malice and he subsequently provided a bitter and biased account of the priests' activities to Musgrave, the loyalist historian of the rising.[90]

However, Needham was also remembered as a 'liberal landlord' and a 'kind friend of the poor in his extensive estates'. He eventually succeeded in November 1818 to the family titles and estates, including the demesne at Mourne Park outside Kilkeel and the ground rents of Newry, then the most

89 Bowen, *The Protestant crusade*, p. 6; Donald F. Durnbaugh, *The Believers' Church: the history and character of radical Protestantism* (New York, 1970), pp 161 ff.   90 Kevin Whelan, 'The Wexford priests in 1997' in Swords (ed.), *Protestant, Catholic and dissenter*, pp 172–3, 179–81; see Musgrave, *Memoirs of the Irish rebellion of 1798*, pp 298, 380–1.

prosperous inland town in Ulster. In 1822 he was created earl of Kilmorey and Viscount Newry and Morne (sic), the subsidiary title a reminder of the unique office he held in the church: hereditary lord abbot of the exempt district of Newry and Mourne. The exempt district was a most unusual anomaly outside the parochial structures, giving Kilmorey exceptional authority as a layman. Bordering the dioceses of Armagh, Down and Dromore, it covered 102,539 acres, and encompassed the parishes of Kilcoo, Kilkeel, Kilmegan and Newry, and four benefices. Kilmorey's medieval authority went unchallenged in the church, his only assistance in administering his ecclesiastical patrimony provided by the dean of Dromore as 'official principal, vicar general and commissary general' of the exempt district. Kilmorey grandly commemorated his elevation in the peerage with the 'Kilmorey chapel' in Adderley, Shropshire. He was buried there ten years later in 1832. He had made no reforms in his own church territory in Ireland but sweeping reforms were on the horizon.[91]

VI

In 1795, the rector of Gowran, County Kilkenny, commenting on the clerical neglect of the laity in many parts of the diocese of Ossory, reported, 'The people are enveloped in ignorance and superstition without any intermediate order between rich and poor'.[92] The over-burdening diocesan structures, widespread pluralism and absenteeism among the clergy, and increasing discontent in the general populace over the collection of tithes, made reforms of the diocesan, parochial, educational and tithe system inevitable from the 1830s on. Already, the laity had expressed their unhappiness with the state of affairs during the period between 1780 and 1830 with their support for the new proprietary chapels in towns and cities, by taking the initiative in many new church building programmes, through their enthusiasm for new waves of evangelical revival and new concerns for mission and charity, and even, in some instances, in the support received by the Wesleys and Methodism and the decision by a small few to secede to the Kellyites, Darbyites and other bodies that emphasized the contribution of the laity to worship, witness and mission. As it faced the abolition of tithes and the consequent loss of income and disestablishment the Church of Ireland may have appeared an unhealthy body at the institutional level but in the lives of the laity it contained the seeds of a new life and activity.

91 *Dictionary of National Biography*, xiv, p 156; Godkin, *Ireland and her churches*, pp 466–7.
92 Leslie, *Ossory*, p. 272.

8

The laity in a changing society, 1830–1900

W.G. Neely

In the century between 1800 and 1900 the Church of Ireland changed from being a state church of privilege and unequally distributed wealth to a constitutional church where the laity had a place at every level of church government. Reform had swept away the corruptions of past centuries. The clergy on set stipends were expected to be hard working administrators and pastors. By the last decades of the nineteenth century new organisations to cater for the needs of men, women and children had become a feature of almost every parish life. It had been a century nevertheless of often unwelcome change where the very existence of the church had seemed to be in question. R.B. McDowell commenting on the impact of disestablishment wrote of the church 'Its adherents were suddenly forced to accept the freedom, responsibilities and burdens associated with membership of a voluntary church.'[1]

Many had believed that it would never survive the change. The distinguished Catholic bishop of Kildare, James Doyle, had written in 1823 an open letter to the lord lieutenant, the marquis of Wellesley, in which he passed judgement on the Church of Ireland 'This church deserted by the legislature has since not ceased to tremble for its very existence' … She does not answer the ends for which any Christian church has ever been erected … She apprehends that they might new model her constitution'.[2] There was a widespread conviction that disestablishment would lead to its downfall. In fact the church was awakened to the danger and revitalised its life and ministry. Critics like Bishop Doyle may have scorned its spiritual worth but in fact the Church of Ireland was developing a profoundly Biblical understanding of its faith that inspired a great number of its members and motivated them to that loyalty which R.B. McDowell noted 'the earnest self sacrificing devotion to their church displayed by many members of the Church of Ireland'.[3]

---

1 R.B. McDowell, *The Church of Ireland, 1869–1969* (London, 1975), p. 4. 2 W.J. Fitzpatrick, *The life, times and correspondence of the Right Revd Dr Doyle* (2 vols, Dublin, 1880), i, p. 275. 3 McDowell, *The Church of Ireland*, p. x.

In 1830 the Church of Ireland had a membership of 805,264 people or about 12 per cent of the total population with a 24 per cent average in the northern counties, a percentage which remained remarkably stable to the end of the century. However the decline in overall population brought about by emigration and accelerated by the Famine led to further decline in the number of church members. The Census of 1861 recorded 693,300 as members of the Church of Ireland which further declined in 1871 to 667,900, but the percentage of overall population had hardly altered.

Church members continued to make a disproportionate and important contribution to national life. R.B. McDowell has calculated that 250 members of the General Synod in 1871 owned between them one million acres. Church people were significant in many aspects of administrative and professional life: 38 per cent of the Civil Service, 54 per cent of bankers, 30 per cent of accountants, 26 per cent of merchants were members of the church as were 25 per cent of the police and 60 per cent of the army. The legal and medical professions had a totally disproportionate membership, 60 per cent of barristers, 50 per cent of solicitors, 50 per cent of medical doctors. The church was well represented in the world of theatre, artists and literature. Amazingly one-third of all clergy in the country belonged to the Church of Ireland.[4]

The members of the Church of Ireland were very equally distributed throughout the country as Donald Akenson commented 'the laity of the Church of Ireland were both powerful and sparse.'[5]

Table 1 Population distribution by ecclesiastical province, 1831

	Anglican	Catholic	Presbyterian	Others
Armagh	500,020	1,760,067	637,607	15811
% of total	17	60	22	
Dublin	177,930	1,063,681	2,517	3162
% of total	14	85	2	
Cashel	111,813	2,220,340	966	2454
% of total	5	95		
Tuam	62,301	1,383,624	1266	381
% of total	4	96		

Source: Report of the Commissioners of Public Instruction H.C 1835 iii.[6]

The Church of Ireland presence in Armagh, despite the existence of a larger Presbyterian population (22 per cent as against 17 per cent) was by far and away

4 Ibid., pp 4–5.   5 D.H. Akenson, *The Church of Ireland: ecclesiastical reform and revolution 1800–1885* (London, 1971), p. 65.   6 Tabulated in Akenson, *Church of Ireland*, p. 65.

the strongest in the country. Dublin's 177,930 population represented 14 per cent of the Leinster total but in Munster and Connacht the Catholic majority was overwhelming at 95 and 96 per cent. Emigration and the Famine hit the Catholic community the hardest and this led to a slight change in the ratio of Church of Ireland members to Catholics. In 1834 there were 13.25 church people to every 100 Catholics in 1861 there were 15.35 to every 100.[7]

The Famine of the 1840s could not but have a profound effect on the laity of the Church. The estates of some of the wealthy were brought to bankruptcy by the government's insistence that the local rates must meet the costs of relief. The Encumbered Estates Act of 1848 was necessary to allow them to escape from an impossible burden of debt. Families that had been in some western counties for generations were forced to sell out or greatly diminish their estates. People were unable to pay rents and some of the landlords were ruined. The burden of tax fell hard on the clergy who had lost all income and had to be rescued by funds subscribed by the laity and members of the Church of England. The Famine came at a time of great religious tension in the heady atmosphere created by the evangelical zealots of the Second Reformation. Neglect of the peasant by all secular and religious authorities gave the evangelists their opportunity. The movement was a new feature of life in the 1830s and was the product of a Biblical inspired intensity of religious feeling among a considerable section of the Irish Protestant society. Nobility like the earls of Roden, Farnham and Enniskillen became passionate and active promoters of evangelical Christianity. It drew into its work members of landlord families and women were often its most active workers. They took a leading role in promoting the work of new movements like the Hibernian Bible Society, the Irish Society and the Scripture Readers' Society. Indeed the most vigorous of the proselytising bodies was the Ladies Auxiliary of the Irish Society.[8] The lay rector of Dingle, Lord Ventry, gave a new direction to the campaign by creating what became known as the Dingle settlement where converts were organised into a community. It was here that converts became known as 'Soupers' when a local Protestant lady began selling cheap food to the poor. The movement began in 1831, grew rapidly under the leadership of the Revd Thomas Moriarty and by 1838 numbered 170 families.[9] The newspapers in the west of Ireland took up the issue and attacks became increasingly scurrilous on both sides. The evangelical archbishops of Tuam, Le Poer Trench and Lord Plunkett, recruited a body of like-minded clerics who wholeheartedly participated in the campaign. Bitterness increased with Archbishop McHale's violent reaction to the foundation of the Achill Island settlement in 1834. The scheme was made possible by the sale of the land to Edward Nangle by the local landlord.[10] Many

7 Ibid., p. 209.   8 Desmond Bowen, *Souperism: myth or reality* (Cork 1970), p. 80.   9 Ibid., p. 84.   10 Ibid., p. 90.

long established clerical and lay families were deeply disturbed by the movement as they saw it as upsetting relationships that had existed amicably for generations. It was this atmosphere that gave some justification to Akenson's judgement that 'the Church of Ireland was not merely a minority church, it was surrounded by a sea of hatred.'[11] Certainly the controversy over souperism remained an issue to modern times. In a rare editorial on the Famine the *Irish Ecclesiastical Journal* on 1 May 1847 commented on how adversity had drawn all sides together 'animosity, political and religious has disappeared at the approach of the scourge. There has been an unexampled readiness on all sides to forget old divisions and co-operate cordially in the work of mercy. Considerable sums of money have been raised in this country and our fellow subjects in England have been prompt and active in their aid.'[12]

The charge of souperism was denied by many clergy and leading laymen. Protests that it was untrue came from both the Dingle and Achill missions. In truth the destitution and starvation were too real to do other than encourage the simple relief of human need. Clergy and laity lost their lives from famine fever, as a result of their involvement in relief work, amongst them the daughter of the local doctor in Ventry Dr Neilson, who despite constant labour for the starving had his home attacked by a distraught mob because of his sympathy for the Second Reformation.[13]

A modern assessment makes an attempt at fair judgment and declares 'a large number of resident landlords not only gave of their time generously in sitting on relief committees, grand juries, boards of guardians but especially in the years 1845–7 provided private assistance in the form of food, money, and seed or rent abatements.'[14] Nevertheless much that was to the credit of church members in the areas of distress throughout the country was forgotten in the bitter legacy of the Famine that did so much to portray the Irish landlord as one of the great persecutors of the poor. Hostility towards the Church of Ireland did indeed become intense in the years after the Famine.

The Emancipation Act of 1829 was seen by Archbishop Lord John George Beresford as making inevitable the disestablishment of the Church of Ireland. He dedicated his considerable energies to a twofold policy, political resistance on the one hand and on the other an efficient church proficient in pastoral care, with a spiritually awakened laity. This was a policy that could not succeed without a well motivated clergy and a supportive laity. This period witnessed an unparalleled growth of lay and in particular evangelical interest in the affairs of the church and after disestablishment a considerable transfer of power to the laity. The laity were for the most part hostile to disestablishment. There were

11 Akenson, *Church of Ireland*, p. 66.　12 *Irish Ecclesiastical Journal*, iv (1847), p. 5. 13 Bowen, *Souperism: myth or reality*, p. 186.　14 Christine Kinealy, *This great calamity – the Irish Famine 1945–52* (Dublin, 1994), p. 165.

few who shared the views of Sir William Gregory 'I had the strongest objection to the state church of a minority.'[15]

Lay influence had existed in the very considerable powers of the crown over church patronage and parliamentary control over church affairs. This influence had not always been beneficial. Indeed the alienation of church funds after the dissolution of the monasteries through lay impropriation had been a major hindrance to the provision for pastoral care. Erck in his *Ecclesiastical register* of 1830 had recorded 115 parishes wholly impropriate of whom forty-two had no provision for clergy and 560 parishes had impropriate rectorial tithes. Altogether about one-third of the total 2450 parishes had funds alienated to the laity. At disestablishment £778,887 17s. 10d. was paid as compensation to the holders of impropriate tithes. Lay attitude to tithes had long been hostile as the struggle with the Irish parliament over the tithe on grassland for cattle grazing witnesses. In the late-eighteenth century Bishop Woodward's hostility to the landlords as having little real sympathy with the aims and needs of the church sprang from the same conviction.[16] This traditional attitude may well indicate a certain apathy to the suffering of the clergy during the tithe war. There appears to have been only limited local support for the financial distress of the clergy. There were large contributions from England and without government support the clergy would have been ruined. Indeed radical members of the church had played their part in attacks on the clergy in the press and in public agitation against the tithe. The tithe war was the first determined attack on the political rights of the clergy after 1829. There is little doubt that the press brought the clergy into contempt as 'Black crows' the oppressors of the poor. There is not enough evidence as to how the laity reacted to these scathing attacks on the wealth and greed of their clergy. Parliament was comparatively easily persuaded to recognise the Church Temporalities Act of 1833 as a necessary reform of an unjustifiable distribution of wealth in the established church.

The Church Temporalities Act 1833 did much to prepare the church for the great change that would follow disestablishment. The Ecclesiastical Commissioners administered the endowments of suppressed bishoprics and benefices, the taxation of bishops and clergy with more than £300 a year income. Despite the membership of the archbishops of Armagh and Dublin and four other bishops the committee was dominated in practical work by the three paid lay commissioners. The church for the first time had a civil service of secretary, treasurer, two architects and twenty-five clerks who supervised payments for church heating, the expenses of worship and the wages of sextons and parish clerks. Whilst not in control of anything like all income they administered considerable sums e.g. in 1852–3 their revenue was £122,000.[17]

15 Elizabeth Coxhead, *Lady Gregory* (London, 1961), p. 4.   16 Richard Woodward, *The present state of the Church of Ireland* (Dublin, 1787), p. 54.   17 Akenson, *The Church of*

Complaints about commissioners salaries and expenses became a regular feature in the *Irish Ecclesiastical Gazette* but their charge of 5 per cent was in fact a very modest one. All construction work throughout the church had also to have the approval of their architects. The first three commissioners were men who had distinguished careers. The two appointed by the government were J.C. Erck, secretary to the Board of First Fruits, and a senior fellow of Trinity College, Francis Sadlier. The third, W.C. Quinn, was the nominee of the two arch-bishops.[18] The full committee in which the bishops were joined by the lord chancellor of Ireland and the lord chief justice seldom met. Never before had the administration of the church been so much in the hands of it's lay servants. The power of the laity, though considerable, had been largely exercised through its patronage which had been shared with the crown and the bishops.

Table 2 Patronage of livings in the eighteenth century[19]

Patrons	Crown	Lay	Bishops
Armagh	119	113	319
Dublin	86	107	421
Cashel	69	103	327
Tuam	8	21	272

Altogether throughout Ireland in the 2,436 benefices the bishops appointed 1,339, more than 50 per cent, but the power of the landlords was not limited to patronage, for no rector could hope to exercise his ministry without the support of the local landlord. This power was exercised indirectly but with the Ecclesiastical Commissioners every parish was under lay management for the first time. It was preparing the way for the new select vestries and the Representative Church Body. Moreover no significant change in the affairs of the church had been possible without the consent of the Irish Parliament.

Once the very existence of the establishment was threatened it became essential for clergy and laity to come together if the Church was to survive. This they did in a very remarkable way. It was not only leaders like the dukes of Abercorn and Leinster and Lord Cairns who helped form the new constitution of the church but throughout the country there was the deep sense that their church had been betrayed and indeed pillaged. In every parish this was the prevailing sentiment. In Kilcooley in County Tipperary young Mary Ponsonby could write in an attempted novel in sheer weariness at the controversy 'Gladstone what thou hast to do, do quickly'.[20] The crisis bonded laity and

Ireland, pp 194–5.   **18** Ibid., p. 195.   **19** Ibid., p. 64.   **20** W.G. Neely, *Kilcooley: land and people in Tipperary* (Belfast, 1983), p. 117.

clergy together in a way unknown since the restoration of church and monarchy in 1660. To some it was the church of 'Lift thy banner church of Erin' but to others also it was the opportunity to create a church more in accord with their hearts desire, a truly Protestant Biblical church. Colonel Fox, a prominent evangelical, would have none of this 'Celtic nonsense' and declared there that his church was 'the grand old church of the settlers'.

Some laity were deeply distrustful of the clergy and were far from accepting the teaching of the church as valid. In 1841 during a dispute with rector of Ballygawley over confession and absolution they simply refused to believe what the formularies of the church clearly stated. Even the intervention of Primate Lord John George had no effect on their determination to resist what they saw as a misinterpretation of the teaching of their church.[21] Throughout the *Irish Ecclesiastical Journal* the debate on this issue, along with baptismal regeneration and the nature of priesthood, dragged on with weary monotony. Bitter opponents like Lord James Butler, Colonel Fox, Thomas Lefroy and to a lesser extent Master Brooke were guaranteed a majority lay vote in the general synod after disestablishment. Lord James shocked the *Irish Ecclesiastical Gazette* by the violence of his attack on the Primate in 1871. Indeed Marcus Beresford made no effort to conceal his dislike for the lay representation in the synod in its opening years. The intervention of the dukes of Leinster and Abercorn in securing voting by houses in exchange for the two-to-one representation of the laity saved the church from disastrous measures. Indeed the voting by houses preserved Prayer Book teaching again and again in the Synod in the 1870s. The violence of the attack ultimately produced a lay reaction though the synod could be guaranteed to react to any hint of Romanism. In the vote on chancel screens at the sanctuary steps in 1879 the laity voted 130 against and only twenty-nine for but the resolution was defeated by a very narrow clergy majority seventy-eight to seventy-three votes.[22]

It was never easy to be sure that the synod truly represented lay opinion at large. In April 1874 the Defence of the Prayer Book organisation presented a petition to the synod signed by forty peers, eighteen baronets, thirty-eight deputy lieutenants, seventy-one J.P.s and 704 gentlemen of rank as well as 6,000 others. These were opposed to tampering with the Prayer Book. Lord James Butler was never really in sympathy with church teaching though he and his associates were elected to Dublin Synod and Council as well as to general synod. He began to attend Merrion Hall in 1878 and scornfully the *Irish Ecclesiastical Gazette* stated that he was one of those of whom it might be said 'They went out from us but they were not of us' and accused him of 'pride, self will, impatience and ill judged zeal'.[23] Very different was their obituary on Master

---

21 Armagh Public Library, Armagh, Beresford Papers, vol. iv, p. 30.   22 *Irish Ecclesiastical Gazette*, June 1879.   23 Ibid., 1 August 1878.

Brooke at his death in 1881, a strongly Biblical Protestant who was nevertheless 'a churchman to the last' and 'all his life a student and a learner.'

In general any accusation of Romanism received vocal and indeed violent support. There was a widespread suspicion among church people across the whole island of any high church, especially Tractarian, teaching as leading to Rome. The name of Pusey was enough to arouse anger. In 1894 violent objections were raised by the furnishing of the new iron church of St Clement's, Belfast with demands that the bishop refuse to consecrate until the chancel gates and the two steps on which the holy table was raised were removed. The bishop of Down surrendered to mob violence. It is amusing to record that when the protesters came to the consecration service they passed over Cardinal Newman's 'Lead kindly light' in silence but strangely enough hissed at the Old Hundredth and at the mention of the Virgin Mary in the Apostles Creed.[24] When church wardens wands were introduced to St Mary Magdalene's, Belfast there was a stamping of feet and an element of the congregation marched out. Innovations were regarded as evidence of Romanism in quite a few parishes. In Down Cathedral the windows depicting the Apostles and the Virgin Mary were smashed and subsequently removed.[25] Though it provoked no mob violence the opposition to the cross raised on a stand before the Holy Table in St Bartholomew's, Dublin, was nevertheless virulent and backed by a strong section of lay opinion. Such ultra Protestant agitation was to be found in every part of the country. There was often a distinct reluctance to accept episcopal authority. In Cork the parish of St Nicholas refused to accept their duly elected rector. In 1895 Bishop Alexander of Derry, after a quarter of a century of faithful ministry, was bitterly disappointed when Orange Order objections to his chosen speakers at a proposed church congress led to opposition in both his own synod and the general synod and his abandonment of the project.[26] In Dublin parishes like Harold's Cross and Sandford were constantly on the watch for 'popish' practices. The Revd Tresham Gregg, who the archbishop of Dublin had tried to silence, had a congregation only to ready to listen to his violent denunciations of popery in the former chantry chapel of St Mary's. There were nevertheless laity of high church outlook. In 1842 Lord Adare tried to purchase the Rock of Cashel to make it a school to promote tractarian views. He with William Sewell and Lord Emly were prime movers in the establishment of St Columba's College. Whilst they represented a minority, men such as Bishop Jebb were widely respected by the laity to whom they preached traditional church doctrine.

Nowhere was the loyalty of the laity to the church as they understood it more evident than in the work of church building in Belfast and Dublin, quite a number of country churches were rebuilt largely as a result of landlord

24 Ibid., 23 June 1899.   25 J.F. Rankin, *Down cathedral* (Belfast, 1997), p. 132.   26 Eleanor Alexander, *Primate Alexander* (London 1913), p. 278.

initiative. Notable trustee churches were built in Dublin and Belfast. In Dublin Sandford Church was built by George Sandford an Irish man who had a successful career in Somerset. He was of evangelical conviction and built the church in 1826. Others were built in the 1830s – Baggotrath, Trinity Church, North Strand, Crinken 1840 and St Matthias 1843. Two of the trustee churches were built to provide worship for those of high church conviction – St John's Sandymount 1850, St Bartholomew's 1867. Others were of no particular theological emphasis, no less than twenty-two, were built between 1824 and 1893 of whom three were also trustee churches.

Preachers' books, whilst too erratic to give much scope for statistics, nevertheless gave valuable insights into the worship experience of the laity. In 1884 the returns from Rathfarnham were: Christmas Morning Prayer & Evening Prayer 360, Holy Communion ninety-three; Easter Morning Prayer & Evening Prayer 200, Holy Communion fifty-nine.[27] This illustrates the general tendency for communicants to be about a quarter of that at morning and evening prayer. In general communion was celebrated only once, occasionally twice a month and attendances were very low. Castleknock in 1886 had an attendance between eleven and twenty-three on Communion Sundays as against at Christmas sixty-two and Easter seventy-three. Douglas parish in Cork in their visitation return in 1862 gave forty-five as the yearly average communicant attendance but recorded 160 Easter communicants and 163 Christmas communicants in 1888. In the visitation Castleknock returned a parish population of 334 plus 110 outsiders giving a total of 444 with an average Sunday congregation of 250, just over half attending each Sunday.[28] This would seem to be about the attendance rate of the average church. Fashionable churches like St Stephen's Dublin, seemed to do much better. In 1845 Christmas communicants at two celebrations totalled 369 and Easter 335. In 1876 it was 308 at Christmas and at Easter in 1877, 333.[29] A fairly constant rate was maintained across the thirty years. Attendances in the noted evangelical churches were particularly good. Holy Trinity in the days of John Gregg's ministry had communicant attendances at Christmas and Easter of seven to eight hundred and a Communion Sunday attendance of three to four hundred. Indeed the church had to be extended to cater for those who wished to worship there. The most remarkable example of evangelical enthusiasm was the three thousand who flocked to hear Achilles Daunt in the Dublin Exhibition Hall. Those who didn't come early failed to gain admission. Attendances at Whitsunday communions were better than average. St Stephen's had 135 communicants in 1868, Rathfarnham in 1845 had 425 in church and ninety five communicants on Whitsunday. Attendances are

27 R.C.B., P 533/8, preacher's book, parish of Rathfarnham, Dublin.   28 R.C.B., P 352/8, preacher's book, parish of Castleknock, Dublin; R.C.B. P 331/8, preacher's book, parish of Douglas, Co. Cork.   29 R.C.B., P 346/8, preacher's book, parish of St Stephen's, Dublin.

recorded for 1 January, the feast of the Circumcision, Rathfarnham 178 in 1845, St Stephen's Dublin 293 communicants in 1845 and Castleknock sixty-four in 1876. Indeed throughout the century there was little variation in communicant practice. Dalkey by 1895 introduced communion every Sunday and other churches moved to twice monthly communions. Ash Wednesday and Good Friday were well supported. A number of southern churches continued daily services, mostly in the morning. Westport in 1897 had an attendance in a typical week of 5,7,4,6. St Nicholas Cork 1868 – 14,11,14,18,15. St Stephen's Dublin in 1877 – 19,17,15,11. Such services may well have depended on charitable bodies in association with the parish. Innovations like children's services or weekday Harvest Thanksgivings were introduced in most of the parishes. Westport by 1897 had a Wednesday Harvest with an attendance of 264, and a children's service in 1893. Rathfarnham had a children's service in 1884. What does appear is evidence of active lay participation in worship but with little attention paid to communion. Even on the great festivals the number communicating are seldom more than half of those attending and often as low as a quarter.[30]

The rapid growth of Belfast in the nineteenth century awakened local laity to the need for church extension to accommodate worshipers. Such church building was promoted by Dr Drew of Christ Church and Bishop Knox but lay support was evidenced in the patrons who paid £300 or more to the fund. Six out of seven were laymen including leading landlords like the marquis of Hertford, the marquises of Downshire and Donegall among them. The vice patrons who paid £100 pounds or more number thirty-eight laity represented by four of the nobility and leading families like Ward, Montgomery and Dobbs. They employed Charles Lanyon as their honorary architect. Such was his desire to promote the work that he gave his services free.

In 1858 there were only three churches in Belfast and one in Ballymacarrett. In that year Drew called for the establishment of a society and within six months £13,400 had been raised. In all about £32,000 were expended on new churches until the society ceased its activities in 1863.[31] These included the Magdalene Asylum, St Matthew's and Trinity church in Belfast and thirteen others in country towns and districts. In 1862 Sir William Ewart of a prominent linen family with Robert Cassidy a lawyer and Sir William Johnston took a lead in funding the Belfast Church Extension and Endowment Society. They raised £50,000 and by 1886 had raised £155,000 and had endowed or built ten churches in the city. They spent nearly £22,000 on mission halls to provide for the rapidly developing poor districts. The inspiration of this society seems to have been primarily a lay one though Bishop Knox in his long episcopacy gladly supported all their endeavours to provide for the pastoral and spiritual needs of

---

30 R.S. Gregg, *Memorial of John Gregg* (Dublin, 1878), p. 174.   31 F.R. Wynne, *Spent in the service* (London, 1876), p. 225.

the city.[32] This work reached its culmination in the vision of a cathedral for the city. The Bill passed the general synod in 1899, when it was claimed Belfast had still not been accorded justice. Its 92,000 church people had only twenty-seven churches as against Dublin's forty nine and two cathedrals.[33] Sir Robert Bateson, a keen supporter of the Church Extension Society, argued 'It was only by the efforts of their poorer brethren that Belfast merchants had been able to make large fortunes. When the poorer man needed their assistance had they not the right to call upon the wealthy merchants to give them their assistance? … After all they were dependent on their labour for the very wealth they enjoyed.'[34]

New churches were rapidly built to serve the poorer districts of Belfast – St Mary's, Crumlin Road 1865, St Stephen's, 1869, Mariners and St Andrew's, 1870, St James's, 1871, Willowfield, 1872, St Matthew's, Shankill Road, 1872. Attendances in the new churches were not always good. A major problem was widespread poverty. The church people were not always welcoming. The Revd Thomas Roe commented 'see how cold these church people are to one another.'[35] Many complained, as in Dublin, that they had no suitable clothes to go to church in. In 1850 St Patrick's, Ballymacarrett, had only an average attendance of 200 and in 1835 only fifty communicants at Christmas and Easter communions.[36] Christ Church did better but then its rector, Dr Drew, was the most noted evangelical in the city. In 1838, 400 parishioners attended on Easter Sunday and there were 180 communicants, a higher percentage than usual as so often was the case in evangelical churches. Indeed Christ Church had a Sunday school with 400 children and sixty teachers, about half of the available pupils. There were also separate Sunday Schools in the afternoon for adult males and females. No less than 430 attended the men's classes. The primary concern of the children's classes was catechism and Biblical knowledge.[37] One of the great annual events was the Easter Monday excursion, the only holiday that most enjoyed. There are descriptions of thousands of children from different Sunday Schools following their banners to York Street Station.

A dedicated pastor could always make headway. The Revd Charles Seaver in St John's, Laganbank, deliberately chose to work in one of the poorest areas. In 1859 he saw the communicant attendance doubled as a result of the revival.[38] Like MacIlwaine, the evangelical rector of St George's, he highly approved of the movement which he described as 'an awakening of the mind of the community to a due sense of the importance of revealed truth evidencing itself in an increased love for the means of grace.'[39] Bishop Knox was equally

---

32 Based on preacher's books cited in n. 27–9 above.   33 *Report of Church Accommodation Society* (Belfast, 1843), p. 9.   34 *Handbook of the United Diocese Down, Connor & Dromore* (Belfast, 1886), p. 34.   35 S.P. Kerr, 'The Church of Ireland in Belfast 1800–1870' M.A. thesis, Edinburgh University, 1975.   36 Ibid., p. 128.   37 Ibid., p. 128.   38 Ibid., p. 130. 39 Ibid., p. 148.

delighted in the sudden leap in the number of confirmees from around 250 to 750 in that year. Visitors like Provost Salmon and Archdeacon Stopford of Meath came north to evaluate the movement. On the whole they were approving but Stopford recognised an unhealthy and unbalanced spirituality commenting on an hysteria amongst mill girls evidenced in long hours of prayer and hymn singing 'often till long past midnight in crowded and ill ventilated assemblies.' Their working day commenced at six o'clock in the morning, in often dangerous conditions. The archdeacon had reason to be concerned.[40] D.H. Akenson saw the revival as giving a new character to the witness of the laity 'within the Church of Ireland the most important administrative effect was the strengthening of the position of the layman.'[41] As never before they took leadership in prayer meetings, Bible classes and cottage meetings. Indeed he claimed that the revival lay behind the hostility to the clergy after 1870 in the new general synod and the attempt by a considerable number of its members to seize control of the church.

In Ulster church attendance seems to have been highest in major provincial towns. St Mark's Armagh varied from 1,000 to 600 at Morning and Evening Prayer, though very often in the century there was a Sunday attendance of 2,000. By contrast the number of communicants was very low. On Christmas Day 1859 attendance at Morning Prayer was 960 and a third were communicants. Easter 1860 recorded 980 at Morning Prayer, 850 at Evening and much the same communicant rate at 390. The numbers were not unduly increased by soldiers. When separate services were arranged for them after 1878 attendances were around 100. Saints' days were seldom celebrated but attendance at Ash Wednesday 1860 were 130 and Good Friday 420. Harvest Thanksgiving introduced in 1884 on a Sunday were morning 648 and evening 589 by no means exceptional for the parish. Choral festivals involving other parishes were introduced in 1865 and recorded attendances from 1,200 to 1,700 in the following years. In 1890 to counteract falling attendances a fortnight of mission services produced between 660 and 1,024 on each night. An innovation was a daily children's service during the mission.[42]

St Ann's Dungannon had nothing like the numbers recorded in Armagh, typical was 4 January 1880 when attendances were Morning Prayer 351, Evening Prayer 278, Holy Communion forty-five. Attendances on Ash Wednesday were 70, Good Friday 146, Easter 409 with 134 communicants and Christmas 322 with 160 communicants. Harvest Thanksgiving was held on a Tuesday with 200 in attendance. In 1886 this was changed to a Wednesday when 516 attended. Children's services were innovated in 1880 but were not a huge success and were discontinued in 1887. Sunday School examination could produce an attendance of 300 but the congregation at the special services at

40 Ibid., p. 148.   41 Akenson, *The Church of Ireland*, p. 208.   42 Preacher's book, St Mark's, Armagh, local custody.

4.15 p.m. were beneath the hundred. In 1890 daily services were held during Holy Week but the average attendance was 24 rising to 94 on Good Friday. The experiment was not repeated in 1895. An innovation of 1885 was a pre-confirmation service when a hundred candidates attended. Choral Festivals were also popular in Dungannon when introduced in 1880 with 600 attending rising in subsequent years to 900.[43]

Other important parishes like Ballymena kept no attendance records until 1897. They then averaged 360 at Morning Prayer and 280 at Evening Prayer. Prior to this communicant numbers were recorded in a monthly service with an attendance which fluctuated from thirty-five to sixty-nine. By 1897 even these numbers had declined to twenty or thirty. An 8 a.m. celebration had been innovated at first in Advent and Lent but in 1894 it was celebrated every Sunday with an attendance of about eight. Major festivals were celebrated with a communicant average of fifty. A new rector in 1865 brought about a marked improvement in communicants at Easter and Christmas which rose to over 200. A Sunday harvest service was introduced in 1875. In 1881 a nightly Holy Week service was instituted.[44]

Smaller churches followed much the same pattern. Kildollagh in Connor diocese, consecrated 1855, had an attendance in 1859 of 110 on Christmas Day with forty-five communicants. Indeed a rather higher percentage than the larger parishes. Seventy-two attended Evening Prayer. At Easter 1860 114 came to morning service and fifty communicated with 106 at Evening Prayer. In the rest of the century attendances fluctuated in Easter 1876 only sixty-eight attended of whom sixteen communicated. Attendances improved following the institution of a new rector in 1885. As might be expected much depended on attitudes to the incumbent.[45] Antrim parish, like Ballymena in a predominantly Presbyterian community, had much the same percentage attendance as the larger parishes. In 1885 Easter figures were 152 with forty-five communicants, 1887 Christmas 210 morning and evening with forty-three communicants. Saints' days were celebrated with an attendance of between three and ten. Most parishes ignored the Saints days. Innovations followed the usual pattern. Wednesday Harvest Thanksgiving 1875 rose to 450 in 1892. Children's service 1887 and Carol Service 1896.[46]

In Belfast the new parish of St Mark's, Dundela, kept little record of attendance figures with the exception of Christmas and Easter. Communions were celebrated twice monthly with a typical attendance in 1864 of thirty-four and fifty-three, Christmas 1866 had an attendance of eighty-six and twenty-five communicants but the parish was growing rapidly. By Easter 1891, 350 came to

43 Preacher's book, St Ann's, Dungannon, local custody.   44 P.R.O.N.I., Preacher's book St Patrick's, Ballymena.   45 P. R.O.N.I., Preacher's book, Kildollagh, Connor.   46 Preacher's book, Antrim local custody.

Morning Prayer and 453 Evening Prayer, but with only fifty one communicants. Harvest Thanksgiving, introduced 1886, grew steadily in popularity until in 1893 there were 676 in attendance.[47]

Another growing congregation was that of St Philip and St James Holywood, diocese of Down, consecrated 1844. Like many parishes Sunday attendance figures were often ignored. Communion was celebrated first Sundays only with communicants fluctuating from thirty-three to sixty-seven. Christmas Day 1847, 170 attended with a 50 per cent communicants of ninety. By 1875 Communion was celebrated twice monthly with attendances varying from twenty-three to eighty-six. Daily services in Holy Week were introduced in 1866 when the whole fortnight of passiontide was observed. Attendances fluctuated from twenty eight to fifty daily with 200 on Good Friday. A new rector, the future Archbishop Crozier, was instituted in 1881. He was a dedicated pastoral minister. Though no doubt helped by growing population attendances improved throughout his ministry. About 100 to 160 soldiers attended from Palace Barracks. On 19 June 1887, 501 came to Morning Prayer of whom 125 were soldiers. In 1889 the rector made a determined effort to improve attendances and a special mission fortnight was held with innovations like a men's service, attended by 460. Attendances were 200 at the lowest which rose to 800. In the same year on 26 May Sabine Baring Gould, the high church author of 'Onward Christian soldiers', was invited to a special Sunday when 1,600 people attended between morning and evening service. A Friday evening harvest was attended by 650. By Holy Week 1894 attendances averaged 100 a night with 350 on Good Friday.[48]

Such surveys of Preacher's Books, whilst defying statistical analysis by their erratic nature, nevertheless, indicate a vigorous parochial life with well-attended churches. As elsewhere in Ireland communicants were comparatively few in number even in large congregations like St Mark's, Armagh. Christmas and Easter attendances were large but even then seldom more than one-third were communicants. Attendances were maintained throughout the period and fresh life was stimulated by new introductions of holy week services, children's services, harvest thanksgiving and choir festivals and parade services for boys brigade and church lads brigade. Nevertheless, one gets the impression of highly conservative congregations where change came gradually.

The nineteenth century saw the coming of age of the laity. On the eve of disestablishment at the invitation of the archbishop of Canterbury the archbishops and bishops who came to confer on what should be done agreed that without the participation of the laity in the governance of the church they could not hope to survive. Two prominent laymen attended that meeting, the duke of Abercorn and Earl Cairns.[49] The dukes of Abercorn and Leinster were by popular

47 Preacher's book, St Mark's, Dundela, local custody.   48 Preacher's book, St Phillip and St James, Holywood, local custody.   49 J.C. MacDonnell, *Life of Archbishop Magee* (2 vols, 1896), i, p. 219.

5 James Hamilton (1811– 85), first duke of Abercorn.

consent the most influential voices in the lay convention. They negotiated with
some difficulty voting by houses on issues of faith and worship in exchange for
a representation of two laymen for each clergyman elected to the synod and to
the diocesan synods. This was in the eyes of such a prominent churchman as
Archdeacon Lee of Dublin a concession against all precedent. In a debate in the
Irish Ecclesiastical Gazette he was assured by Bishop Reichal the scholarly
champion of the laity that they had taken part in the synods of the early church.

Vestries were transformed from agencies of local administration to bodies
with control over all matters of fabric, fixtures and finance. Despite those limitations they could not be ignored in the running of the parish. Indeed one
clergyman claimed that they were an invention of the Devil. The *Irish Ecclesiastical
Gazette* in 1899 quoted Bishop Crozier when he said 'In no other church of
Christendom are the laity given more governing power than in our own and in

no other church do clergy and laity so often meet to discuss church affairs on perfectly equal terms.' In a disendowed church the parishes could not be sustained without the active financial support of the laity. It is to the credit of the laity that all over the country they rose to meet the needs of the new situation.

J.C. Beckett in his *Anglo-Irish tradition* surveyed the late nineteenth-century laity:

> Not only were the landlords predominantly Protestant but among professional men and among leaders of commerce and industry the number of Protestants were out of all proportion to the strength of the Protestant population as a whole. Even at a much lower level Protestantism and prosperity seemed to go together. In many a country town where Protestants formed only a tiny proportion of the population they owned the most flourishing businesses and lived in the best houses and lower still the Protestant workman commonly regarded himself and was sometimes regarded by others as marked off from his Catholic mates by superior cleanliness, honesty and industry.[50]

Sean O'Casey recorded how his working-class mother, strove to maintain standards of decency and cleanliness. Miriam Moffitt in her study of the Church of Ireland community of Killala and Achonry also notes how the Protestant farmers with small holdings that kept them little above the poverty line still tended to live in better houses than similarly situated Catholic farmers.[51]

The recognition by the Dublin poor of a decline in wealth did much to fuel their violent Anti-Roman attitudes. This packed Harold's Cross and Sandford churches and encouraged the Revd Tresham Gregg, 'the flail of popery'. Such anti-Roman sentiments had largely motivated the working men who formed the Dublin Protestant Operatives Association in 1841. Such anger and fear was found at every level of society from the duke to the road sweeper. John Synge growing up in the Dublin suburbs was shielded by his Protestant mother from every contact with Catholic children. He moved in a closed circle of small landowners, Dublin professionals and businessmen. So protective was his mother that she refused to allow her children to attend school, but educated them herself with daily prayer and Bible reading. Such attitudes were strongest amongst evangelicals and inspired their hopes that a 'Second Reformation' was about to take place in Ireland. Their religious convictions were both deeply and sincerely held. The third earl of Roden provided daily Bible studies for his workers and was deeply committed to the Orange Order. It was after a large demonstration at Castlewellan when he rode out to greet them that the incident

50 J.C. Beckett, *Anglo-Irish tradition* (London, 1976), p. 119. 51 Miriam Moffitt, *The Church of Ireland community of Killala and Achonry 1870–1940* (Dublin, 1999), p. 23.

at Dolly's Brae took place as the Orangemen made their way home. Thirty Catholics were slain by the armed demonstrators. This incident in 1848 increased the government's unease and determined them in 1850 to pass an act of parliament prohibiting Orange parades. Roden was dismissed from the bench of magistrates but neither he nor the earl of Enniskillen would resign as deputy grand and grand master of the Order. It was an Order dominated by members of the Church of Ireland. The leaders were nearly all landed gentry or aristocracy. The campaign to repeal the act was led by another evangelical landlord William Johnston of Ballykilbeg. In 1864, 14,000 Orangemen defied the government and marched to Bangor where Johnston addressed them calling for resistance to the Act. In 1868 he was imprisoned for his refusal to obey the law and so crowned with martyrdom he was elected M.P. for Belfast under the banner of 'long live the gallant Johnston and the artisans of Belfast.'[52] He agitated in parliament until in 1872 he secured the repeal of the Act and became the undisputed leader of the Orange Order. His passionate belief in personal liberty is well illustrated by his support for his daughter when she converted to Rome.[53] He defended her right to worship according to her conscience and sent her in his carriage to chapel despite virulent criticism from fellow members of the Order.

Colonel Saunderson was another evangelical landlord with a penchant for preaching in his estate chapel. At his death the future Archbishop Crozier published a collection of his sermons. He did not join the Order until the Phoenix Park murder convinced him that it was a necessary defence against prevailing disorder. He saw that Unionism needed an alliance between the landed interest and farmers, labourers and working men. 'Christian and especially evangelical conviction bound the employer to his employee and helped to create a moral community out of a disparate workforce or a disparate tenantry.'[54] It was a view shared with the Crichtons, Archdales and Maxwells. With Orange support he was elected M.P. for North Armagh and became the real leader of the Unionist party. He owed his religious convictions to his mother, a daughter of the earl of Farnham who was a passionate believer in the Second Reformation who posted lists of converts on his estate notice boards. He was even more deeply influenced by his wife, a daughter of Lord Ventry, also a supporter of the Protestant crusade. Conversion and marriage happened at much the same time. He was one of the leading agitators in the general synod for purging from the Prayer Book the dregs of Rome. Groups of landlord families created areas of evangelical belief that criss-crossed the country. The Powerscourts in Wicklow, the Farnham, Saunderson, Maxwell, Crichton connection in Cavan, Monaghan and Fermanagh, the Annesleys and Rodens in County Down were typical examples. There were equally strong family groupings in professional and business circles.

---

52 K. Haddick Flynn, *Orangeism: the making of a tradition* (Dublin 1999), p. 275.   53 Ibid., p. 284.   54 Alvin Jackson, *Colonel Saunderson* (Oxford, 1995), p. 181.

Even the historian W.E.H. Lecky was described as rushing off to hear the great evangelical preacher the Revd John Gregg in Trinity church.[55]

The Quaker biographer Braithwaite stated 'After dinner there was a sermon and forthwith the company dropped to their knees … the description will give you some idea of the state of society in Dublin. I should imagine that these Bible readings are extensively supplanting card games and other amusements.'[56] W.B. Yeats acknowledged the power of Bible study among the people he had grown up with 'for the people of the Irish Protestant minority who recognised themselves as living in a permanent state of theological war the Bible had an even greater significance than it had for their English neighbours'. Bible classes were almost a necessity in every parish and *de rigeur* in evangelical ones. The Ulster Revival of 1859 not only encouraged confirmation and communicant life but gave Bible study a place in working class communities that endured right up to the First World War. Chaplains in 1914 were amazed by the earnest Bible studies amongst soldiers of the Ulster division. Bible classes became a common place in many parishes. They became a feature of the Church of Ireland Young Men's Christian Association founded in 1849 by such notables as Sir Joseph Napier, Lord Chief Justice Whiteside and William Digges La Touche. This was especially active in Belfast and Dublin where the needs of young men in the cities for support and recreation were a major motivation. Similar needs lay behind the establishment of the Girls Friendly Society in 1876. This organisation had been founded in Winchester by Mrs Townsend whose father had been a rector in Kilkenny. The impulse for the Mothers' Union came from the same diocese and the first branch in Ireland was established in Bray in 1877. By the end of the century the Boys Brigade and Church Lads Brigade had been founded and became an ever expanding interest in the larger parishes of the Church of Ireland.

Much of this religious intensity was generated by strong minded women with a deeply Biblical faith. The author John Synge's mother taught her children out of the Bible everyday. His brother Sam went out as a missionary to China but John's faith was shattered on reading Charles Darwin as a teenager. The world of absolute certainties was gone, never to return.[57] Lady Powerscourt was in many ways the leader of her family in evangelical conviction but they refused to follow her when she joined the Plymouth Brethren. There were others strongly Protestant but not evangelical in outlook. A good example was Elizabeth Smith with a highly critical and intelligent mind revealed in her often acerbic comments in the *Diary of a highland lady* and her subsequent Irish diary. They show how such a woman played an important part in estate management at Baltiboys in County Wicklow. In the Famine years like many other Irish

55 *A memoir of W. H. Lecky by his wife* (London, 1909), p. 15.   **56** J.B. Braithwaite, *Memoir of John Joseph Gurney* (2 vols, Norwich, 1855), pp 326–7.   **57** Edward Stephens, *My Uncle John* (London, 1974), p. 36.

women she did much to alleviate the suffering of those who lived on the estate.[58] Indeed clergy wives and daughters and other ladies from the landlord class worked to bring relief and some gave their lives as they became victims of the cholera and typhoid epidemics. The best landlord families had a paternalistic attitude to their tenants believing they had a duty to be caring. In the years that followed the Famine many families were burdened with debt brought about by extravagant living coupled with loss of rents. Quite a few such families gave up the unequal struggle. The final blow had been the huge rate charges imposed by the government's decision that each district would bear the costs of relief.

The letters of Somerville and Ross gave an account of how their two families and their friends tackled the new world after the Land Acts had released their tenants from dependence. Such families shared a determination to keep the houses they loved and to preserve the demesnes left to them. It was this determination that drove the two women to authorship, but in their family they were not alone. Hildegarde Coghill exported her violets all over the British Isles, Violet and Hebe qualified as doctors. Sir Jocelyn Coghill turned to photography and Sir Egerton Coghill became a painter as did Rose Barton a cousin of the Martins who went to Paris as Violet Martin had done to train as an artist. Rose Barton has claimed her place in the history of Irish Art as has Jack Yeats.[59]

Edith Somerville and Violet Martin were typical of many non-evangelical church women. Regular church goers, supporters of their parish church with Bible reading and family prayers at home, a pattern to be found in many a Big House. Lady Gregory came from a family of ardent supporters of the Second Reformation, the Peirses of Galway and indeed in her youth had been a Sunday school teacher as many others of her social class had been. The Church of Ireland owes much to the support and practical work of such ladies. Whilst a large number were evangelical there were others like Mrs Alexander who had deeply held church convictions of the Bishop Jebb school. She corresponded with John Keble who edited her *Hymns for little children*. The noted vicar of Leeds Dr Hook was another of her mentors and her friendship with William Archer Butler, first professor of Moral Theology in Trinity College, Dublin, helped her to develop those church principles she held to her dying day. In her hymns the spirit of that school of churchmen find their best expression. Their simplicity in theology together with her awareness of the significance of the Christian year and her love for Christ made her an abiding influence on world Christianity. It would hardly be an exaggeration to say that this laywoman was the most powerful influence for good to be nurtured by her church in the nineteenth century.

58 Elizabeth Grant, *The highland lady in Ireland: journals 1840–50* (Edinburgh, 1991), pp 276–7.   59 Gifford Lewis, *The selected letters of Somerville and Ross* (London, 1989), p. xxiv.

Whilst most women exercised their influence in home and family there were others like Agnes Jones whose determination, strength of character and ability made an important contribution to the advancements of the Victorian era. She grew up in an evangelical family in Fahan, County Donegal and earned the esteem of Florence Nightingale who invited her to come to Liverpool to reorganise the large workhouse hospital. Florence said of her on her death in 1868 'She is the pioneer of workhouse nursing ... In less than three years she had reduced one of the most disorderly hospital populations in the world to something like Christian discipline such as the police themselves wondered at.'[60] Another pioneer was Mrs Anne Jellicoe who devoted her life to establish women's education on an equal footing with men and achieve university education for women. She came from a Quaker family but found in the Church of Ireland the support she needed. Archbishop Trench and the dean of the Chapel Royal, Hercules Dickinson, gave her the encouragement to carry out her plans. Dickinson indeed was Warden of Alexandra College from 1868 to 1903. Mrs Jellicoe throughout her life was concerned both with education and providing employment for the poor. In 1861 she had taken a leading role in the establishment of the Queen's Institute to provide training in art and commerce for women. In 1866 she succeeded with the support of the archbishop in establishing Alexandra College and subsequently the Governesses Association of Ireland and Alexandra School. All of these involved an immense struggle in which the Lady Superintendent remained the driving force. The college produced a succession of headmistresses as determined to forward the cause of women's education as Mrs Jellicoe herself. She succeeded in persuading Trinity College, Dublin, to establish the Trinity examination for women in 1870 but failed to persuade them to grant degrees to women. This only became possible from 1880 with the act of parliament creating the Royal University of Ireland. It had been her life wish to see women graduate but she did not live to see it. At her funeral Archbishop Trench said 'She could not know that it had been given to her to trace out a great work.'[61]

Another visionary step had been taken in 1840 when Lord Adare and his cousin, William Monsell, had set out to create a new kind of school which became St Columba's College in Dublin. They succeeded in recruiting a man with a vision of what a school should be, William Sewell, professor of Moral Philosophy in Oxford. They charmed him with the Protestant society of Limerick. 'A society full of life amiability, talent and real goodness' was how Sewell described it.[62] His beau ideal was 'an Irish gentleman, well born, well educated and with his natural tendencies modified by English association is

60 Alexander, *Primate Alexander*, p. 127.   61 Anne O'Connor and Susan M. Parkes, *Gladly learn and gladly teach* (Dublin, 1985), p. 32.   62 Lionel James, *A forgotten genius. Sewell of St Columba's and Radley* (London, 1965), p. 77.

6 St Columba's College staff, 1862.

perhaps one of the most perfect example of civilised human nature.'[63] He saw
a school as a place of culture and the formation of Christian character. He
bought works of art and antiques to grace St Columba's College. The table set
with silver and all the refinements of contemporary taste was to create an
environment where boys would grow up with good taste. More important was
daily worship, based on the Book of Common Prayer with sung services to
catch the imagination of the pupils. Masters were encouraged to share the
interests and recreation of the boys. They were to be brought up in a tradition
of true religion and enlightened politics. One of the early aims had been to
provide an Irish speaking clergy to evangelise the nation. Irish language and

63 Ibid., p. 78.

culture became a feature of the school curriculum. Sewell envisaged St Columba's as an Oxford college fellowship rather than an English public school. The archbishop of Armagh, Lord John George Beresford, became a generous patron and a high churchman like Professor Todd, a keen supporter. Unfortunately the school was almost wrecked when Lord Adare and Monsell followed Newman on his conversion to Rome. Adare became a bitter convert seeking to bring up his son in the Catholic church, forbidding his evangelical Protestant mother to correspond with her son when he went to school in Rome.[64] His efforts failed, his son rebelled and insisted on going to Oxford and grew up a conventional member of the Church of Ireland with love affairs with the prairies of Buffalo Bill and yachting. Sewell felt compelled to resign from the school and Archbishop Beresford withdrew his support. The school survived the crisis and played a part in providing the sons of Irish clergy and gentry with an enlightened education.

The census of 1861 returned 8,412 landlords of whom 8,159 had been born in Ireland 46 per cent were given as resident on their estates and a further 25 per cent as resident on an estate elsewhere in Ireland. The number of absentees has been greatly exaggerated for propagandist purposes. Indeed some of the largest landowners in this group were model owners. They were often far removed from the caricature portrayed by the Land League and the nationalist press. Thomas Connolly and the Marquis Conyngham took care to keep their tenants satisfied. In 1881 the earl of Portarlington accepted the Griffith valuations and in consequence his rental fell by 17 per cent. Indeed landlords were often advised not to increase tension by raising rents and shared the attitude of the Revd John Moore, agent of the Annesley estate in County Down: 'the agent should do all in his power to advance the temporal and spiritual interest of the people.'[65] In an age when on the whole agricultural incomes increase J.S. Donnelly claimed 'the tenant farmer gets the lion's share of the benefits.' The tenants belonged overwhelmingly to the Catholic community 77 per cent, 13 per cent were presbyterian and only 10 per cent Church of Ireland.

In 1855 the *Irish Farmer's Gazette* wrote 'each succeeding year seems more eventful than the last and gives practical proof of the rapid strides improved agriculture is making in Ireland.'[66] Some modern economists have judged that by keeping rents too low land was undervalued and the industry depressed. W.E. Vaughan has estimated that at a time when property valuation increased 11 per cent rental income fell 11 per cent. There has been a revaluation of the Victorian landlord in modern times and a contention that the propaganda of the Land League was grossly over played. Some priests who were often leaders in the attack on the landlords acknowledged that there were good owners. Father Nolan said that Viscount de Vesci was 'a very good, kind, humane feeling man

64 Lord Dunraven, *Past times and pastimes* (2 vols, London, 1922), i, p. 8.   65 W.E. Vaughan, *Landlords and tenants in mid-Victorian Ireland* (Oxford, 1994), p. 109.   66 Ibid., p. 16.

who had never rackrented.' Others praised in County Laois were Lord Castletown, the marquis of Lansdowne and Lord Stanhope. Father Thomas O'Shea said of Sir Charles Coote of Castlefin 'If the landlords everywhere were like him you would not have any need for a Land League.'[67] The earl of Dunraven claimed that if one was prepared to talk over the problems in a friendly way all could be resolved. There was almost no agitation in Ulster outside Donegal. One must not give the impression there were no injustices. In the peak years of the Land War 1879–1882 there were 11,320 outrages and 11,215 evictions. Some landlords saw this as essential to save their estates. In fact the outrages were less than in the years after the tithe wars and the Famine between 1846 and 1849, there had been 60,000 outrages and 750 murders. In Donegal were found two examples of the worst and the best of landlords. Lord Leitrim was utterly ruthless, any default was followed by an instant notice to quit. The Poor Law Inspector claimed that the result was 'to check all enterprise and improvement of any kind.'[68] Lord Leitrim was a petty tyrant whose murder was judged by the R.I. C. sub Inspector to have been almost inevitable. It was the prelude to the bitterest stage of the Land War that time when Mary Ponsonby of Kilcooley spoke of murder lurking outside the demesne wall. The clearance of Glenveagh by its landlord though motivated by the desire to make the estate viable, left a long memory of landlord injustice in County Donegal. By contrast John Hamilton in Donegal was the model of all a landlord should be. He succeeded to his estates as a child with a considerable fortune accumulated by wise management. He had been brought up by his Packenham grandmother, sister of the duke of Wellington, who had made a convinced evangelical out of him. Indeed he was highly critical of the Church of Ireland, regarding it as corrupt and not truly Christlike. Like many others who belonged to the church he had serious doubts about infant baptism. He was rejected as a candidate for ordination by the bishop of Raphoe but devoted the rest of his life to promote a living relationship with Christ amongst his tenants. He established Sunday schools and Bible classes. One indeed was attended by 1,000 of his tenants. His passion for improvement absorbed all his fortune. He built 100 model houses, engaged in huge drainage schemes and land improvement. During the Famine he fed 2,000 as a consequence of his good management only one person died on his estates.[69] In hard times he reduced the rents but the estate ended up heavily in debt. His heirs had little reason to thank him for his benevolence. He tried to hold the line between Orangemen and Ribbonmen with some success and was known to keep the peace by personally reasoning with large bands of armed men.

67 J.W.H. Carter, *The Land War and its leaders in Queen's county* (Portlaoise, 1994), p. 7. 68 Vaughan, *Landlords and tenants in mid-Victorian Ireland*, pp 101–4.   69 Dermot James, *John Hamilton of Donegal 1800–84* (Dublin, 1995), p. 151.

Elizabeth Bowen claimed that a passionate love of place characterised the Irish landlord and probably a majority allied with that a sense of responsibility for their tenants. Of course Lord Leitrim was not alone in ruthlessness. Lord Lucan became infamous during the Famine for his indifference to the tenants he drove from their homes. Coffin ships were often the result of bad management rather than deliberate malice. In fact the Land Acts did almost nothing for the peasants. The real beneficiaries were the farmers, shopkeepers and the lawyers. Many landlords in the west of Ireland were, like the Somervilles, nearly ruined by the loss of rents. The Encumbered Estates Act enabled much land to be sold and a great deal came into the possession of merchants and lawyers more exploitive by far than the families they replaced. The Somervilles were forced to rent out their estate for years and only returned after the Land Acts to tenants who now owned their holdings. Both sides found it awkward. The Somervilles felt that the former tenants were ungrateful for past kindnesses. The tenants hardly knew how to handle the new state of affairs. When the Somervilles invited the children to a traditional party the parish priest urged the parents not to send them. At first none appeared but gradually they trickled in but the familiar world was gone for ever.

Bishop Alexander saw the Land Acts as a plot to destroy the landed gentry and so the church but in fact most survived until the First World War. The Land League was however denounced from the floor of the general synod as Anti-Christ and the duke of Leinster in 1881 lamented 'The plunder of the Irish Church and the late landlord spoilation attempt had their support'. Archbishop Knox with his experience in Belfast was far from convinced that the church was so dependant on the landed interest and in his synod address in 1891 stated 'I do not hold that the Church of Ireland is dependent solely on it's titled followers or generous landlords.' There were 'thousands upon thousands of Christians among her merchants, her cultivated scholars, intelligent artisans, mechanics who clung with unshaken fidelity to the faith of their forefathers.' The *Irish Ecclesiastical Gazette* of April 1888 urged the importance of encouraging subscriptions from all classes.' It will make their attachment to the church even stronger when farmers, artisans, labourers and domestic servants are giving something. Landlords were of greater significance in the parishes of the west of Ireland as Miriam Moffitt illustrated in her study of Killala and Achonry. Indeed in the editorial of 1863 the *Irish Ecclesiastical Gazette* urged

> that Protestant landlords select if possible Protestant tenants, Protestant employers should seek Protestant servants and labourers for surely Protestantism should be a link of union between those who profess it and it would be a most unreasonable and unchristian practice which would not benefit those who are one with us in faith and hope and in the most sacred duties of religion to be also partakers in any temporal benefits which one can bestow.

It was this very policy which created the population of small farmers in scattered pockets throughout the country as in south Sligo as noted by Miriam Moffitt and the largely Palatine population of Kilcooley in the Slieve Ardagh hills of County Tipperary.

This loss of political power and control of local government and police turned the gentry with new found enthusiasm to church affairs. W.E. Vaughan in his study of Victorian landlords states 'The opportunity created by the reorganisation of the Irish Church after 1871 was however eagerly seized by the landlords who played a part in its government at all levels from select vestries up to the general synod which was the largest regular gathering of Irish gentry in Dublin since 1800'.[70] The laity for the most part responded to the needs of the church though unusually the siocesan synods in Tuam and Limerick in 1883 failed to achieve a quorum. On the whole they responded with considerable generosity in church building and endowments. In many ways the general synod was to them what the Irish parliament had been to their ancestors. Vaughan claims they lacked the powers of a real aristocracy and diverted their energies to farming to restore their lost incomes but they were in no way a decadent society. They saw their future in Empire building in the army and political service. The great soldier hero of the Victorians was Sir Garnet Wolseley converted to evangelical faith by his mother in an impoverished upbringing in County Louth.[71] Many officers shared such religious convictions. On the whole there was vibrant life in the determination of their class that they should not sink into insignificance in a predominantly Catholic nation.

Disestablishment far from weakening the Irish church gave it a new confidence in itself. One sees that reflected in the *Irish Ecclesiastical Gazette* of 1874 when the 'Church notes' for January gave a glowing report of church life in Dublin, where churches had been crowded, services had been earnest and hearty. More churches had been decorated for Christmas than ever before. Many had held Christmas Eve carol services. There had been prolonged prayer meetings, Midnight Communions in more than one church. 'There is much proof that God has not forsaken the old Irish church but is still working in her and by her.'[72] The church in Belfast was also striving to meet the needs of that rapidly growing industrial city with a new vigour. In parishes like St Matthew's, St Patrick's Ballymacarrett, St Luke's and St Mark's Dundela. In February 1874 the *Gazette* recorded what it described as a new kind of mission in St Philip and St James's Hollywood. Five days of morning and evening services with Holy Communion on Wednesday and Sunday as well as a daily prayer meeting in the school house at 9 am. The mission was conducted by the Revd Mr Wynne.

---

70 Vaughan, *Landlords and tenants in mid-Victorian Ireland*, p. 220.   71 Morris Arthur, *The life of Lord Wolseley* (London, 1924), p. 2.   72 *Irish Ecclesiastical Gazette*, Feb. 1874.

That St Patrick's Cathedral should have been restored by Sir Benjamin Lee Guinness and that Christ Church and the new Synod Hall should have been built by the distiller Henry Roe provides evidence that the Church of Ireland had moved into a new age where industry and commerce counted for more than the aristocratic and landed interest. The tradition of evangelical piety was part of the Guinness inheritance. 'Whether they were at St Anne's, Clontarf, their quiet house on Dublin Bay or in their handsome house on St Stephen's Green the atmosphere in which the Guinnesses lived was distinctly pious, serious yet far from solemn. Frivolity was as remote from Sir Benjamin Lee as it had been from his father. Their guiding impulse was high minded and their comfortable lives demanded constant recognition of God's grace and thanks for his bounty. Their surroundings were opulent but their lives were sober – in some ways austere – and the day began and ended with family prayers'.[73]

Desmond O'Dowd in his book on Celbridge gave his judgement on that parish at the end of the century, 'As an organisation of Protestant believers it saw the century out as a leaner more independent, democratic and effective force'.[74] John Crawford in his study of the Dublin parishes has endorsed the wealth of anecdotal evidence with sound statistical data set out in table 3.

Table 3 Church Attendance as percentage of Church of Ireland population in Dublin.[75]

Area of City	1831/34	1861
South West	35.9	55.2
South East	45.9	61.7
South Central	47.2	52.4
North West	11.2	13.8
North East	33.8	46.8
South Suburbs	39.8	58.5
North Suburbs	34.8	55.2

Sources: Commission on public instruction, Ireland, 1835; Census of population, 1861; R.C.B., Visitation returns, preacher's books

His earlier study of St Catherine's parish reveals a community of skilled artisans, cabinet makers, print and machinery workers, and employees of Guinness, as well as clerks and policemen. It had a vestry dominated by merchants and

73 Patrick Lynch and John Vaizey, *Guinness's Brewery in the Irish economy* (Cambridge ,1960), p. 182.   74 Desmond O'Dowd, *Changing times: the story of religion in nineteenth century Celbridge* (Dublin, 1997), p. 57.   75 John Crawford, 'Aspects of the Church of Ireland in Victorian Dublin'. Talk given to Church of Ireland Historical Society 13 November 1999.

manufacturers a long way removed from its patron, the earl of Meath, at the beginning of the century. It also reveals in the old heart of the parish an underworld of grinding Protestant poverty in a report in 1860. Its author stated 'During the first quarter I have visited many poor Protestants who are in a very bad condition for the common necessities of life, many with large families who cannot attend church for want of clothing.'[76] In days of industrial depression there were considerable numbers of church members in Belfast living in tumble down kitchen houses in abject poverty struggling merely to live. Belfast had changed from a predominantly presbyterian community to a much larger city with a considerable church of Ireland community that had flooded in to provide labour for the ship yard, the mills and other factories.

There was a growing recognition of the need in a democratic age to win the support of the working class especially in Belfast and Dublin. Much of this was little more than good natured paternalism through such bodies as St Patrick's Cathedral Church (Dublin) Working Men's Society reported in the *Irish Ecclesiastical Gazette* of 1891 and the Ballymacarrett church institute in that ship yard parish which sponsored seven lectures in 1892 chaired by Mr G.W. Wolff of Harland and Wolff ship yard. There were a number of such well intentioned enterprises in the cities. The social Service Union united some of these in 1899. It focused attention on the evils of child drunkenness and over crowded housing in its Dublin meeting.[77]

The two major conferences Belfast 1893 and Dublin 1899 both tried to cater for working men. In Belfast a mass meeting for working men was organised for one evening. The theme of the conference was 'adaptability of Christianity to modern needs.' It was addressed by the bishop of Raphoe and Colonel Saunderson. The Dublin conference included in it's main programme a number of sessions on social concern, housing of the poor, intemperance, gambling, the family, schools and the welfare of young people at work. There is however an atmosphere of well meaning middle class paternalism in their approach. That rarity of a clergyman with sympathy to socialism the Revd Patterson Smyth complained in 1899 'We have been busier about trying to get the masses to the church than to show those masses what the church really is.' He gave voice to socialist criticism: 'We have long ceased to seriously expect any help from the church.'[78] Bishop Knox of Down and Connor was sure that in the future only the mobilisation of the laity could enable the church to carry out its ministry. He licensed the first lay reader in Ireland for St George's Belfast in 1876 'to read prayers and to read and explain the Holy Scriptures in the school or other rooms within the same and generally to render aid to the incumbent in all

---

76 John Crawford, *St Catherine's parish, Dublin, 1840–1900: portrait of a Church of Ireland community* (Dublin, 1996), p. 20.   77 *Irish Ecclesiastical Gazette*, 3 Dec. 1899.   78 Kerr, 'The Church of Ireland in Belfast 1800–1870', p. 114.

ministrations and other offices which do not strictly require the services of a minister in Holy Orders.' In 1862 he held a conference in Belfast to promote a greater involvement of laity in the affairs of the church. He also encouraged cottage meetings and the appointment of district visitors.[79] In 1874 a conference was held in Dublin in the Rotunda by the Association for the Operation of Lay Help but little progress had been made towards the general institution of an office of lay readers by the end of the century.

A few rectors felt the problems of working parishes were so great that they created structures involving laity to meet the needs. One outstanding example was Richard Irvine, rector of St Stephen's Belfast. In 1878 the *Irish Ecclesiastical Gazette* published an account of his aims and methods – well attended Bible classes, Sunday School, cottage meetings, temperance societies, penny savings bank. At the same time Mrs Olivia Hill from London had organised a prison gate mission in Belfast.[80] When Seagoe parish, Portadown held a tea party for it's parish workers one hundred were in attendance.

Love of Ireland strongly motivated much of the Anglo-Irish literature. Maria Edgeworth set out to celebrate the Irish character with such success that Sir Walter Scott followed her lead in Scotland. The novels of Charles Lever and Lady Morgan had the desire to capture the society they knew. Sir Samuel Ferguson turned to the Celtic past. J.M. Synge and W.B. Yeats were fascinated by the same traditions. Whilst having little interest in the society they grew up in Oscar Wilde and G.B. Shaw were nevertheless products of that society. Shaw reared in a conventional church home became a convinced atheist at the age of ten. Æ. Russell shared Sir Horace Plunkett's passionate desire to improve the economic life of the nation. Sir Horace a largely nominal churchman had that strong sense of duty and responsibility that made him work tirelessly for the co-operative movement in which he saw the future hope of rural Ireland.

In the professions others made a valuable contribution both to Irish life and the church as in the case of the architects Sir Charles Lanyon and Benjamin Woodward. The legal profession did much to shape the character of the General Synod notably at the time of disestablishment. J.T. Ball, Sir Joseph Napier and five other judges took a lead in drafting its constitution. Indeed that profession did much to set the Representative Church Body on a firm footing. Ball, the lord chancellor of Ireland from 1875 to 1880, was also an M.P. for Trinity College, Dublin, and served as the assessor of the general Synod for many years. His son F.E. Ball made a significant contribution to local and church history. Another lawyer Lancelot Studdart gave a life time of service as the reporter on synod affairs to the *Irish Ecclesiastical Gazette*.

79 *Irish Ecclesiastical Gazette*, 1 Jan. 1878.   80 Kerr, 'The Church of Ireland in Belfast 1800–1870', p. 114.

7 J.T. Ball (1815–98), lord chancellor of Ireland.

Yet despite this confidence and vitality most church members shared a sense of insecurity because of political efforts to solve the Irish problem. Despite the leadership in home rule agitation by Parnell and Isaac Butt the majority saw the movement only in terms of threat.

The Church was swept into a panic campaign against Home Rule. Virtually every select vestry in the country passed resolutions condemning the Bill and the general synod summoned a special meeting which rejected the proposed legislation by a landslide majority. The laity had no difficulty in accepting the view of leading Church of Ireland bishops that it was a plot to destroy their church. In the general synod of 1893 the Primate in his address declared that it was 'a Bill to suppress the Protestant faith'. William Alexander, then bishop of Derry, addressed a huge assembly in the Albert Hall, London condemning Home Rule as a plot to establish a Catholic Irish Republic. Only a minority of lay members of the church did not endorse such views. Indeed the *Irish Ecclesiastical Gazette* in 1880 expressed its horror that Parnell should have been returned to represent the diocese of Dublin in the general synod. The fact that he was elected indicated that there may have been a body of church support for his land league policy at that time but it could also have a consequence of local loyalties to his family.

It had been a century of awakening for the laity of the Church of Ireland with a growing awareness that privilege carried social and spiritual responsibility.

However misguided to others the Second Reformation had been a recognition of a mission to the whole nation. They felt that in their deeply Biblical faith they had something to give. Indeed they had a feeling that they had a vital part to play in every aspect of the nations life. It was a conviction shared by very many of the laity, though, as W.J. McCormack recognised in his biography of Sheridan Le Fanu, this could lead to an exaggerated sense of their own significance: 'They were an intricate if limited social group less grand than they may have thought but nevertheless powerful in business, in the professions, in education.'[81] It was the conviction of W.B. Yeats that they were 'no petty people' and J.C. Beckett acknowledged that 'Ireland without them would not only be different but a poorer country.'[82]

The shock of disestablishment was a traumatic experience, hard to appreciate in later generations when the church by law established was a mere memory. Mrs Alexander in the hymn she wrote for Derry cathedral for 1871 spoke for many

Fallen fallen fallen is now our country's crown
Dimly dawns the new year on a churchless nation.[83]

Despite this feeling of betrayal and rejection the church remained determined to assert its place in the nation 'Ireland is not more theirs than ours. We must glory in our difference, be as proud of it as they are of theirs.'[84] All in all it was an invigorating time to belong to the Church of Ireland in the transformation of the place of the laity in church offices and in coming to terms with profound political change.

81 W.J. McCormack, *Sheridan Le Fanu and Victorian Ireland* (Oxford, 1980), p. 7.
82 Beckett, *Anglo-Irish tradition*, p. 143. 83 Alexander, *Primate Alexander*, p. 183.
84 Beckett, *Anglo-Irish tradition*, p. 143.

9

Disestablishment and the lay response

Kenneth Milne

R. B. McDowell, writing in 1975, identified the census year of 1911 as a point at which the Church of Ireland might take stock of its position.[1] Statistics showed that the church's population (like that of the country at large) had fallen since 1871 from 667,998 to 576,611. But there had been significant shifts in distribution throughout the island. Church of Ireland population in Connacht had fallen from 35,931 to 19,010, Similarly, there had been steep decline in three counties of Munster: Clare, Kerry and Limerick had fallen from 16,775 to 10,300. In Leinster, there was an absolute and relative decline in Church of Ireland numbers, and while in Dublin county and city figures remained static, percentage of the total population of the area fell from 19.5 per cent to 16.5 per cent. Even in Ulster, the Church of Ireland figure fell, if only marginally, while increasing its share of the population from 20.4 per cent to 23.1 per cent, though these figures conceal regional decline in Donegal, Fermanagh, Monaghan and Cavan, from 99,061 to 60,820. Dramatically, however, the Church of Ireland population of Belfast trebled between 1871 and 1911, rising from 26.6 per cent of the population to 30.5 per cent. Half of the church's population resided in the area soon to be designated Northern Ireland.

Decline in what became the Irish Free State, later the Republic, accelerated between 1911 and 1926, the Church of Ireland population in this jurisdiction falling from 250,000 to 164,215, a decrease of 34 per cent. By 1961, a further decline of 36 per cent had occurred, bringing the figure to 104,016. However, in Northern Ireland the absolute and relative increases of the preceding half-century were maintained (though at a much more modest level) and the 1961 census showed the increase in population (though not in percentage of population) continuing, from 338,724 in 1926 to 344,800 in 1961. By this time, three-quarters of the members of the Church of Ireland lived in Northern Ireland, one half of them residing in Antrim and Down (including the city of Belfast).[2]

---

1 R.B. McDowell, *The Church of Ireland 1869–1969* (London, 1979), pp 119ff.   2 Figures taken from McDowell, *Church of Ireland*, pp 119ff and W.E. Vaughan and A.J. Fitzpatrick

It was to be expected that such a stark demographic slump in the southern state would sap morale. Certainly, the concomitant closure of churches and reduced numbers of clergy occasioned much grief. But it would be wrong to state categorically that the Church of Ireland was demoralised in general. Without doubt, the transfer of power into nationalist hands in 1922 was a traumatic experience for most members of the church, especially in those areas where the murder and house-burning of Protestants was a feature of the 'Troubles'. The avowed policy of the Irish Free State government to gaelicise the country, and the ready acceptance by politicians of Catholic teaching as the basis for social regulation, created (or threatened to create) a society in which many, if not most, Protestants would feel excluded. And so there were large numbers of people who emigrated, landowners big and small being conspicuous among them. Nor did emigration cease with the political turmoil. Economic necessity replaced political pressure as a factor driving many to emigrate, and was no respecter of denominations. Studies of the Church of Ireland population in Kerry and Wexford, carried out in the 1970s show emigration to have had an enormous impact on the social structure of Church of Ireland parishes.[3] Other factors combined with emigration (or migration to the towns) to further the erosion of Protestant population in the years immediately following independence. The withdrawal of the agencies of the crown, for instance. Not only military and naval personnel, but others such as the coastguard service, whose members, with their families, could contribute up to 58 per cent of parish members in those very parts of the island where Church of Ireland numbers were thinnest.[4]

The regulations of the Catholic Church governing mixed marriages, particularly as expressed in the *Ne Temere* decree of 1908, played a key role in the Church of Ireland's demographic decline. In an environment such as that of the twenty-six counties, where mixed marriages are common, the obligation imposed on both partners to bring their children up in the faith and practice of the Catholic Church has had a considerable demographic impact. Anecedotal tradition in the

(ed.) *Irish historical statistics: population 1821–1971* (Dublin, 1978). For analysis of the 1991 census figures, north and south, see J.L.B. Deane and R.E. Turner, 'The 1991 census and the Church of Ireland', in *Search: a Church of Ireland Journal*, xix, no. 1 (Spring 1996), pp 26–47. 3 H.W. Robinson, *Study of the Church of Ireland population of Ardfert 1971* (printed privately, [1972]) and *A study of the Church of Ireland population of Ferns* (printed privately, [1975]). For treatment of the social composition of the Protestant population in the post-independence period see F.S.L.Lyons, 'The minority problem in the 26 counties', in Francis MacManus (ed.), *The years of the great test: 1926–36* (Cork, 1967), pp 92–103; Liam Kennedy, Kerby A. Miller, with Mark Graham, 'The long retreat: Protestants, economy and society, 1660–1926', in Raymond Gillespie and Gerald Moran (eds), *Longford: essays in county history* (Dublin, 1991), pp 31–61, and, with particular reference to the landed classes and crown services, R.B. McDowell, *Crisis and decline: the fate of the southern unionists* (Dublin, 1997). 4 Miriam Moffitt, *The Church of Ireland community of Killala and Achonry 1870–1940* (Dublin, 1999), p. 22.

Protestant community, and indeed much family experience, suggested that this was so. Research published by the Economic and Social Research Institute in 1970 gave a more statistically-based picture, showing that to explain Church of Ireland marriage and demographic patterns, (or, for that matter those of any 'other denominations') by reference to emigration and low marriage and birth rates, was unsafe. To quote B.M.Walsh, author of the report 'mixed marriages occur in Catholic ceremonies ... while the census data on percentages married will contain no such bias.'[5] Another commentator put it in a more homely fashion: 'No wonder Protestants [in Kerry] at first sight would appear to be less fertile when a quarter of them have children being reared as Catholics.'[6]

World War I also played its part in the Church of Ireland's demographic decline. There is scarcely a parish church without its roll of those who died, and who died at an early age. The personal grief that was occasioned by these losses was compounded by the difficulty that independent Ireland experienced in attempting to come to terms with memorialising the great numbers of Irishmen, Catholic and Protestant, who died in the 1914–18 War. Many decades were to pass before a government leader could say, as Seán Lemass did in 1966, that he and others had been guilty of an injustice to those who had volunteered to fight, and, he added, that in fairness to their honour, it should be said that 'they were motivated by the highest purposes'.[7]

Yet the response of Protestants to nationalist Ireland's ignoring of the Irish war dead was not one of demoralisation. Rather did it take the form of an indignant, if muted, defiance, which many of them expressed by the wearing of the poppy, and some, though to a lesser extent, by the fervent singing of 'God Save the King' at armistice day services. This latter manifestation of emotion was not congenial to all Protestants, who felt that it politicised what was essentially a religious commemoration.

Similarly, demoralisation had not been the response of the church's laity to that earlier, and, in the eye's of its leadership at least, equally catastrophic circumstance, the disestablishment of the church. There were those who dreaded it, and who identified with Mrs C.F. Alexander's disestablishment hymn

> Look down, Lord of heaven, on our desolation!
> Fallen, fallen, fallen is now our Country's crown,
> Dimly dawns the New Year on a churchless nation,
> Ammon and Amalek tread our borders down.[8]

---

5 B.M. Walsh, *Religion and demographic behaviour in Ireland.* The Economic and Social Research Institute, paper no. 55 (May, 1970), p. 27.   6 Robinson, *Ardfert*, p. 4.   7 J.J. Lee, *Ireland 1912–1985: politics and society* (Cambridge, 1989), p. 369.   8 Quoted in p. M.H. Bell, *Disestablishment in Ireland and Wales* (London, 1969), p. 158. In fairness to Mrs Alexander, it

II

Mrs Alexander was expressing the view of the Irish ecclesiastical establishment, as was to be expected of a bishop's wife at the time. As things turned out, granting the Church of Ireland its independence from state control was to open all sorts of possibilities to the laity that few of them had anticipated. Indeed, the newly disestablished church brought with it the apotheosis of the laity, or, depending on your point of view, the prospect of lay tyranny.[9] However, the *Quarterly Review*, opposed to Gladstone's measure, clearly perceived the seat of lay power to lie elsewhere when it editorialised that 'An established church means government of the church by the laity [i.e. parliament] and is the surest preservative of religious liberty against clerical domination'. While it was said in the house of commons that one of the great advantages of establishment was that it protected ministers of religion from the 'tyranny' of lay members of the church![10]

Whatever prospects disestablishment may have held out for the enhancement of the role of the laity, the lay membership of the established church had not espoused the government's plans for the Church of Ireland with any greater degree of enthusiasm than had their clerical brethren. There is no evidence to show that even a substantial minority of the laity were seduced by Gladstone's proposals for a form of church government in which they would be represented. Once, however, the die was cast, the laity were quick to claim a voice in the setting up of the procedures whereby, under the Irish Church Act, a constitution for the church was to be devised.

When disestablishment became a live issue there was considerable lay participation in the debate. As early as November 1868 a group of influential laymen, meeting at the provost's house in Trinity College, Dublin, formed a consultative committee to co-operate with the bishops in opposing disestablishment. Leading figures among them were the provost himself (Humphrey Lloyd, a distinguished physicist), Anthony Lefroy, the senior of Trinity's two M.P.s and William Brooke, master in chancery. These men continued to play a significant part in the controversy. The following April, as proposed by the consultative committee, a conference of lay delegates elected by diocesan synods was held at the Exhibition Palace in Earlsfort Terrace.[11] At this conference,

must be remembered that she wrote many other hymns and was author of 'Once in Royal David's city', 'There is a green hill far away;' and 'All things bright and beautiful'. 9 W.C. Magee to J.C. MacDonnell, 23 Sept. 1869, in J.C. MacDonnell, *The life and correspondence of William Connor Magee, archbishop of York* (2 vols, London, 1896), i, pp 236–7. 10 *Quarterly Review*, cxxvi no. 252 (1869), pp 559–88. The *Quarterly's* fears must have appeared justified if, as the *Irish Ecclesiastical Gazette* claimed in the following year, the disestablishment of the Irish Church gave rise to a rash of publications in England calling for lay participation in convocation (23 Feb. 1870); *Hansard III*, 195 (1868–9), col. 902 (15 April 1869). 11 *Irish Ecclesiastical Gazette*, 22 April 1869.

which the bishops attended, a committee was set up to protect the church's interests as the disestablishment legislation, introduced at Westminster on 1 March 1869, went through its various stages. A London agent was appointed to co-ordinate the efforts of the committee and its supporters in parliament and to obtain amendments to the bill. It was an extremely hard-working group and met frequently, at times daily. Among its concerns was the protection of the financial interests of such laity as the members of cathedral choirs, stipendiary singers 'who would be thrown in their old age into a state of destitution by the withdrawal of their present incomes.'[12] Other categories of lay employee affected by disendowment and disestablishment were parish clerks and sextons, henceforth dependent for their incomes on the new ecclesiastical commissioners, whose tardiness in despatching salary warrants was at one stage a cause of concern to the *Irish Times*.[13] At a somewhat loftier level was the cost of compensating the lay holders of advowsons most of whom lost their rights of patronage under clause 18 of the Irish Church Act, and whose interests claimed the solicitude of parliament.[14]

The Irish Church Act received the royal assent on 26 July 1869, and within weeks the archbishops had issued mandates summoning their provincial synods of clergy (considered by Archdeacon Lee of Dublin, a leading figure in all of these transactions, to be 'the old national synod of the Church of Ireland'.[15] The combined provincial synods met at St Patrick's cathedral, Dublin, for three days from 14 September 1869. The question of lay involvement in determining church matters soon arose. While a minority of those attending held the view that such issues ought to be the preserve of the clergy only, the synods decided that under the prevailing circumstances of the Church of Ireland, the co-operation of the faithful laity has become more than ever desirable.[16] The laity were working towards this and while the clergy were preparing for the provincial synods, representatives of the laity petitioned the archbishops to convene a lay conference to address the question of lay representation and participation in the governing of the church. The archbishops complied, and the parishes appointed lay delegates to diocesan synods that returned 417 representatives to a lay conference held in the Antient Concert Rooms in Dublin on 12 October 1869. This conference determined the manner in which laity would be chosen for the convention soon to be held to devise a constitution for the disestablished church, the number of diocesan delegates being roughly speaking proportionate to diocesan population. To some extent it set the pace for the future by

12 R.C.B., Minute book of the standing committee of the church conference, 16 April–30 July 1869, minute of 17 April 1869. 13 *Irish Times*, 17 November 1869. 14 *Hansard III*, 195 (1868–9), cols 1414ff. 15 Lee, *Journal of the General Convention*, pp v–ix. 16 D.H. Akenson, *The Church of Ireland: ecclesiastical reform and revolution, 1800–1885* (New Haven and London, 1971), pp 277–8.

recommending that the forthcoming convention should have before it a draft constitution prepared by a committee comprising two lay and two clerical representatives from each united diocese, the archbishops and bishops, and other 'leading persons'.[17] In the event, these 'leading persons', thirteen in number, were drawn largely from the legal profession.

From 5 to 28 January 1870 this drafting committee met and it is evident from the minutes of its proceedings that much lay expertise and energy were deployed to prepare the church for its new-found freedom. There was considerable nervousness on the part of the clergy, which, while not always expressed in such dramatic terms as those of Archbishop Magee, and quoted above, yet lingered for at least a generation, so that even a decade after disestablishment, when the views of the clergy were canvassed, 141 expressed the view that lay power in the church was 'excessive'.[18] Allotting to the laity their proper place in the scheme of things occupied much of the time of those concerned with formulating voting procedures. Some members of the drafting committee would have excluded the laity from all matters concerning doctrine and church discipline. Yet there were voices in the church that took a different view, including that of the highly-regarded historian G.T. Stokes, who maintained that the laity had a part to play, not only in the legislative process, but also in teaching and preaching,[19] while the bishops made clear from the start that they were in need of the 'aid and prayers of their lay brethren'.[20] The *Gazette* editorialised that the laity had already given evidence of appreciating the trust reposed in them by the archbishops.[21]

In the end, an accommodation was reached between lay and clerical interests, whereby the judicious provision of a system of 'voting by orders' prevented either clergy or laity from making unilateral decisions, while a bishops' veto, elaborately provided for, yet, up to this time of writing never used, quelled the anxieties of those most worried about the balance of power. Such checks and balances ensured that while on the face of it voting power in the house of representatives was skewed in favour of the laity, who had two seats for every clerical one, voting by orders gave the clergy (as, indeed, it did the laity) a veto. The 2:1 ratio was not, in these circumstances, a particularly contentious issue, it being generally conceded that the lay members found attendance at synod less convenient than the clergy, an argument borne out by a study of attendance figures which shows that over the years a higher percentage of clerical than lay representatives has attended.[22] The validity of the argument that voting by

---

17 Lee, *Journal*, pp v–ix. 18 R.C.B., MS A14; Akenson, *The Church of Ireland*, p. 297. 19 G.T. Stokes, *The work of the laity in the Church of Ireland, especially in regard to questions of faith and discipline* (Dublin, 1869). 20 Lee, *Journal*, p. 4. 21 22 April 1869. 22 *Administration 1967: the report of the advisory committee on administration to be submitted to the general synod of the Church of Ireland* (Dublin, 1967), p. 13, showed a higher percentage of clerical than lay

orders protected lay prerogatives was to be clearly demonstrated, as we shall see, both by lay influence on liturgical revision and, perhaps surprisingly, as a brake on the opening to women of participation in the administration of the church.[23]

It has been suggested that such a generous provision for lay representation ensured that others besides the local squire would make their way into the councils of the church.[24] In the nature of things, it was the landed and professional classes that formed the lay representation in the convention, as indeed they were to do in the general synod for generations to come. They were, said the *Daily Express*, 'men of European reputation in the world of science ... country gentlemen and men of business ...',[25] though, of course, the middle classes had their say in the drawing up of addresses and petitions by diocesan synods and vestries. There was at least one short-lived attempt to muster working-class support for the church's welfare. Revd Tresham Gregg, a renowned evangelical, convened in late 1869 a meeting of 'the Protestant operatives of Dublin' in order, as an advertisement in the press put it, 'to initiate a new movement for the recovery of the church's property'. Gregg told those who responded to his invitation that where others had failed, they, 'who came from the lower orders of the people' might succeed. But it was very late in the day to attempt to turn the tide, and though the meeting was well attended, the audience comprised many 'women and boys' and nothing came of it.[26]

The convention conducted its affairs in a businesslike manner, due very largely to the forbearance of its archiepiscopal chairman (Beresford) and its able honorary secretaries, lay and clerical. This was the more creditable, given the innovative nature of the body. As the *Gazette* put it: 'Let us imagine a house of commons, composed entirely of new members, who had no experience of legislation or of the forms of the house, and who were summoned to discuss questions which had hitherto been entirely beyond the region of legislation.'[27]

As the draft constitution made its way through the convention the main occasions of heated debate were those that had taken most time in the drafting committee, and the *Gazette* applauded 'the deep interest shown by the laity in the proceedings as auguring well for the future prosperity of the church.'[28] Moderate men such as Professor J.H. Jellett, who would in 1881 succeed Lloyd as provost of Trinity, threw themselves into debate with enormous energy and

---

attendance in the sample period 1960–5. A similar exercise carried out by the present writer on the attendance figures for 1990–5 showed the same pattern.   **23** See pp 236–9 below. **24** Akenson, *The Church of Ireland*, p. 283.   **25** *Daily Express*, 4 April 1870. The (Dublin) *Daily Express* took a strongly unionist and Protestant line, and by comparison with, say, the *Gazette*, leaves an impression of a lack of objectivity. But the extent of its coverage of debates, whether in the convention or the general synod was second to none, and constitutes a valuable source.   **26** *Irish Times*, 3 Nov. 1869.   **27** *Gazette*, 23 Feb. 1870.   **28** *Gazette*, 23 Feb. 1870, p. 29.

learning, and by their tact and skill they managed to satisfy, or at least conciliate, such strongly held lay views as those conveyed to the convention in an address with 171 signatures and which stated that 'the laity will not possess their due influence in the government of the said church under the proposed constitution', and held in particular abhorrence the fact that the laity were to be 'associated with two orders of ecclesiastics each separately possessed of powers equal to theirs'.[29] The constitution that emerged from the convention's deliberations, recognisably that which operates today, placed the laity, or, rather, lay*men*, at the heart of the decision-making processes of the Church of Ireland. It also embodied full recognition of lay rights in the workings of the church's judicial processes. Consequently, it went without saying that lay participation at diocesan and parochial levels was provided for. Furthermore, the convention saw the first public stirrings of lay claims to have a part in the formulation of doctrine and its liturgical expression, and this was, for some of the clergy, and in particular for the archdeacon of Dublin, William Lee, a bridge too far. When debate moved into the sphere of prayer book revision it seemed to men such as Lee (and there were others) that more was at stake than the balance of power between clergy and laity in the running of church administration, but rather that very survival of the disestablished church's to claim to a place in Catholic Christendom was in jeopardy.

There were those, laity prominent among them, who were fired by a concern to protect the church from a perceived incipient ritualism, deemed to be currently infecting the Church of England, and which gave rise to a royal commission and to restraining legislation for that church in 1874.[30] The ritualism issue had already surfaced in Dublin, where Archbishop Trench engaged in lively controversy with a number of the Dublin laity, arising from a demand by Mr L.F.S. Maberley that the archbishop should condemn a devotional manual given to a member of Maberley's domestic staff by one of the clergy of St Stephen's parish. Trench refused to do so, and thereby deepened yet further the suspicion with which he was already viewed in certain evangelical circles.[31] While it was not unexpected that a newly independent church would address the matter of Prayer Book revision, the Maberley controversy heightened feelings on both the Catholic and Protestant wings of the church, and lines of battle on this issue were rapidly drawn up, with the laity conspicuously on the Protestant side.

When the convention met for its second and final session in October 1870 those who were hesitant to embark on liturgical revision were criticised.

29 Petition received by the convention on 24 Mar. 1870 from 'inhabitants of the neighbourhood of Dublin' (R.C.B., former 'Convention box', misc items, loose).   **30** 37 & 38 Vict., *c*.85, *An act for the better administration of the laws respecting the regulation of public worship*. This statute was more concerned with improving legal procedure in the matter of ritual than with imposing restrictions.   **31** See Bell, *Disestablishment in Ireland and Wales,*

Disparaging references were made to Archbishop Trench, and these were reported with considerable satisfaction by the *Daily Express* which called for action to ensure that the Church of Ireland had a Book of Common Prayer in 'perfect accordance' with the thirty-nine articles.[32] The revision issue was initiated at the convention by the introduction by Master Brooke of a memorial subscribed by almost 4,000 vestrymen calling for action to preserve the scriptural, Protestant and episcopal nature of the Church of Ireland.[33] This provoked increasing pressure for change, in which northern lay voices, such as that of the Ulster landowner John Bloomfield, were much to the fore, and allegedly Romish doctrines of baptism, eucharist and absolution came under fire. An amendment proposed by Bloomfield more specifically calling for the rejection of 'dogmas' such as the real presence, priestly absolution and a necessary connection between regeneration and baptism, though gaining wide lay support, was defeated. As one modern commentator has it, the laity showed impressive confidence in their ability to debate complex theological issues![34] However, as the result of a compromise amendment proposed by another northern layman, the duke of Abercorn, the remit given to the committee set up to consider revision was less prescriptive. 'Brooke's committee', as it came to be called, comprised thirteen clerical and thirteen lay members, the latter predominantly moderate evangelicals or liberals. Some, such as Brooke and Joseph Napier[35] were lawyers, the latter a former lord chancellor of Ireland. The others included academics such as Andrew Hart, a senior fellow of Trinity, and several landowners. The bishops declined to participate in the deliberations of the revision committee, preferring, they said, to consider its report in due course in 'an independent and unprejudiced manner'.[36] The major casualty of this compromise was clerical, none other than Archdeacon Lee, a major figure in the re-constructuring process of the church who, as befitted the archdeacon of Dublin, was a stalwart supporter of Archbishop Trench. Lee was unable to accept that the laity should have a place in determining matters doctrinal, and withdrew from the convention, never again to participate in the synodical procedures of the church.

The new committee's methodology was to prepare and discuss papers, and while it is clear from a study of the proceedings that divisions ran deep, few of the discussion papers emanated from the lay members.[37] By the time the Brooke committee's report came to the general synod, which first met in 1871, it was

---

pp 187–8. 190–1.   **32** *Daily Express*, 18 Oct. 1870.   **33** R.C.B., Convention minutes. **34** R.L. Clarke, 'The disestablishment revision of the Irish Book of Common Prayer' (Ph.D. thesis, T.C.D., 1989), p. 90.   **35** Napier, 'a fervent evangelical', was at the same time a doughty defender of the ordinal as it was set out in the prayer book (McDowell, *The Church of Ireland 1869–1969*, pp 28, 64); Clarke, 'Disestablishment revision', p. 284.   **36** *Daily Express*, 22 Oct. 1870.   **37** Clarke, 'Disestablishment revision', pp 104–5.

clear that the divisions had not been healed,[38] and synod set up its own, larger, revision committee, on which eight of the thirteen laymen from the original committee served. But Bloomfield was now a member, as was another redoubtable Ulster evangelical, Edward Saunderson of Cavan, scion of the notably evangelical house of Farnham. Also included was Judge R.R. Warren, whose prudence had originally marked him as a reluctant revisionist, and who like such other legal luminaries as a former lord chancellor of Ireland, J.T. Ball, and Lord Justice Fitzgibbon, were for years to come to be influential in preserving the doctrinal equilbrium of the church from over-reaction to controversial liturgical practices. Of considerable importance was the fact that this time round the bishops participated and were *ex officio* members of the revision committee.

The sessions of the general synod in 1872 and 1873 were marathons, lasting for thirty and thirty-one days respectively, and much of the time was devoted to the debate on Prayer Book revision, lay and clerical opinion diverging sharply on isues such as auricular confession and the Athenasian Creed. Many of the laity viewed auricular confession as a horrific Roman practice, while at the same time wishing to remove the damnatory clauses of the Athenasian Creed. As Richard Clarke has put it, 'the laity for the most part provided the sound and fury of the debate, but little of the content'.[39] They were in many cases inspired by evangelical fervour, and emboldened by the increasingly significant share of the church's financial burden that they were being asked to carry.

It was at this formative period in the church's life that the charter of the new Representative Body was granted, giving the laity, with the bishops and other clergy, a key role in the church's financial affairs And, just as the laity from the legal world brought their acumen to bear on constitutional and liturgical issues, so also did leading representatives of the world of business and finance contribute their expertise in matters economic. The Representative Church Body put it squarely to the laity that henceforth the sustentation of the ministry of the church would depend heavily on their generosity, and to this the laity responded willingly. But the wish for a voice in calling the tune in return for paying the piper was clearly evident . Nonetheless, when, on 30 June 1878, the revised Book of Common Prayer became the authorised (and only authorised) liturgy of the Church of Ireland, there were few clergy who, whether they deplored some of the newly imposed anti-ritual canons, or lamented that revision had not sufficiently met their concept of Reformation teaching, were not prepared to live with it. Only a handful took the opportunity to move to other provinces of the Anglican Communion.

These unprecedented developments in the life of the church were unfolding at a time of impending political crisis when Irish nationalism was in the

38 Ibid., p. 118.   39 Clarke, 'Disestablishment revision', pp 199–200.

ascendent. Increasingly disenchanted with the drift of political affairs, whether national or local, many of the the leading lay figures of the Church of Ireland found a new outlet for their talents and energies in the restructuring of the church and the laying of sound financial foundations. Some had a background in the armed services, and their administrative experience came to be valued in the parishes and dioceses. Had the established Church of Ireland got its way, and successfully withstood Gladstone's policy, would the breaking of the link with the state, inevitable at some stage, have occurred at such a propitious time from the church's point of view?

The Representative Church Body and the general synod were and are voluntary bodies, but neither could operate effectively without a professional bureaucracy, and so disestablishment brought with it the need for a Church of Ireland 'civil service', which has been from its inception almost entirely staffed by laity. Both at central and, indeed, diocesan levels, there is a substantial amount of administrative work to be done and it has tended to be laymen and laywomen who, sometimes in part-time, sometimes full-time capacity, have been employed to discharge these duties. In 1993 the general synod provided a means by which the contribution of the laity could be formally acknowledged when it gave the archbishop of Armagh, as primate of all Ireland and Ordinary of St Patrick's cathedral, Armagh, the right to appoint up to six honorary lay canons of that cathedral 'such appointmments to be in recognition of particular and distinguished service to the Church of Ireland'.[40]

The newly devised constitution not only provided laymen with an *entrée* to theological debate, but also gave them a voice in every important decision made by the church, from the election of bishops to the care of parish finances. However, while it would be unhistorical to condemn the church too strongly for excluding women when these processes were originally set in place, given that they were similarly excluded from formal public debate in every sphere, it has to be admitted that the church has not, until very recently, been to the fore in promoting their cause. Leaving aside the question of ordaining women, against which theological arguments are advanced, there can have been no theological reasons for excluding them from the franchise within the church. Was there any 'suffregette' movement in the Church of Ireland, seeking votes for women in synod and vestry? Not that we know of. Certainly, the women of the time, such as those prepared for higher education by Alexandra College, founded in 1866 with the influential support of Archbishop Trench, were not lacking in confidence, and soon made their mark on Irish society in a number of ways, social and intellectual. But if there were murmurings at being excluded from the councils of the Church of Ireland, no record of such discontent has come

40 Chapter 3 of 1993.

to light, nor has any evidence of an incipient 'women's movement' such as is discernible in the Church of England from the beginning of this century.[41]

It was, indeed, several years after women had obtained the vote in parliamentary elections that the first moves were made to admit them to general and select vestries in the Church of Ireland. No less a figure than J.A.F. Gregg, bishop of Ossory, but later to be one of the church's most distinguished archbishops, must be given credit for promoting the issue,[42] and the bill which he proposed to the general synod of 1920 (a year when the country was in political turmoil) would have made women eligible for membership of vestries and for appointment to the position of parochial nominator, thus giving them a voice in the nomination of incumbents. However, an amendment restricted the concession to admission to vestries,[43] causing one synodsman to rail against the illogicality of a situation in which 'an educated woman may select an ignorant ploughman as nominator to select the clergyman to whose ministrations she is to be limited (sic), but the ploughman may not select her for the post of nominator ...'[44] Furthermore, to quote the *Gazette*, 'the bill was constantly attenuated in committee, and emerged from that ordeal giving not more than six seats on the vestry to women', a restriction that remained in force until 1960.[45] Indeed a proposal to have the whole matter postponed for two years to allow for local discussion, though defeated, gained considerable, if insufficient, lay (not clerical) support.[46]

In 1928 a bill to admit women to diocesan and general synods ran into trouble in the general synod, and on its second reading was referred to the standing commitee of the synod for its consideration.[47] The standing commitee reported back in 1929 to the effect that it was divided on the issue, and 'in order to avoid giving a false impression of agreement' deemed it better that it should not propose legislsation.[48] Lord Glenavy, vigorous protagonist of the cause, and, incidentally, the assessor (that is, legal advisor) to the president of the synod, did so, however, asserting that he had heard no logical arguments against what he was advocating. There were, indeed, many opposition speeches, ranging from those who claimed that women themselves did not want the measure, to the allegation (a recurrent one) that this was the thin end of a wedge that would lead to women's ordination.[49] The bill failed to get a second reading (the laity

41 See Brian Heeney, *The women's movement in the Church of England 1850–1930* (Oxford, 1988). I am grateful to Mr J.G. Briggs, former chief officer and secretary of the Representative Church Body, for his comments on the paragraphs that follow.   42 *Gazette*, 21 May 1920, p. 327.   43 Chapter 2 of 1920.   44 *Gazette*, 21 May 1920, p. 327.   45 Ibid., p. 338. The author recalls being present at an Easter vestry meeting at which one woman above the permitted quota was 'elected'. She was eliminated and the next man on the list (who had fewer votes) replaced her.   46 *Journal General Synod, 1920*, pp lxiv–lxv. 47 *Journal General Synod, 1928*, p. lxxviii.   48 *Journal of General Synod, 1929*, p. 204. 49 *Irish Times*, 15 May 1929.

voting against), and the battle, if not the war, was lost for the time being:[50] for twenty years, in fact, until 1949, when the persistence of Lord Glenavy succeeded in having legislation passed. Again, lay resistance was stronger than clerical, voices claiming that it was time enough to give women a place in the government of the church when they asked for it, and citing the attendance of Princess Elizabeth at a race meeting on the Sabbath as evidence that women's influence would not necessarily be for the best. But the rector of Greystones and future bishop of Kilmore, E.F.B. Moore, argued for the complementariness of the male and female contributions which would ensue, and such arguments won the day– but not before the archbishop of Armagh and president of the synod, the same J.A.F. Gregg who had helped to secure access to vestries for women in 1920, had felt it necessary to rebuke some speakers for unseemly and flippant speeches.[51] In 1960, when the constitution of the church was amended, updated and codified all references in the constitution to 'laymen' were deemed to include laywomen.

There is little to suggest that the women of the church had been greatly stirred by these matters, the women's movement as we know it not having attained anything like its present influence. And even when it did, many of the men and women who espoused women's entitlement to eligibility for all orders of the ordained ministry were anxious that the debate should be conducted on theological rather than sociological terms, aware that the most cogent opposition was couched in the former. Helped, no doubt, by a changing climate of opinion inside and outside the church the legislation to render women eligible for ordination to the priesthood and the episcopate had a fairly clear passage through the general synod in 1990,[52] the opposition stemming from both the evangelical and Catholic wings of the church. Such alliances are, however, rare, and rather than the general synod being an assembly along party lines, it in many respects shows itself to be a parliament of independent members. Even in the heightened political climate of recent decades, when members from the separate political jurisdictions of Northern Ireland and the Republic of Ireland have disagreed in open forum, polemics have been rare. Nor has the result of potentially contentious votes been predictable. Admittedly, the members of the church in the twenty-six counties are more generously represented than those in the north. But that would scarcely explain the relative ease with which, for instance, a frank report on sectarianism which did not pull its punches where

50 The votes cast were: Ayes, clerical 92, lay 58; Noes clerical 56, lay 69 (General Synod minutes, 14 May 1929. I am indebted to the Assistant Secretary, General Synod, for this information). 51 *Irish Times*, 12 May 1949. The relevant general synod statute was Chapter 8 of 1949, 'To provide for the eligibility of women for election to lay offices in the Church of Ireland'. 52 Chapter 1 of 1990, 'To carry into effect a resolution of the general synod of 1989 to enable women to be ordained as priests and bishops, and to make the consequential

aspects of the loyal institutions were concerned was received by the house in 1999.[53] The report acknowledges that 'our own history and the history of the Orange Order, in its origins and growth, have been intertwined.'[54] Martin Maguire's essay below discusses the influence of the Orange Institution and the Masonic Order on the Church of Ireland laity of Dublin in past years. This influence, particularly that of the loyal institutions, endures in all counties of the historic province of Ulster, and is especially strong in Northern Ireland where many current members of the Orange Order are also members in good standing of the Church of Ireland. But the 1999 report also makes clear that the stance of the Church of Ireland and that of the loyal institutions differ considerably where ecumenism is concerned.[55]

The general synod is a legislative and deliberative body, and, while on occasion providing a safety-valve for the expression of anger and indignation tends to be measured and decorous in its proceedings, and has maintained this characteristic in both good times and bad. More open to question is whether or not it will continue to attract sufficient laity to its membership. One reason for anxiety on this score is the demand that attendance at meetings for several days, generally in Dublin, makes on the time and money of members. Younger members of the church in particular find it increasingly difficult to take time off mid-week from earning their livelihood, a factor that increasingly impinges on women as well as men. To date, efforts to address the matter of reforming synodical structures have failed to attract a consensus. Service on select vestries, which are at the heart of lay participation in the administration of the church may also lose its appeal, but not for the same reasons. The agenda for a select vestry meeting is carefully circumscribed by the constitution of the church, and it could be that the vocation of the laity as the people of God calls for a wider definition of the part that they are expected to play. Ministry, both of the clergy and the laity, is under examination by the general synod. A summit on ministry is being held in the autumn of 2002. If new possibilities of service by the laity emerge, then the church's structures must facilitate rather than inhibit them.

III

If women had to wait for fifty years after disestablishment before being admitted even to the most modest echelons of ecclesiastical administration, they found (as did their male counterparts) many opportunities for service in other spheres of church life. The Girls Friendly Society, founded in 1877 on a Church of

amendments to the formularies of the church'.   53 *Journal of General Synod, 1999*, pp 168–200. 54 Ibid., p. 183.   55 Ibid, pp 171, 181, 183–4.

8   The General Synod in session (R.C.B.).

England model, had in mind the welfare of girls in employment, often away from home. It was very largely a society founded and run by women. Similarly the Mothers' Union, which transcended class distinctions, had its beginnings in England in the 1880s, and soon spread to the Church of Ireland. For boys and men there came into being the Dublin Working Boys' Home and Harding Technical School (1879), initially for the welfare of young men 'earning small wages as apprentices', and which had its equivalents in other towns and cities. The Church of Ireland Men's Society, though never as pervasive an influence in the church as the Mother's Union, catered for their husbands and for other men. And, for those (and there were many) looking for employment, there was the Church of Ireland Labour Home and Yard founded in Ringsend, Dublin, in 1899 'to provide a place where any man desirous of work may be allowed to obtain it' (admittedly on production of a ticket issued by a clergyman or a subscriber). Late nineteenth-century initiatives for the young were the Church Lads' Brigade, which was specifically Anglican, and the Boys' Brigade, which wasn't. These were joined in the early twentieth century by the scout and guide movements, and each of these youth organisations drew heavily on dedicated laity, who provided recreation and companionship for children, many of them from what would now be termed 'deprived' backgrounds. Nor should we overlook an organisation that, unlike those listed above, had its origins in

Ireland, the Girls' Brigade, founded by Miss Margaret Lyttle at Sandymount Presbyterian Church in 1893, and which Church of Ireland parishes soon adopted, until, in 1908, the Brigade was formally established.[56]

Countless numbers of men and women, particularly the latter, taught in 'Sunday School'. No longer the provider of basic literacy skills as well as church teaching that it had been in the days before widespread elementary education, the Sunday School had by late nineteenth century become an adjunct to Sunday worship. Sometimes those who taught in Sunday School taught also in the parish National School. A high proportion of the National School teachers of the Catholic Church were members of religious orders, but, unlike many other churches of the Anglican Comunion, the Church of Ireland experienced scarcely any revival of the religious life[57] and it was as individual members of the church, not in religious congregations, that the laity played their vital role in providing the parish with its school. Similarly with secondary schools, though in far fewer numbers, since grammar schools were the preserve of the better off or academically distinguished until well into the twentieth century. Again, whereas the provision of secondary education for Catholic children was largely the preserve of the orders, the Church of Ireland counterpart was the (largely lay) board of governors. New management structures have brought the lay teacher out of the classroom and into the board room as well, and statutory developments in the Republic have stressed the fact that education is a partnership between parents, teachers and trustees, each having a share in management, so that in many parishes the school management board stands alongside the select vestry as a focus of lay involvement.

As with education, so also with medicine, the Church of Ireland laity had a very considerable involvement, founding and administering many of the hospitals in the voluntary sector in much the same way as the Catholic religious orders were doing. The Adelaide Hospital, whose charter gave it an identifiably Protestant character, while by no means an exclusively Church of Ireland institution, came to have a very special position in the life of the church, and there were other hospitals like it throughout the country. The foundation of St Ultan's children's hospital in 1919 in Dublin owed an enormous amount to the work of Dr Kathleen Lynn, a daughter of the rectory, who was a member of the Irish Citizen Army, and whose revolutionary politics were motivated by her social conscience. Through the founding of orphanages, and homes (whether for the old, the mentally ill or for unmarried mothers), the needs of various forms of social deprivation were met, sometimes by individuals such as

56 *The growth and development of the Girls' Brigade, Ireland 1893–1983* ([Dublin], 1983), p. 4.
57 Only two religious communities, both for women and both in Dublin, took root within the Church of Ireland: the Community of St Mary the Virgin, in St Bartholomew's parish, and (deriving from it) the Community of St John the Evangelist connected with St John's church,

Elizabeth Mageough, founder of the Mageough Home for elderly ladies in Dublin, and Mrs Smyly, who established children's homes, or by corporate voluntary effort. In this way the endeavours of the religious orders were matched, and though the orders were more clearly church-related, and called for a particular kind of discipline and self-sacrifice, yet they were similarly comprised for the most part of the laity.

Nor was the lay contribution to the life and witness of the church confined to the island of Ireland. As Patrick Comerford's essay above shows, since the early eighteenth century (in the case of the Society for the Propagation of the Gospel) and early nineteenth century (where the Church Missionary Society is concerned) Irish auxiliaries of English-based missionary societies had been established in the Irish church, and supported their work, not only with funds but with personnel. An assessment of the Church of Ireland's missionary effort published in 1970 recorded the fact that seventy-six members of the church were working overseas, lay teachers and doctors among them, and that almost £170,000 was contributed to that work by the Irish parishes.[58] The missionary work undertaken by graduates of Trinity College, Dublin, and others, lay and clerical,under the auspices of the Dublin University Far Eastern Mission (1886) and to Chota Nagpur in India (1890), was especially remarkable, the latter resulting in a hospital, four schools and a theological college, heavily dependent, especially in their early days, on lay men and women of the Church of Ireland, and all of which continued to serve independent India. Today, lay personnel from the Church of Ireland continue to work overseas in various aspects of voluntary service. In some cases they would not regard themselves as missionaries in the traditional sense, and indeed would see what they do as having no 'religious' connotation, except in the broadest sense of the term. But still there are those working overseas whose motivation is the fulfilment of the Christian gospel. In 1999 the parishes contributed about £500,000 pounds to the annual Church of Ireland Bishops' Appeal for overseas development which supports long-term overseas projects while also attempting to alleviate the sufferings caused by current disasters. In that same year, one and a half million pounds was contributed to the work of the missionary societies.

IV

When reviewing Fr Michael Hurley's book on Irish Anglicanism for the *Irish Times*, Bishop Richard Hanson found Professor Augustine Martin's essay on Anglo-Irish literature 'a depressing story for members of the Church of Ireland

Sandymount.   58 Thomas McDonald, 'The church overseas' in Michael Hurley S.J. (ed.), *Irish Anglicanism 1869–1969* (Dublin, 1970), p. 93.

in its record of failure by the church to inspire or adapt itself to the needs of its great literary sons and daughters'.[59] A more limited theme, that of the contribution such writers made to the Church of Ireland's self-understanding, is more appropriate to this essay. For, if we accept W.B. Yeats's claim for the Protestants of Ireland that 'we have created most of the modern literature of this country' and the claim put with somewhat less hyperbole by Augustine Martin, who wrote of 'what the Church of Ireland has done not only for Anglo-Irish literature, but for the political and cultural well-being of our country as a whole'[60] then what follows could be a who's who of the literary giants of modern Ireland. But for our purposes the list must be confined to those writers who helped the church to a deeper understanding of itself or whose Church of Ireland background enabled them to make a distinctive contribution to Irish literature and thereby to the shaping of Irish society. Historians were prominent among them, and while this is a field in which major clerical names, such as those of H.J. Lawlor and St J.D. Seymour have honoured places, equally distinguished figures have been drawn from the laity. They include Alice Stopford Green, a clergyman's daughter and nationalist historian, A.J. Otway-Ruthven, probably Ireland's leading medievalist in her generation, J.C. Beckett, professor of Irish History at the Queen's University of Belfast and F.S.L. Lyons, avowedly Church of Ireland, who, during his years as provost of Trinity College, Dublin, evinced a clear commitment to the place of the college chapel in university life.[61] It is worth remembering, too, that W.E.H. Lecky was once a student in the divinity school at Trinity, though his thinking led him into a different system of beliefs.[62]

Mention of Lecky illustrates a difficulty that cannot be avoided when we seek to identify the religious as distinct from other cultural influences that helped determine the contribution of writers of Church of Ireland origins. This difficulty is alluded to by J.C. Beckett (himself a practising member of the church) and is especially relevant when we come to consider those whose writing was in the field of imaginative literature. Beckett referred to Anglo-Irish authors as figures who 'belonged, by birth and inheritance if not by conviction, to the Church of Ireland'.[63] Terence Brown has explored the extent to which the Anglo-Irish writers are, or are not, marked by their religious as distinct from their cultural and political experience. Since, as he believes, few Irish writers have explored the field of Christian belief and practice other than in the terms of conflict between authority and freedom, as defined by Joyce,[64] Anglican

59 *Irish Times*, 16 May 1970, p. 9. 60 Hurley, *Irish Anglicanism 1869–1969*, p. 124. For their advice and comments on the following paragraphs I am grateful to Professor Terence Brown, Professor Nicholas Grene, Professor W.J. McCormack and Professor Christopher Murray. 61 F.S.L. Lyons, *Ireland since the famine* (London, 1971), p. 6n. 62 Donal McCartney, *W.E.H. Lecky: historian and politician 1838–1903* (Dublin, 1994), pp 12–17. 63 J.C. Beckett, *The Anglo-Irish tradition* (London, 1976), p. 140. 64 Terence Brown, 'The Church of

writers were, at least by the period under review in this chapter, as it were immune, since the only authority against which they protested was that of state rather than church censorship. The right to freedom of thought, however grudgingly acknowledged by some church figures, was considered by late nineteenth-century Protestants to be their entitlement, and they were for the most part spared the stimulus of ecclesiastical pressure. But, as Terence Brown has written, there is a 'very significant, if indirect, sense in which the experience of the Church of Ireland and the Irish literary tradition can be said to have been fruitfully associated at one time',[65] going on to remark that simply to name the writers identified with that imaginative awakening 'is to remind one of how great was Protestant Ireland's contribution to the literature of the period – Standish O'Grady, Lady Gregory, Douglas Hyde, W.B. Yeats, John Synge, Séan O'Casey.' But to what extent can their contribution be attributed to their Church of Ireland roots?

Brown's view was that until recent decades little scholarly consideration had been given to this basic question, but that a theory was in process of formulation to the effect that the emergence in late Victorian Ireland of numbers of writers of Protestant background was part of a development in the British Isles as a whole, in which the powerful influence of the evangelical movement was steadily being undermined. He cites Vivien Mercier as a leading proponent of this theory, and quotes Yeats as exhibiting the symptoms: 'I am very religious, and deprived by Huxley and Tyndall, whom I detested, of the simple-minded religion of my childhood, I had made a new religion, almost an infallible church of poetic tradition ...'[66] Synge, who came of strong evangelical lineage, said something not altogether dissimilar: 'Soon after I had relinquished the Kingdom of God I began to take a real interest in the Kingdom of Ireland.'[67] Roy Foster has referred to the possibility that Yeats might be located 'in a particular tradition of Irish Protestant interest in the occult, which stretched back through Sheridan LeFanu and Charles Maturin, took in WBY's contemporary Bram Stoker, and carried forward to Elizabeth Bowen: all figures from the increasingly marginalised Irish Protestant middle class, from families with strong clerical connections ...'[68] The writing of someone like Elizabeth Bowen would, perhaps, lead us to qualify somewhat Terence Brown's statement that, since the mid-nineteenth century, 'there are no works of modern literature that could be said to emerge directly from the complex of concerns, ideas and

Ireland: some literary perspectives', in *Search: a Church of Ireland Journal* iii, no. 2 (Winter, 1980), p. 5.   **65** Ibid., p. 12.   **66** Ibid., p. 14. Declan Kiberd has written of Mercier's projected two-volume study of Anglo-Irish literature that it would have been a cogent account of the workings of the Protestant imagination as a force in the shaping of modern Ireland. See Vivian Mercier, *Modern Irish literature: sources and founders*, ed. Eilís Dillon (Oxford, 1994), p. vii.   **67** Ibid., p. 16.   **68** R.F. Foster, *W.B. Yeats: a life* (Oxford, 1997), i,

feelings that have preoccupied Irish Anglicanism in the period.'[69] He himself has said of *The last September* that it was an expression of the hope that the Anglo-Irish might have some role to play in the new Ireland,[70] contrasting Bowen's hopes with Edith Somerville's 'stern resignation to Anglo-Ireland's demise'.[71] Brown also, in this context, draws attention to Lennox Robinson's play 'The big house', as catching the mood of defiance and intellectual defence, rather than resignation in the face of isolation and impotence.[72] Molly Keane, who writes of that same social world, albeit at a somewhat later stage, manages to do so without, so far as one can tell, ever referring to the religious element in the life of the Anglo-Irish: no clergy appear in her pages, nor do those who do appear ever go to church!

W.B. Yeats and Samuel Beckett must surely count, with Joyce, as the Irish literary titans of our time. Convincing claims have been made for the influence of his early environment on the young Beckett, much of it spent in south County Dublin and Trinity College, both milieus discernibly Anglo-Irish in his day. Beckett's radio play 'All that fall' evokes, according to Nicholas Grene, a 'specifically Protestant suburbia', Mrs Rooney and Miss Fitt attending the parish church where they 'knelt side by side at the same altar' and 'drank from the same chalice'.[73] Grene has shown that there was a definably religious strand to Beckett's cultural inheritance, and he sees Beckett as having in common with Yeats a certain lapsed Protestantism: 'The theology of Yeats and of Beckett is violently, even polemically heterodox.'[74] Professor Grene argues the case that 'the Protestant grounding' of Beckett's radio play 'All that fall' has a parallel in the equivalent importance that R.F. Foster has claimed for Protestantism in the shaping of Yeats's imagination. W.J. McCormack suggests that the Protestantism of County Wicklow, was to J.M. Synge what that of Foxrock was to Beckett.[75] But the decline of the Foxrock Protestant community portrayed by Beckett is a far cry from the burnt-out houses of Yeats. Unless, of course, we remember the burning of Sir Horace Plunkett's house in Foxrock during the troubles. Like Yeats, a member of the first senate of the Irish Free State, Plunkett, entitled to be called the founder of the co-operative movement in Ireland, was, unlike Yeats, a unionist, and paid dearly for it.

While Yeats might lament the passing of the great houses, Louis MacNeice, a young poet, and son of a Church of Ireland bishop,[76] was somewhat dismissive of what they had stood for, claiming that 'in most cases these houses

p. 50.   69 Brown, 'The Church of Ireland', pp 6–7.   70 Terence Brown, *Ireland: a social and cultural history* (London, 1981), p. 111.   71 Ibid.   72 Ibid., p. 119.   73 Nicholas Grene, *The politics of Irish drama: plays in context from Boucicault to Friel* (Cambridge, 1999), p. 180. 74 Ibid., p. 189.   75 W.J. McCormack, *Fool of the family: a life of J.M. Synge* (London, 2000), see especially pp 66–7, 76–7, 96–9.   76 J.F. MacNeice, bishop of Cashel (1931–4) and Down, Connor and Dromore (1934–42).

maintained no culture worth speaking of nothing but an obsolete bravado, an insidious bonhomie and a way with horses.'[77] Yet a biographer has detected something of the bishop's faith in the young MacNeice, who certainly found in his father much to respect.[78] Understandably, for Bishop MacNeice, to quote a recent critic, 'was a man of integrity, intelligence and personal courage' the last attribute being seen most conspicuously in his refusal to subscribe to Ulster's Solemn League and Covenant in 1912.[79] The poet found in the writings of the early Christian fathers intellectual 'nourishment'.[80] Furthermore, his sympathetic interest in one of the great Caroline divines, Jeremy Taylor, a predecessor of his father's in the diocese of Dromore, betokens a taste for a certain Anglican approach to theology.[81] The rector's son, 'banned for ever from the candles of the Irish poor',[82] biblical and other religious allusions are frequent in his poetry. While an ambivalence towards religion is evident in his work, it betrays a similar ambivalence towards the country itself, never more poignantly expressed than in the lines

> Why should I want to go back
> To you, Ireland, my Ireland?[83]

These lines, as do many others, justify Michael Longley's assertion that MacNeice did not feel at home on either island,[84] a dilemma in the poet's life explored by F.S.L. Lyons,[85] and not unknown to other Anglican intellectuals of his generation, including, perhaps, Lyons himself uncomfortable for those concerned, but providing them with a distinctive perspective. Today, MacNeice is being rediscovered as a most telling commentator on the religious and political environment that he grew up in and was to experience, however intermittently, throughout his life. He is, if anything, more relevant than ever.

   It would be hard to find two more contrasting milieus than those that produced, respectively, Louis MacNeice and Seán O'Casey. The former, with his public school and Oxford background, familiar with the corridors of ecclesiastical power, the latter born and bred in the modest circumstances of inner-city Dublin. Both writers were acute critics of Irish society, but it was O'Casey who, in the words of a dean of Christ Church cathedral, Dublin, 'immortalised the hopes and fears, the loves and hates, of the plain people of

---

77 Louis MacNeice, *The poetry of W.B. Yeats* (Oxford, 1941), pp 104–5.   78 John Hilton, 'Louis MacNeice at Marlborough and Oxford', in Louis MacNeice, *The strings are false: an unfinished autobiography* (London, 1965), pp 243–4.   79 Barry Sloan, *Writers and Protestantism in the North of Ireland: heirs to Adamnation* (Dublin, 2000), p. 173.   80 Ibid., p. 282.   81 Ibid.   82 'Carrickfergus', in *Louis MacNeice: poems selected by Michael Longley*, ed. Michael Longley (London, 2001), pp 22–3.   83 From 'Autumn Journal', in Longley, *MacNeice*, p. 40.   84 Longley, *MacNeice*, p. x.   85 F.S.L. Lyons, *Culture and anarchy in*

this city'.[86] O'Casey may not have owed the Church of Ireland as much as did MacNeice, yet he made no secret of his debt to one of its clergy, the Revd Edward Morgan Griffin, a man of strong social conscience who spent much of his ministry as rector of St Barnabas's, in the docklands area of the city. Dedicating *Pictures in the hallway* to Griffin, O'Casey described him as 'a fine scholar; a man of many-branched kindness, whose sensitive hand was the first to give the clasp of friendship to the author.'[87] Much of the religious thought that the young O'Casey encountered locally was of an evangelical nature, and, according to at least one biographer, the contribution made by Griffin, a high churchman, to the young man's intellectual development was to lead him to a churchmanship akin to his own.[88] Furthermore, the East Wall area in which he grew up, where the Great Northern Railway had its southern terminus, was home to many northern Protestants, so that he was aware of sectarian feeling, whether orange or green. The class against whom O'Casey directed so much of his criticism was not that of the big house, but of the Protestant (and other) commercial and industrial élites, whose social attitudes, to his mind, in no way accorded with their religious protestations. He was also angered by the neglect of the Irish language by the clergy of his church. Church of Ireland allusions in his writing are not far to seek, particularly in his first play, *The harvest festival* (never staged and now largely forgotten). Here, the playwright, promoting the interests of labour and the workers, used the device of the annual harvest thanksgiving service as a dramatic device, rather clumsily, a critic claims, in comparison with his more subtle treatment of the Easter festival in *Red roses for me*. According to Ronald Ayling, *The harvest festival* is 'a retrospective analysis of a Church of Ireland community in Dublin at a time of industrial unrest.'[89] In the parish church of St Burnupus, central to the action in *The silver tassie*, we are looking at Griffin's St Barnabas, now demolished.

The intellectual contribution of the laity that has been sketched above is necessarily a select one. Furthermore, it is confined to the written word, and takes no cognizance of intellectual activity expressed through music, on canvas or in glass. The composers Charles Villiers Stanford, Dublin born, and Charles Wood from Armagh, made an enduring contribution to Anglican devotional life and deserve mention, as do the contributions made through stained glass by

Ireland 1890–1939 (Oxford, 1979), chap. 5, 'Ulster: the roots of difference'.   86 Kenneth Milne (ed.), *Christ Church cathedral, Dublin: a history* (Dublin, 2000), p. 338.   87 Seán O'Casey, *Pictures in the hallway* (New York, 1949).   88 My passages on O'Casey owe a great deal to Ronald Ayling, 'Seeds for future harvest: propaganda and art in O'Casey's earliest play' in *Irish University Review*, x, no. 1 (Spring, 1980), pp 25–40, and Alan Simpson, 'O'Casey and the East Wall area of Dublin' in ibid., pp 41–51.   89 Ayling, 'Seeds for future harvest', p. 21. For more details of O'Casey's early years see Martin B. Margulies, *The early life of Seán O'Casey* (Dublin, 1970).

Evie Hone (who eventually found her spiritual home in the Catholic Church), and Catherine O'Brien also of An Túr Gloinne. Nor should one overlook the spiritual potency of the sculptures of Oisín Kelly, or of the paintings of Mainie Jellett, a formative influence in bringing cubism to Ireland, some of whose early exhibitions was held in St Bartholomew's parochial hall in Ballsbridge thanks to the interest shown in her work by Canon Walter Simpson.[90]

The 1870 constitution of the newly disestablished Church of Ireland gave to the laity an unprecedented role in church governance. A century or so later, the *Revised Catechism* accorded them what might be termed a wider brief. In response to the question: 'What is your work as a lay member of the Church of God ?',[91] the response is 'To take my part in its worship, labours and councils, according to the grace that God has given me, and to pray, work and give for the spread of his kingdom.' The Catholic Church has in the aftermath of Vatican II sought to look afresh at the place of the laity in the church, and the phrase 'people of God' has become current. Ironically, perhaps because it has for so long accepted lay participation in church government at all levels, the Church of Ireland has been slow to address the need for a fresh study of the place of the laity. If, however, the laity are fully to discharge the obligations set out in the new catechism, they need to be equipped for the task. To put it bluntly, they need to be theologically competent, and the more active the laity are in pastoral matters, the more theologically competent they need to be.

North and south, the emergence of an increasingly highly educated population has transformed the relationship between government and citizen and between church leadership and church member. All churches, the Church of Ireland among them, have yet to exploit to the full the benefits that can accrue to the church's work from the spread of education among the laity. On the contrary, churches have been slow to engage with the questioning of doctrine and the questioning of authority that education encourages. We live in extraordinarily perplexing times. On the one hand, there is a perceptible 'dumbing down' that permeates the media, both print and electronic. At the same time, there is unprecedented interest in those areas of literature, broadcasting and cinema that seek not only to entertain us, but also to make us think. Platitudinous though it may appear to say so, it has to be repeated that the church must take account of the intellectual mutations of the society in which it ministers, and must also take account of the particular societies that are emerging in Ireland. The pulpit is but one of the voices with which the church speaks, and the pulpit has its role, but it competes for listeners in a very strenuous environment. Furthermore, the pulpit is largely, though not entirely, the preserve of the clergy. The other

---

90 Kenneth Milne, *St Bartholomew's: a history of the Dublin parish* (Dublin, 1963), p. 92.
91 *Revised Catechism*, question 15.

9 Mainie Jellett (1879–1944)

channels of communication are more readily available to the laity, indeed, may well provide their livelihood.

Hence, the importance of theology as an academic option in the higher levels of secondary education, and of the opportunity for lay members of the church to continue such studies at university and elsewhere. Hence also the value of the theological courses for laity that are offered by the Braemor Institute in association with the Church of Ireland Theological College, and by several dioceses, and which are attracting considerable enrolment. The lay theologian is a virtually novel figure in Ireland, but given the massive contribution, outlined earlier in this chapter, that the laity have made to intellectual life in general, it can be expected that they will in due course redress the serious lack of theological thought and writing that at present so inhibits the contribution that the Church of Ireland might be making to the evolution of a changing society on this island.[92]

92 I wish to express my gratitude to Professor Christopher Murray of University College, Dublin, and to Professors Terence Brown and Nicholas Grene, of Trinity College, Dublin, for their comments with regard to the references to poets and dramatists. The opinions expressed are, of course, my own.

10

Lay spirituality and worship, 1750–1950: a reading people

John Paterson

About forty years ago the writer went with a college friend for a weekend visit to his home in the country. On Sunday morning church duties were duly attended and the afternoon was free for recreation. It had been intimated, however, that, after the evening meal, we would sit around the fire with the other members of the family while my friend's father would read aloud a goodly section from the Psalter. This was a normal Sunday evening tradition of the house and guests were expected be present. After this period of devotion we engaged in conversation until it was time to retire. Such an exercise in an earlier generation might have been common enough in many Church of Ireland households, particularly in rural areas. By the 1960s, however, such communal corporate piety had become decidedly unusual. Radio and television had already begun its exclusion of conversation so that, while families may still have been present together, they sat quietly as a faraway voice or picture commanded their attention. It is remarkable that radio and television, which together have done so much to keep religion alive in a largely secular age, are also largely responsible for the significant decline in corporate prayer. On BBC television and radio, 'Songs of Praise' and 'Sunday Half Hour' have made alternative provision for those who might formerly have read the scriptures together or gathered around a piano to sing hymns. Families have been individualised and devotion has become entertainment.

Twentieth-century writers tended to prefer the concept of *spirituality* to the older term *personal devotion*. Indeed that form of it often called *Celtic spirituality* had a high revival in the 1990s. *The Oxford dictionary of the Christian Church*,[1] however, considers most definitions of *spirituality* to be less than satisfactory, believing that the word needs more careful analysis than it normally receives. It is more properly used to refer to people's subjective practice and experience of their religion and of their relationship with God. Certain groups, according to

1 F.L. Cross and E.A. Livingstone (eds), *The Oxford dictionary of the Christian Church* (3rd edn, Oxford 1997).

the dictionary, such as religious orders may foster schools or types of spirituality[2] but the editors have problems with what is often called 'lay spirituality' or 'married spirituality'. For the purposes of this chapter *personal devotion* will be the preferred term – as being the absorption of ideas from the reflections of the thoughts and writings of others rather than based on an individual's original thinking.

I

An examination of the history of the Churches of the Anglican Communion cannot but notice that delving into its story is rather like assisting in an archaeological dig in theology. If one, as it were, digs a deep hole and examines the rings one discovers various theological stances that each predominate over others for a number of years and then change: usually a pattern of puritan-evangelical followed by catholic-liberal. Thus at the very bottom the early Reformation years were heavily influenced by the Calvinism learned by divines who had been exiled for trying to evade Henry VIII's non-papal Catholicism. Cranmer, Ridley and Latimer were by no means the most Calvinistic and puritan among the founders of the English Reformation but it was they and not the more catholic-minded bishops who were to shape belief during the reign of Edward VI. The path of Anglicanism was showing distinct signs of narrowing. Even under Elizabeth, never much given to favouring Protestants, a distinctive Calvinism prevailed until the time of Richard Hooker, though even he had no wish to disinherit his Church from the real benefits of the Reformation. The seventeenth century and the reign of the Stuarts provide the next layer of the dig. The work of the Caroline Divines was important in showing that the Reformation, though important in the defining of Anglicanism, was simply one theological stratum through which it passed – but not its sole defining theology. Caroline theology was a Protestantism that consisted rather in the negation of Rome than in the appropriation of the new orientation of religion produced by the Reformation. After the 1660 restoration it could not even cope with the new dissent. Restricting civil rights to Anglican communicants had the effect of profaning the sacrament rather than of extending Anglican principles.

In the immediate post-1750 period covered in this chapter we shall, for example, see evangelicalism prevail and have its exemplar in William Wilberforce. Yet Alexander Knox, thriving towards the end of the same period, would keep alive the older Caroline tradition. By the time of disestablishment in 1870 a neo-Calvinism, especially among the laity, was to prevail and shape the Church for almost one hundred years. Its lay leader, often more recognised for

---

2 For example the Ignatian method of the Jesuits.

his powerful political oratory and his cultivation of the Orange Order than for his theology, was the County Cavan landowner, Colonel Edward Saunderson. A theological examination of the theological outlook of these three laymen will help us discover some of the changes that shaped the personal devotion of members of the Church of Ireland over this two hundred year period.

The post-Reformation period set an important distinction between Catholic and Protestant devotional books and journals. Catholic Counter-Reformation books tended to be pious treatises on the lives of the saints or on miracles. Early Protestant devotional material, often puritan-inspired, was by contrast designed to emphasise the responsibility of the individual soul before God. It was meant to be literature that would both reflect and stimulate the religious changes that were happening and that would also provide a degree of warmth in what must often have been dry and dull services in the parish church. Protestant devotion was, however, essentially an individualistic thing, even for those who were members of a church possessing a common liturgy. Both types would survive to provide devotional stimulation well into the nineteenth century and the period of this study.

The events of the Reformation must have had a shattering impact on the devotional lives of ordinary people. A church supreme in every area of life, though perhaps not quite so corrupt as later generations might infer, had its infallibility and power severely questioned. Civil legislation was imposed upon liturgy, ritual and ecclesiastical polity, though it was to prove less easy to legislate for personal devotion. On Sunday 2 June 1549 the Mass was in Latin. Seven days later in the same building it was supposed to be in English. What would have happened to the private piety of the people during those seven days? One can only assume that it went on much as before. Deep-seated devotion does not change radically in one week. The growth in individual religion, which had begun in the later middle ages, and which had increased after the Reformation, emphasised the responsibility of each soul before God. The principal theological effect had been the production of a religious literature intended to stimulate the mind rather than the senses. The idea of the visual had indeed been virtually eclipsed. The dominant Calvinism of the English reformers meant that church buildings were thoroughly Protestantised by the removal of colour and visual artistry. Stone altars were smashed, to be replaced by simple wooden tables; statues of the saints (though not of the nobility) were destroyed; and whitewash, literally and metaphorically, was liberally applied, the situation, despite the Caroline Divines, not radically changing until the nineteenth century.[3] In Ireland, where fewer medieval churches were in sound repair, the damage must have been even more incalculable.

3 For contrasting opinions compare E. Duffy, *The stripping of the altars: traditional religion in England, 1400–1580* (London, 1992) with a review by G.R. Elton in the *Journal of Ecclesiastical History* xliv (1993), pp 719–21.

It is difficult for today's worshipper to appreciate the weight of authority that was given to the Bible and to the Book of Common Prayer up to modern times. The Bible was not just read but huge sections were memorised. So too was the Prayer Book. And though the Prayer Book never aimed at being a theological treatise on the shape of the ministry it provided three services for the ordination of its bishops, priests and deacons. Though it was never intended as a treatise on methods of prayer it gives strong emphasis to both Eucharist and Daily Office as the daily staple diet of prayer, psalmody and scripture. It is a biblically based book, with huge sections of scripture printed out in full for those who could read. Indeed if the Articles are recognised as being an appendix to the book itself, the divisive issues of the Reformation and puritan periods were largely avoided. In every edition – 1549, 1552, 1559 and 1662 – it probably had to be so if some sort of inclusiveness was to be hoped for even if not always achieved.

For some in later generations this inclusiveness proved inadequate. It was to drive a John Wesley to 'found' the zeal of Methodism where Church was defined by a common religious experience in a society. And John Newman had to move to the certainties and tidiness of a pre-Vatican II Catholicism. Nevertheless the Book of Common Prayer of 1662 and its subsequent revisions throughout the whole of the Anglican Communion until almost the present day gave Anglicans an opportunity to explore and experiment while keeping them free from undue rigidity and uniformity. It can even be argued that some of the events that presently polarise the Communion into divisive groups have arisen only since the gold-standard pattern of 1662 and its conservative derivatives, such as the variations of the 1920s, have been lost.

The vital principle of Bible and Prayer Book, so tragically missed by the modern churchgoer, was that neither were books taken from a shelf on entering church. Both were well-worn personal possessions, companions and guides, which were as much used in the kitchen as in the church. The Book of Common Prayer in particular was not just a collection of services but a guide to living, covering every area of life from the cradle to the grave.

The sixteenth century began a type of literature that was to survive up to modern times. Ever since the break with Rome books of a more controversial nature had become popular. With stories of martyrs under both Mary Tudor and Elizabeth abounding it was inevitable that laudatory books from both sides of the divide would appear in what had become a time of inexpensive and easy print. Chief of these, from the Protestant point of view, must be John Foxe's *Book of martyrs* first published at Strasbourg in 1554, and in England in 1563. Its chief object was to extol the undoubted heroism and endurance of the Protestant martyrs of Mary's reign. Its homely style, vivid descriptions of the sufferings imposed on the victims of 'papist tyranny' and relatively inexpensive printing ensured it a wide readership even into the early twentieth century. Despite its clear bias it still remains a major source reference for historians through its preservation of early Protestant oral tradition and documents.

As the Reformation progressed the fear of Rome lessened. Memories of the Spanish Armada dimmed and puritanism/Calvinism no longer seemed to provide all the answers a questioning mind might ask. In the early seventeenth century the 'Caroline Divines' began what they believed was a return towards the historic standards of the 1549 Book of Common Prayer and a definite and planned departure from the more extreme teachings of certain of the reformers. The movement, though, can be said to have found its first thinker as early as 1585 who Richard Hooker was appointed master of the Temple in London. His life's work there was eventually to be published in 1594 as *Of the laws of ecclesiastical polity*. It was not simply a rebuttal of puritanism but a systematic presentation of an ecclesiology and theology that was in conformity with the Book of Common Prayer and the Elizabethan settlement and which survived through the evangelical movement until it was newly revitalised by the Tractarians in the nineteenth century.[4] Hooker's theology may have been the foundation on which this renewed Anglicanism would be built but it was William Laud who would become its undoubted leader. The chief spiritual writers of the movement were men with an eirenic outlook though still utterly opposed to Presbyterian polity. Among them were Jeremy Taylor, 1613–67, bishop of Down and Connor, Lancelot Andrews, 1555–1626, bishop of Winchester, and Thomas Ken, 1637–1711, bishop of Bath and Wells and a noted hymn writer. A Dublin layman, James Bonnell, whose biography was on the Charter School reading list as late as 1824, was a devout follower and disciple.[5] Much of the best Caroline teaching that served later generations of the faithful was expressed by their poets: John Donne, 1571/2–1631, later dean of St Paul's, and George Herbert, 1593–1633, rector of Bemerton near Salisbury, who almost daily walked the few miles to attend Evensong in the cathedral. They have left us some of the most beautiful mystical writing of the age. Their expression of religious emotion, though strictly disciplined, was never totally suppressed and many of their verses later became hymns.[6] Monasticism may have disappeared from the Anglican religious scene but in the Caroline writers its ordered spirit has lived on, especially in the cathedrals where the daily round of services has ensured the continuance of a Benedictine-type of the monastic *opus Dei*. The result was a Christian life that was solid and serious, even at times a little scrupulous with most prayer in set authorised forms. But there is little sense of any ongoing relation with the living Lord, and little encouragement for extempore prayer. Caroline Anglicanism was Christianity for adults. There was, however, one

4 H.R. McAdoo, *The spirit of Anglicanism* (London 1965). See also McAdoo in Geoffrey Rowell, (ed.), *The English religious tradition and the genuis of Anglicanism* (Wantage, 1992), pp 105–25.   5 For Bonnell see Raymond Gillespie's essay above. His lay churchmanship will be compared with that of Alexander Knox (early nineteenth century) and contrasted with that of Edward Saunderson (late nineteenth century) on pp 259–61, 271–3.   6 E.g. Donne's *Wilt thou forgive that sin?* and Herbert's *King of glory*.

brave attempt at living in community in these years. At Little Gidding in Huntingdonshire the Ferrar family, comprising some forty persons lived a systematic rule of devotion and work from 1625 until 1646 when it was dispersed under Oliver Cromwell.

Perhaps the most famous legacy of the movement was Jeremy Taylor's *Holy living* and *Holy dying*. Here was a characteristic expression of Anglican devotion that insisted on well-ordered piety while stressing temperance and moderation in all things. The books' beautiful prose, so clearly written yet possessing rhetorical vigour and powerful imagery, made Taylor one of the most significant writers and preachers of the day. No writer from the Caroline period ever had more influence on the devotional lives of so many – even into the twentieth century; yet few today seem to know more than their titles and fewer still have read them. Other books from the same school of thought were the *Private devotions* of Lancelot Andrews, 1555–1626 and, though a century later, William Law's *Serious call* (1728), which might be described as the final fling of the Caroline tradition. Technically later, by accidental discovery, was the publication of the poetry and reflections of Thomas Traherne. Though he lived from *c.*1636 until 1674, he had been regarded as a minor contributor to the Caroline school of thought until two of his manuscripts were discovered in a second-hand shop in London in 1895 and were realised for what they were. Published in 1903 and 1908 his poems have aroused intense interest and are remarkable for their penetrating sense of the glory of God.[7] They have never been more popular than at the present day.

Despite the interval of the Cromwellian commonwealth period, the Caroline liturgical influence on many parts of the Church of Ireland was to be significant,[8] especially in Christ Church Cathedral, Dublin.[9] It is worth noting the number of Dublin parish churches of this period with daily services, often as early as 6 am. Such services are usually provided only if they are felt to be needed and will be reasonably well attended so they must have supplied a devotional need. This situation had notably changed by the early nineteenth century where only the two cathedrals appear to have maintained regular daily worship. Preacher's Books for the period do not usually indicate numbers but those with knowledge of the two Dublin cathedrals over the past half-century would be aware that any growth in weekday attendance is a recent development.

7 The story is well told in A.M. Allchin, and others, *Profitable wonders: aspects of Thomas Traherne* (Oxford, 1989).   8 F.R. Bolton, *The Caroline tradition of the Church of Ireland* (London, 1958).   9 K. Milne, (ed.), *Christ Church cathedral Dublin, a history* (Dublin, 2000), especially chapters x and xiii.

II

The eighteenth-century church of the period of the Enlightenment is not normally best remembered for its piety. The many-copied prints of church life as lampooned by artist William Hogarth or the lives of the clergy described by novelists such as Henry Fielding and others[10] tell of latitudinarian bishops and 'high and dry' parsons. 'God, virtue and morality' were the theological themes of the day with little about sin and grace and salvation through Jesus Christ.

> In literature of this kind there are numerous descriptions of priestly indifference: the Squarson, a compound of Squire and Parson, who lived his comfortable life as an honest landed proprietor, took a lively part in his neighbourhood's more or less robust pleasures, hunted ate and drank, at the best the worldly-wise adviser of his flock. ... Sunday came as a slight interruption in the agreeable round of days. His well-worn dialogue with the 'Amen-clerk' was soon finished ... The state of the Church fabric answered to the nature of the service. Often enough green mould crept over leaning walls.[11]

Warmth in faith was needed yet a majority of the clergy would have continued to agree with the eighteenth-century Bishop Joseph Butler (1672–1752) that enthusiasm was a very horrid thing – and dangerous too.[12]

The University of Oxford in the course of its history has spawned no less than three movements of religious reformation: the sixteenth-century Reformation, the eighteenth-century evangelical movement and nineteenth-century Tractarianism. It has often been said that the evangelical awakening was this very enthusiasm of which so many of the clergy were afraid. To call the movement a 'party' is to define it with sharp limits. Rather it consisted of those who strove for a warmer religious feeling, all who were spiritually minded, yet exercised self-control of mind and body, of time and talents. They were like-minded clergy and laity who supported each other in pockets all over the ecclesiastical map. Where they emerged (and usually they came in clumps) they transformed church life within their parishes – multiplying Sunday services, introducing weekday meetings and founding societies for spiritual and charitable purposes. Evangelicalism stressed conversion rather than baptism, the scriptures rather than tradition and reason, the word rather than sacrament as the main channel of grace, and penal substitution[13] as the only acceptable theory of the atonement of Christ. By the

---

10 *Tom Jones.* See also *The vicar of Wakefield* (Goldsmith) and *Parish Register* (Crabbe).
11 Y. Brilioth, *The Anglican revival* (London, 1933), quoted pp 8–9 from *The story of the Catholic revival*, a rather partisan history of the Oxford Movement by G. Kelway, published 1915.   12 See R.W. Church, *The Oxford movement* (London, 1892), pp 3f.   13 A theory of

1830s its London headquarters was patronised by bishops, peers, members of parliament and the great and the good, yet it was linked with its humblest 'auxiliaries' in the remotest parishes of the land. The Delegates and representatives would enjoy the great excitement of the London May Meetings where notable orators would treat their audiences to feasts of argument and flows of soul.[14]

Clapham (then a commuter village outside London) and Cambridge were its first two strongholds. In Clapham a group of like-minded friends found a comfortable retreat after work in the London banks or, the most famous, William Wilberforce, in parliament. One cannot doubt their religious convictions. They united a sincere and active piety that did not hesitate to surround itself with all the pleasures that riches could give. But with all this they subjected themselves to a detailed self-control and used their time and worldly goods as a talent entrusted to them. The members of the 'Clapham Sect' formed a most honourable page in the history of evangelicalism. We need only think of the tough and finally victorious fight against the slave trade that made William Wilberforce's name immortal. Other undoubted achievements included the founding of the Church Missionary Society (1799), the British and Foreign Bible Society (1804) and many local moral welfare associations. Wilberforce (1759–1833) must be regarded as the premier lay moulder of theological reflection in the late eighteenth and early nineteenth century church. His faith, however, was shared by those who would have stood far aloof from later pietistic evangelicalism with its strong Calvinist flavour. Wilberforce brought warmth of feeling to a Church whose public worship often seemed more like a code of behaviour than a reflection on the things of God. In the most secular of London's places and occasions he could speak of the love of God without ever boring his hearers.[15] The long descriptive title made plain the nature of his book and of his theological position, *A practical view of the prevailing religious system of professed Christians, in the higher and middle classes in this country, contrasted with real Christianity.* This was a layman's book, in which practical questions were preferred to those of doctrine. Wilberforce may have made many people feel uneasy but not so uncomfortable that they would not listen. His lifestyle matched his beliefs and he died in 1833, the year his bill to abolish slavery was approved by parliament. This older concept of evangelicalism penetrated deeply throughout the length and breadth of Britain and Ireland and was widely admired, even by those whose style of theology was profoundly different.

> Though doubtless, in certain points, I entertain a view different from them, I can safely say, that that they belong to the elect of the earth, and

the atonement that Christ died *instead of us* rather than *for us.* **14** A.J. Symondson, (ed.), *The Victorian crisis of faith* (London, 1970), chapter 2, Evangelicalism **15** C.J. Stranks, *Anglican devotion* (London, 1961), p. 15.

I say now, what I should desire to say on my deathbed, *sit mea anima cum istis.*[16]

Even before Wilberforce's death considerable changes in the style of evangelical spirituality had taken been taking place: a pietism evolved that would be not just world denying but strongly anti-Catholic. The strong social passion had also been dissipated, and despite the perseverance of some individuals in the working-class districts of Manchester and Liverpool, the movement became identified with fashionable society and spa towns. Irish evangelicalism in addition developed a proselytising agenda of work among and mission to the Catholic poor – the 'Second Reformation Movement' – largely supported by the earls of Farnham and of Roden and other members of the aristocracy and prosperous businessmen.

III

The Church of Ireland in the years before and after the Act of Union, as by law established, was a set of strange contradictions – principally of many separate interests and movements. The anomaly of an Anglican state church in an overwhelmingly Catholic country seemed to be a cause of no great concern to any of its members. It was an unreal bond, however, for it in no way prevented a spirit of independency and division growing up leading to the formation of unofficial societies and congregations which inevitably would divide the church's energies. Most visible was the great gulf that existed between the state-appointed bishops and clergy who were within the diocesan and parochial system and the ministers and strong lay supporters of the new independent proprietary chapels then emerging. The two groups lived in different worlds. They held totally different theologies. The former was erastian in politics, largely dry in theology and trusting in the legal ordination of the clergy and the institution through which they worked. The latter was pietistic, emphasising personal conversion and the right of the individual to private judgement.

One description of parochial church life by an historian never enthusiastic about the established church may well exaggerate reality:

The external appearances were but too sadly emblematic of the spiritual condition of the church. Where Divine service was performed it was conducted in a careless and a slovenly manner. Everything about it was cold, formal and lifeless. The 'duty' was done because it *must* be done, but in such a hurried careless way, as to show that it was most irksome to those

16 C. Foster, *The life of John Jebb* (3rd ed., London, 1851), p. 61.

appointed to minister in sacred things. The clergy, for the most part, belonged to families of the aristocracy and the landed gentry, the younger sons ... going into 'the Church' ... for the chance of its 'prizes'.... The prizes were certainly magnificent.[17]

Contrast this with a description of the proprietary chapels from a surprising source. The 1868 *Freeman's Journal Irish Church Commission* report into the temporalities enjoyed by the Church of Ireland provides a surprisingly warm approbation of the proprietary chapels. Its author, Sir John Gray, was as scathing as Godkin about centuries of Church of Ireland oppression and greed yet he wrote concerning the Dublin chapels:

> The largest Anglican congregations in the city are those which attend ... what are termed Proprietary Churches, supported altogether by the private contributions of those who come as worshippers ... The Ministers of these Churches are better paid by pew rents, on an average, than are the best paid of the State endowed Ministers of these dioceses. It is computed that more than half the Church-going population of Dublin, including all the more intellectual classes ... are 'hearers' at these voluntary Chapels, and that three-fourths of the Evangelical Anglicans hold pews in them, and never dream of entering a parochial Church. Dublin affords in fact, the best illustration of what voluntaryism might effect from religious, as distinct from political, Protestantism, if men would have but trust in the power of the faith they profess to believe divine and not place their reliance on the fleshy arm.[18]

IV

Alexander Knox (1757–1831) was an anomaly in an evangelical age, especially in Ireland. Knox was born at Derry[19] on 17 March 1757, where his father was a member of the city's corporation. Though a descendent of the Scottish Presbyterian reformer John Knox, his theology was of a completely different complexion. Nor should he be thought of as a member of the 'high and dry' school, rather an eminent lay theologian and sacramental churchman of the school of thought of James Bonnell.[20] By his breadth of vision Knox remarkably was able to retain the friendship of both John Jebb, the high-church bishop of Limerick and also of John Wesley the 'founder' of Methodism. For a layman of

17 J. Godkin, *The religious history of Ireland* (London, 1873), p. 219.   18 *The Freeman's Journal Irish Church commission* (Dublin, 1868), pp 369ff.   19 *Dictionary of national biography*, though Brilioth, *The Anglican revival*, p. 46, says Limerick.   20 See Gillespie, above p. 133.

the period he was widely read in theology. At an early age Knox for a time became a member of Wesley's society though claiming that a growing disposition to think for himself caused him to leave before he had reached the age of twenty. Weak health – he was subject to periodic epileptic fits – meant that he received no formal education though his writings prove that he managed to pick up a considerable knowledge of the classics and of general literature. For a while he threw himself into politics in support of parliamentary reform in Ireland and was a good speaker, as well as writer.

In 1797 he renewed his friendship with Jebb, begun when both had been at school in Derry, and, down the years, it is clear that Knox was to exercise a significant influence on the bishop's thinking and writing. Following the passing of the Act of Union in 1800 Knox retired from politics and devoted himself entirely to the study of theology, living somewhat as a recluse in lodgings in Dublin's Dawson Street where he became a parishioner of St Ann's church.[21] Though always wary of the Calvinism of some of the evangelical school of thought, he had close friendly relations with English evangelicals such as Hannah More and William Wilberforce and with the La Touche family of Delgany in Ireland. Knox was admired by many as an admirable conversationalist and people flocked to his lodgings in Dawson Street. He frequently lamented upon the general deadness of church services as conducted in his day and rebelled against the identification of churchmanship with toryism. His ideal was the theology of the Caroline divines and, though an admirer of the great continental Catholic spiritual writers such as Francis de Sales, he had no tendencies towards or thoughts of ever joining the Catholic Church.[22] Knox's publications, thus, were largely in defence of Church principles such as belief in baptismal regeneration (1820) and on the *Use and import of the Eucharistic symbols* (1822). The thrust of his theological understanding was that 'our vitality as a church is in our identity with the church catholic'. It was this that led G.T. Stokes to write in the *Contemporary Review* (August 1887) that a very real connection can be made from Wesley to Knox, from Knox to Jebb, and from Jebb to Hugh James Rose, Newman and Pusey. Dean Church impugned the theory but came to allow that Knox may have anticipated some of what was afterwards taught by the leaders of the revival.

Knox, though well disposed towards evangelicals in general, heartily detested the Calvinism that had come to show itself in Irish evangelicalism and which was most strongly expounded in the sermons of James O'Brien, bishop of Ossory (1834). Knox's belief that justification is a gift of righteousness that is

---

21 The east window of the church is dedicated in his memory.   22 Brilioth, *The Anglican revival*, p. 44, makes the interesting point that those brought up in the old-fashioned High Church tradition, e.g. Pusey and Keble, produced fewer converts to Rome than those from Calvinist backgrounds, e.g. Newman and Faber.

imparted rather than *imputed*, sacramental rather than legal, caused him to fall foul of the entire Irish evangelical school of thought. Bishop O'Brien, indeed, did not mince his words when in 1834 he wrote 'there is scarcely anything in Mr Knox's volumes on the doctrine of justification which is not erroneous either in itself, or in its intended application'. Robert Daly, rector of Powerscourt and later bishop of Cashel, in a letter to Archbishop Whately said, 'I honoured him for his deep personal piety … but feel very thankful that I was delivered from the erroneous doctrines of his school'.[23]

Knox would have allowed that the world of pietistic evangelicalism, while holding to the essential orthodoxy of the faith, gave rather over-strong emphasis to certain areas of it. The 'gospel' was reduced from being the whole work of Christ to a narrow interpretation of the atonement (penal substitution) and to an emphasis on justification by faith alone. Was it no longer enough to trust in the sacramental grace of one's baptism, to receive the Eucharist at least on a number of occasions during the year, to believe the Christian message, to practise personal prayer and attend public worship on a regular basis? While recognising the desirability for personal faith Knox believed that this new evangelical emphasis was proclaiming as mandatory a necessity for a personal, spiritual breakthrough, leading to a new way of life and the rejection of the things of this world with all its vanity. It was a puritanism he believed to be contrary to the ethos of the Book of Common Prayer and of the United Church of England and Ireland, yet which has survived in many places to the present day and to attract adherents of all sorts and conditions. Unlike the Methodist movement, which produced its leaders largely from among tradesmen and farmers, the Church evangelicals were frequently from the 'aristocracy' and from the 'upper' and 'higher middle' classes, people whose financial support was essential for their chapels and their religious works.

V

Revivalist movements were a common Protestant phenomenon. So too were the tensions and even splits that they created within church life. For their supporters inner certainty was to be found in the believing converted individual – layman as well as priest – but not in the Church as body corporate. Many of the leaders of the movement were indeed members of the clergy but unless they were 'converted' and had experienced personal salvation they were not considered to have any special spiritual authority. A much-remembered example of one of the early evangelical clergy was Peter Roe of St Mary's Church,

---

23 Both quotations are from W.A. Phillips, *History of the Church of Ireland* (3 vols, Oxford 1933), iii, pp 334–5.

Kilkenny who pioneered clerical meetings and organisations such as the Bible Society and the Sunday School Society. Thus, although the movement brought a new enthusiasm for devotion and contributed lasting values, it also proved a source of tension and was ultimately responsible for a significant change in the theological outlook of the Church. This would seriously manifest itself in the years leading towards disestablishment in 1870.

Pietism had made these significant and permanent gains from the late-eighteenth century through the establishment of proprietary chapels and religious societies and they proliferated from the early 1800s. The chapels, as we have seen, were essentially preaching houses built by public subscription or maintained by wealthy individuals but which had neither constitutional existence nor parochial rights, their clergy simply holding an episcopal licence to preach and having the (sometimes reluctant) consent of the incumbent of the parish. Among the better-known chapels in Dublin was the Bethesda in Dorset Street (erected in 1786, subsequently a cinema and a wax museum). Its minister from 1805, W.B. Mathias, attracted a large and influential laity who imbibed a gospel of personal conversion and penal substitution in the death of Jesus Christ. The provost of Trinity College forbade his students to attend but one of his Fellows, J.H. Singer, later bishop of Meath, was to be a strong supporter both of this theology and also of the later phenomenon of the 1859 Ulster Revival. As late as the opening years of the twentieth century the rector of St Mary's, whose chapel of ease (the black church) was barely one hundred yards from the Bethesda, would still be advising his parishioners to avoid attendance. Another chapel was the Magdalene Asylum (1835) in Leeson Street (now totally demolished and replaced by an office building). Trinity Church in Gardiner Street, which had been built in 1839, was given a district in 1847 and became well known as a preaching house for John Gregg, later bishop of Cork. Since 1908 it has served as an employment exchange. As late as the year 1900 there were still in Dublin eight proprietary chapels surviving as independent places of worship.[24] Even today three trustee churches (as they are now known) still survive in the diocese.[25] Most were centres of pietistic evangelicalism and ideally suited as a base for the earnest preacher and a gospel-seeking congregation.

> The vehement gesticulation and impassioned tones with which some deliver themselves.... have still the effect of awakening the attention of the hearers, persuading them that the things spoken, be they what they may, are eminently important to the speaker, and so to them also.[26]

24 This figure excludes the many hospital and college chapels, most of which are listed as having public services. 25 Crinken (Evangelical) and Sandymount St John (Anglo-Catholic), both nineteenth century, and St Catherine's (Charismatic) whose trustee position dates only from the 1990s. 26 *Christian Examiner*, July 1826, pp 55ff.

Religious literature was also often equally impassioned. An examination of the religious papers for the early years of the nineteenth century seem more notable for advertisements for books on religious controversy than religious devotion. Their pages are more filled with the contents of anti-Roman tracts and concerned with stories of conversions[27] than for manuals of prayer and devotion. Was there a connection between anti-popery tracts and the struggle for Catholic Emancipation that had become such a feature of Irish life after the Act of Union in 1800? What people might read would vary, not simply through rank or wealth, but by what was available locally at a given period. That poverty and illiteracy both abounded through much of the nineteenth century can be found in accounts of how the poor lived.[28] Yet books are regularly recorded among the very few worldly possessions of even the poorest homes.

One of the best accounts of semi-literate Victorian poverty, although not published until 1913, must be Alexander Irvine's *My lady of the chimney corner*. It is largely an account of his parent's marriage at the time of the 1847 famine, his mother (from a Catholic family) able to read, his father Protestant and illiterate, and of their grinding poverty in a hovel in a laneway (Pogue's Entry) in the town of Antrim. Like their neighbours around them they were devout and God-fearing, even Sabbatarian, though actual churchgoing meant little more than ensuring that all twelve children were baptised in the parish church. On Sunday afternoons, however, following the one significant meal of the week, Anna Irvine would read aloud to the family. The Bible and *Pilgrim's progress* were their sole book possessions and both were much quoted. They were supplemented by 'improving literature' distributed by the local Methodist tract distributor, a Miss Clarke. This too would be read to all that would listen.

To ensure that the poor might have what might be regarded as 'suitable reading material' Protestant evangelicals had established subsidised publishing houses. Among the poor, books would often be read aloud so that everyone in the room might receive benefit. *The Christian Examiner*, piously Protestant and evangelical, was among the journals used by booksellers and printers to make known their own publications. As late as 1840 *The Christian Oratory*, selections from the works of Jeremy Taylor, was published. This was in fact a series of prayers, mounted on board, to be hung in cottages, ready for daily use. It is typically described in an advertisement in *The Christian Examiner* as 'useful for the Peasantry, and is recommended to Landlords, Clergymen, and others interested in the spiritual welfare of the people'. Even more interesting might have been a three-volume set of books, published in London in 1841, which has sadly proved unobtainable for examination. An Irish censorship board might surely have closely examined 'An essay on sex in the world to come', by the Revd G.D. Haughton.

27 *Christian Examiner*, April 1827, has a highly dramatic account of the reception of a Catholic convert into the Church of Ireland in Christ Church Cathedral, Dublin.   28 R. Loeber and M. Stouthamer-Loeber, 'Fiction available to cottagers' in B. Cunningham and

Raymond Gillespie in 'The religion of Irish Protestants: a view from the laity, 1580–1700'[29] makes the important point that lay personal religion will often differ considerably from the official views of churchmen and theologians. The whole story of the beginnings of modern hymnody and chancel choirs in the nineteenth century and the abolition of the old gallery choirs and bands would support such a view.[30] These events were fraught with major clerical/lay disputes, and are well exemplified in the fictional writings of authors of the day.[31] Sometimes the opposition may not have been simply an objection to organs and chancel choirs but more perhaps a feeling that a sense of great loss had happened with the passing of the world of the gallery bands. The high degree of illiteracy before the founding of a national education system in the nineteenth century makes it clear that printed books were not necessarily everyone's source of popular devotion, whereas all could memorise a hymn with a good tune.[32]

The eighteenth-century Methodists, and evangelicals such as Watts, Newton and Kelly, had shown the importance of putting the gospel words of the New Testament into song for the people of God. Their repetitious words and tunes may not appeal to some modern singers[33] but they formed a major part of popular devotion until they were supplemented at the beginning of the Oxford Movement by the publication of John Keble's *Christian year*, Rosetti's poems and Heber's hymns. Heber's poems indeed, according to Owen Chadwick, were written not for the congregation but for the bedside. Yet they, among others, have provided us with the material that gave us the setting of Victorian parlour life, which is such a feature of nineteenth-century novels. One only has to turn to the novels of Thomas Hardy,[34] Rudyard Kipling,[35] and even D.H. Lawrence[36] to discover the impact that hymns made on the lives of the people portrayed.

Keble's *Christian Year*, first published in 1827, was the first major attempt among the 'high and dry' school to appeal to the feelings and not just to the intellect. Keble was a shy but brilliant young fellow of Oriel College, Oxford – so shy that even those who best liked him misjudged his qualities. When under pressure he liked to unburden himself of some of his thoughts in poetry. From 1818 and over a number of years these poems had been published. In 1827, rather reluctantly, he allowed them to be gathered into one volume where his

M. Kennedy (eds), *The experience of reading: Irish historical perspectives* (Dublin, 1999), pp 124–72.   **29** in A. Ford, J. McGuire, and K. Milne, (eds), *As by law established: the Church of Ireland since the Reformation* (Dublin, 1995).   **30** The first collection of hymns for use in the Church of Ireland dates from 1856 and formed the basis of what was to become known as the *Church Hymnal* (2nd ed., Dublin, 1873).   **31** E.g. Hardy, Eliot, Kipling.   **32** For a more detailed story of gallery bands, see I. Bradley, *Abide with me* (London, 1997), pp 28–52.   **33** Though see *Church hymnal* (5th edition, Dublin, 2000), at no. 104.   **34** *Far from the madding crowd.*   **35** *Puck of Pook's hill.*   **36** *Hymns in a man's life*, quoted in Bradley, *Abide*

readers might experience 'the soothing tendency in the Prayer Book'. The liturgy had, he believed, the power to calm and steady the spirit and to reduce the cares of this world to its proper proportions. The popularity of the verses was almost instantaneous yet it is not always easy to follow their train of thought and harder still to make out any consistent body of doctrine from them. Many are today unquoted while others have become much-loved hymns: 'New every morning', 'Hail, gladdening Light', 'Sun of my soul' and 'Blest are the pure in heart'[37] are among the best known. The best of them have the ring of a simple, heart-felt devotion unknown since the hymns of Thomas Ken. His beauty of character impressed all that came into contact with him yet he never received preferment other than the country living of Hursley near Winchester. His advice on spiritual matters, always given with great diffidence, was widely sought after. His work and life and his commitment to the Church of England, even after the secession of Newman to Rome, ensured that Tractarian devotion became more widely accepted and acceptable to many.

Poems that had been written to be read privately now came to be put to tunes and sung corporately as the piano became part of the furnishings of any a rising middle-class family. They were sung around the fire on a winter Sunday evening. Their style, however, was beginning to change. The effects of the 1859 Revival in Ireland together with the more exuberant songs of Moody and Sankey, which followed the success of their first mission to England in 1873, were to eclipse the more reflective offering of the earlier writers. It was often not so much emotion as emotionalism that was reflected in their verses. What is so noticeable about the hymns of the 1860s and later is the number that lose the objectivity of the majesty of God. They begin with 'I' or 'My' and deal with largely subjective themes. Today's gospel songs have further increased this tendency to place the emphasis more on the worshipper than on Christ. John Mason Neale, translator of many of the ancient Office hymns from the Latin, believed that many hymns seriously encouraged dangerously subjective emotionalism and frequently peddled false doctrines. Yet evangelical hymn singing was to form a devotional norm for the Sunday evenings of many people – even up to the advent of television in the 1950s. Certainly, apart from the Bible, no other devotional method has done more to influence the views and mould the theology of the average person. Hymns once learned are rarely forgotten – even at twenty-first century football matches. Cecil Francis Alexander embarked on her scheme for teaching the children in her Sunday school when she commenced her series of hymns that would illustrate the Apostles' Creed. 'All things bright and beautiful' complemented 'maker of heaven and earth', 'Once in royal David's city' 'born of the Virgin Mary' and 'There is a green hill' 'he suffered'.[38] The last named with its fourth verse,

with me, pp 217–18. **37** *Church Hymnal*, nos. 59, 699, 72 and 630. **38** See *Church Hymnal*,

'There was no other good enough ...', has been described as perhaps the most brief and perfect description of the atonement outside the pages of the New Testament. Perhaps less attractive is the emphasis on death and sin in her children's hymns, but this was as common as death itself in Victorian times.

It was in poetry that the Oxford movement began as writers like Mrs Alexander, in common with the revivalism of John Wesley, encouraged Anglicans not to be ashamed of their religious feelings. At the heart of the preaching and writing of Keble and Newman and Pusey was a concern for personal holiness and a call for the renewal of spirituality. They saw the calendar of the Christian year and the Church's seasons as a proper framework for worship and learning. Keble's own *Christian year* first published in 1827 had become staple devotion for many throughout the nineteenth century. The very core of Tractarian spirituality was that we become by grace what Christ is by nature: we are transfigured by the divine indwelling within us. We are not simply reasoning animals, but beings that see, feel, contemplate and act. *Maxims from Dr Pusey's writings*, edited by M.F. Sadler and published in 1882, shows knowledge of the writing of continental writers who influenced Tractarian devotion. 'The daily round' (1884) divided the day into five parts: a passage from scripture, what the passage means, thoughts to bring home the general lesson, a prayer and ends with a verse of a hymn. Such books were full of nuggets of wisdom intended to influence for good those who might read them and anticipate the modern work of the Bible Reading Fellowship and the Scripture Union. Irish clergy prominent for their Tractarian sympathies included Richard Travers Smith of Saint Bartholomew's, Dublin,[39] and Henry Dickenson, vicar of Saint Ann's, Dublin, who were early supporters of the value of retreats or quiet days for both clergy and lay people. This was at a time when retreats were still a relatively new devotional concept within the Anglican tradition and highly suspect to people like Thomas Mills, editor of *The Church Advocate* and John Duncan Craig (minister at the old Molyneux chapel in Bride Street). At a time when the Church of Ireland was at its lowest-ever period of sacramental life and its most extreme period of pietistic evangelicalism parliament decided to end the 'eternal' union which it had set up between the Churches of England and Ireland only seventy years earlier and to disestablish and disendow the Irish part. That disestablishment happened is now regarded as both justified and inevitable – the 1861 census had shown it to represent no more than one-eighth of the total population of Ireland – but that it happened at this particular period was to have repercussions that would colour church life for almost a century.

nos. 25, 177 and 144.   **39** R.T. Smith, *Advent and Lent* (Dublin, 1883), and *Lessons in thought and prayer* (London, 1895).

VI

The nineteenth century shows a significant increase in the power of the laity in the church. In part it may have happened because the provincial convocations of the Church of Ireland, unlike those of England, had not been permitted to meet since 1716. There was thus no natural governing body with authority. In part it may also have occurred through the influence of the proprietary chapels (particularly in Dublin) where there was an educated and affluent laity, which by paying for its own spiritual needs exercised virtually a total independence from both parish and diocese. At any rate, a coherent concept of 'authority in the church' had most definitely broken down. The eighteenth century legacy of episcopal rule meant that bishops were often remote within and frequently absent from their dioceses and, all these things taken together, the true nature of a properly functioning ecclesial community had been seriously undermined. The ministers of the Episcopal chapels had encouraged their lay members to work independently in founding missionary and evangelical societies (not always under episcopal patronage). This outlook also assisted those societies that had been responsible for the proselytising activities of the Protestant crusade and the 'Second Reformation' campaign of the 1840s, though here with the enthusiasm of the then archbishop of Tuam, Dr Le Poer Trench. It also was aided by the extraordinary events of the 1859 revival in Ulster. This revival had made a particular impact on the faith of all classes of people. Too often it has been seen simply as an event happening among the less educated sections of the population, but the 'gentry' too were affected – even if they did not usually succumb to the more extreme side effects such as barking and mooing like dogs and cows when caught up in the fervour. Thus both proprietary chapel and revival gave to many members of the laity such an identity and forcefulness in public speaking and writing in matters of theological controversy that any deference to the learning of the clergy, even of the bishops, was becoming a thing of the past.[40] Added to this, when disestablishment happened the financial maintenance of the Church naturally fell to its lay membership and the sense of lay authority was thus even further increased.

When the archbishops summoned the two provincial Convocations of clergy to meet on 14 September 1870 it soon became clear that in any new governmental structure members of the laity would inevitably have to be given a very full voice – even in matters of doctrine. As a protection again hasty decisions it was decided that there should be 'voting by orders' and that, for certain items, a majority of all three houses would be required rather than a simple majority of all present.

40 See the R.C.B. '1859 Revival' collection of pamphlets.

A lay conference, also summoned by the archbishops, was called for 12 October 1869 with 417 representatives attending. This in itself was a victory for moderation since some of the laity had wished for lay leaders to be the convenors of the parliament of the disestablished church. Discussion ranged on whether or not the bishops should be permitted to sit as a separate house, or be considered a part of the clergy. Wiser counsels prevailed and this meeting of the laity accepted that it should be the role of the archbishops to be the convenors of future church assemblies. A ratio of two lay to one cleric was insisted upon for membership but even Archbishop Trench accepted that voting by orders would ensure that the preponderance of laity over clergy would not be a matter of substance. The final request of the lay conference was that two clerics and two laymen from each diocese would meet with the bishops to draft a constitution to be submitted to a Church Convention.

This Convention of bishops, clergy and laity was summoned to meet in February 1870. It was becoming clear that a deep tension was developing between the laity and some of the clergy on one side and the bishops and some of the clergy on the other side as to where final authority would lie. The draft constitution had provided, as desired by the national synod, that a total right of veto be given to the bishops, in that no motion could be deemed passed unless a majority of the bishops voted in favour. This, together with the right of the bishops to vote as a separate house, secured the reluctant consent of the bishops though Archbishop Trench feared as inevitable the opening up of the most solemn truths of theology for discussion by unlearned and uncultured county squires.[41] The country squires, however, were also becoming resentful and now began to speak of 'the bishops' veto', as if an episcopal right to vote would be some despotic blunt instrument rather than a democratic right exercised in exactly the same way as votes by orders of the clergy and laity. One midlands landlord, F.G. Bloomfield, moved an amendment that the bishops' veto be overturned simply by the houses of clergy and laity re-passing any motion vetoed by the bishops. After a stormy and heated debate on 25 February the right of (but not the necessity for) the bishops to vote if they so wished was affirmed but with some restrictions. It was left to the duke of Abercorn, a moderate evangelical, one of Ireland's largest landowners and twice lord lieutenant of Ireland, to use his diplomatic skills to help resolve the crisis. He proposed that the bishops should require a two-thirds majority among themselves to sustain a veto beyond one year – in effect no less than a majority of eight out of the then eleven members. Also, if over two sessions of the synod an episcopal vote prevented a measure from passing, the bishops were required to give their reasons in writing. Such a measure was offensive (and may by some have been intended to be offensive) to the nature of authority in an episcopal

41 *Richard Chenevix Trench: letters and memorials* (2 vols, London, 1888) ii, p. 104.

Church. For the time being, however, expediency had won but a power struggle was becoming inevitable. Where the actual battleground would be was at first not clear. One, in the sphere of worship, was quickly found.

Personal holiness in preparing for Holy Communion became the first potential cause of rupture in the unity of the post-disestablishment Church of Ireland. In March 1870 what would now be regarded as a harmless manual of preparation for confirmation was given to a servant girl in St Stephen's parish, Dublin. Her master, a Mr Maberly, an extreme Protestant and no admirer of Archbishop Trench, implied that it recommended confession to a priest. He is often accused of using the affair as an excuse to entrap the archbishop into condemning both the clergyman (Dr L.B. Weldon) and the book. Archbishop Trench declined to do either – despite receiving a protest signed by 420 of the clergy, 529 noble and professional men and some 3,000 registered vestrymen. His final response was to indicate that he would resign the archbishopric rather than narrow the teaching of the prayer book or the limits of legitimate theological belief. Dr Weldon subsequently became curate assistant of St Bartholomew's and a noted preacher but never received parochial preferment in the Church of Ireland. Trench's sympathies were obviously with him for, while still curate-assistant in St Bartholomew's, he made him a canon of Christ Church from 1882 to 1887, the year he received his preferment to a parish in the diocese of Salisbury.[42] The clerical objectors, nearly 25 per cent of the total clergy, is an indication of the massive swing away from the Church of Ireland's older Caroline tradition that had happened with the Evangelical Revival. The argument burned fiercely throughout the summer of 1870. For the first time the possibility of Prayer Book revision was now being accepted even by many who did not wish for it.

William Brooke, Master of the Rolls represented an evangelical tradition that propagated what was in effect a Reformation fundamentalism.[43] Initially he had opposed any suggestions for revision. Now between the first and second meetings of the Convention he began to have a change of mind and circulated a 'memorial' intended for a wide readership. It professed a desire that there should be no alteration in the comprehensive nature of the church but argued that its theological basis was never intended to be wide enough to embrace error. If the Book of Common Prayer therefore seemed to give even small support to error then a committee ought to be appointed to consider the matter and to make it report to the general synod of 1871. Brooke's 'memorial' attracted over 3,000 signatures representing a broad and influential band of churchmanship from all over Ireland; most of them people uninfluenced by membership of the Dublin proprietary chapels.

42 H.E. Patten, *Fifty years of disestablishment* (Dublin, 1922), pp 30–1. Weldon was later honoured by being made Donnellan Lecturer in T.C.D. for the years 1894–5.   43 R.L. Clarke, 'The distestablishment revision of the Irish Book of Common Prayer' (Ph.D. thesis,

The Convention met again on 18 October. On 27 October, whilst regretting an intervention from the chairman of the Protestant Defence Association, Lord James Butler,[44] that the Prayer Book contained 'rubbishy nonsense', the Convention nonetheless accepted the Brooke Memorial to set up a committee which would report to the first general synod in 1871. The bishops declined to be involved in any way in its proceedings. Twenty-six members were elected, thirteen each of the clergy and the laity. Among the laity Dublin lawyers and country landowners predominated, the latter being rather unkindly dismissed by Bishop Alexander with the comment that they had more knowledge of practical agriculture than of theology. Archbishop Trench's biographer, perhaps even more unfairly, described it as containing few names known much beyond the bounds of their own parishes.[45] However, he astutely pointed out[46] that a body about to cease to exist (the Convention) should appoint a committee to report to a body (general synod) that did not yet exist and which itself therefore was not even in a position to seek the presentation of such a report was not just an absurdity but a legal impossibility. All such arguments, however, were swept away in the whirlwind and tempest that had been raised throughout the country by Archbishop Trench's refusal to condemn either Dr Weldon or the doctrine that both plainly believed to be consistent with teaching of the Book of Common Prayer. The walls of Dublin were covered in graffiti referring to 'Puseyite Trench' in language more often reserved for the papacy. The battle lines had been set months before the new general synod was even due to meet.

If it has sometimes proved difficult in this essay to ascertain accurately the theological views of the laity before the mid-nineteenth century the same cannot be said of 1870 and the years following. The work of the Convention and then of new general synod gave both time and opportunity for lay members to express their views publicly and for the media to record them in detail for posterity. Both bodies were overwhelmingly evangelical, though far from the evangelicalism of a Wilberforce or a Wesley. Disestablishment evangelicalism was more firmly based on *differences* that could be emphasised between the Church of Ireland and contemporary Catholicism.

Despite the affection professed on all sides for the Book of Common Prayer the Maberly affair was still too fresh in members' minds when the first General Synod met. Debate on the Brooke proposals began on 20 April 1871 though from the outset it was clear that they were not going to have an easy passage. Everything centred on sacramental liturgy: presence, penance and practice, on which the lay representatives had strong, if not always informed, views. On presence the Brooke report would have committed the Church to a doctrine of receptionism; on absolution the recommendations were to omit reference to

T.C.D., 1989.)   **44** A landlord noted more for his exuberant language than for any knowledge of theology.   **45** *Richard Chenevix Trench*, ii, p. 138.   **46** *Richard Chenevix Trench*, ii, p. 137.

absolution from the ordinal and from the ministry to the sick to ensure that it was the penitent rather than the priest who would decide on how conscience should be comforted; ceremonial practice was an area without the niceties of theology and so the anti-ritual canons were more easily devised. Richard Travers Smith, vicar of St Bartholomew's, Dublin, believed that doctrinal changes were about to be made which would compromise the Church's position as a part of catholic Christendom. Far from leading the Irish church into popery, his influence was rather to preserve her heritage. The bishop of Ely, Edward Harold Browne, wrote to him in 1872:

> God grant that the Church of Ireland may take your wise warnings and those of other wise men. If once she settles down into a mere Calvinist sect, she will have given the Church of Rome far more than that Church could have dreamed of in her brightest dreams of conquest in Ireland.[47]

Another writer described Smith as:

> ... a sound churchman and a really learned theologian, though not a brilliant speaker, who by sheer weight of superior knowledge, earnestness, and absolute sincerity claimed and won the attention and respect of those who were most opposed to what they considered his high church proclivities.[48]

As was expected, the work of the Convention and then of the new general synod gave both time and opportunity for lay members to express their views publicly and for the media to record them in detail for posterity. The work of the Master of the Rolls, William Brooke, has already been noted but his role following his report was more that of a figurehead. Dublin lawyers were prominent and their valiant work did much to save the inclusiveness of the disestablished church. Sir Joseph Napier was one such. His background was that of trustee chapel, but his views were moderate, based on legal considerations, and it was these he used to oppose alterations to the ordinal that might have strained inter-Anglican relations. Other members of the laity whose views helped moderate difficult situations included Judges Longfield, Warren and Ball, the earl of Courtown and the duke of Abercorn. The ultra-revisionist party included Lord James Butler, Colonel ffolliott and Colonel Edward James Saunderson.

In each of the areas of presence, penance and practice none was more vociferous than the County Cavan landlord Edward Saunderson. Though not involved at the beginning of the revision movement, Saunderson quickly

---

47 Quoted in Kenneth Milne, *St Bartholomew's: a history of the Dublin parish* (Dublin, 1963), p. 19.   48 William Sherlock, *The story of the revision of the Irish Prayer Book* (Dublin, 1910).

established himself as the most accomplished orator among the laymen, with ffolliott, Bloomfield and Butler normally serving as his lieutenants in debate. He was also unusual among the laity in that he *initiated* a number of the revision proposals.[49]

The Saunderson[50] family fortune and estates were founded by Alexander Sanderson in 1618, first in County Tyrone but would later be more securely built on the sequestration of the O'Reilly lands in County Cavan on the Fermanagh border. The estate provided a power-base for the family's near three-century long parliamentary representation. It was helped by an alliance with the major County Cavan landlords, the Maxwells (the lords Farnham), and in 1826 by the marriage of Alexander Saunderson with Sarah, a niece of the fifth Lord Farnham. This not only guaranteed the Saunderson family a parliamentary voice but more importantly determined its religious as well as its political outlook. By the early nineteenth century the Farnham family, like the earls of Roden, had become evangelicals of the pietistic type, rabidly anti-Catholic, sponsoring the 'Second Reformation' and encouraging and giving shelter to converts.

Edward Saunderson was born on 1 October 1837 at Castle Saunderson on the Cavan-Fermanagh border[51] but spent his formative years in France where ironically, considering the family's evangelicalism and his own later outlook, he was often to be educated by Jesuits. His schooling, however, though haphazard was excellent, concentrating on languages in a way that would make him a natural orator. In 1865 he married Helena de Moleyns, a daughter of Lord Ventry. They were deeply devoted to each other, finding spiritual consolation in a shared evangelical faith that was openly lived and proclaimed and the small chapel in the grounds of Castle Saunderson became a place where he preached frequently and persuasively. His relations with the Catholic clergy and laity of County Cavan, as indeed his care for the well being of his Catholic tenants, were often in marked contrast to the recognised bigotry of the Farnhams. In this early period Saunderson felt no need to be a part of the Orange Order. Rather, he showed sensitivity towards the mid-nineteenth century need for new Catholic places of worship throughout Ireland and in his own area freely provided land for church-building projects.

After Church disestablishment he became a member of the Kilmore diocesan synod and also of the newly established general synod, a body that helped him develop his oratorical skills and indeed enabled him to build up political connections that would prove of value in later years. Like many a later evangelical

---

49 Clarke, 'Disestablishment revision', p. 283.   50 The family name began as the familiar Sanderson, not becoming Saunderson until a mid-eighteenth century unsuccessful attempt to lay claim to a dormant peerage. Alvin Jackson, *Colonel Edward Saunderson* (Oxford, 1994), p. 11n.   51 A house and estate now derelict but soon to become a centre for both branches of the Irish boy scouts.

preacher Saunderson, using rhetorical devices, effectively conveyed a simple message using humour and passion. In general synod he became the principal lay figure in the Prayer Book revision debates and exercised a charismatic leadership. He was frequently intolerant of painstaking negotiation and was happiest as an unrestrained and swashbuckling advocate of his own principles. Often carried away by his own oratory, he could be offensive to members of other churches, even when seeking only to apply his opinions exclusively to the Church of Ireland. Condemning any doctrine of Real Presence in the Eucharist at a synod meeting in April 1873 he caused great offence with a rhetorical question:

> Was it possible that in the nineteenth century they were to believe that a priest could turn a piece of bread into the body of Christ, and could they say to those who knelt before him, 'Here is your God – eat Him'?[52]

More than any other speech this was the one that exposed the actual thinness of any true ecumenism towards his Catholic neighbours. It was probably this speech more than any that probably brought about his electoral defeat at the hands of a Home Ruler in 1874. This was a personal humiliation that also marked the beginning of moves towards membership of the previously ignored Orange Order. Saunderson, whose political ideal had previously been a cross–sectarian loyalism to the union, was now seen, when it became politically expedient, to pander to Protestant exclusivism, becoming one of the chief architects of a type of loyalism that still survives. Colonel Edward Saunderson was a militia officer who never saw war service and one whose skirmishing was confined to debates in the synod hall in Dublin and the houses of parliament in London. Despite his hard line faith and politics he was neither ruthless nor reckless but he did help fashion a religious and political landscape that, in both instances, is still recognisable in modern Ireland.

VII

If the evangelicals were lay-led, the Tractarians were essentially clerical and hierarchical, which may have been one of the reasons why the movement never gained a strong following among the Irish laity. In Dublin, apart from four churches,[53] it was looked upon with great suspicion so that the merest liturgical change was felt to be incipient Romanism. Outside Dublin the faith and practice

---

52 Quoted in Jackson, *Colonel Edward Saunderson*, p. 41.   **53** St Bartholomew's, St Bride's (demolished) and Grangegorman All Saints'. Sandymount St John was not to become a part of the group until the early twentieth century.

of the Tractarians were really unknown but the suspicion nonetheless existed that following their teaching would lead people into the arms of the Catholic Church. None of the lay members of the new general synod could ever have been classed as Tractarian in belief. A devout layman influenced by Tractarianism, however, Henry Roe, a Dublin distiller, would be the benefactor who would build the synod a meeting hall where his most cherished work, the 1871–8 restoration of Christ Church cathedral, would be excoriated.

The principal and original aim of the Tractarians had been to promote the practice and the piety of the Book of Common Prayer and especially to encourage frequent reception of Holy Communion after due preparation. Ceremonial was at the very bottom of their list.[54] Yet not even Christ Church cathedral, Dublin, otherwise so much influenced by the Caroline return to the practice of the Elizabethan settlement and its liturgical layout, seems to have celebrated the Eucharist more than once a month and at the festivals, even up to the early nineteenth century.[55] Jonathan Swift had perhaps been more aware of traditional Anglicanism when in the 1740s he introduced a weekly early celebration at Saint Patrick's cathedral.[56] Devout preparation but infrequent reception was to remain the practice among the Church of Ireland laity until the middle years of the twentieth century. More frequent reception was regarded as definitely high church. Three societies were to work for more frequent communion: The 'Irish Guild of Witness', founded by Rosamund Stephen in 1918,[57] the English 'Parish and People'[58] movement through its Irish branch and 'Cumann Gaelach na hEaglaise' which promoted services in the Irish language. What began to be called a parish communion, at the hour of the main morning service, became more common. Manuals of preparation for devout reception were regularly published. Yet except for a small number of Dublin or Belfast churches it was rare until recent years to find the Eucharist as the principal service on more than one Sunday in the month.[59] A daily Eucharist, as was celebrated in St Bartholomew's church, Dublin for more than one hundred years, was so unusual as to be regarded with deep suspicion.[60]

---

54 Newman in his Anglican days, up to 1845, is said never celebrated the Eucharist other than at the north end of the altar and wearing scarf and hood.   55 Milne (ed.), *Christ Church cathedral Dublin*, pp 197–8.   56 Phillips, (ed.), *History of the Church of Ireland*, iii, p. 191.   57 Her private library formed the nucleus of the R.C.B. Library and the Guild's archives are also there.   58 P.J. Jagger, *A history of the Parish and People movement* (Leighton Buzzard, 1978).   59 In 2002 a Eucharist as the principal service of each Sunday is celebrated only in the cathedrals of Belfast, Cork, Dublin Christ Church and in a handful of churches in major conurbations.   60 In 2002 a daily Eucharist is maintained only in the two Dublin cathedrals, in one Dublin parish church and one in Belfast (all such services being of recent vintage).

VIII

In the twentieth century there has been a significant renewal of spiritual devotion among members of the Church of Ireland. Yet, apart from the writings of three of the clergy, George Otto Simms (archbishop of Armagh until 1980), Michael Lloyd Ferrar (a descendent of the Ferrars of Little Gidding and warden of the Divinity Hostel in Dublin until his death) and Cosslett Quin, much of whose writing was in the Irish language, little of this spiritual renewal has come from the pen of Irish authors. A layman who was Irish by birth, Belfast-born and probably the most popular author of the century, must be C.S. Lewis whose 1940s wartime talks on radio were widely followed and whose books are still in demand. For him Christian faith was always linked with the call to discipline and prayer. None of them has had any obvious successor in the present day Church of Ireland and it is to the other Anglican Churches of these islands that Irish Anglicans have to look for devotional material. One book widely read was Archbishop William Temple's *Readings in St John's Gospel*,[61] which is a devotional rather than intellectual commentary. Evelyn Underhill was of decisive importance in making known the classical texts of Christian mysticism.[62] Her work has encouraged an interest in mystics of previous centuries, such as the Lady Julian of Norwich. Contemporary writers such as Rowan Williams and Andrew Louth have written scholarly books that are practical as well as academic. The poetry of T.S. Eliot and R.S. Thomas has gained a wide audience, while two archbishops of Canterbury – Ramsey and Coggan – have bridged the gulf between Biblical theology and sound spirituality. The Anglican tradition has also shown itself to be more open to the spirituality of other traditions than at any previous period. Remarkably a kind of underground ecumenism in spirituality helped bring the Churches more closely together. In the final years of the twentieth century Anglican spirituality passed through an identity crisis questioning the very efficacy of prayer. Notable among those who have helped us work through this period were Alan Ecclestone, W.H. Vanstone and H.A. Williams, CR. They reminded us that the important thing is that we do not grow in prayer by reading books but only by praying and loving. To learn in any other way is to deceive ourselves. We know God through his communicating of himself to us. This is the pathway of spirituality, the way of prayer and of all worship. Great theologians such as Augustine and Anselm slip naturally from speaking *about* God to speaking *with* him. There is no awkwardness in the transition. Theology needs spiritual devotion and devotion requires sound theology: without a combination of both there lurks the danger of both superstition and fanaticsm.

---

61 London, 1939.   **62** E. Underhill, *Mysticism* (London, 1911) and *Worship* (London, 1935).

If theology is important so too is literary formation. The quality of the prose and the poetic styles of devotional writers since the Reformation have been enormously influential in the forming of the English language as well as in providing food for thought. Few have ever better mastered prose and poetry than Taylor or Traherne. Yet, like the others, they were not trained in some intellectual hothouse as a race apart. They went to school and to university with those whose lives would be devoted to commerce and the professions. It was this that, perhaps unlike the present system of theological colleges, united the Anglican priest and devotional writer so firmly into the contemporary scene. It was never difficult for writers like Keble and Mrs Alexander to live in close relation to people of all classes around them and to speak to their condition. They had a sympathy and an understanding towards the devotional needs and problems of ordinary people that could never have been obtained in any other way. The aim of the best Anglican writers of every tradition was to make people think deeply and sincerely about God and about themselves. They tried to hold a balance between reason and emotion that was often lost in the more extreme polarised ends of the Anglican spectrum.

The haven that Anglican devotion has always found in both Bible and Prayer Book has been of immense importance. It has denied the possibility of any one aspect of religion being stressed to the neglect of another. The call to justice has been as incisive as the call to prayer. The Reformation aimed at putting a copy of the Bible into every house and it was to the Bible that Anglican writers turned for a determining of doctrine, yet without the more extreme fundamentalist approach that would treat the text as a magical inerrant formula discovered by an individual's private judgement. The Prayer Book worked towards the same end. It was not intended as a handbook of offices for the clergy but a basis of those family virtues and prayers that until comparatively recent times were a regular feature of religious households. Old-fashioned churchmen and women were not keen on complicated spiritual direction. They learned a sense of duty and of personal responsibility that helped them lead a moral and upright life and be a wholesome influence in the community. The decline of corporate family prayer, reading and hymn singing began with the advent of radio in the 1920s and was accelerated by television in the 1950s. By the 1960s Protestant family prayers were so unusual that the writer, accustomed to radio and television but not to family prayers, was so taken by surprise by the communal reading of the psalms during his visit to his friend's country home.

11

'Our people': the Church of Ireland and the culture of community in Dublin since Disestablishment

Martin Maguire

A group of two hundred young men and women of Clontarf parish, attending a talk in 1957 on mixed marriages, were warned that 'once we begin to get involved in the question of a mixed marriage, we are immediately dealing with the Roman church's standards, which are very different from, and lower, than our own; and as we enter into arguments and negotiations we must come down to the lower standard so losing the 'Protestant Integrity' which is our birthright'.[1] The answer, the young adults were advised, was to make your friends exclusively amongst 'our people and within the church community'.[2] This essay explores the various meanings and cultural forms which attached to 'our people' and 'community' within the Church of Ireland.

The Church of Ireland community enjoyed an assured sense of its own superiority, derived in part from the evangelical tradition which formed a central part of its Protestantism and in part from its success in surviving disestablishment and creating an effective structure for a self-governing community of laity and clergy.[3] It was also a community which took its religion seriously. For most people religious identity is less a matter of precise beliefs than one of different social practices. What was most distinctive about the Church of Ireland community was its very solemn approach to Sunday, when mornings were spent at a service of worship of prayer more often than Eucharist, and afternoons at gospel halls and Sunday school. In the early years of the twentieth-century Dublin had eight gospel halls the most popular of which was the Merrion Hall of the Plymouth Brethren, its central pulpit facing the tiered galleries, seating a congregation of over two thousand.[4] The Merrion Hall Sunday afternoon drew in a predominantly Church of Ireland congregation

---

1 *Clontarf Parish Magazine*, March 1957. 2 Ibid. 3 Alvin Jackson, *Ireland 1798–1998* (Oxford, 1999), pp 220–1. 4 Peter Costello, *Dublin churches* (1989), pp 110, 226.

attracted by the Plymouth Brethren emphasis on an essentially pessimistic though inspirational preaching of the gospel. More than any arcane theological dispute it was the sombre Church of Ireland Sunday, shunning the frivolities of sports and picture-houses, which marked it out as a distinct, and more serious, community. Whereas issues of morality and authority have fuelled divisions within Catholicism, it is liturgical revision that has fuelled most controversy within the Church of Ireland.[5]

The self-confidence thus nurtured enabled the Church of Ireland to over-come the rapid erosion of its formal status in Ireland. After disestablishment removed its state under-pinning the Church of Ireland was sustained, as a community, not only by the formal structures of synodal government but also by the informal networks of charitable, social and cultural organisations. The Church of Ireland parishes in Dublin generated an array of political, social and religious organisations, societies and clubs. Many of those who were members of these various societies regarded some, or all, of them as agents of a divine will. However, in this essay they are framed in terms of an entirely human function and agency. Through an examination of these complex networks and their operation within the parishes of Dublin, this essay seeks to reconstruct the communal culture of the Church of Ireland; 'our people'; and the sense of concerted human lives which attaches to 'community'. The city has been chosen because it was there that life is most sociable and community most elaborate. In Dublin city voluntary organisations linked social classes, churches, neighbourhoods and workplaces in networks of often elaborate complexity. Also, the Church of Ireland, despite the cultivation of an image of eccentric rural gentility, was primarily an urbanised culture.[6]

Unlike Belfast, Dublin did not have recognisably Catholic or Protestant areas. A comparison of the Catholic and Protestant residents in each of Dublin city's twenty wards between 1891 and 1926 shows quite a high degree of similarity in the distribution of the two population groups. What Dublin did have however were recognisably middle class areas in the suburbs and working class areas in the inner city. The differences in the dispersal of the two population groups are the result of socio-economic rather than sectarian forces; middle class Protestants lived in middle class areas along with middle class Catholics. Working class Protestants lived in working-class areas with working -class Catholics. In Dublin a person's address would give no clue to religion but could reveal socio-economic class.[7] In order to focus in on the functioning of these community organisations at the local level several of the Dublin parishes are considered in detail, with occasionally reference to other parishes. These

5 See Kenneth Milne's essay above.   6 *Population (Ireland). Census of Ireland, 1911*, H.C. 1912–13, cxiv. Report, pp xlvi, l.   7 Martin Maguire,'A socio-economic analysis of the Dublin protestant working class 1870–1926' in *Irish Economic and Social History* xx (1993),

parishes are St Jude's in Inchicore, a skilled working-class suburb in Kilmainham
to the south of the city; St Matthew's in Irishtown in the Pembroke township,
a mix of working class and middle class; St George's in the north inner city,
formerly well-off middle class but by the end of the nineteenth century a centre
of working-class poverty and decline; St Kevin's in the south inner city, a
strongly low-church parish with again a mix of working and middle class; and
the parish of St John the Baptist in Clontarf in the middle-class northern
suburbs. Thus the contrast is between poorer working-class parishes and the
better-off middle-class parishes. Clontarf was the only one of these parishes to
experience growth in the hundred years after disestablishment. Between the
census of 1901 and the census of 1926 the Church of Ireland population of
Clontarf virtually doubled from 1,187 persons to 2,024 persons.[8] By 1928 the
parish facilities were barely coping with the pressure of the rising parish
population.[9] By contrast the inner city parishes had to cope with a decline in the
number of their members, particularly the better-off. This reflects the
migration of the middle classes to the outer suburbs. In 1891 St Michan's
'formerly a rich parish' had withered into a parish of the 'struggling poor'
Protestants.[10] In 1899 the parish of St Matthew in Irishtown was suffering the
drain of its middle class parishioners to Rathmines, leading to recurring
problems of poor collections.[11]

Where Church of Ireland parishes were virtually all self-governing republics
in their finances the flight to the suburbs of the middle classes undermined the
ability of the inner city parishes to sustain the communal organisations which
were vital to their survival. This is reflected in the quality of the ubiquitous
parish magazine. Clontarf parish magazine was a substantial, quality production
with illustrations, on good paper, printed in letterpress which, even in the
shortages of the 'Emergency', was maintained as a monthly issue. In the poorer
parishes, like St James's or St Matthew's, the magazine were far less substantial,
often only one or two pages, which were bulked out by being inserted into
church or missionary magazines such as *Home Words*, a Church of England
magazine featuring daring deeds by plucky missionaries in exotic corners of the
Empire. During the early 1920s St Matthew's parish magazine was actually
hand-written and reproduced on a rotary duplicator. These magazines were the
messengers to the community, recording not only the cycle of the church year
and the work of the parish organisations, but also the achievements of parish
children in exams, prize winners in Sunday school, the movement in and out of

Table 2.   8 *Census of Ireland, 1901, part 1, area, houses, population ... vol.1 province of
Leinster, No. 2 county of Dublin*, No. 2a city of Dublin, table xxix; *Saorstát Éireann, census of
population 1926* vol.ii Part 1–religion, table 12.   9 *Clontarf Parish Magazine*, May 1928.
10 Revd. Robert Walsh, *The ancient church of parish of St Michan, a sermon preached ...
Sunday May 10th 1891* (Dublin, 1891).   11 *St Matthew's Parish Magazine*, Nov. 1899.

the district of the parishioners, weddings and births and funerals, and detailed listing of the parish contributors to parochial funds.

As a political community the Church of Ireland in Dublin was Conservative and Unionist. However Dublin Conservatism was not an exclusively middle and upper class phenomenon. After changes in the electoral law increased the numbers of those qualified to vote, and also restricted the opportunities for corrupt practices, Dublin Conservatives organised, in 1883, the City and County of Dublin Conservative Workingmen's Club to mobilise the Protestant working class of the city. The Dublin Protestant working class, Church of Ireland for the most part, were 'rough' rather than 'respectable' both in their politics and in their recreation. The clubhouse in York Street off St Stephen's Green was the scene of a spectacular riot in the election campaign of November 1885. In preparation for election night the club had been draped in Union flags and bunting. As a crowd of nationalists besieged the club, demanding the lowering of the flag, the members within responded with a hail of bricks, bottles and, ultimately, gunfire. Time and again the club membership showed that it preferred the excitement of mobilising the Protestant community to the drab tedium of electoral canvassing. Though the club did have as its object the 'provision of rational recreation' for the Protestant working class, for the membership leisure meant beer and billiards. Gambling was a passion that led to frequent disorder and fighting. However this working-class club did see itself primarily in terms of creed rather than class, identifying with a wider Protestant community which embraced the Orange Order, the Y.M.C.A., the Church of Ireland, and the various political organisations of Conservatism (always Conservatism and not Unionism, interestingly). The club refused membership to Catholics and remained suspicious of any contact with Catholic working-men's clubs. At the core of its sense of the political community to which it belonged was not conservatism but a militant and uncompromising assertion of Protestantism, especially an evangelical and low-church Protestantism.[12] Hence members willingly turned from heckling nationalists in the ward elections to Dublin corporation to barracking 'Ritualists' in All Saints church, Grangegorman; in St Bartholomew's, Ballsbridge; or the notorious Anglo-Catholic Fletcher le Fanu of St John's, Sandymount.[13]

Partition was a severe challenge to the concept of who exactly were, within the Irish Protestant community, 'our people'. Although the creation of the Ulster Unionist Council in 1905 had already effectively partitioned Unionism, Dublin saw itself as the organisational and cultural centre of the Church of

---

12 John Crawford, *St Catherine's parish Dublin 1840–1900: portrait of a Church of Ireland community*. (Dublin, 1996), pp 49–50.   13 On the history of the Conservative Workingmen's Club see Martin Maguire, 'The organisation and activism of Dublin's Protestant working class, 1883–1935' in *I.H.S.* xxix (1994–5), pp 65–87.

Ireland political community.[14] The City and County Conservative Club in Dawson Street, the Dublin Constitutional Club and the City of Dublin Unionist Registration Association in Leinster Street, and the Unionist Association in Grafton Street all reflected a rich and continuing tradition of political organisation and activism.[15] Ulster Covenant day and the attitude of Ulster loyalists to their fellow Protestants in the rest of Ireland had led to a very heated debate in the Sandymount and Irishtown Christian Association.[16] That exclusion from home rule was not a tactic by the Ulster Unionists but was in fact their objective was finally brought home at a Dublin loyalist rally in November 1913 when, in speech after speech, Bonar Law, Carson and the other leaders of Ulster Unionism emphasised that Ulster would go it alone. Momentarily cowed by the enraged response of the Dublin loyalists (the Ulster leaders were reportedly drenched in spittle as they left the hall) Carson merely repeated his meaningless assurances that Ulster would not sell out southern loyalists.[17] The Conservative Workingmen's Club were active supporters of the Southern Unionists Committee (reputedly the wild men of Dublin Unionism), formed during the Convention of 1918 in a final desperate bid to reaffirm the Union and prevent partition.[18]

The eclipse of the Church of Ireland as a political community in Dublin was not as total as Buckland suggests.[19] Even before the third Home Rule Bill Dublin Unionism had begun to re-invent itself as a middle class 'Municipal Reform Party', under which banner it had some success in the Dublin corporation elections but was especially successful in the suburban townships.[20] This pre-pared the ground for the re-emergence of ex-Unionists, after the establishment of the Irish Free State, as independents and Businessmen's Party T.D.s. Major Bryan Ricco Cooper was an independent T.D. for Dublin South from 1923 until his death in 1930. This same constituency also returned J.P. Good (formerly the Unionist M.P. for Rathmines) as the Businessmen's party T.D. from 1923 to 1937. In the senate the ex-Unionists formed an independent group under the leadership of Senator Jameson.[21] The Businessmen's Party was never electorally significant. But it was an important indication of the political development of the Church of Ireland community. Most members of the Businessmen's Party

14 Jackson, *Ireland 1798–1998*, p. 231.   15 R.B. McDowell, *Crisis and decline the fate of the southern Unionists* (Dublin, 1997), p. 33.   16 *St Matthew's Parish Magazine*, Nov. 1912. 17 *Dublin Daily Express*, 29 Nov. 1913; Lennox Robinson, *Bryan Cooper* (London, 1931), pp 83–5.   18 Martin Maguire, 'The Dublin Protestant working class, 1870–1932: economy, society, politics' (M.A. thesis, University College, Dublin, 1990), pp 187–8.   19 Patrick Buckland, *Irish Unionism 1: the Anglo-Irish and the new Ireland, 1885–1922* (Dublin, 1972) p. 272.   20 Maguire, 'The Dublin Protestant working class, 1870–1932', pp 158–76.   21 Brian M. Walker (ed.) *Parliamentary election results in Ireland, 1918–92* (Dublin, 1992) pp 110, 116, 120; Donal O'Sullivan, *The Irish Free State and its senate: a study in contemporary politics* (London, 1940), pp 428–9, 514–15.

ended up in the Fine Gael party. The Dockrells became a political dynasty within Dublin, representing various south city consitituencies from 1918 through to 1977 and moving from Unionism via the Businessmen's Party to Fine Gael. Not all Protestants were Fine Gael supporters and Fianna Fáil: the Republican Party had its attractions. The emphasis that Fianna Fáil gave to nurturing indigenous manufacturers through protectionism certainly won it some supporters in the commercial and business world and amongst the working class Protestants. In Dun Laoghaire-Rathdown consituency Lionel Booth was the Fianna Fáil candidate and T.D. from 1954 to 1969. Booth's background lay in motorcar assembly, one of the protected industries. Another Protestant candidate run by Fianna Fáil in the same constituency was Neville Keery who later went on to serve in the European commission. Fianna Fáil may have calculated that running Protestant candidates would undermine Protestant support for the Fine Gael candidates, the Protestant Percy Dockrell and the conservative and pious Catholic Liam Cosgrave.

This evolution of the Dublin's Protestant political community from Unionism to a non-sectarian middle class 'value for money and sound business principles' political culture underlines the genius of the middle class for compromise and, in the context of Dublin's Church of Ireland community, the fact that the period of the war of independence was not one of overwhelming crisis. From 1920 a curfew curtailed social activity whilst being Protestant and loyal was little protection in the escalating war of terror and counter-terror. The meeting of the St Matthew's registered vestry men in April 1921 ended abruptly at 7.45 p.m. as 'all hurried home being urged forward along the road by fear of the Black and Tans'.[22] With the truce and treaty normal life returned. St Matthew's parish magazine featured a witty article (with a hint of bravado perhaps) on which public building of the city would be most appropriate for the Free State parliament.[23] Across the city in Clontarf the early summer months of 1922, as civil war erupted, were spent in planning the parish fete and the Church Association outing to the Featherbed mountains.[24] Holy Trinity Church Rathmines announced proudly in 1924 that it was 'free of debt and encumbrances, pulsing with parochial life and organised in every detail'.[25] The Conservative Workingmen's Club, rapidly shedding its working class name and identity, spent 1922 on improving its facilities and amusements in order to make the premises more congenial to wives and 'our lady friends'. The club remained an exclusively Protestant establishment, though less fervently evangelical, and as it declined into a middle class club became social rather than political in its activity.[26] Though still conservative in their politics the Church of Ireland could

22 *St Matthew's Parish Magazine*, April 1921.   23 *St Matthew's Parish Magazine*, Feb. 1922.
24 *Clontarf Parish Magazine*, June 1922.   25 Revd E.C. Hodges, *Holy Trinity Church Rathmines centenary booklet, 1828–1928* (1928), pp 23–4.   26 Maguire, 'Organisation and

be proud of the role 'our people' played in the state. That the first president of Ireland, Douglas Hyde, should be Church of Ireland was regarded with a quiet pride even if many were less than happy with the new state.

In 1887 it was estimated that were four thousand Orangemen in Dublin, organised in ten lodges.[27] In 1911, despite the presence of the Grand Lodge and about seventeen lodges, including the elite Trinity College Dublin lodge, Orangeism was inert. The yearly submission of the same figure for the affiliation fees of the Dublin Orange Order lodges (about the same as the Derry city lodges) suggest a stagnant membership. The same grand officers are returned, the same Dublin Church of Ireland parish clergy are listed as grand Chaplains. Political activity was fitful and desultory. In 1904 an attempt by the Dublin city lodges to organise a political committee to work the voter register and consolidate the Orange vote never got off the ground.[28] Though politically impotent Orangeism survived in Dublin after independence, perhaps as social and welfare centres. The Grand Orange Lodge had already withdrawn northwards, consolidating its political power within the Ulster Unionist Council, and also reinforcing the Dublin view that Orangeism was an 'Ulster' rather than an all-Ireland Protestant movement. In the Irishtown area the Loyal Orange Lodge 566 and the Royal Black Perceptory lodges 55 and 980 were still meeting in 1930.[29]

As might be expected the main social organisation of liberal middle class (male) Protestant opinion, the Grand Lodge of Free and Accepted Masons of Ireland, continued to thrive. Despite the political presence of the leading Freemasons J.H.M. Campbell Lord Glenavy, chairman of the Senate, and Maurice Dockrell in the Dáil, it could no longer expect the easy access to political power that it had in the years of the British regime, when it succeeded in amending the third home rule bill to prevent any national administration acting against Freemasonry.[30] In the years 1919 to 1923 there was an unprecedented surge in the number of new members and new lodges being formed, shades perhaps of hatches being battened down. Despite the occupation of the Grand Lodge by republicans during the civil war the Freemasons could note in the 1923 report on the 'great improvement in the state of things in the last year'. The bi-centenary year of 1925 was celebrated by a service in St Patrick's cathedral attended by three thousand Freemasons, and addressed by D'Arcy, lord primate of All-Ireland. By now the main worry was not the authorities in

---

activism of Dublin's Protestant working class', p. 85.   **27** *Dublin Daily Express*, 14 Nov. 1887. 28 Orange Lodge of Ireland, general half-yearly meetings, 1901–1911. N.L.I., IR363g17. **29** *St Matthew's Parish Magazine*, July 1930. Some records of the Dublin lodges and the Grand Lodge survive in the Grand Lodge Belfast but most are in P.R.O.N.I.. Though some scholars have been given access to the P.R.O.N.I. records they are, it seems, officially closed. Until these records are made freely available any conclusions about Dublin Orangeism can only be tentative.   **30** Grand Lodge of Free and Accepted Masons of Ireland, *Annual*

the Free State but rather an incipient partition of Freemasonry. The majority of Freemason lodges were now in Northern Ireland and they objected that the Board was 'too much a Dublin crowd'. There were also reports that the Antrim Freemasons, forgetful perhaps of which organisation they had joined, were staging public parades in their masonic regalia. The Board was reorganised, though their continued to be complaints that the northern members were poor contributors to Masonic charities based in Dublin, preferring to fund their own.[31]

Royal landmarks such as the death of Queen Victoria in 1901 or the coronation of Edward VII in 1902 prompted extravagant displays of loyalty in the Church of Ireland parishes in Dublin.[32] Though no doubt feeling betrayed by the British political establishment after 1922 the Church of Ireland community in the Dublin parishes continued to maintain an emotional link with the crown and empire. The Dublin Grand Lodge of the Freemasons sent a sympathetic telegram to Buckingham Palace during the king's illness of 1928 and in Clontarf all parish entertainments were cancelled 'on account of the dreadful gloom everywhere felt on the death of His Majesty King George V'.[33] The most powerful and emotional bond with Great Britain, and within the Church of Ireland community in Dublin, were memories of the First World War.[34] Parish organisations had responded with energy and enthusiasm to the war. Working parties had knitted furiously to provide soldiers with woollen socks, sick and convalescent soldiers had been visited and plied with cigarettes, boys' organisations became recruiting bases for the services.[35] Wednesdays, across Dublin, became a day of special service and intercession where the names of those serving from the parish were specially mentioned and prayed for.[36] In Clontarf the Bible and Literary Association devoted its meetings to military subjects; 'an infantry soldier in training', 'submarine and aircraft', 'the royal engineers'; and concerts of patriotic songs were held.[37] After the war Remembrance Day became one of the most solemn occasions in the year, one which strengthened the sense of being a special community and, despite national independence, maintained the close identity between the Church of Ireland and the community of the British Empire. Armistice Day, focused initially on the site of the former statue of King William of Orange on College Green, became a powerful demonstration of both the emotional intensity of the war experience and the survival of the Dublin loyal community. Early in 1919 the archbishop of Dublin

Report, 1912; *Parliamentary Debates*, 12 Dec. 1912.   31 Grand Lodge of Free and Accepted Masons of Ireland, *Annual Reports*, 1913–25.   32 *St Matthew's Parish Magazine*, Feb. 1901, August 1902.   33 Grand Lodge of Free and Accepted Masons of Ireland, minute book, 6 Dec. 1928; *Clontarf Parish Magazine*, Feb. 1936.   34 *Irish Times*, 5 Oct. 1990, 'Interview with Dr Donal Caird'.   35 *Clontarf Parish Magazine.*, Nov. 1914, May 1915.   36 *Clontarf Parish Magazine.*, 1914–18; *St Matthew's Parish Magazine*, 1914–18.   37 *Clontarf Parish Magazine*, Feb. 1915.

issued guidelines on war memorials for the parishes, suggesting that 'every parish ought to have its own parochial memorial, upon which should be inscribed the names in alphabetical order of all from the parish, whatever their rank or class, who died in battle in our defence'. He vigorously opposed the suggestion that the memorial should record the names of all those who served rather than those only who died.[38] Across the Dublin parishes plaques and cenotaphs were raised often at considerable expense. Clontarf parish spent £600 on a carved memorial cross situated in the church grounds, recording all those who died (to which were later added those who died in the Second World War); panelling the chancel in oak with again the names of the dead and a further plaque recording those who served and survived. As the smoke rose from the burning ruins of the Custom House the memorials were dedicated in a solemn ceremony by the archbishop.[39]

If, as seems to be the case, the numbers of the Irish war dead are based on the casualties of the Irish regiments then the participation of Irish Protestants in the war is greatly underestimated. A great many of these volunteers chose to enlist in British regiments, perhaps for family reasons. Where these memorials of the dead list the regiments to which they belonged then the potential for underestimation is apparent. The memorial in St Barnabas's in the North Docks lists twelve men of the parish, of which six only are listed as serving in Irish regiments.[40] The loss of a great many young men to a population which was already unstable was traumatic. The Conservative Workingmen's Club lost 180 members in the war.[41] In Clontarf parish 178 men enlisted of whom twenty-eight were killed. In Rathmines parish 500 men enlisted of whom sixty were killed. Throughout the 1920s Armistice Day was marked by solemn religious ceremonies, including the tolling of the church bells. In Irishtown laying a wreath at the war memorial became part of the ceremonials of the school year. In St George's parish church Remembrance Sunday, inaugurated by the synod in 1929 as the Sunday prior to November 11, brought together congregations of over one thousand. Gradually Remembrance Sunday took on a social as well religious aspect. The Conservative Club (it dropped 'Workingmen's' in 1927) marked the day by a special bar extension and extensive decorations of the British flag and red, white and blue bunting.[42]

Supporting the missions and missionaries acted as another important link between the Dublin Church of Ireland community and a wider world. There were a great many missionary societies active in the parishes; the Zenana

38 *Clontarf Parish Magazine.*, Jan, Feb. 1919.   39 *Clontarf Parish Magazine.*, Oct.1919, June 1921.   40 A.Garrett, *In ages past, the story of North Strand Church* (Dublin, 1985), p. 64. 41 Maguire, 'The Dublin Protestant working class, 1870–1932', p. 187.   42 Ibid., p. 190; *Clontarf Parish Magazine*, Nov. 1923–1929; *St Matthew's Parish Magazine*, July 1926, Nov. 1927; *St George's Parish Magazine*, Dec. 1939; Hodges, *Holy Trinity Church*, pp 23–4.

Missionary Society, the Church Missionary Society; the Mission to Lepers, the Colonial and Continental Church Society, the South American Missionary Society, the Irish Church Missions, the British Syrian Mission, and the Bible Churchmen's Missionary Society were all active in Irishtown in the 1930s.[43] There were also a great number of magazines on the missions; *The Gleaner, Awake, The Round World* (for children), *Mercy and Truth* (the medical mission of the CMS), the *Church Missionary Quarterly* (which featured exciting yarns of missionary daring) and the *Dublin University Missionary Magazine*.[44] Parishes were encouraged to support 'Our Own Missionary' a particular individual missionary in whom they took particular interest. Letters and visits from these missionaries provided news from exotic corners of the British Empire and constant reassurance of the good that was being done by their missionary efforts in combating witch-doctors in Africa or heathens in India. Clontarf parish, through the Church Missionary Society, helped to support the Revd Lavy and his family in Peshawar in India. The Children's Mission in the same parish was visited by the Revd A.W. Smith, working in Yoruba in West Africa. St Matthew's helped to support Miss Darley in China and Miss Ethel Bleakley in Bengal in India. Parish magazines carried news from the exotic regions of the world in the long and often intensely descriptive letters from their 'own missionary', occasionally accompanied with photographs.[45] These missionaries and their news maintained a bond with the British Empire and also a reminder that the Church of Ireland community though small remained part of the world-wide community of Anglicanism. The foreign missions were more popular in the Dublin parishes and better supported than the missions to Belfast, which because of its phenomenal growth was in desperate need of clergy, preachers, scripture readers and especially churches.

In the new independent Ireland the Church of Ireland community's political discourse became conservative and defensive, though by no means cowed. The Grand Lodge of the Freemasons organised a bi-centenary festival in 1925 which assembled 3,000 Freemasons for a service in St Patrick's Cathedral and a banquet which toasted 'all the Grand Lodges which live under the Union Jack' and finished with 'God Save The King'.[46] During the Eucharistic Congress of 1932 the title of the Church of Ireland came under attack from some Catholic commentators. The response of the Church of Ireland was forceful. Special sermons on the historical claims of the Church of Ireland were preached on successive Sundays in January 1932 in the Dublin parishes and in St Patrick's cathedral where there was also organised tours of the historic landmarks within.

43 *St Matthew's Parish Magazine*, April 1932.   44 *Clontarf Parish Magazine*, Feb. 1915. 45 For example *Clontarf Parish Magazine*, June 1905, Feb. 1915, Summer 1948; *St Matthew's Parish Magazine*, May 1921, Feb. 1924.   46 Bro. W. Clarke, *Bi-Centenary festival of the Grand Lodge of Ancient Free and Accepted Masons of Ireland* (1925).

Parish Church Associations sponsored lectures on St Patrick and the early Irish church. During April special services for children were held in order to 'bring home to them the greatness of the traditions which are theirs as members of the Church of Ireland'.[47] Later in the year, in October, a conference in commemoration of the 1,500 anniversary of the coming of St Patrick was held in the Mansion House which included an historic pageant defending the church's title and traditions.[48] Ironically it was de Valera's new 1937 constitution which 'recognised' definitively and finally the claim of the church to be the 'Church of Ireland'. The Church of Ireland was prepared where it saw it necessary to be critical of the new state. A particularly controversial policy of the government which was criticised by the Church of Ireland was the Hospital Sweepstakes which was seen as state-sponsored gambling cloaked by charitable ends. Nevertheless relations were generally cordial and state support for denominational primary schooling and teacher training proved vital to maintaining the Church of Ireland as a separate community.[49] The survival of its own denominational parish schools, more than any other factor, served to preserve the sense of a Dublin Church of Ireland community as the daily routine of delivering and collecting children at the school gates created social networks, revived old friendships, and laid the basis of new ones. Nevertheless, although it still enjoyed a sense of superiority, the Church of Ireland community in Dublin found itself living under a political ideology which they had played no part in shaping, unimportant and overlooked by the new political establishment, with no opening into the wider community of the 'nation'. Proud as many were of the status of Church of Ireland figures like the first president Douglas Hyde, agreeing with Senator W.B. Yeats that they were 'no petty people' yet no longer in control of their world, they reduced the horizons of the Church of Ireland to the size of their own community. Parochialism became a way of opting out of a world that was probably hostile, towards a closed, introspective familial society.

Voluntary associations can be divided into those which intervene in the community in the pursuit of objectives, and those which are primarily sociable and aimed at facilitating face to face contact. In the Church of Ireland in Dublin city interventionist organisations were, for the most part, charities formed and directed by the middle class but aimed and directed at the working class. Many of these charities which intervened in the Protestant working class communities were formed in the later nineteenth century and were denominationally exclusive, a response to the fear that poverty made the supposedly irreligious working class vulnerable to proselytism. For these interventionist charitable

47 *Clontarf Parish Magazine*, March 1931, Jan & April 1932.   **48** W. Bell & N.D. Emerson (eds), *The Church of Ireland A.D. 432–1932: report of the conference held in Dublin 11–14 October 1932* (Dublin, 1932).   **49** Kurt Bowen, *Protestants in a Catholic State: Ireland's privileged minority* (Dublin, 1983), pp 135–41.

organisations the Church of Ireland community had a wide embrace and 'our people' included the poorer and even rough elements across the city, but the relationship was unequal and paternalistic. The richer suburban parishes were encouraged to 'adopt' the poorer inner city parishes. St George's parish had many of its Protestant poor relieved by the parish of Monkstown in the south suburbs of the city. In the depressed 1930s the parish was also helped by the Alexandra School girls adopting poor families with children and by the Rathfarnham Parish Guild of Youth delivering Christmas parcels. Clontarf parish helped the inner city parish of St Thomas through an annual collection.[50]

Some of the poorer working-class parishes supported friendly societies which encouraged saving, offering a small dividend to regular savers, and acting much like an early credit union. Poorer parishes also ran 'Dorcas Clothing Clubs' which encouraged members to save for new clothing, keeping up a smart appearance being seen as vital to self-respect and to employment prospects.[51] Other charitable societies were the Protestant Orphan Society, the Samaritan Fund (to provide nurses for the sick poor) the Country Air Association (to provide holidays in Bray County Wicklow for poor Dublin Protestants) or the Smyly Homes for poor Protestant children.

The middle class who formed and ran these charities often saw their own comfort as a reward for moral qualities which the working-class, who did not live in comfort, lacked. There were many forms of working class leisure which were not simply regarded as distasteful but were thought actually sinful. Drink especially was the great symbol of degeneracy and much more amenable to restraint than abstract 'sin'. The most sustained campaign amongst the Church of Ireland working class therefore was that of the Church of Ireland Temperance Society (C.I.T.S.). For the C.I.T.S. the drunkenness and intemperance which were endemic amongst the working class were seen as the cause of, rather than as a response to, poverty. The campaigns of the C.I.T.S. were designed firstly to evangelise the working-class by Biblical preaching and secondly to restrict working-class access to drink by campaigns on Sunday closing and by contesting applications for licensed premises. The C.I.T.S. as a middle-class organisation believed that whereas its own class was amenable to rational argument the working-class would only respond to coercion.[52] Apart from local temperance societies the main vehicle of the campaign in the parishes was the Band of Hope which aimed to inculcate the habit of abstinence in the young.

One of the oldest of the charitable organisations linking the middle and working class and founded by the Church of Ireland was the Association for the

---

50 *St George's Parish Magazine*, Aug. 1932, Feb. 1933; *Clontarf Parish Magazine*, Apr. 1906, Jan. 1917.   **51** *St Matthew's Parish Magazine*, Jan. 1899, Nov. & Dec. 1926, Feb. 1929; *St George's Parish Magazine*, Nov. 1928.   **52** Elizabeth Malcolm, *'Ireland sober Ireland free'*, *drink and temperance in nineteenth-century Ireland* (Dublin, 1986) p. 289.

Relief of Distressed Protestants (A.R.D.P.). It was established in 1836 to 'afford relief to necessitous members of any Protestant denomination who shall not reside as a member of a family with a person not a Protestant; by means of grants of money, coal, provisions, tools, clothing and household necessities'.[53] All parishes ran 'poor and coal funds' but the A.R.D.P. was the most popular causes for charity sermons and special collections. The Christmas collection in Clontarf parish always went to the A.R.D.P.

Attitudes began to change towards the last decades of the nineteenth century as a new attitude began to emerge amongst the middle class towards the poor and poverty.[54] The poor were accustomed to charity as personal and spontaneous alms-giving. Increasingly however, as it became the main point of contact between the poor and the middle class, charity became bureaucratised and manipulative. The rationalisation of charity implied there was something wrong with a spontaneous and undemanding generosity. There had to be a response in the recipient which repaid the donor's investment. Church of Ireland charities were not unaffected by this transformation. What the A.R.D.P. demanded was that the poor 'remember who they were and what was expected of them as Protestants'.[55] The thrust of the application form the A.R.D.P. used to assess the requests for assistance was not to determine the level of distress, or the relief it warranted, but rather to determine the moral worthiness of the applicant, were they 'our people'?:

> How long is the applicant known to the recommender?
> Does applicant regularly attend divine service?
> Are the children sent regularly to weekday and Sunday school?
> Is applicant a member of any Scripture class Temperance or Benefit Society?
> Is applicant in the habit of daily family prayer and reading the Holy Scripture?
> Is applicant of clearly sober and industrious habit?[56]

The purpose of this depth of inquiry was to 'separate the indigent, incapable physically morally or mentally of self-support, who should go to the poor law,

---

53 Association for the Relief of Distressed Protestants, articles of association (R.C.B., MS 535); G.D. Williams, *Dublin charities* (Dublin, 1902); Kenneth Milne, *Protestant Aid: a history of the Association for the Relief of Distressed Protestants* (Dublin, 1989), p. 4; on the Church of Ireland and the working class charities see, Martin Maguire, 'The Church of Ireland and the problem of the Protestant working class of Dublin, 1870s–1930s' in A.Ford, J.McGuire & K. Milne (eds), *As by law established the Church of Ireland since the Reformation* (Dublin, 1995), pp 195–203. **54** Stephen Yeo, *Religion and voluntary organisation in crisis* (London, 1976), p. 211. **55** Milne, *Protestant Aid*, p 4. **56** Association for the Relief of Distressed Protestants (A.R.D.P.) *Annual Report*, 1875 (R.C.B., MS 485).

and the poor wage-earner in need of temporary help'.[57] Thus charitable giving became deformed into a weapon for social control and was used to impose middle class patterns of behaviour and discipline on the working class. Middle class charitable activists confused morality with happiness.

An example of the more coercive response to working-class poverty was that of the Church of Ireland Labour Home and Yard, established in 1899 by the Church of Ireland in St Matthew's parish in the working-class suburb of Ringsend. Though the Labour Home and Yard was organised by Dublin clergy of the Church of Ireland and was under church control it was managed on a daily basis by the English evangelical organisation, the Church Army.[58] The labour-yard at Ringsend offered work to any man willing to undertake it and in return provided food, shelter, and a pittance wage. The object of the yard was 'to render impossible the complaint that any honest man is starving in the city owing to want of work'.[59] The work offered was chopping wood at a wage of tenpence per day and a meal. The qualifying 'honest' reveals the coercive attitude becoming prevalent in a middle class frustrated by the persistence of poverty and by the apparent failure of the working-class to respond to moral exhortations. That the function of the Labour Home and Yard was to police the poor rather than relieve distress is apparent in both the principles on which the Home and Yard operated and those of the Church Army who undertook the running of it. The Home and Yard was originally intended to be exclusively for men of the Church of Ireland but as men would 'undoubtedly declare themselves Protestant for the purpose of admission' it was decided that while it was primarily for members of the Church of Ireland all men who were willing to attend daily prayer and Mission Service on Sunday would be eligible for admission to the Yard. From those in the Yard 'suitable cases' would be selected for the permanent accommodation in the Home. Those selected were not to associate with those in the Yard.[60] Reaction in St Matthew's parish was mildly sceptical, it was felt that the yard was too far from the city centre where the worst poverty lay. Parishioners were encouraged to purchase the firewood from the yard, where it quickly piled up as no-one took the responsibility of actually selling it.[61] Parish collections became the usual way of supporting the yard as it became simply an evangelising shelter for the poorest of the working class and the labour element was abandoned.

A reflective and more intelligent response to poverty was that of Revd Paterson Smyth of St Ann's on Dawson Street. He was strongly influenced by the Christian Socialist movement in the Church of England, which regarded

---

57 A.R.D.P. *Annual Report*, 1902, p 7.   58 Church of Ireland Labour Home and Yard, committee minutes, 21 Feb. 1899 (R.C.B., MS 535).   59 *Church of Ireland Gazette*, 22 Sept. 1899.   60 Church of Ireland Labour Home and Yard, Committee minute book 21 Feb.1899–25 Sept. 1899 (R.C.B., MS 535).   61 *St Matthew's Parish Magazine*, Aug. 1899,

the state as a sacred organism and believed it a Christian's duty to ensure that the workers got their fair share. Speaking at the 1899 Church of Ireland conference on the subject of 'the Church of Ireland and the poor' he announced the formation of the Church of Ireland Social Services Union.[62] The role of the Social Services Union was not to mitigate the results of poverty but to attack poverty itself.[63] Paterson Smyth saw poverty not as a result of immorality but as a social problem requiring more than a moral response.[64] A branch of the Social Services Union was formed in Clontarf in 1905. Prominent in the Clontarf branch were W.J. Dollar and Alderman Healy, both parish church-wardens, both conspicuous Unionists in Dublin corporation and both active in the Municipal Reform group. The original concept of Paterson Smyth was summarised in the motto 'educate-agitate-operate' by which was meant education about the causes of poverty, agitation by the Church of Ireland on ending poverty, and the public to operate effectively in response to that end. In the hands of Dollar and Healy the Social Services Union in Clontarf turned into an election machine for the approaching Poor Law Guardianship elections. The Poor Law system and the incumbent guardians were attacked for failing to weed out the undeserving poor and safeguarding the interests of the ratepayers.[65] An effective branch of the Social Services Union was established eventually, though not of the type envisaged by Paterson Smyth. Instead of a propagandising body with a social mission offering a critical insight into poverty it was in fact a conventional charity which used the money collected to create bursaries for the respectable poor of their own parish.[66]

As the newly independent state increasingly (albeit reluctantly) took responsibility for the health and welfare of the citizens, the charitable role of the Church of Ireland declined. The broader sense of community, which identified the Protestant poor of the inner city as still being, despite their wretched condition, 'our people', was in decay. The removal of the Protestant middle-class to the suburbs meant that the class upon which these interventionist charities relied were becoming less aware of, and therefore less concerned about, working class poverty. The only poverty visible was that of the local, their own parish, usually elderly or widows. Even the existence of a Protestant working class in Dublin was doubted. The self-identity and social values of the Church of Ireland community in Dublin revolved around a parochial and middle class notion of respectability. As a consequence 'our people' increasingly took on a

Jan. 1900; *Clontarf Parish Magazine*, Jan. 1900, Jan. 1915.   **62** *Authorized report ... Dublin 1899;* Peter d'A Jones, *The Christian Socialist revival, 1877–1914* (Cambridge, 1968) p. 125. **63** *Authorized report of the Church of Ireland conference held at Limerick 1902* (Limerick, 1902). **64** Revd J Paterson Smyth (ed.), *Social service handbook, first series, issued by the Church of Ireland Social Service Union* (Dublin, 1901).   **65** *Clontarf Parish Magazine*, Apr., May 1905, Aug. 1906.   **66** *Clontarf Parish Magazine*, June 1907.

cultural and symbolic significance. As the charitable organisations declined the voluntary community groups which now flourished were primarily associative, facilitating leisure and social contact.

Most parishes sustained an extraordinary range of social organisations, most of them branches of a national society. In the 1930s St George's, a poor inner city parish, could still maintain sixteen different societies; the Change-Ringers (ringing out one of the most famous peels in Dublin), Boys' Brigade, Girls' Brigade, Life Boys, Old Boys Union, Dorcas Society, Girls Friendly Society, Parish Guild of Youth, Men's Social Club, Missionary Union, St George's Parochial Society, the Y.M.C.A., and a Young People's Social Club.[67] A well-off parish such as Clontarf supported an even more luxuriant growth; Ladies' Bible Class, Mothers' Union, Zenana Working Party, All Day Working Party, Hosanna League, Sower's Band, Girl Guides, Girls' Brigade, Girls' Working Party, Brownies, Girls' Club, Band of Hope, Children's Scripture Company, Gleaner's Missionary Union, Young People's Union, League of Pity, Guild of Youth, Rangers, Special Service, Church Association, Dramatic Society, Pierrot Troupe, Bible Reading Union, Ping Pong Club, Minstrels' Troupe, Winter Social Club, Chess Club, Football Club, Sunday School Teachers Class, Lawn Tennis Club, Badminton Club, Hockey Club, Boys Brigade, Old Boys Union, Young Men's Bible Class, Church of Ireland Men's Society, men's Study Circle, Life Boys, Arts and Crafts Society.[68] The years from 1918 through the 1920s saw a very energetic period of re-building or founding many voluntary organisations and societies. This was in part an effort of renewal after the loss of impetus in community organisations during the war years, but it was also a defensive 'circling the wagons' as the political changes brought Catholics to power. For the young there were companies of the Boys' Brigade in virtually every parish though companies of the Girls' Brigade were not so ubiquitous. The Clontarf parish company of the Girls' Brigade was not formed until 1937.[69] Life Boys were the junior branch of the Boys' Brigade and most parishes could also sustain an Old Boys Union of former members. The Boys' Brigade under the motto 'Sure and Steadfast' was founded in Glasgow in 1883 as a Protestant and imperialist boys movement to further 'the advancement of Christ's Kingdom among boys and the promotion of habits of obedience, reverence, discipline, self-respect, and all that tends towards a true Christian manliness'. The link between the Protestant churches, the military, the empire and the Boys' Brigade was vividly demonstrated in the 1899 annual parade in the Metropolitan Hall in Abbey Street. Under a banner proclaiming 'Discipline-Manliness-Religion', reviewing the march past and the drilling were side by side the primate of the Church of Ireland and Lord Roberts, hero of the Afghan

67 *St George's Parish Magazine*, Oct. 1933.   68 *Clontarf Parish Magazine*, Mar.1943.
69 *Clontarf Parish Magazine*, Jan. 1937.

Wars and now commander-in chief of the British forces in Ireland.[70] The Boys' Brigade prospered well into the years of independence, underlining the continuing sentimental links with the empire. In St Matthew's parish in Irishtown 1924 was the most successful year ever for the Brigade in terms of recruitment. In Clontarf the existing company of the Boys' Brigade was added to by an Old Boys Union in the same year. Up to the late 1950s the march out by the Boys' Brigade on Founder's Day in October halted the traffic from Adelaide Road to St Patrick's cathedral. However the successful transition into the independent state and the continued vigour of the Boys' Brigade might also be due to the less sentimental role of the Brigade in securing employment. Members were taught commercial skills such as book-keeping and shorthand and these classes were well attended. The Dublin Battalion maintained an employment agency for the boys and employers (many of them former members) were encouraged to ask there first for junior clerks, apprentices or assistants.[71] Within the commerical culture of Dublin there were firms which were recognised as Protestant enterprises. The Royal Bank of Ireland, the Hibernian, and the Munster and Leinster were the Protestant banks, and Brookes Thomas, Henshawes, Hills and Dockrells dominated hardware (a particularly Protestant sector).

Discussion and debate on current topics, a mixture of amusement and exhortation, formed the staple of most of the associations aimed at youth and young adults such as Christian Endeavour, the Young Men's Christian Association, the Young Women's Christian Association, and the parish Church Associations. They often followed an announced programme of scriptural, scientific and topical subjects, a judicious mix of secular and religious themes. Topics for discussion seem to have been chosen to encourage participation without becoming overly contentious and possibly divisive, that is to say they were primarily to facilitate debate as a leisure activity. The associations for the young were formed to encourage and enable young people to socialise exclusively within the community, amongst 'our people', and to maintain secular networks that would prove useful in the future. Typically, the objectives of the Church of Ireland Men's Society were

(a) to band churchmen together in a common effort to promote the glory of God and to help forward the work of the church
(b) to foster the practice of Christian brotherhood and conduct, and to promote opportunities for social intercourse amongst members and associates
(c) to provide for the systematic commendation of members and associates on change of residence.[72]

---

70 *St Matthew's Parish Magazine*, April 1899. 71 *St Matthew's Parish Magazine*, April 1899, June 1924; *Clontarf Parish Magazine*, May 1924, June 1925, Jan. 1927. 72 *Clontarf Parish Magazine*, Jan. 1910.

In Irishtown and in Clontarf parishes debates on the role of women in society or on the labour question were popular in the pre-war years. These were leavened by what would be recognised today as very dangerous demonstrations of X-Rays and an illustrated lecture on Manchuria.[73] During the war years the subjects became more military. After the war, as the political situation in Ireland became more uncertain, relevance began to edge into the debates; 'Dublin's social problems' or 'politics and the Church of Ireland' were debated in 1918 in Clontarf's Church Association. Contemporary, though less immediately relevant subjects, continued to feature during the 1920s. The July-October 1927 programme for the Clontarf Young Men's Study Circle included 'the state and the individual', 'business and morality', 'is patriotism a Christian value?', 'socialism', 'gambling and betting' and 'evolution and the Bible'.[74] In November 1929 the parish Church Association enjoyed 'a night full of information about the wonderful Italian politician' in an address from the Revd Aldhouse entitled 'A night with Mussolini'.

In 1929, in an attempt to both make the church more relevant to the young and to promote involvement, the Church of Ireland held a special Youth Conference where the role of young people in the church and their problems, could be aired. The two main issues that emerged from that conference were firstly the problem of 'finding employment for our young people on leaving school' and secondly 'the representation of women on the Synods of the Church'. This led to attempts to get younger representatives elected to select vestries but, due to the poor response, the bid failed.[75] It is clear that for most young people the social dimension of these associations was of greater importance than the didactic. Participation in the lectures, debates and discussions always required considerable cajoling and persuasion. These were generally the winter programme. By contrast the summer programme of day excursions to beauty spots with picnics and games, were always hugely popular. Social and sporting clubs with no pretence to any other function than providing recreation, but which were exclusively available to Protestants, were the most successful. Thus by the 1930s most parishes supported a variety of very popular cricket, tennis or badminton clubs in the suburban parishes or soccer and snooker clubs in the city parishes. Associated with these were dances, whist drives and other social events. Badminton has made many matches in the Dublin Church of Ireland community.

The most widespread voluntary society, and the one which seemed to many to best embody the ethos of the Church of Ireland community, was the Mothers' Union. The Mothers' Union had been founded in 1872 in England by Mary Elizabeth Sumner (*née* Heywood), an aristocratic philanthropist married

---

73 *Clontarf Parish Magazine*, Nov. 1904, Oct. 1907; *St Matthew's Parish Magazine*, Jan.1899, Dec. 1913. **74** *St Matthew's Parish Magazine*, Mar. 1927. **75** *St Matthew's Parish Magazine*, Feb. & June 1929, Feb. 1930.

at the age of nineteen to George Henry Sumner, rector of a parish in Hampshire. Initially a parochial movement it was launched as a diocesan movement in 1887, the same year that the first Dublin branch was founded in Raheny parish. It became one of the most characteristic lay societies within Anglicanism as, facilitated by the empire, it spread all round the world. The Mothers' Union brought together mothers from social classes normally separated by a gulf of social conventions. The objectives of the Mothers' Union were

1 To uphold the sanctity of marriage.
2 To awaken in mothers a sense of their great responsibility in the training of their boys and girls, the future fathers and mothers of the empire.
3 To organise in every place a band of mothers who will unite in prayer and seek by their own example to lead their families in purity and holiness of life.

After a conference on marriage in 1909 the Mothers' Union interpreted their first objective as meaning opposition to divorce and that therefore divorced or separated woman could not be members.[76]

The Mothers' Union branches in the Dublin parishes tended to be social gatherings, used primarily to integrate the newly arrived parishioners. Membership was not confined to mothers only and adult women, married or single, attended. In some of the Dublin branches the second objective was modified so as to drop the reference to the 'future fathers and mothers of the empire' and to read simply 'fathers and mothers of the future'. The golden jubilee of the Mothers' Union in 1937 was celebrated in Dublin by a pageant in the Mansion House. The performance of music and ballet, directed by Lennox Robinson, depicted the 'gradual purification of woman's outlook and aims' in scenes depicting women in prehistoric times, in Babylon, in pagan Rome, Tudor England, and then finally, in the perfection of womanhood, the Mothers' Union.[77]

Women were also vital in fund-raising for church and school, and in church decoration and maintenance. Fund raising by the 'ladies of the parish' in Irishtown in 1925 generated sufficient income to install new lighting in St Matthew's church, clear the accumulated overdraft and still leave something in hand. Between 1900 and 1930 the 'ladies of the parish' in a succession of fetes, concerts and other events raised enough money to build a new school, paint the church, renovate the organ, repair the boys school, and by 1930 begin the building of a new rectory.[78] Invariably women were also the collectors for the

---

76 Owen Chadwick, *The Victorian church: part two 1860–1901* (London, 1970), pp 192–3.
77 *St Matthew's Parish Magazine*, Dec.1923, Feb. 1924; *Clontarf Parish Magazine*, Oct. 1931; *St George's Parish Magazine*, Oct. 1937. 78 *St Matthew's Parish Magazine*, July 1923, July 1926, April 1930.

missionary and charitable societies. Without this voluntary activity by women the Church of Ireland as a living community would have died. However if, as has been argued here, the Church of Ireland in Dublin abandoned a critical engagement with irish society to become an introverted and familial community, then membership of conventional organisations such as the Mothers' Union does not reflect the vital role that women played in sustaining that community. Whereas men dominated the formal structures as clergy and hierarchy, churchwardens, synodmen and select vestry, it was women who dominated the informal voluntary structures and answered the need for religion to serve a social purpose. Indeed it could be argued that class differences were becoming less important to the Church of Ireland community than gender differences. Socio-religious associations played a far bigger part in the lives of women than in the lives of men. Women made these clubs and societies warm and attractive places where the Church of Ireland community, especially the young, could find identity and mutual support. Most of these clubs and societies had either all-women or mostly women committees. These associations, rather than the select vestry, were the backbone of the parish community. They catered for every age group, both sexes, all sorts of special interest and sporting activities, literary discussion circles, and associated them in an extensive network of overlapping membership which reinforced communal identity and solidarity. They institu-tionalised, in a way that formal church services could not, what it was to be a member of the Church of Ireland community. They also had the unintentional consequence of fragmenting the ideal of the Church of Ireland as a single community into a multiplicity of communities which were exclusive to particular age or interest groups.[79]

The common denominator in all of these social organisations was exclusive-ness, the clubs and societies were for 'the parishioners and their Protestant friends', only Protestants were welcome.[80] However it should not be supposed that the exclusiveness of the Church of Ireland community reflected some sort of siege mentality. It was not only the Church of Ireland that equated Protestantism with respectability. As the *Church of Ireland Monthly Magazine* proudly noted, members of the church had a general reputation for honesty and good citizenship, were held in high esteem in Irish society, and exercised an influence far beyond their numbers.[81]

The Second World War was an uncertain time for the Church of Ireland community in Dublin. Neutrality in a war in which Britain was engaged was

---

79 David Hempton, *Religion and political culture in Britain and Ireland from the Glorious Revolution to the decline of empire* (Cambridge, 1996), p. 140. 80 *Clontarf Parish Magazine,* Oct. 1924, Nov. 1933; *St Matthew's Parish Magazine,* April 1923, Aug. & Dec. 1931, June 1932; *St George's Parish Magazine,* Oct. 1933; *St James Parish Magazine,* Oct. 1940. 81 *The Church of Ireland Monthly Magazine,* Sept. 1939.

unprecedented. It also meant that the experience of war was very different to that of the Church in Northern Ireland. In Dublin the war was experienced vicariously. The local Air Raid Precautions unit were convinced to store their gas masks elsewhere than the parish hall in Clontarf. The 1941 bombing of North Strand was near enough to be exciting, but not near enough to be frightening. The rector of Clontarf, J.B. Neligan, through the war in a series of sober and reflective editorials in the parish magazine, decried the insidious propaganda which was already demonising the German people and portraying the war as a Christian crusade against paganism rather than as the result of the failure to practice Christianity.[82] For many in Clontarf parish the war was experienced through the suffering of 'Our Own Missionary' Ena Williamson, captured by the Japanese in China. The parish magazine carried regular reports of the plight of the prisoners of war under the Japanese and later, when Ena Williamson was traced to a camp in Hong Kong regular reports conveyed whatever news was to hand. The Freemasons annual dinner sent messages of support to the brethren in England and toasted 'the army, the navy and the air force'.[83] The Life Boys in St James's parish had a talk from a visitor on the horrors of the blitz.[84] Prepared stoically to meet whatever the future would bring, the main concern of the diocesan authorities in the darkest days of the war was that in the event of the evacuation of Dublin, Church of Ireland children would be sent to church homes. In the parishes shortages and the blackout meant a decline in the social organisations. In Clontarf as the Mothers' Union began to fail a 'Fellowship of Marriage' for young married mothers, who might feel that the Mothers' Union was too stodgy, was equally unsuccessful in generating support. In the inner city parishes, especially St Paul's in the Smithfield markets, the misery and want of the war years was extreme but the appeals for help to the suburban parishes got a poor response.[85] Many of the Church of Ireland clergy served a chaplains to the British forces, but the most immediate experience of the war for the Church of Ireland community in Dublin was through those members of the parishes who joined the British services. Censorship allowed no direct reference be made in parish magazines to those absent on war service but Remembrance Sunday acquired a new significance and continued to be the best attended service of the church year. In Clontarf parish a prayer list was maintained. 115 parishioners served in the British forces, including twenty-six women. Of these nine were killed in action, including two of the women. After the war their names were added to those of the First World War on the memorial cross in the church-yard.[86]

By 1944, with victory for the allies now certain, the Church of Ireland in Dublin could begin planning with confidence for the future. A Youth Conference

82 *Clontarf Parish Magazine*, Oct. & Nov. 1939; June 1940; Feb, 1941.   83 Grand Lodge of Free and Accepted Masons of Ireland, *Annual Report*, 1940.   84 *St James's Parish Magazine*, June 1941.   85 *Clontarf Parish Magazine*, Jan. & Feb. 1942.   86 *Clontarf Parish Magazine*,

worked on a plan of campaign for reconstructing a post-war world in better accord with the will of God. The war served to loosen identification with the British state and warmed relations with the Irish state and its representatives. Especially important in this was the support which the state continued to give to denominational education and church control of schools and teacher training. In Clontarf a school fund-raising event was opened by Tom Derrig T.D., Minister for Education, and Oscar Traynor the local Fianna Fáil T.D., J.B. Neligan, writing of the contribution which the Church of Ireland would make to the post-war Ireland, called on the Church of Ireland tradition of enlightened patriotism exemplified by Thomas Davis and Jonathan Swift.[87] The declaration of the Republic in 1948 and the departure from the Commonwealth in 1949 did lead to some objections to the deletion of the king from the state prayers in the Prayer Book, but it was not as traumatic as would have been the case in the pre-war years. The emotional ties to the crown were waning though not yet severed. The death of George VI in February 1952 passed virtually unnoticed, but there was not a Church of Ireland parish hall in the country that did not show at least once, and probably a great many times, the three-hour newsreel film of the coronation of Queen Elizabeth II. Missionary activity maintained a sentimental sense of community with the empire. Clontarf's 'Own Missionary' Ena Williamson returned from her wartime captivity to recover, then went to India as China became closed off under the communists. Her reports from India are far less hearty than those from pre-war China and there is a sense of a world becoming strange. The parish also supported Miss Maud Parsons in Kenya, her fearful reports of the Mau Mau presaged the ebbing of the imperial tide in which missionaries like her had swam.

The Second World War proved in fact to be a watershed for the Dublin Church of Ireland community of even greater significance than the transition to national independence. The war period broke the momentum of the many associative organisations which had become the main locus of social interaction of 'our people'. Post-war shortages further prolonged the hiatus in activity. In Clontarf the Mothers' Union (or the Grandmothers' Union as it was now derisively called) resisted all attempts at revival. The parish tennis club struggled to 'keep the Church's young people together in healthy fellowship'. The Church Association, a vital bridge into parish life for newcomers, had also fallen into disuse. An uplifting lecture on the mission to lepers did not get any response, but a Halloween dance proved more successful.[88] In St George's parish the Boys' Brigade and its junior company the Life Boys declined, due in part to the movement of population to the suburbs. Membership of the Girls' Brigade also ebbed.[89] In St Kevin's parish on the South Circular Road the

June 1945.   87 *Clontarf Parish Magazine*, Feb. 1944, Nov. 1945, Summer 1947.   88 *Clontarf Parish Magazine*, Sept. 1946, Jan. Oct. & Dec. 1947; Mar. 1950.   89 *St George's Parish*

Young People's Christian Endeavour Society struggled to survive. Women increasingly dominated the membership and sub-committees until eventually it became exclusively women. The roll-book shows a gradual dispersal of the membership, with fewer and fewer in the immediate area.[90]

The Protestant exclusiveness which was the common hall mark of the Church of Ireland community associations reflected not only the sense of superiority that was inherent in the church, which equated Protestantism with respectability, but also the fear that contact with Catholics was leading to marriage and therefore a loss to the community. The inspiration of many of the interventionist charities of the Victorian period had been the fear (or hope) that the desperate poor were susceptible to conversion. As the state took responsibility for much of the welfare that had fallen to charities it was increasingly feared that marriage to Catholics was in fact a far more significant factor in conversion as almost always the children were reared as Catholics and sometimes even the Protestant spouse would eventually convert as well. Thus whole families were lost to the community. The decree *Ne Temere* proved a powerful inspiration to Protestant fears of assimilation into a Catholic culture. The thinly veiled bigotry of the Catholic archbishop of Dublin John Charles McQuaid, the Tilson case, and the Fethard on Sea boycott revived and gave added life to those fears. McQuaid made it clear that he regarded Protestants as posing only slightly less a danger to the faith of Catholic Ireland than communists. The Tilson case arose out of a marriage between a Protestant, Ernest Neville Tilson and a Catholic, Mary Joseph Barnes. Both had signed the *Ne Temere* promise to bring up the children as Catholics. However the couple fell out, there was a gap of nearly twenty years in their age, and Tilson took three of the four children to the Protestant Mrs Smyly's Home. His wife sought an order in the High Court for the return of these children. Justice Gavan Duffy ruled that the *Ne Temere* promises to bring up the children as Catholics were cognisable by the High Court and he ordered the return of the children who would continue to bring up by their mother as Catholics. In 1957 the local Catholic clergy and bishop led an economic boycott of Protestants in Fethard-on-Sea in Co. Wexford after a local Protestant woman, married to a Catholic, had refused to have her children enrolled in the Catholic school. She fled, first to Belfast and from there to Scotland, taking the children with her. It was alleged by the Catholic clergy that the whole local Protestant community had actively assisted her flight from her husband and her promises to raise the children as Catholics. The boycott was condemned by de Valera but it revealed overtly the usually covert sectarianism which lay beneath the surface of daily life.[91] The dangers

Magazine, Nov. & Dec. 1946. **90** St Kevin's Young People's Christian Endeavour Society, minute book and roll book, (R.C.B., P43/8/3/112). **91** John Cooney, *John Charles McQuaid, ruler of Catholic Ireland* (Dublin, 1999), pp 87, 245–6, 321–5.

of social contact with Catholics became a subject of urgent sermonising to the young.[92]

It should not be assumed, as has been by leading loyalist commentators such as the Revd Ian Paisley, that the demographic decline of the Church of Ireland was determined solely by religious and political differences. The Church of Ireland community showed, in an exaggerated form, the general trends within the Irish population which were causing a continuing decline; high emigration and high celibacy. It was not only the Church of Ireland community that found the independent state uncongenial and offering no future as emigration became virtually a national exodus. Also, like the Irish population as a whole, the church community had a very high number who never married, lifelong celibacy was becoming a national characteristic. Adding to these forces of decline was the lower fertility of the Church of Ireland marriages. This had been first brought home by the publication of the 1936 census information on marriage, fertility and religion.[93] The *Church of Ireland Monthly Magazine* had commented in 1939 on these disturbing trends and suggested that the church help young married couples financially in setting up homes, perhaps even offering a grant for each child. This aid, with an employment bureau, would secure the bedrock of the church community, the working class.[94]

Previously published research on the enumerator returns of the 1901 and 1911 census shows that marriage patterns were the most significant factor in explaining the decline in the numbers of working class Protestants in Dublin city.[95] In brief the research found that there was a high level of marriage between Catholic and Protestant in the working class areas of Dublin, as high as 18 per cent of households. The dominant pattern was for Protestant men to marry Catholic women. Most of the children of these marriages were raised as Catholics. This may reflect the view that religion was 'women's business' and that therefore the mother (Catholic) decided the religion of the children. The research also shows that in the period before independence most Dublin Protestant women from the working class preferred to marry British soldiers, suggesting that the military barracks were a social centre for the Protestant working class. These marriages meant a loss to the Dublin Protestant community as the soldiers tour of duty ended. Thus, even before the creation of the independent Irish state, marriage patterns were creating a demographic instability.

Using a variety of sources an inference of what precisely was happening in one parish, Clontarf, can be drawn. The records are the census enumerator

92 *Clontarf Parish Magazine*, Mar. 1911, Oct. 1950, Mar 1957; *St Matthew's Parish Magazine*, April 1929, Dec. 1930. 93 Thomas Keane, 'Demographic trends' in Michael Hurley SJ (ed.), *Irish Anglicanism 1869–1969* (Dublin, 1970) pp 168–78. 94 *Church of Ireland Monthly Magazine*, Oct. 1939. 95 Martin Maguire, 'A socio-economic analysis of the Dublin protestant working-class 1870–1926' in *Irish Economic and Social History* xx

returns, marriage, baptismal, and burial records, the sustenation fund donations listed year by year in the parish magazine (which serve as a proximate listing of the parish community), and after 1948 the yearly listing of the Church of Ireland households street by street. An examination of the 1901 census returns in the middle class suburb of Clontarf shows no evidence of mixed marriages.[96] What the marriage register of the parish church, St John's, does show is an extreme localism in choice of marriage partner, often from the same or adjoining parish, sometimes even from the same street. This suggests that the associative emphasis of the parish organisations was very successful in so far as it ensured that leisure and social inter-action was exclusively Protestant. However such a narrow and inward-looking social circle meant that the parish, which had a growing church community, had a surprisingly low rate of marriage, and a low birth rate, as shown by the baptismal register.[97] The rector of Clontarf parish J.B. Neligan blamed the demographic decline, which he first noticed in his own parish in 1940, on the reluctance of the young to make the commitment of marriage. The yearly trends in the parish show the number of communicants, excluding Christmas and Easter, showed a steady increase year by year during the 1930s and 1940s. The expansion of suburban house-building in the 1950s further strengthened the numbers of the church community in the parish. Yet the number of marriages remained at a steady average of around ten marriages a year right through from the 1930s to the 1950s. In only one year, 1948, did baptisms exceed burials. If it were not the continual influx of new families brought into the parish by the move to the suburbs, the Clontarf Church of Ireland community would have actually declined.[98]

The individual donations to the parish sustenation fund, between 312 and 384 per annum, provide a rough census of the church community in Clontarf year on year. In the fifteen year period 1910-25, which covers the First World War and the War of Independence, the lists show a stable core of about 50 per cent of the households. This core actually grows more stable through the 1920s; of the 312 who made a donation in 1910 47 per cent were still in the parish in 1914; of the 388 in 1914 who made a donation 51 per cent were still in the parish in 1920; and 68 per cent of those who donated in 1920 were still there in 1925. The permanent core in the 1950s is smaller but still significant, 41 per cent of households continue in the parish from 1950 to 1960. From 1957 the marriage register required a record of the intended place of abode of the married couple. Of the one hundred marriages in the Clontarf marriage register

(1993), pp 56–60.   96 N.A., Census of Ireland 1901, Enumerators returns, city of Dublin DED 23/1–57; DED 24/1–11. 'Evidence of mixed marriage' is where there is a member of the household, related to head of household by blood or marriage, who is of a different religion, either Catholic or Protestant, though not of a different denomination.   97 Registers of St John's parish, Clontarf.   98 Clontarf Parish Magazine, April 1940, Feb. 1944, Jan. 1943,

from 1957 to 1968 sixty were staying in Dublin, eighteen going to Britain and sixteen to other parts of Ireland. What the parish of Clontarf shows therefore is a community which relied on a stable, though slowly ageing and declining, core to maintain the many societies and associations which created the networks holding the community together. What we see is the slow dissipation of a community. The most recent research on mixed marriages suggests that the exclusiveness of the Protestant middle class began to break down in the 1950s and early 1960s as the number of such marriages increased.[99] This same research also concludes that though mixed marriages have increased they are still few. This conclusion cannot be sustained for the Dublin Church of Ireland community where as many as 75 per cent of marriages celebrated in the parish churches have been mixed marriages.

The 1960s is the period when Ireland finally emerged from the Victorian period. Affluence created new forms of entertainment along with greater mobility. Leisure was privatised. For the young age differences became more important than religious differences. For the relatively affluent young the urban environment now offered a range of leisure activities which were exciting, non-denominational, even non-religious. New forms of association and leisure were rapidly generated in the commercially run dance halls, cinemas and clubs. The family as the centre of amusement declined rapidly as increasingly the young did things together whilst parents did things together, often at home, usually watching television.

The community of the Church of Ireland had relied on a network of associative voluntary organisations, denominationally exclusive, to generate and sustain a sense of community. 'Our people' had withdrawn from a critical role in Irish society and settled for being, in essence, a club. However a rethinking of the relationships within the Church of Ireland community and between it and the rest of Irish society can be seen in the reaction to the Orange Order's controversial parades at Drumcree and in the bicentenary commemorations of the 1798 rebellion. That these too were 'our people' at Drumcree has been a shock to the complacency of the Church of Ireland in Dublin and the rest of the south. It has opened up a division in the community of the Church of Ireland between north and south. For many Church of Ireland people in the south the identification of their community with Orangeism is profoundly alien. On the other hand the extent to which members of the Church of Ireland community were active in the events of 1798 was a significant theme in the bicentenary commemorations. The cultural community of the Church of Ireland

Mar. 1944, May, 1945, May 1946, May 1947, May 1948, April 1950.   **99** Richard O'Leary, 'Change in the rate and pattern of religious intermarriage in the republic of Ireland' in *The Economic and Social Review*, xxx no. 2, (April 1999), pp 119–32.

is perhaps being redefined in a way in which 'our people' are becoming an urbane, intellectual, tolerant and liberal leavening of Irish society, offering a spiritual home to the like-minded.[100]

100 My thanks are due to Revd Tom Haskins for granting access to the records of St John the Baptist parish Clontarf; Revd John Crawford for his suggestions and for comments on an early draft; Barry Lyons for access to the records of the Freemasons; Valerie and Rex Coghlan, Albert and Rosemary Fenton for their personal insights and responses, Celia Keenan for her interest and her support.

12

Buildings and faith: church building from medieval to modern

Paul Larmour & Stephen McBride

The development of ecclesiastical buildings over the centuries has been determined by many factors including not only significant historical, theological and liturgical influences but also the dictates and whims of architectural style and fashion. This survey seeks to briefly trace the changing styles of architecture in the Church of Ireland over the past three to four hundred years,[1] before highlighting a few special moments in the course of the nineteenth century when the normally harmonious relationship between clergy, architects, and laity became disrupted.

MATTERS ARCHITECTURAL[2]

Without dealing with the vexed question of original provenance it is a fact that, in the aftermath of the Reformation, the Church of Ireland found itself in ownership of almost all the medieval parish churches and cathedrals in Ireland. Although most stand now as maintained ruins, having been transferred to state care in the nineteenth century, some are still in active use as places of worship by the Church of Ireland. These are some of the most important examples of early church architecture in Ireland. They include Clonfert cathedral in County Galway (fig. 10) which boasts the finest Romanesque portal in Ireland in its twelfth-century main entrance; Tuam cathedral, County Galway, which although now largely a nineteenth-century building, retains within its choir the grandest chancel arch of the Romanesque period in Ireland; Christ Church

---

1 There is no single text confined to the entire architectural history of the Church of Ireland, but for a general background to church architecture in Ireland see the following – B. de Breffny and G. Mott, *The churches and abbeys of Ireland* (London, 1976); and R. Hurley and P. Larmour (eds), *Sacred places – the story of Christian architecture in Ireland* (Dublin and Belfast, 2000).   2 By Paul Larmour.

10 Clonfert cathedral, Co. Galway. Twelfth-century Irish Romanesque doorway with late medieval tower above.

11 St Canice's cathedral, Kilkenny. Mid thirteenth-century Gothic.

cathedral, Dublin, and St Patrick's cathedral, Dublin, which although both very much restored in the nineteenth century, represent the only thirteenth-century churches in Ireland designed on a truly grand scale, and St Canice's cathedral, Kilkenny (fig. 11), in style the purest Gothic cathedral in Ireland, with one of the few medieval interiors that retains any of the original atmosphere.[3]

The dissolution of the monasteries following the Reformation in the early sixteenth century signalled the end of the medieval era in Ireland. The unsettled political and religious situation in the century or so that followed was far from conducive to new architecture of any sort, let alone church building, and since medieval parish churches and cathedrals had passed to the established church, few new churches were needed, except in new areas of settlement. Nevertheless, some notable churches were built.

3 For medieval cathedrals of the Church of Ireland see R. Stalley, *Architecture and sculpture in Ireland 1150–1350* (Dublin, 1971); and J.G.F. Day and H. Patton, *The cathedrals of the Church of Ireland* (London, 1932).

12 St Columb's cathedral, Derry, 1628–33 with tower, spire and
chancel added in the nineteenth century.

The Plantation of Ulster in the early seventeenth century saw a unique
survival of late Gothic style in the cathedral built in the re-founded city of
Derry, while the end of that century saw several Dublin churches being built or
rebuilt in the incoming classical manner. St Columb's cathedral in Derry
(fig. 12)was initially built between 1628 and 1633 by William Parrott, who was
presumably also responsible for its design. It was designed in what was by then
an already archaic English style, characterised by its detailing of an Elizabethan
Gothic type, and although it has had later additions such as the tower and spire,
and chancel, all from the nineteenth century, it still stands as the largest
seventeenth-century church in Ireland. Other survivals of Gothic styling, a
rather old-fashioned trait of the time, sometimes referred to in Ulster as
'Planters' Gothic', can be seen in smaller churches of the early seventeenth
century in Ulster, such as Clonfeacle parish church in Benburb, County Tyrone
(1618–22) built by Sir Richard Wingfield, which is the best preserved small-
scale example of the type, and the now-ruinous church at Derrygonnelly,
County Fermanagh (1627) built by Sir John Dunbar. Derrygonnelly is curious

13 Middle Church, Ballinderry, Co. Antrim, 1668.

14 Middle Church, Ballinderry, Co. Antrim, 1668, interior.

in that it displays, in the one building, a 'Gothic survival' east window and a Renaissance-style west doorway of Italian inspiration, both newly built at the same time, one clearly a feature from the past, the other a sign of things to come.[4] The most perfect example of a seventeenth-century church in Ireland, albeit much restored in 1902, is the Middle Church at Ballinderry in County Antrim (figs 13, 14), consecrated in 1668, our solitary example of an essentially Jacobean type of structure. Its plan is a simple rectangle, its overall form is barn-like and its exterior finish is plain. The interior, lit by square-headed three-light and five-light windows, has a wide stone-paved aisle and retains part of its original Jacobean-style fittings including a remarkable three-decker pulpit topped by a canopy, and high box-pews of Irish oak with wooden latches on the doors.[5]

The church at Ballinderry is a very plain building with a lack of external embellishment, whereas some Dublin churches built only a few decades later were of a more ornamented classical type.[6] They include St Michan's, a medieval church rebuilt in 1686 to the designs of Sir William Robinson, laid out on a Renaissance plan with a classical west doorway, and St Mary's, also designed by Robinson, dating from around 1697. St Mary's is reputedly the first church to be built in Ireland with a gallery, in the manner of the new London city churches following the Great Fire in 1666. The English-born Robinson was the most important architect of his time in Ireland being surveyor-general from 1691 until 1700. His most important building was Kilmainham Hospital in Dublin which includes as part of the overall complex, a chapel which displays a profusion of classical decoration including the only important ornamented Carolean ceiling in Ireland, but with an east window which harks back to the medieval in its tracery pattern.

The eighteenth century, the period of the 'Protestant Ascendancy' in Ireland, coincided for the most part with the great age of Georgian classical architecture here, as variations of the style were adapted for both the simplest country churches as well as the more prestigious and elaborate examples in towns. One prominent church, dating from the start of the Georgian era, is St Werburgh's in Dublin (fig. 15), built sometime between 1715 and 1719. It has been attributed to Thomas Burgh, surveyor-general of Ireland in succession to Robinson from 1700, but it may also have involved Allessandro Galilei of Rome. It is notable in that a quintessentially Catholic design of jesuit origin, derived

4 For some seventeenth-century Plantation churches in Ulster see A.J. Rowan, *The buildings of Ireland: north-west Ulster* (London, 1979).   5 For a detailed and illustrated description of Ballinderry Middle Church prior to its restoration, see F.J. Bigger and W.J. Fennell, 'The Middle Church of Ballinderry and Bishop Jeremy Taylor' in *Ulster Journal of Archaeology*, 2nd series, iii (1897), pp 13–22.   6 See H.A. Wheeler and M. Craig, *The Dublin city churches of the Church of Ireland* (Dublin, 1948); and D. Guinness, *Georgian Dublin* (London, 1979).

15 St Werburgh's church, Dublin, original facade, 1715.

from examples in Rome of a century or so before, was adopted for the façade of a Protestant church, although only the lower part of that façade now survives. The interior of St Werburgh's, which was rebuilt in 1759, possibly by John Jarrett, has been described as the finest Georgian church interior in Dublin. Jarrett, it would appear, was also responsible for what has been described as the finest classical church façade in Dublin, that is the boldly modelled neo-Palladian front of St Catherine's, of 1769.

Beyond the capital, Church of Ireland design was usually more modest in ambition, and ranged from the rather clumsily handled classicism of, for example, St John's, Moira, County Down (1726), the work of an anonymous builder, where an over-sized doorcase pushes up into a window above, to the more sophisticated version of the same western entrance tower-and-spire theme at Newtownbreda parish church (fig. 16) near Belfast (1737) designed by Richard Castle, then Ireland's leading architect. Its elements are more neatly proportioned

16 St John's church, Newtownbreda, Co. Down, 1737
by Richard Castle.

17 Cashel cathedral, Co. Tipperary, 1763 with tower and spire
added 1780–8 by Richard Morrison.

and its handling more assured. Another good, but anonymous example of the
same type is Holy Trinity, Ballycastle, County Antrim of 1756, an example of a
landlord's church, very formally treated, with a Venetian window above a
pedimented entrance; it contains a restrained, and still unspoiled classical
interior. Further good examples of landlord churches in classical style, are those
at Donabate, County Dublin (1758), built by the Cobbe family of Newbridge,
with an arcaded octagonal private gallery at the west end, for their use only,
replete with a corner fireplace and plasterwork incorporating the family crest,
and Coolbanagher, County Laois (1785), built by Lord Portarlington of Emo,
to the designs of James Gandon, although its original interior has been altered.

Elsewhere, St Peter's, Drogheda, County Louth, dating from 1748, originally
designed by Hugh Darley but with a later spire added by Francis Johnston,
ranks as one of the finest provincial town churches of the mid-eighteenth
century, while Cashel Church of Ireland cathedral, County Tipperary (fig. 17),
is important as one of the few cathedrals of the eighteenth century in Ireland.

Its main body was built in 1763 while its complex classical west front incorporating a tiered tower and spire was added in 1780–8 by Richard Morrison, one of the most important Irish architects of the time.

The essence of these and most other Georgian churches of the establishment, was a simple rectangular plan, usually with a gallery at the entrance end or round three sides, together with a very much reduced sanctuary or chancel, compared with medieval practice, thus emphasising the importance of the 'Ministry of the Word' as distinct from ritualistic concerns. The inclusion of a rather medieval-looking spire on the exterior of many of these otherwise purely classical buildings is somewhat anachronistic, but it follows the precedent of some of the new London churches by Sir Christopher Wren and his successors, and serves to provide a picturesque landmark in the Irish town and landscape.

Although some eighteenth-century churches were virtually style-less, being built in the plain vernacular tradition of the country and resembling at times little more than a barn, the prevailing fashion among the architecturally aware was for some form of classical style, whether assembled from Renaissance sources, which was the most common approach, as in the examples already mentioned, or based more directly on antiquity as exemplified by the Primate's chapel at Armagh, which was designed by Thomas Cooley in 1771 to resemble a small Roman temple like that of Fortuna Virilis in Rome.

One alternative fashion however, was for a revived form of Gothic styling that recreated some of the features of medieval design and echoed its picturesque qualities, but without any concern for archaeological correctness. This Georgian form of rather superficial Gothic design is commonly referred to as 'Gothick' to distinguish it from the genuine Gothic of the middle ages and from the more serious and scholarly Gothic Revival which was to follow in the nineteenth century.[7] The nave and tower of St Patrick's church in Glenarm, County Antrim of 1763 appears to be the first instance of such a Georgian Gothick church in Ireland,[8] but the most accomplished example is undoubtedly St Malachy's church in Hillsborough, County Down (fig. 18), of 1773. Laid out on a cruciform plan, towered and spired, this is one of the best eighteenth century churches in Ireland, remarkable for the Gothick fittings of its interior which include box pews, a hexagonal pulpit, a throne and an organ. It has been attributed to the English amateur architect Sanderson Miller, who was known in his time as the 'Great Master of Gothick'. Another delightful large-scale Georgian Gothick interior is that of Downpatrick cathedral, a genuine medieval building which was restored and remodelled in this style in the 1790s by Charles Lilly of Dublin followed by R.F. Brettingham of London.

7 For both the Gothick and Gothic Revival phases in eighteenth and nineteenth century Irish architecture see D.S. Richardson, 'Gothic Revival architecture in Ireland', (Ph.D. thesis, Yale University, 1970). 8 See H. McDonnell, 'The building of the parish church at Glenarm' in *The Glynns* x (1982), pp 31–6.

18 St Malachy's church, Hillsborough, Co. Down, 1773.

19 Kilternan church, Co. Dublin, 1826 by John Semple.

Whereas the eighteenth century had coincided for the most part with the great age of Georgian classical architecture here, with only an occasional foray into the Gothick, the nineteenth century was represented by a variety of mainly medieval-revivalist styles.[9] Although an interest in classical design continued for a while as in the case of St George's church, Dublin (1802–14) by Francis Johnston of Armagh, or St Stephen's church, Dublin (1825) by John Bowden, possibly the last of its type, most of the leading architects looked back to the middle ages for inspiration, in particular to the Gothic period, but there were also limited excursions into the Early Christian and the Romanesque. The early decades of the century were dominated by the extensive church building and re-building

9 See P. Larmour, 'The styles of Irish church architecture in the nineteenth century' in Hurley and Larmour (eds), *Sacred places*, pp 10–13; and A. Rowan, 'Irish Victorian churches: denominational distinctions' in R. Gillespie and B.P. Kennedy (eds), *Ireland, art into history* (Dublin and Colorado, 1994), pp 207–30.

campaign directed by the government-funded Board of First Fruits. A simplified Gothic style was favoured by the various architects of the board, characterised by square towers, thin spires, crude pinnacles, battlemented walls, and pointed windows with elementary tracery and sometimes laid out on a cruciform plan.

The most original creations by the various architects who worked for the board were those by John Semple of Dublin whose handling of the Gothic style was more idiosyncratic than most (fig. 19): he designed St Mary's, known as 'The Black Church', in Dublin (1830) (fig. 20) with an unusual parabolic vaulted interior, and the even more remarkable church at Monkstown, County Dublin (1831) (fig. 21), adorned with towers and turrets, in a variation of the style that is hard to categorise. Other Gothic-style work of the early part of the century includes the Castle chapel in Dublin of 1807–14 by Francis Johnston of Armagh with a very ornate interior, the first neo-Gothic church to be built within Dublin, originally built for the Church of Ireland but later transferred to the Catholic church, and the more simplified, almost toy-like Cahir parish church, County Tipperary, of 1817 (fig. 22), designed by the famous English architect John Nash.

A more serious and archaeologically inspired Gothic Revival style developed in the 1840s following the lead given by the English architect A.W.N. Pugin who believed that a 'correct' medieval setting was the only suitable one for Christian worship. Although, as a convert to Catholicism, Pugin's personal concern was with Catholic church architecture, his ideals regarding the revival of Gothic design were shared by Protestants, including various ecclesiological societies in both England and Ireland, and his liking for a distinctive medieval layout and carefully observed English detail was as readily taken up within the Church of Ireland as it was by the Catholic church. Thus one of his earliest and most committed followers in Ireland was Joseph Welland who from 1843 until his death in 1860 was the sole architect to the Ecclesiastical Commissioners of the Church of Ireland, a new body which had replaced the old Board of First Fruits in 1833. Welland designed over one hundred churches besides numerous enlargements and alterations. Among his larger works are the churches at Lisnaskea, County Fermanagh (1852), Ballymena, County Antrim (1855) (fig. 23), Magherafelt, County Londonderry (1856–8), Gorey, County Wexford (1858–63) (fig. 24), and Zion church, Rathgar, Dublin (1859–62) (fig. 25). These churches, all typical of the early Victorian phase of the Gothic Revival, display a sympathetic use of local materials, with open timber trusses inside and a clear separation of parts on plan with the nave, chancel, robing room and porch all given individual expression outside.

Joseph Welland was followed in his official role in Dublin by his son William and his partner William Gillespie, from 1860 until disestablishment of the Church of Ireland in 1869. They designed many Gothic Revival churches all over Ireland in a High Victorian treatment of the style, the difference now mainly being one of more jagged angularity of form usually coupled with greater variety in materials,

20 St Mary's ('The Black Church'), Dublin, 1830 by John Semple.

21 Monkstown church, Co. Dublin, 1831 by John Semple.

such as bands of different coloured masonry or dressings in brick. Other leading Church of Ireland architects of the High Victorian era working mainly in Gothic style, were Lanyon, Lynn and Lanyon of Belfast who designed St Andrew's in Dublin (1860–6), and William Atkins of Cork, responsible for a number of churches in the 1860s including Killarney, County Kerry (1865–8) and Eastferry, County Cork (fig.26).

Various English architects, some of them leaders in ecclesiological circles, appeared in Ireland from time to time to carry out Church of Ireland works, from small churches to large cathedrals: among the most notable were William Slater who designed St Fethlimidh's cathedral, Kilmore, County Cavan (1857–60) (fig. 27); G.E. Street who designed small churches – at Piltown, County Kilkenny (1859–60) and Ardamine, County Wexford (1860–1) – as well as rebuilding Christ Church cathedral in Dublin (1871–8); William Butterfield who designed St Mark's, Belfast (1876–8); and William Burges whose magnificent cathedral of St Finn Barre in Cork (1865–79) (fig. 28) is perhaps the most spectacular example of High Victorian Early French Gothic anywhere in the British Isles.

Although Gothic Revivalism was the dominant force in the Victorian era there were other alternatives to it within the broad medieval-revivalist spectrum. The

22 Cahir parish church, Co. Tipperary, 1817 by John Nash.

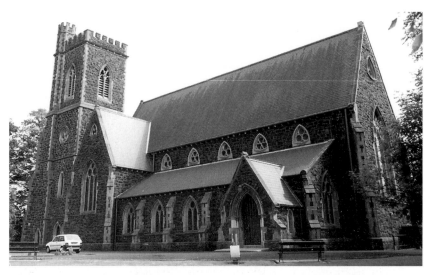

23 St Patrick's church, Ballymena, Co. Antrim, 1855 by Joseph Welland.

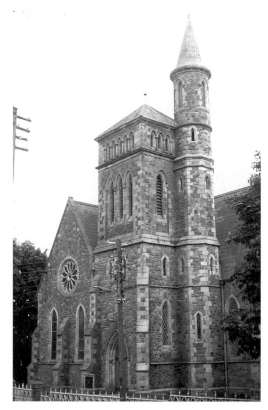

24 Christchurch, Gorey,
Co. Wexford, 1858–63
by Joseph Welland.

25 Zion church, Rathgar, Dublin, 1859–62 by Joseph Welland.

26 Eastferry church, Co. Cork, 1860s by William Atkins.

most popular alternative was Romanesque which came in various forms: Norman, as at St John the Evangelist's, Sandymount, Dublin (1849) by Benjamin Ferrey of London; and Lombardic, based on churches in Northern Italy, as at Sandford Church, Sandford Road, Dublin (1860) by Lanyon, Lynn and Lanyon. One revival which struck a uniquely national chord was the Hiberno–Romanesque, in the manner of early Irish work, occasionally with an attached circular belfry, alluding to the Irish Round Towers of the Early Christian and Romanesque periods.[10] The earliest example of such a Celtic Revivalist 'round tower church', as the type may be called, was St Patrick's Church of Ireland church at Jordanstown, County Antrim (1865–8), designed by W.H. Lynn of Lanyon, Lynn and Lanyon (fig. 29). The arrangement of its attached belfry was

10 For the Hiberno-Romanesque Revival see P. Larmour, 'The Celtic Revival and a national style of architecture', (Ph.D. thesis, The Queen's University of Belfast, 1977); see also J. Sheehy, *The rediscovery of Ireland's past: the Celtic Revival, 1830–1930* (London, 1980).

27 St Fethlimidh's cathedral, Kilmore, Co. Cavan, 1857–60 by William Slater.

consciously based on the twelfth-century example of Temple Finghin at Clonmacnoise, but the overall treatment of the church is very free, with a more complex plan than any early Irish work, which includes an un-Irish curved apse. Most other Church of Ireland examples of the 'round tower church' were even more freely treated, being Gothic in style rather than Romanesque, such as St Patrick's, Ballyclog, County Tyrone (1865) by Welland and Gillespie (fig. 30), and St Patrick's, Kilcock, County Kildare (1869–70) by J.E. Rogers. The most ornate of Hiberno-Romanesque Revival churches was Rathdaire Memorial, Ballybrittas, County Laois (1885) by James Fuller (fig. 31). It has a square tower of Lombardic Romanesque type and its overall plan is equally un-Irish but the west front arcading is based on the twelfth-century church of St Cronan at Roscrea in County Tipperary, and is lavishly carved with Celtic ornamentation.

Historicism was to hold sway throughout the first half of the twentieth century, as the old parade of revivalist styles continued, with little apparent change from the Victorian era. There was of course no special virtue in modernity itself and much historicist church design in Ireland in the first half of the twentieth century was very accomplished in its handling of traditional styles, often characterised by building craftsmanship of considerable quality. Good examples from the Edwardian era include St Patrick's, Castle Archdale, County Fermanagh (1905–8), designed by Thomas Drew in late Gothic style, and the Church of the Good Shepherd, Sion Mills, County Tyrone (1909) (fig. 32), designed by William Unsworth in an unusually elaborate Italian Romanesque style.

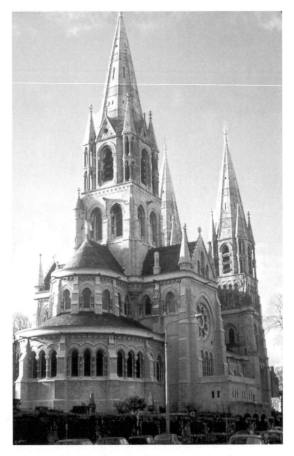

28 St Finn Barre's cathedral, Cork, 1865–79
by William Burges, rear view.

Dating from the inter-war era are St Thomas's church in Dublin (1930–2), designed by F.G. Hicks in a Lombardic style, which achieved a measure of architectural recognition by being selected by the Royal Institute of the Architects of Ireland for the first award of its gold medal in 1932–4, and St Patrick's Memorial church at Saul, County Down (1932–3), designed by Henry Seaver in Celtic Romanesque style (fig. 33). The church at Saul was built to commemorate the 1500th anniversary of St Patrick establishing his first church in Ireland in 432 on the site of a barn, and its distinctive round belfry therefore provides a very appropriate symbol of the early days of the church in Ireland.

A traditional approach to church design clearly suited a largely conservative and backward-looking clergy not only in the Church of Ireland but indeed in all denominations in Ireland, even after the onset of modern design in architecture

29 St Patrick's church, Jordanstown, Co. Antrim, 1865–8
by Lanyon, Lynn and Lanyon.

30 St Patrick's church, Ballyclog, Co. Tyrone, 1865 by Welland and Gillespie.

generally, and continued unabated into the post Second World War era.[11] Thus we had churches of neo-Gothic type in the mid-1950s, such as Orangefield in Belfast (1955–7), designed by Gibson and Taylor, and St Barnabas in Belfast (1955–6), designed by John MacGeagh, impressive in their way but entirely backward-looking by comparison with progressive Continental works of anything up to thirty years before.

Historicism was only brought to an end in the 1960s when church design in Ireland finally caught up with other building types, coinciding to some extent with new liturgical requirements; from thereon a rich variety of 'modern' styles

11 See P. Larmour, 'Twentieth-century church architecture in Ireland', in A. Becker, J. Olley and W. Wang (eds), *Twentieth-century architecture: Ireland* (Munich and New York, 1997), pp 61–5; and for illustrations of some twentieth century Church of Ireland churches in Belfast see P. Larmour, *Belfast: an illustrated architectural guide* (Belfast, 1987).

31 Rathdaire Memorial church, Ballybrittas, Co. Laois, 1885–7 by James Fuller.

32 Church of the Good Shepherd, Sion Mills, Co. Tyrone, 1909
by William Unsworth.

33 St Patrick's Memorial church, Saul, Co. Down, 1932–3
by Henry Seaver.

34 St Ignatius' church, Carryduff, Co. Down, 1964–5 by Donald Shanks.

35 St Gall's church, Bangor, Co. Down, 1964–6 by Edwin Leighton.

36 Knocknagoney church, Co. Down, 1964 by Desmond Hodges.

37 Knocknagoney church, Co. Down, 1964 by Desmond Hodges, interior.

was to enliven the churches built in the rest of the century. Among the more notable examples exhibiting modern styling are the Church of the Pentecost, Cregagh, Belfast (1961–3), with its large glazed entrance gable, and St Molua's, Stormont, Belfast (1961–2), with its tall serrated side windows of abstract design, both designed by Denis O'D. Hanna; St Ignatius's, at Carryduff outside Belfast (1964–5) (fig. 34), designed by Donald Shanks, which has an octagonally planned interior lit by unusual large triangular and kite-shaped windows, and St Gall's, at Bangor, County Down (1964–6) (fig. 35), designed by Shanks's partner Edwin Leighton in the form of a rectangular box with a belfry of abstract design.

Often the modernity of these new churches was one of stylistic appearance only – abstract architectural shapes with 'contemporary' patterns in the windows, and novel forms in the furnishings – with the plan and layout remaining as traditional as ever, but there were exceptions. The church at Knocknagoney near Belfast (1964), designed by Desmond Hodges, was certainly given an overtly modern appearance, with continuous glazing above screen walls, rising to an angular copper roof carried on exposed tubular steel frames (fig. 36, 37). More significantly, however, it was influenced by the new liturgical movement which put the main emphasis on the sacrament of corporate Communion bringing the congregation into a closer relationship with the act of worship than hitherto in the Church of Ireland. This was achieved by means of a square plan with the main entrance, baptistery, choir and holy table placed on the diagonal of the square, and the pews angled to each side to partly embrace the sanctuary.[12] Meanwhile, at the Church of the Resurrection in Elmwood Avenue, Belfast (1963–5), designed for the Church of Ireland chaplaincy of Queen's University by Edwin Leighton of the firm of Shanks and Leighton, the idea of a single Eucharistic room where the laity were enabled to gather around the Communion table took a further step toward realisation, in a thoroughly modern building characterised by a central cubic space articulated by a concrete frame surmounted by a tall polygonal lantern light reminiscent of a traditional church spire (fig. 38).

It was in such inventive blending of old and new ideas that the most satisfying experiments in modern church design were carried out but the scope for new building steadily diminished as the twentieth century drew to a close. At the dawn of a new age, Church of Ireland architecture seems likely to confront new challenges. Changing spiritual needs, together with changing patterns of worship and diminishing resources and numbers, will undoubtedly place new demands on architectural ingenuity and also raise crucial questions about the future of the existing church building heritage of the Church of Ireland.

12 The church at Knocknagoney was a rare instance of a twentieth-century Church of Ireland church being publicised in the specialist architectural press, for which see *The Architects' Journal*, 11 Nov. 1964, pp 1111–14.

38 Church of the Resurrection, Queen's University, Church of Ireland Student Centre, Elmwood Ave., Belfast, 1963–5 by Shanks and Leighton.

MATTERS LITURGICAL[13]

Unlike England, which has a rich heritage of medieval churches still in use, in Ireland many parish churches and cathedrals were destroyed during the numerous conflagrations that took place from the Anglo-Norman occupation to the pre-Reformation period and beyond.[14] The Gothic architecture employed in the design of the churches of the middle ages with its elaborate decoration was gradually replaced by the classical style of architecture favoured by the Renaissance and influenced by the theology of the Reformation. As the Reformation movement took hold, those churches that survived the centuries

13 By Stephen McBride.   14 F.R. Bolton, *The Caroline tradition of the Church of Ireland* (London, 1958), pp 204–11 describes in detail the ruinous state of many of the churches in the aftermath of various campaigns.

39 Middle Church, Ballinderry, Co. Antrim, 1668, pulpit.

of destruction were gradually cleared of the candlesticks, crosses, embellishments and rood screens of the middle ages. Medieval wall paintings were replaced with inscriptions of the Lord's Prayer, Apostles' Creed and the Ten Commandments.[15] There was also opportunity for the self-glorification of the rich in many churches where walls became covered with lists of benefactors and pompous memorial tablets with fulsome inscriptions.[16]

Liturgical, priestly ceremonial was simplified and although Cranmer's Book of Common Prayer of 1549 was initially regarded with suspicion in Ireland, it eventually brought about a style of worship that encouraged a corporate participation. Worship moved away from the objective and sacramental

15 F.H. Crossley, *English church craftsmanship* (2nd ed., London, 1947), p. 10: 'The dislike of colour after the Reformation was sufficiently powerful to ensure its systematic destruction; glass was broken, walls were whitewashed and what furniture was allowed to remain, generally defaced.' 16 A.L. Drummond, *The architecture of Protestantism* (Edinburgh, 1934), pp 37–9.

emphasis of the medieval church and developed into the subjective worship we now associate with Protestantism.

The new emphasis on Bible reading and preaching was reflected in the architectural layout of many churches that were built in the post-Reformation period and it gave rise to a great deal of debate with regard to the positioning of the altar within many of the European Protestant churches at this time.[17] Lutheran churches tended to favour a more balanced approach with altar and pulpit being given equal emphasis while the Calvinist churches were generally fitted with a large pulpit, seating and little else. In Anglican architecture, the chancel in many churches was reduced to a niche or recess containing the Holy Table as there was no longer the necessity to provide an area to accommodate large numbers of priests. Although Canon 81 of the English Canons of 1604 stipulated that a stone font should be provided in churches often it was nothing more significant than a vase or basin placed on a moveable pedestal which was generally kept in the vestry.

The three-decker pulpit (as at Middle Church, Ballinderry (fig. 39), which was largely an Anglican innovation, developed as a direct result of the importance that was now being placed on the reading of the scriptures and preaching during divine worship. This novel piece of ecclesiastical furniture combined the pulpit, a desk for the clerk who led the congregation in their liturgical responses and singing and a reading desk from which the minister conducted the service. As services became longer with the emphasis shifting to the sermon, the need for better seating was another feature of church design. Benches were transformed by richly carved boards which were set at either end and box pews were developed to increase creature comfort and to ward off drafts during lengthy sermons. The squire's pew sometimes had a fireplace set in an outside wall. Over all towered the panelled three-decker with its menacing sounding board.[18]

The principal personality who gave architectural expression to the changes in worship brought about by the Book of Common Prayer was Sir Christopher Wren. Following the Great Fire of London in 1666, Wren had the opportunity to design the replacements for sixty of the eighty-seven churches that were destroyed. Very few churches had been built in England from the Reformation to 1666 and Wren, freed from the constraints of medieval architecture, adopted the basilican auditory style of church, which had already been used in many European Protestant churches. This form of architecture provided a suitable setting for the dignity of the services of the Book of Common Prayer.[19] It is not altogether true to say that the sermon was regarded as more important than the sacraments, but as Sir Christopher Wren wrote, 'In our Reformed religion, it

17 T. Cocke, 'Liturgy' in M. Binney and P. Burman (eds), *Change and decay, the future of our churches* (London, 1977), pp 129–34.   18 H. Braun, *Parish churches, their architectural development in England* (London, 1970), p. 209.   19 For biographical details of Wren, see K. Downes, *The architecture of Wren* (London, 1982), H.F. Hutchinson, *Sir Christopher Wren: a biography* (London, 1976).

40 St John's church, Ballymore, Co. Donegal, 1752 by Michael Priestly.

would seem vain to make a parish church larger than that all are present can both see and hear ... It is enough if they (the Romanists) hear the murmur of the Mass and see the elevation of the host, but ours are fitted as auditories'.[20] In Wren's designs, the altar, or Communion Table, was not the main focus of attention when one entered his churches and this was in contrast to the contemporary Catholic architecture where altars and chancels were given an almost theatrical treatment to emphasise the doctrine of the Real Presence of Christ in the Eucharist. The use of the classical style, which Wren had pioneered in the Church of England, dominated ecclesiastical architecture in the British Isles until the beginning of the nineteenth century (fig. 40).

In the early part of the nineteenth century, however, there were various developments that changed the situation architecturally. In England the established church had to satisfy a demand for more church buildings as a result of the population shift which had occurred due to the industrial revolution. In 1818 the first Church Building Act was passed and £1 million was allocated to build one hundred churches at a cost of £10,000 each.[21] The Church Building

---

20 C. Wren, *Parentalia, or memoirs of the family of Wrens* (London, 1750; facsimile reprint, London, 1965).   21 M.H. Port, *Six hundred new churches: a study of the Church Building Commission 1818–1856, and its church building activities* (London, 1961), p. 21.

Commission was set up to oversee this operation and guidelines were laid down for the building of these churches. Economy of construction and maximum seating capacity were the two main constraints the architects had to work with. Faced with a choice of styles, the Commissioners in the end preferred the Gothic style to the Classical style, not on stylistic considerations but purely on the grounds of cost. A subsequent shift to Gothic was to have more than just stylistic and economic consequences.

The most influential personality involved in the development of the Gothic Revival in the British Isles in the 1830s and 40s was Augustus Welby Northmore Pugin,[22] a prophetic figure who devoted all his energy to propagating a gospel of medieval design philosophy and technique with an evangelical zeal. He believed that it was essential for an ecclesiastical architect to have not only a knowledge of Gothic architecture from the stylistic point of view, but also to know about the Church's liturgy and rubrics, and its rites and ceremonies. This change of emphasis would soon raise a challenge to accepted practises within the Protestant church although Pugin's personal preoccupation was with the Catholic church to which he had become a convert. Meanwhile, within the Church of England a group of men whose collective efforts was to become known as the Oxford Movement, began to question the relationship between the Established Church and State. It was the passing of the Irish Church Temporalities Act in 1833, which sought to rationalise and reorganise the bishoprics of the Church of Ireland that finally sparked off the Oxford Movement.[23] As the teaching of the Tractarians developed, with their stress on Apostolic Succession, ministerial priesthood and the Sacraments, they hoped that the Church of England could act as a *via media* between Protestantism and the Church of Rome but because of their hostility to the teachings of the Reformation, they were soon charged with writing propaganda documents for popery.

The Cambridge Camden Society, which has been described as a 'by-product' and a 'natural development'[24] of the Oxford Movement,[25] was inspired by the sacramental ethos promoted by the Tractarians and also by the antiquarian study of mediaeval Gothic which Pugin had been exploring. The Society was founded by two undergraduates, John Mason Neale and Benjamin Webb in

22 See P. Stanton, *Pugin* (London, 1971) for biographical detail.   23 G. Rowell, *The Vision Glorious: themes and personalities of the Catholic Revival in Anglicanism* (Oxford, 1983), p. 21. 24 B. G. Worrall, *The making of the modern Church* (London, 1988), p. 33.   25 N. Yates, *The Oxford Movement and Anglican ritualism* (London, 1983), p. 15 suggests that the success of the Oxford Movement and the influence it exerted owed a great deal to the Camden Society. 26 The most comprehensive history of the Cambridge Camden Society is to be found in J.F. White, *The Cambridge movement: the ecclesiologists and the Gothic Revival* (Cambridge, 1962). see also E.J. Boyce, *A memorial of the Cambridge Camden Society* (London, 1888), A.G. Lough, *The influence of John Mason Neale* (London, 1962), M. Chandler, *The life and work of John Mason Neale* (Leominster, 1995).

41 Christ Church, Belfast, 1833 by William Farrell.

42 Christ Church, Belfast, 1833 by William Farrell, interior.

1839 with the aim of restoring old churches and influencing the building of new ones so that they would conform to what the ecclesiologists held to be a correct interpretation of Gothic architecture.[26] The society published its own journal, the *Ecclesiologist*, from 1841 until 1867, and in it they outlined their views on every aspect of Church architecture.

Those who were opposed to the tenets of the Oxford Movement and the Camden Society were worried that an undue emphasis was being placed on the Sacraments by the renewed interest in chancels and fonts, while the Ministry of the Word was in danger of being overlooked. The introduction of ritual and ceremonial from the pre-Reformation church along with coloured stoles and lighted candles on the altar infuriated Evangelicals as well as churchmen from other theological parties.[27] The Gothic style, which had been used in the 1820s to build the Commissioners' churches in England without any protest, was subsequently viewed with suspicion by Evangelicals who saw the introduction of medieval architecture and ritual as 'popish error'.

Richard Mant, an Englishman, who was bishop of Down and Connor from 1823 to 1848, was a member of the Church Building Commission and regularly made valuable contributions to its development.[28] He maintained his links and attended occasional meetings of the Commission even after his elevation to the bench.[29] His passion for architecture was a great benefit to the United Diocese of Down and Connor which undertook a programme of church extension to meet the demands of a population explosion in the Belfast area which had grown from around 30,000 inhabitants in 1823 to almost 61,000 in 1834. Bishop Mant had expressed his concerns about the lack of church accommodation in his dioceses to the Board of First Fruits as early as 1830, and one tangible result of his efforts was the building of Christ Church in Durham Street in Belfast in 1833 (figs. 41, 42). In Belfast, before Christ Church was built, in St Anne's and St George's churches only a dozen or so seats out of 2,500 sittings were available to the poor.

The development of the pew and box pew in the post-Reformation period created a social demarcation within parish churches with the largest and most comfortable pews at the front of the building. The smaller, less well furnished benches for the poorer classes were relegated to the back.[30] The local gentry often had their pews situated in the transepts, and occasionally even had a separate exterior entrance built to maintain their distance, an example being the

---

27 N. Yates, *Oxford Movement*, p. 14. See also W.N. Yates, *Buildings, faith and worship* (Oxford, 1991), p. 139. Yates lists the locations where riots occurred because of the introduction of ceremonial. 28 For biographical details of Mant see W.H. Mant, *Memoirs of the Rt Rev Richard Mant, D.D., M.R.I.A., lord bishop of Down and Connor, and of Dromore* (Dublin, 1857). F.R. Bolton, 'Richard Mant (1776–1848), bishop of Down, Connor and Dromore' in *Theology*, lii, no. 341 (Nov. 1948), pp 403–10. 29 Port, *Six hundred new churches*, p. 15. 30 Yates, *Buildings, faith and worship*, pp 36–40.

43 Gartree church, Langford Lodge, Co. Antrim, 1831 by James Sands.

Pakenham family's arrangements at Gartree church, County Antrim (fig. 43). The plight of the poor and their inability to gain entry to a church in Belfast was no different to any other city at that time. The Cambridge Camden Society campaigned vigorously to rid churches of box pews and a paper that was read to the society was prefixed with twenty-four reasons for getting rid of church pews. The author argued that 'pues' (to use their archaic spelling) were invented by people who thought themselves too good to pray by the side of their neighbours: and who were too proud to join in the service of God with such as were poorer than themselves and Pues shut out the poor, who ought, if there be any difference, to be first cared for in church, not last.[31] As well as the spiritual and social dilemma created by pews, the author also hinted that pews provided worshippers with the opportunity to conduct themselves in activities that were not altogether edifying 'many wicked practices have been, and sometimes (it is to be feared) are still, carried on in Pues. Those who sit in them can amuse themselves, or go to sleep, as they will, without a fear that any human should see them'.[32] By the 1850s open benches were favoured by architects designing new churches and in most alterations and renovations, they were used to replace the high sided, closed, box pews.[33]

31 Anon., *The history of Pues* (Cambridge, 1843), p. v.   32 Ibid.,p. vii.   33 P.F. Anson, *Fashions in church furnishings 1840–1940* (London, 1960), p. 93.

44 Architect's original perspective drawing for St Jude's church, Muckamore, Co. Antrim, 1841–2 by Charles Lanyon.

Mant made little progress with the Board or its subsequent body the Church Commissioners and consequently some members of the diocese organised what became known as the 'Great Meeting' which was held in Christ Church in December 1838.[34] The Down and Connor Church Accommodation Society was formed as a result of this meeting, and after only one month the funds of the society exceeded £9,000. It was envisaged that grants of £1,000 would be made to areas that were in most need of church accommodation. The Accommodation Society was initially planned to have a duration of four years and in that time grants were made to twenty projects which produced sixteen new church buildings. Charles Lanyon, county surveyor of Antrim, offered his services to the society and designed the churches free of charge.[35] The churches constructed by the Accommodation Society included Muckamore (fig. 44), Killagan, Whitehouse, Craigs, Glynn, Raloo (fig. 45) and Ballyclug, all in County Antrim; Groomsport, Hollymount and Tyrella in County Down; and Trinity Church in Belfast. (fig. 46) They were all designed in Gothic style, mainly variations of two standard designs, with a minimum of architectural embellishment. Simplicity was clearly of the

34 Anon., *Great meeting of the diocese of Down and Connor, for church extension* (Belfast, 1838).
35 P. Larmour, 'Sir Charles Lanyon' in *Irish Arts Review Yearbook 1989–90*, pp 200–6. P. Larmour, '"The father of Ulster architecture", Sir Charles Lanyon (1813–59)' in *Perspective*, ii, no. 5, (May/June, 1994), pp 53–4.

45 Raloo church, Co. Antrim, 1842 by Charles Lanyon.

essence: as a contemporary commented at the time, 'it is not fine temples that are desired, but humble, at the same time, respectable houses of worship'.[36]

In 1842, Bishop Mant had been invited to become a member of the Cambridge Camden Society, and in October 1842, he established the Down and Connor and Dromore Church Architecture Society to further the study of ecclesiastical architecture.[37] The membership of the society included many who were also members of the Church Accommodation Society. In his opening address to the Church Architecture Society, Mant, aware of the possibility of an adverse reaction to the infant society, avoided any criticism that he was travelling in a Romeward direction by saying 'whatever tends to add dignity and majesty to the houses of God in our land, provided it be free from all superstitious admixture, is deserving of our encouragement: whatever tends to diminish those qualities, is deserving of censure and reprobation.'[38] It might be thought that a diocesan architecture society would be widely welcomed in the church, especially at a time when the Down and Connor Church Accommodation Society was

36 *Ulster Times*, 22 Dec. 1838.   37 Mant's pamphlet *Church architecture considered in relation to the mind of the Church since and before the Reformation* (Belfast, 1843) was favourably reviewed in the *Ecclesiologist* and Mant's desire for the correct furnishing of churches is to be found in several of the 'charges' he delivered to the clergy of his dioceses.   38 *Ulster Times*, 8 Oct. 1842.

46 Architect's original interior drawing for Trinity church, Belfast, 1843
by Charles Lanyon.

involved in a programme of erecting new church buildings in the United
diocese. However, during his inaugural speech, Bishop Mant made favourable
references to the universities of Oxford and Cambridge and these were severely
criticised in the local press. Oxford was still coming to terms with the aftermath
of Newman's *Tract 90* and the Cambridge Camden Society was accused by
many within the church of architecturally developing the Catholic spirituality
of the Oxford Movement in a way that was being unfaithful to the Reformation
and all that it had achieved.

To a 'Protestant' member of the Established Church in Ulster in the 1840s,
Oxford and Cambridge were seen to be bastions of 'popery', and because of
this, for such people, there could be nothing emanating from them that should

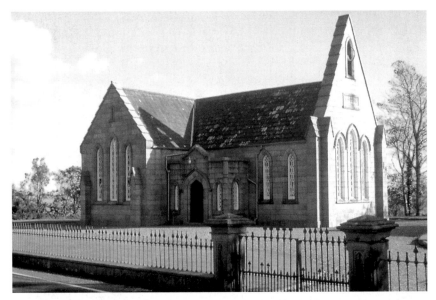

47 Tyrella church, Co. Down, 1842 by Charles Lanyon.

be allowed find a place within the Church of Ireland.[39] The bishop's initial stress on the 'ancient position of the font,' and more dangerously, his passing reference to the communion table as an 'altar' would have been enough to confirm in the minds of those who were cautious of any new innovation, or one that sought to re-establish a medieval tradition, that the Architecture Society should not be given a chance to develop its aims and aspirations.

These were days of unnatural excitement and the Church Architecture Society was judged, and condemned, by some persons, not for what it had done, but for what its accusers imagined it intended to do, and for the supposed evil doings of the Cambridge Camden Society, of which it was represented to be an affiliated branch.[40] Unlike the Church of England, where Catholicism posed little more than a minimal threat, the Church of Ireland had a well developed 'siege mentality' which manifested itself in a fear and suspicion of the Roman Church and this was a theological issue that united high churchmen and evangelicals in the Church of Ireland. There were many who were determined that the perceived 'Romish' architectural practices of the Cambridge Camden Society would not find their way into the Church of Ireland. William MacIlwaine, rector of St George's, Belfast and a noted Evangelical brought the case for the

39 D. Hempton and M. Hill, *Evangelical Protestantism in Ulster society 1740–1890* (London, 1992) and D. Bowen, *The Protestant crusade in Ireland 1800–1870* (Dublin, 1978) illustrate the anti-Catholic polemic that was prevalent at this time. 40 W.H. Mant, *Memoirs*, p. 422.

prosecution of Mant and the Church Architecture Society. He wrote in the *Belfast Commercial Chronicle* under the *nom de plume* of 'Clericus Connorensis'. The *Chronicle* gave him free reign to attack the Church Architecture Society and its main rival, the *Ulster Times* which had given the infant society a very favourable review.

Bishop Mant did not enter into the debate; instead, Lord Dungannon, a vice-president of the Church Architecture Society, who resided in Oswestry and was a generous benefactor of the Church of Ireland, the Revd John Monsell, who was a secretary of the society, and Archdeacon Walter Mant, son of the bishop, rector of Hillsborough and a secretary of the society, all argued on the Architecture Society's behalf. The main areas of contention centred around alterations to the plans and furnishings of Tyrella church (fig. 47) and the links between the Church Architecture Society and the Church Accommodation Society, and between the Church Architecture Society and the Cambridge Camden Society. The *Belfast Commercial Chronicle* was alarmed that the original plans for Tyrella had been altered and seats had been removed. A lectern had also been introduced and the reading desk modified. These apparently innocent changes were seen at the time to be the thin end of a Puseyite wedge. Tyrella church was to become a test case for exposing the influence the Architecture Society had on the Accommodation Society.

Mant's opponents set out to undermine his authority within the diocese and they urged people to withhold their donations to the Church Accommodation Society until the Architecture Society was dissolved. A petition, or 'Memorial' was circulated throughout the United Diocese of Connor, Down and Dromore in January 1843. It stated that the confidence within the United Diocese had been shaken due to the infiltration of the doctrines contained in documents emanating from Oxford and Cambridge. The memorial contained around 1,300 signatures including a peer of the realm, one M.P., eleven deputy lieutenants and forty justices of the peace. The memorialists presented their petition to Mant who met them with a prepared statement, which must have taken over one hour to deliver. He said that most of the people who signed the memorial were of limited intelligence and defective knowledge. Although Mant's reply stated that the memorial would not bring about the closure of the Architecture Society, it did achieve its purpose. The Church Architecture Society dissolved its links with the Cambridge Camden Society and Mant tendered his resignation as a patron of the society.

The Down and Connor and Dromore Church Architecture Society (to give it its full name) was in effective existence only from October 1842 until March 1843. It changed its name in 1845 to the Harris Society and continued to meet until 1849, but it did not create any further disturbance.[41] The weight of public

41 Ibid., pp 425–6.

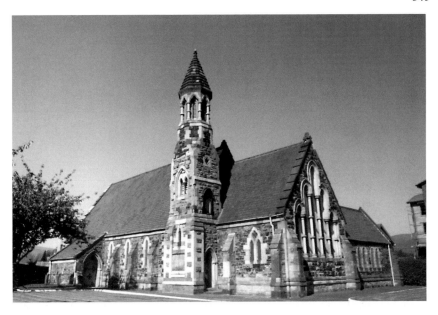

48 St Paul's church, York Street, Belfast, 1851, by Charles Lanyon and W.H. Lynn.

opinion had caused Bishop Mant to be transformed from a bishop who was not going to let his episcopal authority be undermined by 'a mob of uneducated and ill informed people' into a conciliatory figure who was willing to forsake his own views for the good of his diocese.

As a result of the anti-Puseyite feelings that were prevalent in Ulster and throughout the Church of Ireland at that time, we have very few churches, which adopted all the embellishments which were introduced by the ecclesiologists. There were very few Anglo-Catholics in the Church of Ireland in the mid-nineteenth century and architects had to respect the wishes of their clients, many of whom had no place in their buildings for an elaborate rood-screen or a highly decorated chancel and sanctuary. In any case, architects for the Church of Ireland usually had only a fraction of the funds available to their counterparts working for the Church of England.

Despite the generally cautious approach to embellishment and decoration in Irish churches, problems arose from time to time. Although the controversies surrounding the Church Architecture Society had concluded eight years previously, Charles Lanyon's firm found itself at the centre of a new architectural debate in 1851. Lanyon's assistant, William Henry Lynn had specified gable crosses for the design of St Paul's Church, York Street, Belfast but as soon as they were erected by the builder they had been removed by people who believed them to be 'trappings of Popery.' (fig. 48) A report of the consecration

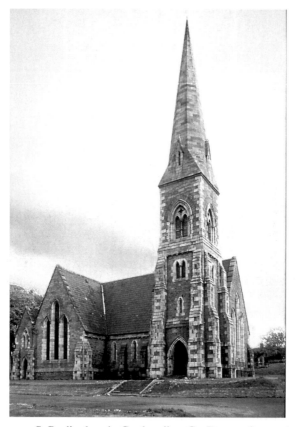

49 St Paul's church, Castlewellan, Co. Down, 1847–53 by
Charles Lanyon and W.H. Lynn.

of the church, which appeared in *The Builder*,[42] noted that 'the gable-crosses
were twice purposely thrown down during the erection of this church.' This
incident provoked Arthur, Viscount Dungannon to write an open letter to the
lord primate of Ireland complaining against the behaviour of people whose
actions he regarded as acts of 'wanton desecration well calculated to excite the
disgust of every sound churchman.'[43] The crosses, which were actually a gift of
the architect, were smashed and Dungannon was incensed that members of
society supposedly acting under misguided reasoning, were unable to
distinguish between the sacred and the profane. To avoid further contention,
the architect replaced them with 'enormous stone finials of questionable taste.'

Just prior to the trouble at St Paul's in Belfast, the architect W.H. Lynn,
again acting for Charles Lanyon, had encountered similar sensitivities when he

42 *The Builder*, ix no. 455 (1851), p. 679.   43 Viscount Dungannon, *Why should crosses on our
churches be objectionable?* (Oswestry, 1851).

50 Ballymoyer Church, Co. Armagh, remodelled 1863–5 by
William Barre.

was asked in 1849 to design finial crosses for St Paul's in Castlewellan, County
Down (fig. 49). The Revd J.R. Moore, brother of the dowager Countess Annesley,
whose family helped to finance the church, was agreeable to the incorporation
of gable crosses but he was aware of the possible difficulties they might cause
and had advised Lynn accordingly:

> I merely throw out the suggestion for your approval, ... I think it would
> improve the appearance of the building very much if you put a cross of an
> oval shape (if correct) or of any other form on the gable next the road, the
> square pedestal will look bare and unfinished.... As there is a feeling
> against crosses, if a circular one like a wheel could be put next the road,
> people who have hot heads and bad eyes might take it for a chimney.[44]

St Paul's, Castlewellan is a good example of a church which was endowed
and financed by a wealthy family who had been influenced by the manifestations
of the Gothic Revival in the architecture of the Church of England and who
were not afraid to adopt them even if it incurred the wrath of local parishioners.

A further episode concerning antagonism toward exterior crosses occurred
when another Belfast-based architect, William Barre designed and had executed

44 P.J. Rankin, *Historic buildings and groups of buildings. Areas of architectural importance in the
Mourne area of south Down* (Belfast, 1975), p. 26.

three Celtic crosses for the apexes on the north, south and west gables of Drumglass parish church in Dungannon, County Tyrone (1865–9).[45] When the builder began to erect them, it was said that some persons, mainly from outside the parish, had threatened to remove them if they were put in place.

Barre's alterations to Ballymoyer church in the diocese of Armagh is another example of a privately endowed church which embodied many ecclesiological influences without any fear of recriminations from local parishioners. The remodelled church has gable crosses on the tower, nave and chancel (fig. 50), while the label-stops of the east window incorporate two crowned figures, one of which is reputed to be Mary, Queen of Heaven. Internally, the corbels supporting the trusses in the chancel are carved in the form of angels in devotional attitude, and the stained glass throughout the building is very Anglo-Catholic in its themes.

Although there were architectural and liturgical disagreements from time to time, this was not always the case. As Belfast's industrial expansion continued throughout the nineteenth century the Belfast Church Extension and Endowment Society[46] was set up in 1863 to provide additional church accommodation in areas of need in Belfast as well as establishing much needed endowments. Eighteen years had elapsed since the closure of the Down and Connor Church Accommodation Society and in that period the population of Belfast had grown in excess of 120,000 of which it was estimated that about 30,000 were members of the Established Church. The eleven existing churches in Belfast could only provide accommodation for 7,500 people and their total endowment income was £600. Belfast contained one twentieth of the total Church of Ireland population while the amount of endowment income in the same area formed about one thousandth of the Church's income.

The 'Belfast problem' as it became known, was tackled by a group of laymen who met on 26 November 1862 in the Belfast office of William Ewart, a prominent linen manufacturer. The initial meeting was chaired by Charles Lanyon, formerly the architect of the Down and Connor Church Accommodation Society and now also a respected public figure. A memorial which outlined the necessity of further church accommodation was drawn up and signed by seventy leading churchmen. In their memorial they requested the Ecclesiastical Commissioners to fund a scheme whereby seven churches could be built. It was proposed that the Commissioners would partly fund the scheme while the necessary sites would be provided free of charge and each church would be endowed for £75 per year.

The Ecclesiastical Commissioners were enthusiastic about the proposals presented to them and the Belfast Church Extension and Endowment Society

45 E.W. Montieth, *Drumglass parish history* (Dungannon, 1967), p. 42.   46 W.Q. Ewart, *Third and final report of the Belfast Church Extension and Endowment Society* (Belfast, 1925).

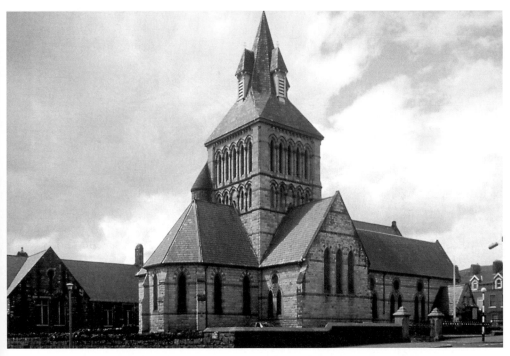

51 St Mary's church, Crumlin Road, Belfast, 1865–8 by William Slater.

was formally constituted at a meeting held on 16 March 1863. A sum of £4,485 was immediately pledged at the conclusion of this first meeting. The first church to be completed was St Mary's church, Crumlin Road, Belfast (fig. 51). It was designed by the English architect William Slater and the foundation stone was laid on 27 October 1865. The consecration by Bishop Knox took place on 26 November 1868 and the preacher was the Lord Primate, Marcus Gervais Beresford. The seven churches[47] completed by the Endowment Society provided accommodation for an additional five thousand worshippers at a cost of over £35,000 (fig. 52). The Society operated for nearly nine years and during its lifetime about £51,000 was raised, of which £24,229 was donated locally. These figures do not include the value of the free sites and the legal expenses, which were given freely by various members of the Society.

Occasionally controversies developed elsewhere, such as that which occurred in 1890 at St Bartholomew's church in Dublin, originally built in 1867 to the designs of another English architect T.H. Wyatt. The dispute arose when a

47 The seven churches built by the Endowment Society were : St Mary's, Crumlin Road (1868), Mariners' church, Corporation Street (1869), St Stephen's Free Church, Millfield (1869), St Andrew's, Hope Street (1870), St James's, Antrim Road (1871), St Matthew's, Shankill Road (1872), Willowfield, Woodstock Road (1872).

52 St Matthew's church, Belfast, 1872 by Welland and Gillespie.

parishioner presented an altar cross which was permitted by the select vestry to be erected just behind the altar but not on it, but was nevertheless the first cross to appear in such close proximity to the communion table in a Protestant church in Ireland.[48]

In general, however, the Church of Ireland as a body – both clergy and laity, and their architects – was united in its suspicion of ritual and its caution toward the introduction of furnishings and fittings alien to its generally 'low church' attitudes, a situation which is only slowly changing today.

48 See K. Milne, *St Bartholomew's; a history of the Dublin parish* (Dublin, 1963).

Index